Political Parties

Political Parties

Seth Masket
UNIVERSITY OF DENVER

Hans Noel
GEORGETOWN UNIVERSITY

W. W. NORTON & COMPANY
Independent Publishers Since 1923

W. W. Norton & Company has been independent since its founding in 1923, when William Warder Norton and Mary D. Herter Norton first published lectures delivered at the People's Institute, the adult education division of New York City's Cooper Union. The firm soon expanded its program beyond the Institute, publishing books by celebrated academics from America and abroad. By midcentury, the two major pillars of Norton's publishing program—trade books and college texts—were firmly established. In the 1950s, the Norton family transferred control of the company to its employees, and today—with a staff of five hundred and hundreds of trade, college, and professional titles published each year—W. W. Norton & Company stands as the largest and oldest publishing house owned wholly by its employees.

Editor: Peter Lesser
Associate Editor: Anna Olcott
Project Editors: Marian Johnson and Maura Gaughan
Copy Editor: Marne Evans
Production Manager: Elizabeth Marotta
Media Editor: Spencer Richardson-Jones
Assistant Media Editor: Lena Nowak-Laird
Media Project Editor: Marcus Van Harpen
Marketing Manager, Political Science: Ashley Sherwood
Designer: Juan Paolo Francisco
Permissions: Patricia Wong
Photo Editor: Ted Szczepanski
Composition: Westchester Publishing Services
Manufacturing: LSC Communications, Crawfordsville

ISBN 978-0-393-93808-1 (pbk.)

W. W. Norton & Company, Inc., 500 Fifth Avenue, New York, NY 10110
wwnorton.com
W. W. Norton & Company Ltd., 15 Carlisle Street, London W1D 3BS

1 2 3 4 5 6 7 8 9 0

To Vivian, Eli, and Sadie
To Chloe and Owen

Brief Contents

Contents

3 Parties in Congress

4 Parties and the Executive

6 Party Machines

7 Formal Party Organizations

8   Party Activists

9 Nominations

10 Presidential Nominations

11 The Party in General Elections

12 Parties and Voters

About the Authors

SETH MASKET is professor of political science and director of the Center on American Politics at the University of Denver. He is the author of *Learning from Loss: The Democrats 2016–2020, The Inevitable Party: Why Attempts to Kill the Party System Fail and How They Weaken Democracy,* and *No Middle Ground: How Informal Party Organizations Control Nominations and Polarize Legislatures.* He teaches courses on political parties, campaigns and elections, and congressional procedure. Masket also contributes regularly to FiveThirtyEight, the *Los Angeles Times,* and the  Mischiefs of Faction blog, and his work has appeared at The Monkey Cage, Politico, and in the *New York Times.* He received his PhD from UCLA in 2004.

HANS NOEL is an associate professor in the department of government at Georgetown University. His research is on political coalitions, political parties and ideology, with a focus on the United States. He is the author of *Political Ideologies and Political Parties in America* and a co-author of *The Party Decides: Presidential Nominations Before and After Reform.* Noel blogs  on political parties and related issues at Mischiefs of Faction, and occasionally at The Monkey Cage. He received his PhD in 2006 from UCLA.

Preface

Only a few decades ago, observers thought political parties were dead, or at least irrelevant. Now, American politics cannot be described without reference to partisan polarization or hyperpartisanship. That transformation in perspective came with a surge in scholarship on political parties—parties in government, in elections, in nominations, as organizations. This book seeks to provide a contemporary perspective while still engaging with the long tradition of scholarship on political parties in America.

We built this book around the ways that we teach about political parties in our own classrooms. We've also drawn on conversations we've been having with each other and trusted colleagues about parties over nearly a quarter of a century. The subject of parties is one that refuses to stand still; parties and the American party system change from year to year; and things dismissed as unthinkable not long ago have become common, such as outsider presidential candidates seriously contesting (even winning) their party's nominations, a president's approval rating remaining unchanged as the country moves from steady economic growth to a pandemic-fueled recession, or adherents of the major parties strongly disagreeing about which candidate won the last election. And yet many of the same motivations that early Americans like Jefferson and Hamilton had for constructing parties still exist today for modern party leaders.

We begin with the observation that understanding political parties is necessary to understanding democratic politics because political actors use political parties to solve the problems that they face. That makes political parties a central feature of nearly every aspect of American politics. Even political actors who are uninterested or disdainful of political parties must reckon with them.

We acknowledge that because parties touch every aspect of the American political system, they are especially challenging to teach and learn about. This book is designed to make those jobs a bit easier. We approach parties from many different angles—as political identities, as legislative coalitions, as campaign organizations, as policy teams, as unwieldy coalitions, and more. We attempt to synthesize classic and contemporary research on the nature of parties in a way that undergraduate students will comprehend, but without oversimplifying complex matters or shying away from challenging questions.

At the same time, it is no secret that parties in the United States are in a state of uncertainty. We aim to be the most contemporary book available, by engaging with those developments, while also acknowledging that the implications of some of those developments are still not completely known. We thus stop short of bold pronouncements or predictions about the meaning of the party changes we attempt to document.

We also show students how political scientists study parties and the tools they use to reach their conclusions. All chapters include a "Political Science Toolkit" feature, shining a light on how scholars measure party behavior and test competing theories. For example, we develop the political science notion of the spatial model, both theoretically and empirically, over several chapters, allowing us to reference the extensive literature that both builds on and challenges it. We hope you'll find these useful.

Also, in keeping with the growing belief in political science that American politics would benefit from more engagement with comparative politics (and vice versa), we try not to treat the United States in isolation. While the book focuses primarily on American political parties, we regularly look at the American case from the comparative perspective. Chapter 5 focuses on questions that demand a comparative answer, such as Why does the United States have a two-party system? And other chapters, when useful, place U.S. political parties in a global context.

We have also made significant efforts to weave in current and timely anecdotes and examples to illustrate concepts throughout the book. For example, we look at partisan responses to the COVID-19 pandemic of 2020 (Chapter 4) and the fault lines that divided the Democratic Party in its 2020 presidential nomination (Chapter 10). We examine the state and national parties' attention to the Georgia Senate runoff elections of early 2021 (Chapter 11) and the party activists on both sides who pressured lawmakers during the Brett Kavanaugh Supreme Court nomination (Chapter 8).

A note on language: The ways that writers, editors, and publishing houses refer to people's chosen identities has varied considerably over time, particularly in the past year. For example, in the past, we have alternately used the terms "African American" and "black" to describe individuals of African ancestry. Following recent style guide changes from the Associated Press, the *New York Times*, Fox News, the *Washington Post*, and others, we have chosen to capitalize "Black" when describing this group of people. Accordingly, we also refer to "Whites" with a capital letter, following the recommendations of the National

Association of Black Journalists, as well as the examples of CNN and several other news organizations. We use the lower-case "white" when it is an adjective referring to such things as white supremacy, white nationalism, and so forth. We recognize that this decision is far from unanimous, but we accept it as the most appropriate for our times. We use "Latinos" to refer to those with Latin American or Spanish ancestry, and we use it to encompass all gender expressions. In accordance with new guidance, we use the terms "enslaved person," "enslaved people," and "slaveowner(s)," rather than "slave," "slaves," and "slaveholder(s)," respectively, to acknowledge the humanity of those whose freedom was denied during this history and to more accurately describe the institution of slavery.

Acknowledgments

Many friends and colleagues assisted us in writing this book. They read portions of the manuscript at various stages and provided feedback on concepts, quick responses on data requests, and general support for the project. We are thankful to Julia Azari, Matthew Green, Gregory Koger, and Jon Ladd, among others. We want to thank research assistants Lise Vitter and Mairead O'Brien, who helped collect data and synthesize materials.

We are grateful to our colleagues who provided detailed feedback on chapter drafts:

Julia Azari, Marquette University
Rachel Blum, Miami University of Ohio
David Darmofal, University of South Carolina
Dustin Fridkin, University of Florida
Michael G. Hagen, Temple University
Hans Hassell, Cornell College
Boris Heersink, Fordham University
Gregory Koger, University of Miami
Francis Moran, New Jersey City University
Jacob Neiheisel, SUNY Buffalo
Barbara Norrander, University of Arizona
Jason Roberts, University of North Carolina
Karen Sebold, University of Arkansas
Vincent Stine, George Washington University
Matthew Wright, University of British Columbia

We also thank W. W. Norton for supporting and nurturing this project—including our editor, Peter Lesser, for his expert guidance and feedback; associate editor Anna Olcott; media editor Spencer Richardson-Jones and assistant editor Lena Nowak-Laird; project editors Marian Johnson and Maura Gaughan and digital project editor Marcus Van Harpen; copy editor Marne Evans; production manager Liz Marotta; marketing manager Ashley Sherwood; book designer Juan Paolo Francisco; photo editor Ted Szczepanski; and text permissions clearer Patricia Wong. Writing about American political parties at this dynamic and fraught time in history has been a real challenge but also a considerable joy. Throughout this process, we have been truly grateful to this fine team for its skill, professionalism, enthusiasm, and excellent taste in dining establishments.

Seth and Hans

Political Parties

1

You Can't Understand Politics without Understanding Parties

How did Donald Trump become president?

Scholars, political observers, and students like you may well be asking this question for many years to come. And indeed, it's a puzzler. Trump didn't have any of the experience held by previous presidents—he had never been in office or served in the military. He was nominated by the Republican Party even though he alienated many Republican politicians and seemed to share few of their public policy views. He had record-high disapproval ratings for a presidential candidate. He won in the Electoral College even though polls consistently had shown him trailing his Democratic opponent, Hillary Clinton, substantially. How did all this happen?

The answer is parties. The reason that only candidates with a certain set of experiences become president is because political parties traditionally screen out inexperienced candidates during the nomination process. The major parties have been doing this for centuries, giving key advantages to preferred candidates. Trump got the Republican nomination because that party's leaders either couldn't or wouldn't screen him out. Although the party was ultimately successful in winning the election, it had very publicly failed in another of its major duties: controlling the nomination process.

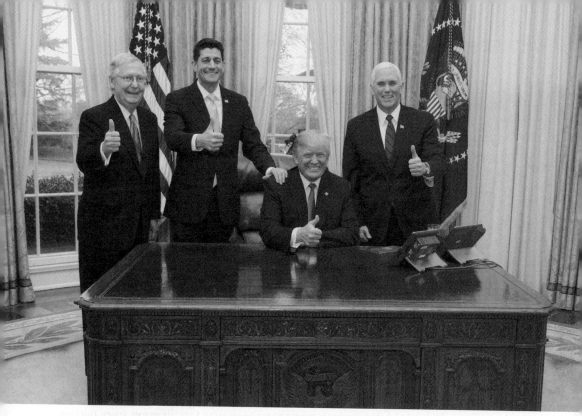

Though Republicans failed to control the nomination process in 2016, their ultimate unity behind Donald Trump helped him win the general election and pass legislation while in office. He is pictured here with former Republican Speaker of the House Paul Ryan, Senate majority leader Mitch McConnell, and Vice President Mike Pence celebrating the passage of the Tax Cuts and Jobs Act of 2017.

Once he was nominated, how was Trump able to get elected? Again, the answer is parties. Despite his high disapproval ratings and polarizing character, Republican voters rallied to their party's choice. Partisanship among American voters today is strong, despite the claims of many voters that they are "independent" or that they "vote the person, not the party." Roughly 9 in 10 Republicans voted for Trump, just as 9 in 10 Democrats voted for Clinton.

We can see an illustration of how strong party loyalty can be in the example of Senator Ted Cruz (R-TX). Cruz, who also ran for president in 2016, notably refused to endorse Trump at the Republican National Convention, and he encouraged other delegates to "vote your conscience" rather than fall in line behind Trump. After this late resistance against Trump's nomination failed, Cruz later found himself on the phone, calling voters and encouraging them to support Trump in the general election. Cruz is just one of several prominent Republicans to resist Trump's nomination yet ultimately support him in the 2016 general election.

3

How did Trump remain in office and manage to secure a number of wins for his governing agenda despite an array of scandals that dwarfed those faced by many previous presidents? How did he end up signing an unpopular tax cut into law and seating unpopular Supreme Court justices? Yet again, the answer is parties. In Congress, partisanship is at a record high. That is, Republican members of Congress vote with each other—and against their Democratic peers—more than any time since the late nineteenth century, and possibly ever. Republicans in Congress, it seems, would accept quite a bit of scandal and nontraditional behavior in the executive branch before they'd be willing to cross party lines and give Democrats a win.

Quite simply, if one wishes to understand how Donald Trump took power, one must understand political parties. Of course, this is not a book about Donald Trump. Nonetheless, for the vast majority of questions about American politics, the answer is closely tied to parties. If you wish to understand how campaigns work, why Supreme Court justices rule as they do, how legislative districts are drawn, or practically anything else about the American political system, parties are at the heart of the matter. This book is designed to help you understand how parties function in American politics today: where they came from, why even people who despise them rely on them for political activity, how parties polarize (and depolarize), how they are similar and different from parties in other countries, and the degree to which parties make democracy both frustrating and functional.

DISAGREEMENTS ABOUT PARTIES GO BACK TO THE BEGINNING

One of the points we will return to frequently is that parties are essential to democracy. This doesn't mean that parties are inherently good or bad, or that we will agree with what they do all or most of the time. These organizations are no better or worse than the people running them. The point is that it's difficult to build and maintain a democracy without political parties.

To understand parties, we find it helpful to start with a few classic texts. The *Federalist Papers* were a series of essays designed to sell the American people on the idea of the Constitution, which was written in 1787 but had not yet been ratified by the states. One of those essays, *Federalist 10*, written by James Madison under the pen name Publius, focused on **factions**, or parties (see discussion below and Appendix, page A-6).

Madison was not a big fan of political parties as he understood them. They emerged naturally enough, Madison felt, stemming from people's innate differences and their varied interpretations of the world. "The latent causes of faction are thus sown in the nature of man," he explains, and they are rooted in "a zeal

Senator Ted Cruz (R-TX) notably refused to endorse Donald Trump at the 2016 Republican National Convention and encouraged fellow delegates to vote their conscience (left). Months later, Cruz made phone calls in support of the Trump/Pence presidential ticket (right).

for different opinions concerning religion, concerning government, and many other points, as well of speculation as of practice; an attachment to different leaders ambitiously contending for pre-eminence and power; or to persons of other descriptions whose fortunes have been interesting to the human passions."

A faction wasn't necessarily a problem; in Madison's framework, if only a minority of the country was attached to it, it could be defeated in elections and in legislatures. But a faction that had the support of the majority (of voters, of elected officials, or of some other aspect of the political system) was a threat to a well-functioning government. "When a majority is included in a faction," he writes, "the form of popular government . . . enables it to sacrifice to its ruling passion or interest both the public good and the rights of other citizens." This would create the "instability, injustice, and confusion" that are "the mortal diseases under which popular governments have everywhere perished."

Madison was hardly unique among the Founders in this view. "If I could not go to heaven but with a party," Thomas Jefferson remarked, "I would not go there at all." Upon his departure from government service, President George Washington warned in his farewell address, "The alternate domination of one faction over another, sharpened by the spirit of revenge, natural to party dissension, which in different ages and countries has perpetrated the most horrid enormities, is itself a frightful despotism" (see Appendix, page A-1).

The Constitution itself contains no mention of political parties. Indeed, the Founders were attempting to build a republic free of, or at least insulated from, the influence of parties. Madison was clearly concerned by the destructive prospects of parties, but importantly he didn't see any way for a country to curtail them while remaining a democracy. Nonetheless, he thought it was possible to limit parties' worst excesses. Many philosophers of his time thought that democracy was impractical on a large scale and was better suited to smaller polities like ancient Athens. But Madison proposed that a large, diverse nation was just the thing to limit parties' excesses. In a small, homogeneous republic, it might be easy for some faction to control a majority of voters and the government, crushing the rights of the minority. It would be much harder to get, say, South Carolina planters, Boston beer brewers, and New York textile workers all together into the same faction. A faction that couldn't sustain a large and diverse coalition would have a difficult time winning an election or controlling the government. The very size of the republic Madison and his colleagues were constructing was, he believed, its saving grace.

Madison takes a similar tack in *Federalist 51*, in which he argues that the division of federal power across three government branches would be key to preventing tyranny. "Ambition must be made to counteract ambition," he argues, saying that a government structurally divided against itself would make it hard for a passionate faction to take it over and use it for its own designs.

These arguments reflect a particular bias among the Founders. They were far more comfortable with a government doing too few things than with one doing too many. And it is essential to remember that the Founders were an unusually wealthy group of early Americans holding a good deal of property. Property was key to the Founders; in *Federalist 10*, Madison says that "the most common and durable source of factions has been the various and unequal distribution of property." And it's essential to remember what *property* encompassed to Madison and most other Founders: enslaved people. In addition to their vast land holdings, many Founders owned dozens or hundreds of human beings, and they were wary of a government that could take away that form of wealth. A strong federal government was not only reminiscent of the tyrannical British government they had recently overthrown, but also posed threats to the Founders' personal long-term interests. Their preference for a government that was thusly *limited*, both in its powers and in the range of areas it could apply them, has cast a long shadow over America's political development.

Like their concerns about government, the Founders' concerns about parties sound familiar today. We regularly hear politicians and pundits lament polarization and partisanship, complaining that it's hurting the government and tearing the country apart. The view of parties as basically an unavoidable evil has held weight throughout American history and has helped to shape many debates and discussions about parties over the centuries.

Political scientist E. E. Schattschneider offered a different, and important, take on parties in his landmark book *Party Government*, in 1942. To Schattschneider, parties weren't some barely tolerable side effect of democracy; they were its *creators*. "The political parties created democracy," he argues, "and modern democracy is unthinkable save in terms of the parties."[1]

What does he mean? Democratic politics in a large nation, Schattschneider says, is functionally impossible without some sort of mediator between the people and the government. People simply cannot deliberate about policy choices on such a vast scale. And it's not because they lack intelligence or education, he says: "An electorate of sixty million Aristotles would be equally restricted."[2] What they need is someone or something to boil down the essentially infinite number of policy choices into a series of simpler options—this candidate or that one, lower or higher taxes, looser or stricter gun laws, and so forth.

Parties excel at this task, argues Schattschneider. Essentially, parties are a sort of conspiracy of the informed against the uninformed, of those who care deeply about politics against the vast majority who find it uninteresting. The informed recognize that they can band together with other informed people who care about some of the same issues, and if they organize well, and work together rather than independently, they can win and control the government.

The benefit for the general public is that the small number of informed people working to put these parties together ends up organizing politics in such a way that the public can then actually participate. Parties provide simplified choices. What's more, parties try to bring people into the political system, recognizing that the more people they convince of their merits and can get to the polls, the better their chances of winning.

Many political observers complain that parties are dominated by insiders who have a penchant for conducting business in secret "smoke-filled rooms," but Schattschneider saw that as a feature rather than a bug. To him, democracy was to be found between the parties, rather than within them, and attempts to make parties more internally democratic and more accountable to their rank-and-file members were silly at best and dangerous at worst.

Over the centuries, American political *rhetoric* has leaned somewhat more toward Madison's view of parties than Schattschneider's, although in several ways Schattschneider's views have proven more accurate. And Madison's anti-party convictions ring a tad hollow given that he and his colleagues, including Jefferson and Hamilton, formed political parties just a few years after publicly condemning them. Parties, they found, were a rather useful tool for getting government work done.

ASSESSING PARTIES TODAY

The views of thinkers like Madison and Schattschneider will reemerge throughout this book. Our own views are somewhat closer to Schattschneider's, although we recognize that there are various ways to evaluate and use parties, and that Schattschneider did not foresee many of the ways parties would change in the late twentieth and early twenty-first centuries.

For one thing, parties have become more polarized than Schattschneider envisioned, perhaps even more than he would have wanted.[3] For another, despite Schattschneider's protests, the parties have become far more democratic internally. Nearly all nominations are decided by primary elections now, instead of by conventions or party leaders, and rank-and-file party members have a great deal more say in whom parties pick and what stances they take. Arguably, this has become a problem for parties. When party leaders seek to do anything that seems like leadership, they are singled out as corrupt or elitist. Moreover, it's not obvious that today's more democratic parties are making better decisions now than they were 70 years ago.

What do we mean by "better" decisions? The party-boss-centered system (see Chapter 6) produced presidential nominees like Abraham Lincoln, Franklin D. Roosevelt, and John F. Kennedy. These candidates could represent the broad range of passionate interests in their fractious parties, win an election, and go on to achieve important party priorities while in office, including seeing the end of slavery, the creation of Social Security, and advancements in civil rights. This is a successful version of party government, and one might legitimately ask whether today's parties are capable of this level of coordination and achievement.

The old system wasn't always successful, however. In addition to Lincoln, Roosevelt, and Kennedy, it also produced nominees like Richard Nixon and Warren Harding, whose scandals would derail policy making and tarnish the reputation of their party for years. Andrew Jackson helped to build this party system in the 1820s and 1830s, and yet his administration repeatedly worked to undermine democratic norms while enshrining cruelty toward Native Americans and African Americans as national policy. Whether the presidential nominees of the past half century have been, on average, of higher or lower quality than those that preceded them is debateable.

Additionally, there's still considerable disagreement over whether political parties are good or bad for democracy. As we will discuss later in this book, parties do reinforce—and even create—division in society. Recent work by Lilliana Mason[4] shows how the party system in the United States, which once helped mitigate divisions in society by grouping different sorts of people within the same party, is now reinforcing societal divisions. In recent decades, parties have become increasingly *sorted* along lines of race, class, wealth, religion, education level, gender, and ideological conviction in a way they never were before. This has further divided American politics and has made members of one party increasingly see members of the other as a threat to the country and less deserving of the protection of its laws.

Yet parties play an important role of protecting democracies, as well. In their recent research, Steven Levitsky and Daniel Ziblatt[5] note that several authoritarians—people with a desire for absolute power and little belief in democracy, coequal branches of government, or a free press—have sought power in American history. These include famous, wealthy populists like Charles Lindbergh, Henry Ford, Huey Long, and others. What prevented them from running credible presidential campaigns were the major political parties, which refused to consider nominating them. These candidates knew enough about American politics to understand that they had little chance of becoming president without the support of a major party, so they channeled their ambitions elsewhere.

Levitsky and Ziblatt provide several examples of parties around the world that have refused to nominate people they considered undemocratic. They provide other examples of parties that have joined with their adversaries to prevent the election of autocrats. In 1930s Finland, for example, conservative parties broke from an increasingly fascist and violent Lapua movement and joined with the more liberal Social Democrats to form the Lawfulness Front. This combined effort by the parties protected Finnish democracy and ostracized the Lapuas, preventing Finland from descending into fascism as many other European governments of the era did. Other parties have distanced themselves from autocratic candidates and movements they considered dangerous for democracy, even though they agreed with many of their policy goals.

Yet parties can also go in the other direction. Sometimes parties see autocratic candidates and movements gaining popularity and calculate that they can win elections by bringing those people into the fold, assuming the candidate can control their worst antidemocratic impulses. The decision by a democratic party to align with an authoritarian candidate is rarely a successful approach in the long run; such alignment helped produce leaders like Benito Mussolini and Adolf Hitler and effectively killed democracy in their countries. Autocrats can rarely rise to power on their own; they require the assistance of a party insider like Giovanni Giolitti of Italy or Paul von Hindenberg of Germany (or Jar Jar Binks of Naboo). Parties have the power to protect democracy, and just sitting back to see what voters think of the candidates isn't always the best way to go about it.

THE BIG QUESTIONS ABOUT PARTIES

Over the course of this book, we will be working to answer several key questions about political parties: What is a party? Why do we have them? Are the parties polarizing? Is the American party system unique? Are parties good or bad for democracy?

What Is a Party?

This is a harder question to answer than it may seem, and political observers and scholars have disagreed about a definition of parties for centuries. We proceed from a particular definition:

> A **political party** *is a coalition of people who form a united front to win control of government and implement policy.*

There are a few important concepts in this definition:

- *A coalition of people*: One of the most important things to understand about parties is that they are coalitions, rather than singular, unified organizations. They contain different sorts of people and groups who do not necessarily agree on everything. The Democratic Party contains environmental groups who favor limiting reliance on internal combustion engines and cars to protect the planet, and labor unions who favor the creation and protection of auto industry jobs. The Republican Party contains libertarians who want to restrict the ability of government to interfere with personal decisions, and cultural conservatives who want to pass laws that make it harder to obtain abortions or use drugs. Both parties are rife with such tensions, which must constantly be managed and negotiated for the parties to function.
- *A united front*: Party members have differing goals and perspectives, but they're willing to set aside some disagreements to work for common goals and candidates who will advance them. Constructing that united front requires extensive negotiation and compromise.
- *Control of government*: Party members are not just involved in politics to have a voice or to "influence a debate." They are in it to win it. They care about their issues but are willing to make some sacrifices to actually win.
- *Implement policy*: The end goal for party members is to actually change the direction of government, whether that means raising or lowering taxes, extending or rescinding rights, building alliances with foreign nations or attacking them, or regulating or deregulating industries. Implementing policy can also mean extending government benefits or contracts to their friends and denying them to their opponents. At their core, party actors have policy goals, and they want the government to implement them.

One might notice that our definition of party is fairly expansive. As has been mentioned, different types of people and groups can be part of the party. So what *isn't* the party? That is, what sorts of political groups and individuals should not be thought of as part of a party?

A group or individual is part of a party if they play a role in affecting whom that party nominates for office and whether that nominee wins the election. But there are a number of political actors who do not play a role in these major party choices. Black Lives Matter, for example, is an activist group devoted to raising awareness about institutionalized racism and the disproportionate violence faced by African Americans in the criminal justice system. Its members, and its message, are notably left-leaning, and more ideologically aligned with the Democratic Party. However, few Democratic elected officials claim membership with the group, and the group has tended more toward public demonstrations than direct lobbying or campaign activity. It would not be accurate to describe Black Lives Matter as a part of the Democratic Party.

Similarly, longstanding interest groups like the American Medical Association (AMA), AARP (formerly known as the American Association of Retired Persons), and the American Automobile Association (AAA) have long histories of political activity and can claim numerous legislative achievements. But they have resisted being too closely affiliated with one political party, and they tend to stay out of nomination battles within the parties. These are just some of the varied groups and individuals who are highly active in politics but are still not part of political parties.

Some groups and individuals may be separate from a party but then become part of one. The environmental movement, at one point, was largely unaligned with a political party, and even tended to be somewhat conservative in its outlook. As David Karol[6] points out, environmental leaders in the mid-twentieth century began working with Democratic-leaning groups to push back on more conservative corporations, compelling the environmental groups to take more liberal stances on a range of issues. Today, most environmental groups are closely tied to the Democratic Party, and many are involved with major party decisions like nominations. We can see a somewhat similar evolution of the National Rifle Association, which was once relatively nonpartisan but today is deeply embedded within the Republican coalition. These examples show how interest groups can change their orientation and affiliation and how parties' membership lines can be quite porous.

POLITICAL SCIENCE TOOLKIT
Why Do We Have Parties?

It's one thing for us to give you our viewpoint about what parties are and how they behave, but it's another to explain how political scientists go about measuring that behavior and testing theories about parties. Here, and in each of the chapters that follow, we will offer a short, standalone section called the Political Science Toolkit. This feature will give an idea of how scholars go about studying parties in a scientific manner. We'll talk about such things as polling techniques, measurements of ideology, formal models, and some statistical methods. This isn't designed to be intimidating or scary or terribly technical, but rather to give readers a sense of how to address important questions in a rigorous way and, hopefully, find some answers. In this Toolkit, we provide a simple model for understanding how legislators behave and why they might form parties.

It's no secret that political parties are unpopular and becoming more so. It's been common for recent politicians to have run for office complaining about partisanship and promising to help America overcome its deep divisions. Unsurprisingly, once elected, those same people became closely associated with partisanship and sometimes even helped foster it. Why is it that parties endure if people keep criticizing them? Political scientist John Aldrich[7] asked exactly this question in his 1995 book, *Why Parties?* Aldrich's answer, which is ours as well, is that political parties solve specific problems that political actors need solved.

Coalition Building The first, most simple problem to solve is *coalition building.* To win an election or pass legislation, politicians need to get a possibly diverse group of people to act together. To show why, Aldrich introduces a simple model of a legislature[8] (although this logic also works in larger legislatures facing more-complicated issues):

A Hypothetical Legislature with an Incentive to Form Parties			
Bills	**Legislators**		
	A	B	C
1	4	−1	−1
2	−1	4	−1
3	−1	−1	4

This figure shows three legislators (A, B, and C) who together have to consider three bills (1, 2, and 3). The numbers 4 and −1 tell us how much each legislator likes a bill—you can think of the numbers as a sort of reward (or penalty) the member would get if the bill passed. Each legislator has one bill that they like very much, and two bills that they'd rather not see pass at all. But they feel more strongly about what they want than what they don't want; each would like their preferred bill to pass 4 times as much as they oppose either of the others. Assuming legislators vote for what they like and against what they don't like, and that passage requires a simple majority, nothing will pass. Bill 1 will fail with Legislator A voting for it and legislators B and C against. Bill 2 gets only B's vote, and so on.

Legislators could make an agreement with each other ahead of time to support all three bills, and they would all be better off. Each gets one thing they really like and has to put up with two things they don't much like, and 2 (4 minus 1 minus 1) is still better than zero. The term for this strategy is **universalism**, since everyone gets their share. Legislatures sometimes work this way. Getting three (or more) people to commit to something might be hard, but it's not impossible.

While universalism might seem appealing, any two legislators will be better off if they permanently team up against the third. If A and B agree to support each other's bills and vote down C's preferred item, they get what they want for the price of only one thing they do not. So A and B get a payoff of 3 (4 minus 1), while C ends up with –2 (4 minus 4 minus 1 minus 1). A and B are substantially better off in this situation than if they had no arrangement at all, and C is substantially worse off.

There are only three votes shown in the table, but things get interesting when we think about how A and B might act in the long term. Every time a bill comes up that one of them wants, they both support it.* If neither of them wants it, they don't. This is called a **long coalition**. The coalition is long because it extends to every vote. As new issues come up, the coalition partners stick together. Sometimes they will have to face internal disagreements, and sometimes they might see a short-term gain by joining the opposition, but in the long run, they are better off by sticking together and guaranteeing they will always be in the majority. Parties are the institution that keeps the coalition together.

Legislator C in the example, meanwhile, soon realizes what it's like to be losing all the time. C can try to win over A or B on a few issues, but if A and B constructed their party institutions well, that will be extremely hard for C to accomplish. It may take an election and the replacement of A or B before C would be in the position to forge a new coalition in which

---

* This book employs "they" as a gender-neutral, third-person singular pronoun, following in the tradition of Geoffrey Chaucer, C. S. Lewis, William Shakespeare, Jane Austen, Walt Whitman, Oscar Wilde, the author(s) of the King James Bible, and many, many others (see Burchfield 2004, Liberman and Pullum 2006, Doyle 2009).

C is a member. That is, the solution to C's problems in the legislature may lie outside the legislature.

Voter Mobilization Building and maintaining coalitions are not the only problems political parties solve. Politicians need voters to turn out, and turnout requires mobilization. Parties help not only to mobilize voters, but to mobilize the specific voters parties need to win. Just as legislators might be tempted to deviate from their party's agenda from time to time, voters might be tempted to vote for someone other than their party's candidate— or not vote at all. Parties can help prevent that.

Candidates also need resources, expertise, and labor to win elections. Parties can provide them. Professional party staff develop expertise running campaigns, and party leaders direct donations to candidates who need them the most. Volunteers knock on doors for specific candidates, but the volunteer trainers who direct them draw on experience from past campaigns and they use funds, technology, and other tools that the party provides.

Coalition building and voter mobilization are critical problems politicians face, but they are only two of them. Throughout this book, we will uncover others and examine how parties act to solve them. We hope this approach will provide you with a rich understanding of why parties do what they do, the tools to evaluate the effectiveness of today's parties, and ideas about potential reforms to America's party system.

Are Parties Actually Polarizing?

Once we understand what parties are and why we have them, we can begin to focus on some features important to their functioning in American politics. One of the most important features, which has received a great deal of attention from journalists, politicians, and scholars, is polarization. It's widely assumed that the parties are growing more polarized, although there are several different ways to understand and analyze this. By many measures—voting patterns in Congress, the policies advanced by presidents, individual voting patterns and party identification, even the rulings of the Supreme Court—our parties are moving further apart. Not only are people and elected officials voting in a strict party-line manner far more than they used to, but those parties stand for more divergent sets of beliefs than in the past. There has probably never been a time when the Republican Party's vision for the United States has looked so radically different from that of the Democratic Party. (Interestingly, though, not all parts of the party system are polarizing. Most state legislatures have polarized over the past few decades, but a handful have become less polarized.)

Today's political system has seen polarization in terms of both party and ideology. The ideological differences between liberals and conservatives are exceptionally sharp today, and those distinctions have aligned with the partisan ones in a way that they did not in earlier generations. Throughout the book we'll examine just what that means for the governance of the country and for its future.

Is the American Party System Unique?

The primary focus of this book is U.S. politics, but looking at democratic and partisan processes elsewhere in the world can shed light on those of America. In particular, we examine the question of why the United States has tended toward a two-party system while other democracies may have three, four, five, or more viable parties. The American tradition of two major parties dominating all partisan offices for over a century is quite unusual.

What's also unusual is the American system of nominating candidates through primary elections. In many other democracies, party staffers select a slate of nominees, and voters just get to vote for the candidates the parties have selected for them. Sometimes voters may only vote for parties, and those parties get to determine who sits in the legislature. American-style primaries have been adopted by several nations in recent decades, particularly in Latin America, although they're still somewhat rare.

We'll look at some of the causes and consequences of the ways that America nominates candidates and elects them to office. We will also look at some of the ramifications of having a president elected separately from the Congress, as opposed to the more common system of voters electing a parliament and a prime minister simultaneously.

Are Parties Good or Bad for Democracy?

This is a fundamental question that voters and the American political system have grappled with since the founding, and it's one that we will return to repeatedly. We proceed from the assumption that parties provide a number of benefits to a democracy and that a *partyless* system would in many ways leave us substantially worse off. However, we are not blind to the many challenges and annoyances parties create. We try to reflect on these in a balanced way throughout the text and to address the question of what roles parties should be playing in the American political system—and what they should be avoiding. We'll look into various anti-party movements, such as the Progressive movement of the early 1900s, which have emerged over the decades; we'll examine what motivated them, how they affected party behavior, and how they ultimately shaped the system we have today. We'll look at more modern anti-party reformers and their ideas, seeking to understand their motivations in weakening the parties and assessing their successes and failures.

We'll also discuss whether party polarization might actually offer some benefits. For example, polarization provides voters with clearer distinctions between the parties. Even if most voters don't really follow individual politicians closely, they have some sense of what the parties stand for, and they know that if they vote a different party into power, they will get markedly different policies. This isn't true during an era of low polarization, such as the mid-1900s. On the other hand, the intense polarization today that may make elections so interesting and useful for citizens may also prevent government from dealing with problems that desperately need addressing.

Finally, we will consider just how involved individual citizens should be in America's party-focused political system. That is, just what is our job as citizens? Are we supposed to make an informed vote every two or four years and then just let elected officials govern? Should we be playing a more active role between elections in protesting or lobbying our officials or trying to shape party nominations? Do the parties really want us involved, or do they consider us a nuisance? What's realistic for us given how few people actually pay close attention to politics?

We hope that after reading these chapters you walk away from this book not only with a healthy understanding of what parties are, how they behave, and what functions they serve, but also why the concept of parties is such a controversial and fraught one. We hope you will find our perspective fresh and apt for the polarized times in which we live, and that you will have a better idea of the value and frustrations of parties, the logic of the party system, and just what would be necessary to change it.

Discussion Questions

1. Judging from the writings of Founders mentioned in this chapter, such as George Washington, Alexander Hamilton, and Thomas Jefferson, to what extent were they correct or incorrect in their predictions about political parties?

2. Political scientist E. E. Schattschneider said that "modern democracy is unthinkable save in terms of the parties." What did he mean by this? Was he correct?

3. What is the relationship between an organization like Black Lives Matter and the Democratic Party? To what extent is the National Rifle Association part of the Republican Party?

4. Describe something that makes parties useful for officeholders. Also describe something that makes parties useful for voters.

5. From what you've read so far, would you consider parties good or bad for democracy? Why?

stances and consist of particular groups of people. Why are Democrats today the champions of civil rights while Republicans are advocates for low taxation and minimal regulation of businesses? Why do Republicans tend to do better in sparsely populated, more rural areas of the country while Democrats do better in more urbanized, densely populated areas? To answer these questions, we need to know about these parties' historical development.

In this chapter, we examine several pivotal moments in the development of American political parties, including the nation's founding, the critical election of 1800, the party collapse prior to the Civil War, responses to the Great Depression, and the civil rights movement. We also seek to explain these pivotal moments as part of party "realignments," a term we'll examine later. These key moments help to reveal how parties are born, how they steer governing agendas, how they select nominees, and how their coalitions shift over time.

CONSTRUCTING PARTIES FOR A NEW GOVERNMENT

As we noted in Chapter 1, the U.S. Constitution contains no mention of political parties, and the Founders wrote eloquently about the need to build a government without them. Nonetheless, after just a few years under the Constitution, those same people who thought parties were a bad idea began to form parties. What began as factions in George Washington's cabinet and congressional alliances surrounding Jefferson and Hamilton soon became known as, respectively, the **Democratic-Republicans*** and the **Federalists**.

Those familiar with the musical *Hamilton* will recognize how these early parties were driven strongly by personality differences (Hamilton and Jefferson despised each other from their first meeting) and identity claims (in the musical, Jefferson derided Hamilton for his citified perspective and for smelling like "new money" and dressing like "fake royalty"; Hamilton hated Jefferson's pretensions as a farmer when he was, in fact, a wealthy slaveowner: "Keep ranting, we know who's really doing the planting."). But those differences also reinforced divergent views about the best direction for the new country. Hamilton and his allies sought to build up the national government's ability to tax and regulate the economy, while Jefferson's group wanted a relatively weak national government but stronger state governments. Each side worked not just to maintain party discipline in the Congress, but

---

* Technically, they were known as just the Republicans. However, the party is not the modern Republican Party, but rather a precursor to the modern Democratic Party. Historians and political scientists often refer to it as the Democratic-Republican Party to distinguish it from the modern Republicans. The Democratic Party today traces itself to this party, and to the Democratic Party formed out of it by Andrew Jackson and Martin Van Buren in 1828.

The factions that formed in George Washington's first cabinet around Alexander Hamilton (center) and Thomas Jefferson (to Hamilton's right) evolved into the first political parties, Hamilton's Federalists and Jefferson's Democratic-Republicans.

also to foster relationships with local notables, journalists, and pamphleteers in an effort to get their message out and elect more people supportive of their goals.

The need to win the presidency in particular spurred two specific organizational moves. When Jefferson lost the election of 1796 to John Adams, he and his supporters vowed to win a rematch. They identified New York as a potential swing state. Electors from New York were at that time chosen by the state legislature, so the Jeffersonians' first move was to organize a party to win legislators in New York. The famed Tammany Hall political organization (see Chapter 6) began in part from efforts by Aaron Burr to organize in New York with an eye toward 1800. In 1800, Jefferson faced Adams again. This time, Jefferson won, in large part due to the switch of New York's 12 electoral votes from the Federalist to the Democratic-Republican column.

But it wasn't enough to just win more electors. The Constitution had not envisioned parties, and so it wasn't set up to accommodate these divisions. Notably, the original institutions called for the candidate who came in second in the Electoral College vote to become the vice president. Each elector had two votes, and the framers imagined they'd choose the two most qualified candidates, without regard for political party. But if the two leading candidates represented different partisan groups, this all but guaranteed that the vice president would be from a different party than the president. After coming in second in 1796,

Jefferson had spent four years as vice president to an Adams administration that he disliked and disagreed with.

Neither party was happy with that outcome, so they separately devised a strategy to select both the president and vice president from their own party. Each party ran a ticket, with a candidate for each office. The Democratic-Republicans ran Jefferson for president and Aaron Burr for vice president. The Federalists ran a ticket of John Adams and Charles Pinckney. Since each elector had two votes, each party arranged for its electors to give one less vote for their vice-presidential candidate. If all of the electors voted according to plan, the winning party's candidates would win both positions.

That move required quite a bit of coordination. In the early years of the republic, electors were not bound to vote for their party's candidates. In 1796, for instance, many electors were extremely idiosyncratic, especially with their second vote. In 1800, there was only one mistake, in which the elector who was supposed to *not* vote for Burr actually did, and Jefferson and Burr tied. The Federalists followed through on the plan, with one elector voting for John Jay. But all 73 of the Democratic-Republican electors voted for both Jefferson and Burr. The tie was resolved in the House of Representatives, which despite being still controlled by Federalists, ended up narrowly choosing Jefferson as president.

In other words, the parties organized in response to the requirements of the political system. National geography, the rules of the Constitution, how each state had adapted to those rules—they all created obstacles and opportunities for parties to organize for victory. For this reason, we sometimes say that parties are *endogenous institutions.* "Endogenous" just means that something has its cause or origin within the system. Parties adapt to the system they are in. (When possible, they adjust the system itself. In this case, the Twelfth Amendment adjusted the presidential election system to accommodate party tickets without any coordination.)

Proto-parties in Early Congress

The preceding example shows how parties may be endogenous to electoral rules; they formed as a way of enabling coordination across different states as factions sought to control the presidency. We can also see parties as endogenous to legislative institutions.

The first Congress convened in March of 1789 in New York City, and by most accounts, voting patterns were somewhat chaotic. Legislative parties were not well organized at that point, and members who voted together on one important issue were likely to oppose each other on the next one. As historian James Young found in his study of the early Congress, members often voted by region or even by residence (members often lived in small "dormitories" with a few colleagues in the early years) rather than by party.[4]

This changed over time, however. Increasingly, members began voting by party. As we discussed in the previous chapter, there are good reasons for voting this way. Putting together a winning roll call vote on each and every bill one cares about is basically impossible, but it's easier to win more often if one is a member of a long coalition united across a wide range of issues. It means that you will lose when your party is in the minority, but you have a good chance of getting your bills passed when your party is in the majority, which allows you to claim credit with your constituents when you tell them about all the work you've gotten done on their behalf.

As party-line voting grew during the 1790s, Jefferson's Democratic-Republicans found themselves increasingly on the losing side of congressional roll call votes, with Hamilton's Federalists proving to be more organized and better able to secure election victories. Jefferson and his allies reasoned that the solution to their problems lay in increasing their numbers in the Congress. The election of 1800 involved not only a critical presidential election, but also sophisticated interstate efforts to coordinate messaging and strategies.

The Democratic-Republicans routed the Federalists in 1800, increasing their share of the 106-member House from 46 to 68 members while seizing a narrow majority of the Senate. Federalists had been the dominant party in the 1790s; after 1800, they would never control either congressional chamber again.

It would be too simple to suggest that the Federalists and Democratic-Republicans emerged completely within the Congress; they were, after all, championing ideas about economic policies, federal government power, and other issues that predated the birth of the United States and were alive well outside legislatures. But these early parties also developed in a way that allowed members of Congress to best capitalize on their capacity for generating ideas, turning out voters, and organizing roll call votes.

The Era of Good Feelings?

In the 1820s parties became more innovative in how they organized elections. By then, the Federalists had almost completely disbanded, and most American politicians identified with the Democratic-Republican party of Jefferson. This was the "Era of Good Feelings," so named because there were essentially no partisan divisions in Washington. But that didn't mean there were no differences in opinion or conflicting ambitions.

In 1824, the Democratic-Republicans' big tent started to get crowded, and four credible Democratic-Republican candidates ran for president: Secretary of State (and son of a Founder) John Quincy Adams, U.S. House Speaker Henry Clay, U.S. Treasury Secretary William Crawford, and U.S. Senator and former U.S. Army general Andrew Jackson. Table 2.1 shows the results.

TABLE 2.1 The Election of 1824

Candidate	Popular Vote	Electoral College Votes	Electoral College Share
Andrew Jackson	41%	99	38%
John Quincy Adams	31%	84	32%
Henry Clay	13%	37	14%
William Crawford	11%	41	16%

As we can see, the most popular candidate was Andrew Jackson. But the Constitution requires an outright majority in the Electoral College, and 99 out of 261 is about 38 percent. When no one wins a majority, it becomes the House of Representatives' obligation to choose from among the top three choices.[5] In the House, each state gets one vote. The House considered Jackson, Adams, and Crawford; Clay didn't make the cut.

Even though Jackson won the most votes, Adams prevailed in the House. His victory came in part from support from Henry Clay, who urged his backers to vote for Adams. Some accused Clay of backing Adams in exchange for being appointed secretary of state. Adams did appoint Clay, but there's a simpler explanation. Clay, and Clay's supporters, liked Adams much more than they liked Jackson.[6] While all four candidates were Democratic-Republicans, they represented slightly different visions. Clay and Adams were more similar to the now defunct Federalists. Crawford and Jackson were more similar to the original Jeffersonians.

This threw the young political system into something of a crisis. The popular vote winner had been denied the election, and there were allegations of corruption in the selection of the new president. The parties were learning an important lesson here about the failure of coordination. What if each of those two factions had run only one candidate?

There's no way to know the answer to that question for sure, but we do know that Jackson backers, who felt unjustly denied by the vote in the House, set out to make sure their votes weren't split again. With leadership from Martin Van Buren, Jacksonians organized a convention to nominate Jackson again in 1828. What's more, the Democrats, as they now called themselves, mobilized voters across the country. Voter turnout more than doubled between 1824 and 1828, jumping from 26 to 56 percent. Jackson defeated President Adams with 56 percent of the popular vote and 68 percent of the Electoral College.

Jackson's loss and redemption illustrate the power of coordination. The population of eligible voters didn't change wildly between 1824 and 1828, and the two major choices didn't change either, but the efforts of the Democratic Party changed the outcome. By coordinating across different potential candidates and agreeing on a nominee, Jackson and his backers reshaped the options the voters had. By encouraging turnout, they changed who the voters were. These events were a stunning testament to the power of a party to affect political outcomes, even if they weren't changing many minds.

Agenda Control

With Jackson's Democrats in control of the White House and the Congress at the close of the 1820s, they began the work of undoing federal regulation of the economy and dismantling the national bank, which had been central to Adams' policies. Meanwhile, a new party, the Whigs, was trying to limit the powers of President Jackson and promote the authority of Congress. At this point, the parties had fairly coherent economic positions, and they had clear views on the various unorthodox powers Jackson claimed as president.

Internally, however, the parties were divided on the crucial issue of slavery. Each party had strength in both northern and southern states, and thus each party found the subject of slavery an uncomfortable one; taking a position would inevitably divide the party. As we noted in the previous chapter, a political party is a long coalition. Each member commits to vote for the policies that other members care about in exchange for support for their own issues. This exchange is easiest when your party is asking you to vote for something you and your constituents don't care about one way or another. But when you and your copartisans care deeply about opposite sides of the same issue, the only solution may be to avoid the issue altogether.

As the nation grew westward, both Democrats and Whigs found it hard to avoid the topic of slavery. Proslavery politicians sought to add new slave states to the nation while antislavery leaders sought to contain or eliminate the institution, sometimes seeking to add free states to counter the representation by the new slave states.

Much of Congress' activities between the 1820s and 1850s can be seen as an effort to keep the issue of slavery from dominating the national discussion. The Missouri Compromise of 1820 set a northern boundary for slavery and set a guideline for admitting equal numbers of slave and free states so neither side would dominate the Congress. A number of decisions, collectively known as the Compromise of 1850, sought an equitable use of the southwest territories won in the recent war with Mexico, admitting California as a free state and ending the slave trade in the District of Columbia but also establishing a federal fugitive slave law. The Kansas-Nebraska Act of 1854 was an attempt to defuse slavery tensions in the Kansas territory by dividing it into two new states that could decide among themselves whether to be slave or free. These legislative actions were all efforts to keep the divisive slavery issue from dominating congressional deliberations and dividing the parties internally.

Yet the parties were evolving in how they discussed slavery. At the time of the nation's founding, many leaders—including Jefferson, Washington, Madison, and others—recognized that they were economically bound to slavery and thus protected it politically, but they were also clearly uncomfortable with the institution, saw it as potentially catastrophic for the nation, and rarely publicly defended it. By the 1850s, however, prominent southern Democrats had emerged as fierce defenders of slavery and had developed an entire ideology to support the idea of human bondage as an inherent good.

Meanwhile, sectional (or geographic) tensions continued to escalate, with increasing violence between pro- and antislavery factions in the Kansas territory, massive public pushback to the Supreme Court's defense of the Fugitive Slave Act, and increased antislavery activism by formerly enslaved people and abolitionists. By the mid-1850s, Democrats in the North began to abandon their party, while the Whigs, straddled across pro- and antislavery portions of the country and, desperate to avoid discussing the issue, collapsed as a party. From their northern ashes, an antislavery coalition calling itself the Republican Party emerged in 1854. The multi-decade, bipartisan effort to keep slavery off the national agenda had ultimately failed; slavery was now the dominant issue motivating national politics.

The 1860 election remains the starkest example of sectional polarization we've seen. Democratic support for the party's nominee was confined largely to southern slave states, and the Republican nominee, Abraham Lincoln, was not even on the ballot in much of that region. Although Democrats remained a potent political force in some northern cities like New York and Boston, Republicans dominated the Union states. The Civil War can be seen as almost as much of a battle between the parties as it was between the states. The Union victory and subsequent extension of voting rights (enfranchisement) to many formerly enslaved people in the South during Reconstruction allowed Republicans to dominate national politics in the decade following the Civil War. The withdrawal of federal government forces from the South following the 1876 election, however, along with Jim Crow laws and the rise of the Ku Klux Klan, suppressed African American votes throughout the former Confederacy, enabling the Democratic Party to return to prominence there. Even though Republicans mostly controlled the White House and Congress through the late nineteenth century, the Democratic resurgence in the South and in many western states would end up making the party system more competitive at the national level.

Candidate Selection

One of the most important decisions a party makes is its selection of nominees for high office. As politicians learned in the election of 1824, failing to coordinate and decide on a candidate can be dangerous for a party or a faction of a party. In subsequent elections, parties worked hard to make sure that their members were united behind a single candidate who could adequately represent most of the factions within a party, but these efforts sometimes failed.

By the 1880s, a popular political reform movement had spread among farming communities in the West and South. Largely an agrarian protest movement in western and southern states, it advocated for farmers, wage workers, and others concerned about massive technological changes and the concentration of wealth and corporate power. This movement would soon call itself the Populist Party or the People's Party, and it fielded a candidate for president and other offices in 1892. Its platform urged a host of reforms designed to ease the plight of impoverished farmers and also to make politics more open and accessible—that is, seeking to minimize corruption and open up politics to outsiders. The Populist Party was the original **populist** movement, in that it framed itself as defending the interests of the common people above those of business and government elites. Other "populist" movements may involve different issues and define the people and elites differently, but their core feature is this framing of conflict between the people and elites.[7] The Populist Party's success caught political observers by surprise; its nominee, U.S. Rep. James Weaver of Iowa, claimed 8.5 percent of the popular presidential vote along with 22 Electoral College votes. The results suggested that though the Populists were not about to win the presidency, they had the power to deprive one of the major parties of a victory. The election results also suggested to the major parties that there was significant benefit to winning over supporters who had voted with the Populist Party.

Over the course of the next few years, the Democratic Party would come to embrace many of the Populist platform's economic planks, if not always the ones based on political reform. In 1896, both the Democratic and Populist parties nominated Nebraskan William Jennings Bryan for president, essentially fusing the parties. The gamble didn't pay off, however. Bryan lost to Republican William McKinley. The Populists were devastated, and their party collapsed. What remained, however, was a transformed Democratic Party.

The results of the 1896 election revealed new sectional division in the country, with southern Whites and western-state farmers forming the Democratic coalition and Republicans representing the industrializing and populous Northeast and Midwest. Republicans typically controlled the White House and Congress during this period, although that control was sometimes undermined by factional splits. Some remnants of the Populist movement would form the Progressive movement of the early twentieth century. This new movement consisted largely of Republicans seeking reform to government, industry, and journalism. The Progressives would constitute an important faction within the Republican Party of the early 1900s. A rift between Progressive and "Standpat" (more traditional) Republicans at that time became wider.

Theodore Roosevelt served as the Republican president between 1901 and 1909, mostly aligning himself with issues associated with Progressivism, including reform of politics and regulation of industries. Though Roosevelt declined to run for reelection in 1908, he reentered politics in 1912 as a Bull Moose Progressive presidential candidate, challenging both the Republican incumbent (William Howard Taft) and his Democratic challenger (Woodrow Wilson). With the Republican coalition functionally split between its Progressive and Standpat factions, the Democrats took the White House with well less than a majority of the vote (see Chapter 9 for more details).

Coalitions and Crises

As we've seen, party coalitions may shift a bit from year to year, but overall they tend to be quite durable, only falling apart during major national crises like the Civil War. Another such crisis occurred in the late 1920s and early 1930s with the collapse of the stock market and the onset of the Great Depression. As the party in control of the national government, Republicans were broadly blamed for massive unemployment, economic contraction, and destruction of wealth, which helped Democrats take over the presidency and large majorities of Congress and state legislatures in the 1932 election. Many scholars identify this voting shift as a realignment. This new party system would define the politics of the next several decades, with Democrats broadly advancing greater regulation over the economy and expanding the social welfare state, and Republicans largely resisting such moves in the name of free enterprise. Social Security (1935), Medicare (1965), and Medicaid (1965) all emerged during this period. Despite the sharp issue divisions of the 1930s, much of this era would be defined by parties with only vague ideological distinctions. Southern Whites, still culturally opposed to the party of Lincoln, would be among the Democratic Party's most staunch supporters, while northern laborers embraced Democrats due to their record during the Depression. Each major party contained large cohorts of liberals and conservatives.

Though the party period of the 1920s and 1930s was largely defined by economic matters, race became a key issue again as civil rights activists and union members pressed for changes in the mid-twentieth century. In particular, though the constitutional amendments passed after the Civil War extended full citizenship and voting rights to African Americans, those rights had been systematically undermined by state and local governments, especially in the

South, for almost a full century thereafter. Many White leaders in the majority Democratic Party of the period sought to ignore or downplay this issue as it threatened to undermine their vast coalition of urban laborers in the North and poorer Whites in the South. Yet, as we saw in the mid-1800s, the issue could only be ignored for so long. With civil rights activists and pro–civil rights union leaders increasing in power and beginning to influence party nomination processes,[8] and with African Americans migrating from the rural South to urban centers in the North—The Great Migration—and becoming more Democratic in their voting behavior,[9] Democratic leaders ultimately backed their causes, resulting in the Civil Rights Act of 1964 and the Voting Rights Act of 1965. Democratic president Lyndon Johnson crowed of these substantial policy victories, but allegedly expressed concerns to his staff that he had just delivered the South to the Republican Party.

Over the next few decades, White southerners would increasingly see the Democratic Party as hostile to their culture and interests and would come to embrace the Republican Party. This shift had profound consequences on American politics and is key for understanding modern American parties and polarization. Many observers of modern American politics find it striking that southern states, one of the strongest regions of support for the Republican Party, was solidly Democratic in the mid-twentieth century, and even a relatively unsuccessful national Democratic candidate like Adlai Stevenson (the Democratic presidential nominee in 1952 and 1956) could count on the support of the South (Figure 2.1) as long as he didn't mention civil rights too often.

In the second half of the twentieth century, the most conservative voters in the nation—southern Whites—shifted their support from the Democratic Party to the Republican Party. Meanwhile, newly enfranchised and generally liberal African Americans began voting in large percentages for Democrats. Over the course of a century, the parties had essentially switched places on the politics of race. The Republicans of the 1850s through 1870s were deeply committed to ending slavery and advancing the rights of formerly enslaved people; by the 1950s through 1970s, it was the Democratic Party that had taken up the cause of civil rights.

These trends brought the party alignment in sync with the ideological alignment, making the Democratic Party more liberal and the Republican Party more conservative, which in turn contributed to the dramatic party polarization we've seen since the 1980s. The parties today have their regional strengths, but at the national level they are about as competitive as they've ever been. In recent decades, control of the presidency and the Congress has been consistently up for grabs in a way that it never has been previously.[10]

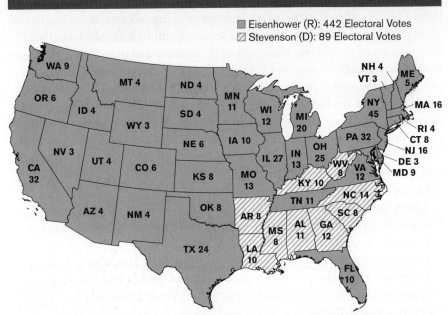

FIGURE 2.1   The 1952 Presidential Election

■ Eisenhower (R): 442 Electoral Votes
▨ Stevenson (D): 89 Electoral Votes

Note: All electoral college maps are included in the Appendix on pages A-20–A-34.

POLITICAL SCIENCE TOOLKIT
Realignment

Throughout this book, we describe parties as coalitions. A party is made up of many **groups**, some of which may disagree with one another. Many of the episodes in this chapter illustrate ways that the party actors have tried to hold those groups together. But the groups that make up a party may sometimes split apart, with one eventually joining the other party. Groups of voters also sometimes cease to be relevant at all, and new groups replace them. Such changes in the composition of the parties are called **realignments**.

"Realignment" is a term that gets thrown around a bit during election coverage and it is often used incorrectly. A realignment is not one party doing unexpectedly well in an election or taking control of all branches of government. Realignment is a change in who is in the party.

Recall the long-coalitions framework we introduced in the last chapter.

A Hypothetical Legislature with an Incentive to Form Parties

Bills	Legislators		
	A	B	C
1	4	−1	−1
2	−1	4	−1
3	−1	−1	4

We argued that in a small three-person legislature where everyone wants slightly different things, two legislators would have an incentive to get together and support each other's policy goals. That would be the basis for a political party. But in the simple example we put together, any two legislators would want to form such a party. So, A-B, B-C, or A-C are all possible parties. A realignment is when one coalition member moves from one coalition to another. If B leaves the party of A-B and joins a new party with C (becoming B-C), that's a realignment.

Real parties aren't made up of only two legislators, but the basic dynamics of party coalitions can be illustrated in this way. Perhaps the most significant realignment in American history has been the shift of segregationist southerners from the Democratic Party to the Republican Party in the mid-twentieth century. A simplified version of those groups is in the following table. In this case, we have replaced the numbers in the table with a general assessment of whether the policy is "good" or "bad" for the group in question. We show three groups that were part of the Democratic Party. (The Republican Party in this period was also a coalition of different groups, but their divisions are not important for this example.)

Coalition Building in the Twentieth Century

		Group			
		Labor (mostly in the North)	Segregationists (mostly in the South)	African Americans	Republicans (business, others)
Policy	Labor Protections	Good	Indifferent	Good	Bad
	States Rights / Jim Crow Laws	Indifferent	Good	Bad	Indifferent

In the 1930s, the New Deal coalition of the Democratic Party included both labor unions and segregationists. Many Black voters were also now voting for Democrats. Despite the Democratic Party's history of supporting slavery and opposing civil rights, Black voters often benefited enough from New Deal labor policies to justify supporting Democrats, especially in the North and for president. The Democratic coalition was held together by a **logroll** between those first two large groups: southern segregationists agreed to support labor laws, even though many southern conservatives were not very excited about them, in exchange for a commitment from northern party leaders not to push on civil rights.

The kind of tacit logroll seen between northern labor and southern segregationists is common in coalitions, but as we have seen with the Whig and Democratic parties trying to avoid the issue of slavery, holding off divisions is not easy. When the political system attempts to avoid an issue that matters to its citizens, someone will find a way to get the issue into the political landscape.

In the case of civil rights, liberal activists in the early twentieth century were frustrated for decades by their inability to advance civil rights legislation (voting protections, anti-lynching laws, and so forth) in the Congress, thanks to that logroll within the Democratic Party between segregationists and labor advocates. Those pro–civil rights activists sought new ways to press the issue both inside and outside the Democratic Party. The subject became harder for the party to avoid as many important Black politicians were winning power within the Democratic Party. In Chapter 3, we discuss New York Rep. Adam Clayton Powell's strategy of forcing Congress to vote on civil rights. In addition, as political scientist Keneshia Grant shows in her book *The Great Migration*, newly empowered Black politicians representing communities that had moved to northern cities in the Great Migration pressed for these issues.[11] And even in communities where the African American population was small, northern liberal Democrats began to pay more attention to civil rights.[12]

Civil rights played a dominant role in the 1948 Democratic National Convention. That year, incumbent president Harry S. Truman was nominated to campaign for his first full term, having taken over the presidency after Franklin Roosevelt died. Northern liberal Democrats pressed for a strong pro–civil rights platform plank. Campaign strategist Clark Clifford argued that support from the new Black voters in northern cities would be critical to winning elections. Southern Democrats were outraged over the new platform but they lost the fight. In response, 35 southern Democrats from Mississippi and Alabama walked out of the convention.

These angry southerners did not immediately join the Republican Party. They had too many ties to the Democrats. They eventually formed the States' Rights Democratic Party, which nominated South Carolina senator Strom Thurmond for president. They wanted to prevent the Democratic Party from further embracing civil rights and have it return to its earlier position on the issue. But the southern, racially conservative part of the coalition repeatedly lost in conflicts with the northern, racially liberal part, driving this group into the Republican Party.

The Republicans, for their part, welcomed new voters. The party had a long-standing disadvantage in party identification and had held majorities in Congress only twice since Herbert Hoover had been president (1929–33). Just as Democrats had seen promise in pursuing Black voters in the North, Republicans saw an opportunity with White conservative voters in the South. In what has been termed the "southern strategy," presidential candidates Barry Goldwater in 1964 and Richard Nixon in 1968 successfully pursued these voters. Before Goldwater, no Republican had won widely in the South since Reconstruction. In a blowout loss to Lyndon Johnson, Goldwater won only five states (Louisiana, Alabama, Mississippi, Georgia, and South Carolina) in addition to his home state of Arizona. Today, those southern states are the most reliable parts of the Republican coalition. This nearly complete reversal of the South in less than a decade is shown in Figure 2.2.

In terms of our coalitions model, then, southern racial conservatives were a core part of the Democratic coalition before 1948, and two decades later, they had begun a steady migration into the Republican Party. Over the past half century, the issues that are relevant to Black voters, racial liberals, and conservatives more broadly have changed. But those who advocate for policies aimed at helping racial minorities have moved into the Democratic Party, while those who oppose many of those policies have moved from the Democrats into the Republican Party.

Politics generally, and party coalitions more specifically, are always shifting in subtle ways. And sometimes a party will simply have a good election year, thanks to a strong economy, or a war, or a clever campaign, or something else. In those years, we'll see support from certain groups shift somewhat, but largely in the same direction. In 2008, for example, Democrat Barack Obama managed to win a majority of voters making over $200,000 per year, a constituency that has usually voted solidly for Republican presidential candidates. But this didn't mark a realignment;

it was rather a reflection of an economic collapse in 2008 that hit people in that income category unusually hard and turned them against the incumbent party. Wealthy voters returned to their previous voting patterns by 2012.

When you're watching or reading about a recent election and a pundit says something about a realignment, you should be skeptical. Then ask yourself (or the pundit): Has there been a shift? Did a group that's been voting with one party for a long time suddenly start voting with the other party? Did some new issue disrupt the old arrangement between the parties? Did politics suddenly get a lot less predictable? If so, then you just might be witnessing a realignment.

INTO THE TWENTY-FIRST CENTURY

Today's party regime, like the one that preceded it, is defined by sharp divisions on economic questions, but also by divisions on social issues such as civil rights, abortion, and gun regulation. As new issues emerge, they get absorbed into these ideological divisions and contribute to even further polarization. The parties are not only more competitive, but also more ideologically distinct from each other than at any time in American history. The policy consequences of shifting from Republican control to Democratic control of the government, or vice versa, have arguably never been greater.

One of the more striking tests of the modern party system's stability was the rise of Donald Trump as a Republican leader. Many party leaders in 2015 and 2016 were deeply skeptical about the wisdom of nominating Trump for the presidency, partially because they assumed (based on polling) that he would lose the election, and partially because he did not seem committed to long-standing Republican policies. While running for president, he advocated for some things that could be considered Republican issues—restricting immigration, lowering taxes, reducing business regulation, and naming pro-life conservatives to federal courts, for example—but also for things that sounded far more like Democratic agenda items, such as massive infrastructure spending, placing restrictions on trade, enhancing the social safety net, and increasing funding and federal responsibility for health care.

The 2016 election itself was a remarkable example of the party system's stability, however, with 90 percent of self-identified Republican voters and 90 percent of self-identified Democratic voters choosing their own party's

FIGURE 2.2   The Realignment of the South: Presidential Voting in 1956 and 1964

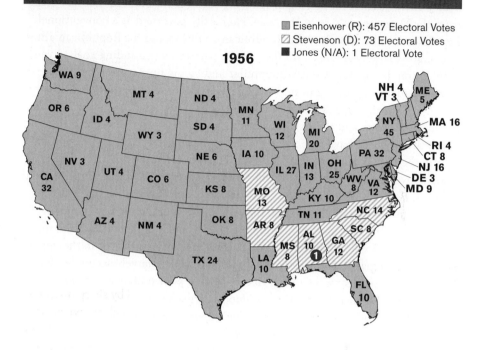

■ Eisenhower (R): 457 Electoral Votes
▨ Stevenson (D): 73 Electoral Votes
■ Jones (N/A): 1 Electoral Vote

1956

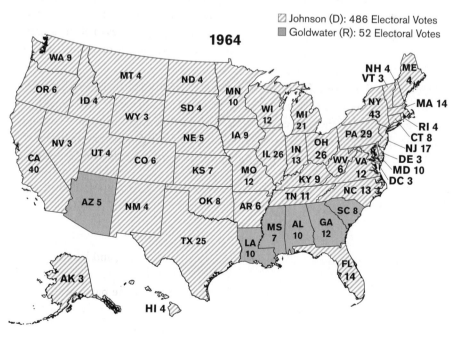

▨ Johnson (D): 486 Electoral Votes
■ Goldwater (R): 52 Electoral Votes

1964

nominee—roughly the same percentages as we have seen in other recent presidential elections. Once in the White House, Trump largely advanced Republican policies, either modifying or ignoring those of his stances that had come from the Democratic side of the aisle. He hardly governed as a conventional Republican, to be sure, but the Republican coalition and his Republican allies in Congress largely steered him toward the party's long-standing goals. Even with Trump being persistently unpopular and facing numerous scandals, a global pandemic resulting in massive unemployment, and impeachment, very few members of Congress or state legislators have switched out of or into the Republican Party, and the party coalitions have largely remained stable.

All that said, we have seen some modest variations in the party coalitions, at least in their areas of geographic strength. Ohio, for example, had been the ultimate bellwether state, voting with the winning party in 28 of the 30 presidential elections between 1896 and 2012. Between 2012 and 2016, however, it shifted sharply right. Although Democrat Hillary Clinton won the national popular vote by two percentage points, Trump beat her by eight percentage points, making the state more Republican than Texas. Shifting voting patterns in the upper Midwest, principally among less educated White voters, largely accounted for Trump's surprise Electoral College victory and for poor polling predictions in those states.[13] Meanwhile, mirroring Ohio, Georgia had been shifting toward the Democrats for some time, so Joe Biden's upset win in Georgia in 2020, while surprising, was not completely shocking. These once reliably red states are changing mostly as their demographics change. Growing Black and Latino populations in Arizona, Georgia, and even Texas are shifting those states. The rightward shift of working-class Whites in the upper Midwest is hardly a major realignment, but all these changes have caused campaigners to rethink which states are safe and which are in play.

Despite such modest shifts, the current party coalitional alignment has proven stunningly durable. It's not clear what new issue or demographic shift would undermine this alignment or even could, or when that might happen. That said, anything that can't last forever won't, and no doubt political observers in the 1850s and 1920s thought those party alignments were quite durable, as well.

Discussion Questions

1. The Electoral College as it functions today bears little resemblance to how it is described in the Constitution. What role did parties play in changing it?

2. What was the major difference between the elections of 1824 and 1828? To what extent did the parties create that difference?

3. To what extent are the parties to blame for the Civil War (1861–65)? Was the Civil War a result of the parties failing or of them succeeding?

4. To what extent do today's political parties stand for what the parties stood for in the 1960s? What about the 1930s?

5. Describe what a "realignment" is. If we're seeing working-class White voters, who used to vote regularly Democratic, increasingly voting Republican, should we call it a realignment? Why or why not?

3

Parties in Congress*

No law passed in the last few decades has had as much political impact as the Patient Protection and Affordable Care Act, often shortened to the Affordable Care Act (ACA) and better known as "Obamacare." From its conception to long after its passage in 2010, the law has been one of the dominant issues of three presidential elections, and promises to create it, expand it, or repeal it have been at the heart of congressional campaigns for more than a decade. In a way, calling the ACA "Obamacare" is misleading. Not because President Obama wasn't an advocate and key player in its passage—he was—but because so many other Democrats were as well. It might more accurately be called Democratcare.[1] Likewise, the Republican attempts to "repeal and replace" the ACA in 2017 were less "Trumpcare" than "Republicancare."

The continuing fight over the ACA illustrates how parties structure almost everything important in legislating. In 2009, both the House and the Senate were working on similar health care bills. (For major congressional legislation, it is common for the House and Senate to start working on bills separately.) The House passed their bill on November 7. The Senate considered this bill, but Democratic Party

---

* And some discussion of parties in state legislatures.

A Tea Party supporter outside the U.S. Supreme Court protesting the constitutionality of the Affordable Care Act in March 2012.

leaders had to satisfy some concerned members of their caucus to reach the 60 votes required to overcome a potential Republican-led filibuster. For instance, Senator Ben Nelson of Nebraska, one of the most conservative Democrats in the Senate, had several objections. Democratic leaders in the Senate and from the White House met with Nelson and negotiated language allowing states to limit funding for abortion and providing additional Medicaid money for Nebraska. Other Democrats had objections as well, and party leaders and the president had to make more concessions.

The Senate narrowly avoided a filibuster and passed their version of the bill. Ordinarily, two slightly different versions of a bill like this would be taken to a joint House-Senate conference committee, where discrepancies could be worked out. But before that could happen, Republican Scott Brown won a special election to replace the late Ted Kennedy as senator from Massachusetts. The Democratic Party strategized and decided that the House should pass the Senate's version of the bill. That meant, however, that members of the House would not be able to negotiate with their colleagues in the Senate and work out any disagreements they had with the bill.

House Democrats agreed to pass the existing bill, but only with the promise of support for a later bill that would make the changes they wanted. For this second bill, Democratic leaders used the "reconciliation" process, which is a procedure designed to let Congress make budgetary changes without the possibility of a filibuster. The use of reconciliation was controversial, but the party in power decides whether it is appropriate. In the end, the House passed the Senate bill, which Obama signed into law on March 23, 2010. And the Senate passed the reconciliation act from the House, which Obama signed on March 30.

Throughout the process, Republicans marshalled strong opposition to the legislation. Since its passage, they have attempted to repeal the ACA more than 70 times. In 2017, Republicans succeeded in eliminating one controversial feature of the bill, the "individual mandate," by using the same tool, reconciliation, that Democrats used to pass the bill.

Obamacare remains a target of Republican campaigns, and protecting it remains a goal of Democrats. In short, the legislative fight over health care in the United States has been, and continues to be, a fight between Democrats and Republicans.

Legislators are like any other large group of people—they need to organize and coordinate if they want to get anything done. Legislators in the United States do this in many different ways. They organize by state, by region, by policy area. They form committees to focus on specific issue areas, and they gather in caucuses to discuss shared interest in everything from fighting cancer to bicycling.[2] But the dominant organizing force in the U.S. Congress is the political party. Parties choose leaders, shape agendas, and help legislators make decisions.

WHO'S WHO IN THE LEGISLATIVE PARTY

The United States has at least 56 legislatures, including those of the national, state, and territorial governments. Notably, these do not include the many other smaller decision-making bodies that govern cities, counties, tribes, schools, and other political districts. Each legislature is different, but the basic party structure they adopt is similar. In this section, we first discuss how parties are organized in the House of Representatives and the Senate before turning to notable examples of parties in state legislatures.

The House of Representatives

The United States Congress is *bicameral*, meaning it has two chambers. The "lower" chamber, or House of Representatives, has 435 members, each from districts with roughly the same population. They are elected to two-year terms in every even-numbered year.

Once they get to Congress, representatives can conceivably organize themselves in different ways. Those from the same state, or same region, can coordinate and strategize together, and in fact they sometimes do. Representatives can organize around policy areas, forming committees to explore their topics—and they do that too. But parties are the most important organizational structure in Congress today.

House Leadership The organization of the House does not receive much attention in the Constitution, which says "The House of Representatives shall chuse their Speaker and other Officers; and shall have the sole Power of Impeachment." The role of the **Speaker of the House** is not elaborated on beyond that half sentence, but the Speaker is the presiding officer of the House, its public face, and second in the line of succession for the presidency, after the vice president. The Speaker usually delegates the day-to-day presiding over debate, but organizational matters are their ultimate responsibility.

While the Speaker's role need not be partisan, in effect, it is. Why? Because although the Speaker is technically chosen by the entire House, each party has their own candidate. That means the majority party's candidate has a built-in majority. The Speaker for the entire House is functionally picked by just the majority party's members.

When legislators arrive for their session in Washington, the members of each party meet in a closed-door session. The Democrats call this meeting a **caucus** and the Republicans a **conference**, but both serve the same basic function. Members of the House who are not in a party are sometimes invited to "caucus with" one of the major parties. These gatherings are where the members come together as a party, and it is at these meetings that legislative strategy is discussed. Leaders are also chosen. If the party is internally divided, then the members may have trouble choosing a leader. But they are meeting as a party, and they can sort out those internal differences before they bring the choice to the floor. There, if everyone in the majority party votes for the leadership candidate chosen by the party, that candidate will win.

We witnessed an interesting test of this in 2018. House Minority Leader (and former Speaker) Nancy Pelosi was something of an unpopular figure in national politics, and many more conservative Democratic congressional candidates ran for office that year by criticizing her and promising to challenge her speakership should their party take the majority. Democrats did take the majority that year, but Pelosi was able to secure the support of most of the dissidents in her caucus by negotiating term limits for congressional party leaders, including herself, paving a path for newer leadership down the road. In the end, 220 House Democrats backed her for Speaker in 2019, a few more than she needed to reclaim the position. A total of 192 Republicans backed fellow republican Kevin McCarthy for the position, and the remaining House members backed a handful of other candidates. Despite the internal dissent, it was a party-line vote that put Pelosi back in the speakership.

And a party-line vote is pretty typical. Figure 3.1 presents data from votes on the Speaker of the House from 1991 to 2021. The data show how partisan those votes are. For each vote, the figure shows the percent of the Democratic and Republican Members of Congress that voted against their party's candidate for the Speaker. In nearly every Speaker election, the percentage for both parties is 0. In a handful of cases, there are a few defections. In recent years, several members in each party have protested their party's candidate, but even then, they are not usually voting for the other party's candidate instead.

Once elected, the Speaker of the House technically speaks for the entire House. But who would we expect them to pay the most attention to? Since their reelection hinges not on the entire House, but on support from their party, we would expect them to pay most attention to the interests of their party. This makes the Speaker the de facto leader of their party in the House. Since they are in a position to set the agenda for the entire House, they set that agenda in the interests of their party. Each party also has a nominal leader, the majority leader and the minority leader, also chosen in the party caucus or conference. The House majority leader functions as second in command to the Speaker, although their precise role depends on the nature of the Speaker's leadership style and on their working relationship. Many Speakers delegate a lot of authority to the

FIGURE 3.1   Members of the House Not Voting for Their Party's Speaker Candidate, 1991–2021

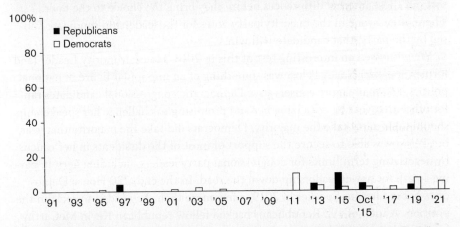

Source: Matthew N. Green and Briana Bee (2016), "Keeping the Team Together: Explaining Party Discipline and Dissent in the U.S. Congress," in *Party and Procedure in the United States Congress*, 2nd ed., edited by Jacob R. Straus and Matthew Glassman (Lanham, MD: Rowman & Littlefield, 2016). Thanks to Matt Green for assistance with this data.

majority leader, who sets the legislative schedule and generally works out the strategy for moving forward with the Speaker's agenda.

The House minority leader is the head of the minority party and the person the minority typically puts forward as their choice for Speaker. Minority leaders have little control over the legislative agenda, but they can shape the minority's response to the majority's agenda, including which amendments to offer and how to coordinate voting on them.

Both parties also select **whips**. The majority whip and the minority whip keep track of expected votes. When a bill comes to the floor for a vote, the leadership of each party wants to know, beforehand, how it is likely to come out. The whips use informal conversations and a network of deputies to keep track of how members are planning to vote. These are called whip counts. If legislation won't have enough votes to pass, the majority may decide not to hold the vote at all. Or they might try to revise the bill to make it more popular or to negotiate with unsupportive members for their support.

The term "whip" comes to the U.S. Congress from the Parliament of the United Kingdom, which in turn imported the language from the world of foxhunting. In foxhunting, the "whipper-in" uses a whip to drive the hounds back into the pack when they might stray.[3] This is effectively what the whip count is meant to accomplish, keeping legislators from straying from the party line, although herding hounds is probably easier than herding members of Congress.

House Committees Congress is also organized into subject-matter committees. Under Congress' traditional procedures, or "regular order," bills are first sent to those committees, which debate the legislation's merits and revise it before forwarding it to be considered by the entire chamber on the floor. Committees are shot through with partisan influence. To begin with, it's the parties that choose committee membership. Specifically, the House Republican Steering Committee assigns Republicans to committees, and the Democratic Party Steering and Policy Committee assigns Democrats. Both of these committees are made up of the caucus leaders discussed above, as well as members representing different parts of the country and levels of seniority. (The Democratic Party Steering and Policy Committee also advises on legislative priorities, while the Republicans do this with a separate Policy Committee.)

Each committee's membership is roughly proportional to the partisan split of the chamber. This means that if the Democrats are in the majority, there are more Democrats on every committee, and the committee chair of every committee will be a Democrat. When the committee meets, the majority party will always be able to prevail on votes if it is united. The chair has considerable power over how the committee will be run and what priorities it will take. The most senior member of the minority party is the ranking member. Since committee membership is assigned by the party leadership, the committee chair and ranking member will be chosen by the leaders. Members who are more helpful to the party (by voting with it or raising money for it, for example) are more likely to get the committees they want.[4]

Beyond appointing members to the committee, party leaders also have control over which bills are sent to committees, and how. The flow of a bill from proposal, to committee, to the floor, and through debate is governed by the leadership. They decide which committee the bill will go to, and as Barbara Sinclair pointed out in *Unorthodox Lawmaking*,[5] bills can be split, sent to different committees, and fast-tracked in various ways, all at the behest of the leadership. Sometimes the leadership will send a bill to a "kill committee"—one that is guaranteed not to pass it—so that the bill will not show up on the floor for a public vote.

In committee, the bill is discussed and revised. Then, should the bill pass committee and be sent to the floor, its debate is governed by a rule, assigned by the Rules Committee. That rule determines how long the bill will be debated, whether (and which) amendments will be in order, and so forth. The Rules Committee is run by the majority party. While most committees have a slight advantage for the majority party, the Rules Committee tends to be dominated by the majority party. In the end, the Speaker of the House can determine the agenda through use of these rules. We discuss how these rules affect legislative agendas later in the chapter.

The Senate

If the House is strongly organized by political parties, then by comparison, the Senate is not. The Senate is known for the power that individual senators wield, making its members less beholden to party leaders than members of the House are. But parties are highly influential even here.

The Senate has 100 members—two from each state—elected to staggered six-year terms. About one-third of the Senate is up for reelection in every even-numbered year. This means that senators can spend less time worrying about reelection than do members of the House. Fewer members and less focus on reelection mean there is less demand in the Senate for managing the workload. Ultimately, the Senate is governed less by party organizations and more by individuals, and any one senator can gum up the works.

The agenda and most other procedures in the Senate are determined by **unanimous consent**, meaning that if any one senator objects, the plan is scrapped. Senators also have the power to **filibuster**, or "hold the floor" indefinitely, preventing any work from being done. As discussed later in the chapter, the mere threat of a filibuster can cause the Senate to move on to a different topic.

Despite the power of individual members, the Senate still has partisan leaders. The ease with which individual senators can go their own way makes whipping and leadership perhaps more important. But unlike in the House, where the influence is formally built into the institutions, party leadership in the Senate is more informal.

After the 2020 elections, Democrats maintained their majority in the House of Representatives and re-elected Representative Nancy Pelosi (D-CA) as Speaker of the House. Following close runoff elections in early 2021 for Georgia's two Senate seats, Democrats won a majority in the Senate and named Senator Chuck Schumer (D-NY) as Senate Majority Leader.

The Senate has no equivalent of the Speaker. Officially, the vice president of the United States is the president of the Senate and presides over the body—although they are rarely in attendance. The Senate chooses a president pro tempore ("president for the time"), who presides and serves the president role. But unlike the Speaker, the president pro tempore is typically held by the most senior member of the majority party, although it is not particularly a partisan role. The president of the Senate is third in presidential succession.

The real leadership in the Senate are the elected Senate majority leader and Senate minority leader, who represent their parties' caucuses (as their counterparts do in the House). If most of the Senate is organized by unanimous consent, someone has to decide what will be consented to. The party leaders do this in consultation with each other. Because of the power of the filibuster (by which a small number of senators can delay or even prevent Senate business), the minority has much more influence in the Senate than in the House (which does not have a filibuster). But the Senate majority leader still has the upper hand.

As with the House leadership, the most powerful tool of the Senate majority leader is **agenda control**; the leader gets to decide which measures come for a vote and which do not. In 2016, when Supreme Court Justice Antonin Scalia died, Senate Majority Leader Mitch McConnell refused to have the Senate consider President Barack Obama's nominee for the position, Merrick Garland. As a result, the seat would not be filled until after the 2016 election, when a new president of McConnell's own party could nominate someone for it. This was certainly a controversial and historically unprecedented use of the power of the Senate majority leader, but it was not an illegal or unconstitutional one.

State Legislatures

Forty-nine of the fifty state legislatures are also organized along party lines, similar to Congress. While every state is different, all but one have bicameral legislatures with a lower house and an upper house that reflect the differences between the House and the Senate at the federal level. That is, the lower house tends to have more members who are elected more frequently, while the upper house tends to have fewer members elected less frequently, sometimes in staggered terms. Party leaders direct legislation through rules and partisan coordination, much like in Congress.

The one exception is Nebraska, which has a unicameral legislature that is officially nonpartisan. In Nebraska, legislators run for office without political labels and do not formally organize as parties in office. Committee chairs and chamber leaders are selected through secret ballots rather than party-line roll call votes. Interestingly, however, as politics in the country has become more polarized, so too has it become polarized in Nebraska. Party organizations outside the legislature still shape political careers and influence who gets elected. But the legislature is not organized in a partisan manner in the way that the Congress is. Nebraska's legislature has 49 senators, fewer legislators than any other state in the country. This may be one reason why the legislators don't need party leaders to help keep them organized.

The most significant variation across state legislatures is in how professional they are. Some state legislatures meet for long terms with members who make it their career. Others meet for a limited period of time, and their members typically have other jobs when the legislature is not in session. For example, state legislators in California are full time, earn $104,118 per year, and meet consistently over the two years between elections, while state legislators in Texas are part time, earn $7,200 per year, and are in session for only 140 days (plus any short special sessions) in a two-year period.

The more complicated the job of the legislature—the more members, the more legislation, the more professional—the more it will need some sort of organization. The next section explores why that is, and why legislators tend to use parties to organize.

WHY PARTIES?

Congress and state legislatures are not required to be run by parties. The Speaker could be a nonpartisan office, and the caucus leadership could have a small role. The Constitution does not mandate that these positions be partisan. So the power of party in organizing Congress reflects choices made by the politicians themselves.

Why would legislators choose parties? As we saw in Chapter 1, parties form to solve problems that are particularly evident in a legislature. Members of Congress would be better off if they agreed to back a common agenda, but they are individually tempted to break from that agenda when it suits them. Sometimes, what is in the best interests of the party is not in the members' short-term interests, even if it is in their long-term interests. A legislator might wisely vote for a bill that is a little bit unpopular in their own district to ensure the support of others on a bill that *is* popular with their constituents. But it can be hard to commit. In practice, members will need an institution to help keep them in line. This institution is a party.

To illustrate why members might want to submit to someone who could help keep them in line, let's look at a case where members lacked such coordination. And, since we often find ourselves taking the side of parties and party leadership in this book, we're going to give an example where you might find those opposing the party leadership more sympathetic.

In the 1950s, the Democratic Party was a coalition that included northerners, who wanted more rights for labor and for African Americans, and southern Whites, who were more conservative on most things, but especially on civil rights. The Democratic coalition was held together in large part by giving northern members what they wanted on labor and southern members what they wanted on race.[6] This compromise kept the party together, but of course it was a problem for African American Democrats, who were frustrated by a lack of attention to, let alone progress on, civil rights issues.

Representative Adam Clayton Powell (D-NY), then one of just a few African Americans in Congress, devised a strategy to bring issues of segregation onto the congressional agenda. Whenever plausible, Powell would introduce an amendment to a bill that would restrict its benefits to states that were not discriminating against Black people. These pro–civil rights amendments created a dilemma for Democrats.

To see why, look at Table 3.1, which outlines the basic preferences of four different groups in Congress. We don't know for certain what everyone wanted at the time, but based on their behavior and what we know about their districts, it's reasonable to make some educated guesses.[7] Each column in the table is the group's rank-ordered preferences. For example, in the leftmost column, northern Democrats want the spending bill with a civil rights amendment first—but would be okay with just the spending bill if they can't have that—and prefer the status quo least.

As the table shows, most Democrats supported the amended bill, while most Republicans opposed it. But Powell's amendment messed that up. Before the bill could be considered, the Powell Amendment would be voted on. At that point, northern Democrats were happy to have the amendment, because they

TABLE 3.1   Estimated Preferences on Powell Civil Rights Amendment

	Northern Democrats	Some Republicans (mostly from New England)	Southern Democrats	Most Republicans
Size	120 members	107 members	78 members	140 members
First Choice	Original bill + Powell Amendment	Original bill + Powell Amendment	Original bill	Status quo
Second Choice	Original bill	Original bill	Status quo	Original bill + Powell Amendment
Third Choice	Status quo	Status quo	Original bill + Powell Amendment	Original bill

and their constituencies mostly agreed with Powell. But southern Democrats would not, since theirs were the states that the amendment would have prevented from getting the funding. Republicans, meanwhile, were probably split on the amendment. Many agreed on the important civil rights reforms. Others might be happy to see less funding go to southern states represented by Democrats.

The key, though, is what happens when legislators with these preferences actually vote. The first vote is on the amendment. The second is on final passage, of either the amended or unamended bill. And at that point, with the preferences in Table 3.1, the unamended bill will pass (with the votes of all Democrats and some Republicans), while the amended bill would not (because southern Democrats join most Republicans to vote against it).

Legislators know that voting for the amendment is equivalent to voting against the bill. Political scientists distinguish this **strategic voting**, in which legislators vote based on the ultimate outcome, from **sincere voting**, in which they vote on the immediate question at hand. Such strategic voting might even be why some Republicans voted for the amendment. Meanwhile, Democratic leaders wanted their members to vote strategically.

In 1956, Congress was considering a bill to provide federal funds for education, and Powell introduced his amendment that would prohibit funds to states that discriminated against African Americans. Democratic whip Richard Walker Bolling recruited former president Harry Truman to sign an open letter urging Democrats to vote against the amendment. Bolling wrote:

> The Powell amendment raises some very difficult questions. I have no doubt that it was put forward in good faith to protect the rights of our

citizens. However, it has been seized upon by the House Republican leadership, which has always been opposed to Federal aid to education, as a means of defeating Federal aid and gaining political advantage at the same time. I think it would be most unfortunate if the Congress should fall into the trap which the Republican leadership has thus set. That is what would happen if the House were to adopt the Powell amendment. The result would be that no Federal legislation would be passed at all, and the losers would be our children of every race and creed in every State in the Union.[8]

Bolling's effort may have persuaded some. Forty-two northern Democrats voted against the amendment, joining 107 southern Democrats. But with support from Republicans and 78 northern Democrats, the amendment passed. At final passage, however, 140 Republicans, not all from the South, switched to oppose the bill. And thus the bill failed.[9] This left Democrats with nothing, when they could have at least gotten the education bill. And, as Bolling's effort indicates, they knew it. So why did so many Democrats not heed their leaders' advice? There are two big reasons.

First, voting strategically is hard to explain to constituents. They would see that their Congress member voted against the interests of Black people. The careful reasoning behind why such a vote was for the best might never be understood. Second, many Democrats agreed with Powell that their party should care more about the civil rights movement. It's one thing to sometimes give up what you want in the interests of the long-term logroll that the party manages. But African Americans were always giving and never getting.

A big part of the Powell Amendment story is what happens when a party is divided over something so fundamental as civil rights. But parties are always divided—over fundamental issues and over issues that may be important to only a few. Ideally, the party seeks to avoid fighting over those issues and to focus on the things that they do agree on—in this case school funding.

Managing Internal Disagreements

Managing disagreement among those who otherwise agree—as in the example of school funding and the Powell Amendment—is the main reason legislators turn to political parties. Political scientists theorize about parties in Congress by exploring the ways a party can prevent legislators from doing what they might otherwise want to do. Political scientists Gary Cox and Mathew McCubbins offer a useful metaphor for the situation legislators find themselves in. In Central China, some workers made their living by pulling boats laden with cargo through less navigable parts of the Yangtze River.[10] A team connected to the boats by ropes could pull several boats a day, and the more they pulled the more money they made. But because it took several people to pull a boat, it was tempting for any one puller to slack off just a little bit.

So the workers found a clever, if sometimes painful, solution. They paid someone to follow them and lash them if they slacked off. Under fear of the whip, each worker pulled harder, and the team could pull enough extra loads that they could afford to pay the whipper and still come out ahead. For Cox and McCubbins, a strong party leadership is a similar clever, if sometimes painful, solution. Party leaders have the power to influence and manipulate members into acting the way that is in their collective best interest.

Of course, this is only wise if the party leaders do, in fact, keep the interests of members in mind. In this way, the party leadership in the House of Representatives (and particularly the Speaker of the House) is like the benign ruler in Thomas Hobbes's *Leviathan*, and Cox and McCubbins titled their book *Legislative Leviathan* for that reason. Without leadership, Hobbes argues, people live in a dangerous world that is "solitary, poor, nasty, brutish, and short."[11] They thus pledge fealty to a leviathan (the king) who will create rules to protect them. But key for Hobbes is that leviathans serve their purpose. If they do not, they are no longer just and no longer deserve the loyalty of their subjects.

How then, to make sure that the leadership does what it is supposed to do? Cox and McCubbins argue that the interests of party leaders are aligned with their members because the members elect the leaders.[12] If the leaders fail to advance an agenda that reelects existing party members and expands their ranks in the legislature, then they will be replaced. If the leadership serves its constituents in the legislature well, they will act together to advance their party interests and thus, they hope, get reelected.

The Cox and McCubbins model of party leadership is sometimes called the **cartel model**, because the party coordinates like a business cartel might. Each member is independent, but they enter into an arrangement to work together, and they end up better for it. The model helps explain why legislators submit to parties. The party prevents fracturing of the sort that the Powell Amendment exposed by empowering leaders to decide whether an amendment will be considered or not. When possible, those leaders can even negotiate compromises between factions like the northern and southern Democrats.

But often, such compromise is not possible at all. The cartel model doesn't say much about what happens in that case. But another approach, called **conditional party government**, emphasizes the consequences of serious internal conflict. The conditional party government model, associated with political scientists John Aldrich and David Rohde,[13] also claims that members will give power to the leadership to accomplish common goals. But Aldrich and Rohde note that legislators will be much more willing to give power to leaders when the party generally agrees among itself.

Boat pullers drag boats off the banks of the Yangtze River in China. As a method to prevent any one boat puller from slacking, a man with a whip would follow the workers and lash any-one who didn't pull his weight.

In particular, Rohde observed that as the Democratic caucus in the House became more homogeneously liberal after the wave of "Watergate babies" were elected in 1974, the younger, liberal members rebelled against the power held by the shrinking group of generally senior southern conservatives. They asked for more power for themselves, but they also empowered the Speaker to push through a common, and more liberal, agenda. Aldrich and Rohde argue that when legislators become increasingly homogeneous, they give leaders more power, and when they have internal disagreements, they wish to keep more freedom to do as they would prefer.

The logic of conditional party government helps explain how the Powell Amendment made it to the floor for a vote. A strong party leadership would have prevented it, but the party leadership was not as strong then, precisely because the members didn't agree enough to empower them. It's one thing for party leaders to prevent minor disagreements from derailing the party coalition. But major disagreements, such as those over civil rights, are not so easily set aside.

Political scientists have continued to revise these models of congressional party organization, especially the conditions in which a party will be strong and those in which it will be weak. For instance, John Patty argues that differ-ent members of the party will differ over how strong they want the party leadership to be.[14] He says the party will settle on the median preference. Frances Lee argues that party voting derives from a team spirit that parties cultivate.[15]

Gregory Koger and Matthew Lebo developed a model of what they call "strategic party government," in which the parties empower their leaders in their desire to be reelected.[16] Even if they don't agree with everything the party leadership might want, they are willing to forgo some of their preferred policies to serve the goal of reelection. That is, they're willing to back their party even on issues they don't agree with because they believe it will help them win their next election. They might even do that if the "condition" of conditional party government is not met, because they need to consider the power of the opposing party. As they put it: "at any point in time, each party will strike a balance between individualism and cooperation that reflects the costs and benefits of each and the strategy of the opposing party."[17]

Internal disagreements are not enough to prevent members from giving party leaders power, Koger and Lebo argue, in part because many of the party leaders' activities don't affect policy outcomes anyway. In creating a party brand, the party leaders amplify differences with the other party, regardless of what policy passes. For instance, Democrats pushed a plan to extend funding for Planned Parenthood in 2015. Since Democrats were in the minority, the plan was "doomed to fail," Koger and Lebo write, but "highlighted opposition among Republican senators in precarious states."[18]

Conflict with the other party can lead even an ideologically diverse party to want strong leadership. Each party will organize not only in response to the needs of their own party, but in response to the other party's organization as well. Koger and Lebo argue that both parties may end up with similar strategies.

POLITICAL SCIENCE TOOLKIT
The Spatial Model: Part 1

The various theories of party organization in Congress all suggest that legislators realize they need leadership to help them coordinate. What strategies can party leadership use to keep their members in line?

We can divide these strategies into two categories—those that induce members to change their behavior and those that do not. To examine and understand these categories, it is important to distinguish and compare what a member wants and what the leadership wants. To help us do that systematically, we can use a tool that political scientists use to discuss political preferences. It is called the *spatial model*.

The basic idea of the spatial model is that we can think of policies as arranged along a line—a continuum. That continuum could represent levels of spending or levels of regulation, but for the sake of illustration, let's say it represents how liberal or conservative the policy is. We can also think of politicians as having preferences for different policies along that line. So any politician has a point on the line that indicates their "ideal" policy positions, and the policy itself has a point on the line indicating how liberal or conservative it is. We can reasonably assume that the politicians will prefer policies that are closer to their ideals over those that are farther away.

This approach allows us to visualize cases where the leadership changes policies to satisfy members; cases where members accept policies that are not ideal but are better than the alternatives; and cases where leaders avoid proposing policies at all, because these first two options are not possible. As we illustrate these concepts, you can see them in the boxes that depict the actions of members of Congress in terms of the spatial model.

In the hypothetical education spending figure below, you can see that some legislators want to spend a lot on education, and others want to spend less. Some may not want to spend anything at all. This means we can put the ideal policies of specific politicians on the same diagram with the policies themselves:

Here, Legislator A would like to spend $650 billion, while Legislator B prefers $700 billion. Legislator C prefers to spend $900 billion. What will happen as the politicians vote on different alternatives?

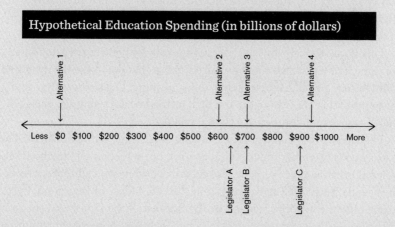

Hypothetical Education Spending (in billions of dollars)

Scholars using the spatial model would make the straightforward assumption that people prefer policies that are closer to their ideal point than those that are farther away. This means that Legislator A would rather spend $700 billion than spend $800 billion. We also tend to assume that people have symmetric preferences, so that Legislator A is indifferent between spending $600 billion and $700 billion, and would prefer spending $600 billion to spending $800 billion, since $600 billion is closer to $650 billion.[19]

Political scientists can identify a number of important implications with just this simple setup. We present two of them here.

It matters what the alternatives are.

A politician may dislike some policy, but do they dislike it more than the alternative? In the figure, Legislator B prefers spending $700 billion over spending $600 billion, and if that lawmaker were to choose between alternative 2 and alternative 3, they would choose alternative 3. But if the alternative is to spend nothing at all, as with alternative 1, the preference would be to spend $600 billion, because $600 billion is closer to $700 billion than zero is.

The existing policy before anyone votes is called the **status quo**. If politicians do nothing, the status quo will remain unchanged. (Though sometimes, if politicians don't act, policy will revert to something else, such as when a law has a built-in expiration or "sunset" date.)

In this example, the decision requires a vote using majority rule. If these three legislators were to choose between alternative 3 and alternative 4, they would choose alternative 3, because legislators A and B both prefer $700 billion to $950 billion. But suppose that the choice is between alternative 4 and alternative 1, so that if the higher budget doesn't pass, nothing is spent at all. In that case, A and B would switch their votes to alternative 4.

This is one reason why legislators often vote for choices they don't like very much. If a problem must be solved, those that don't like the proposed solution may still like it better than doing nothing. Legislators often vote for budgets that they think are too high or too low, for example, because they'd rather spend something than spend nothing at all.

The alternatives that legislators vote on don't come out of nowhere. The status quo is often beyond anyone's control, but someone gets to choose the other alternative that everyone else gets to consider. We call that someone the agenda setter. The agenda setter in the U.S. House of Representatives is generally the majority leadership: the Speaker of the House and the rest of the leadership team. Setting the agenda includes choosing which options are available as well as what order they are voted upon.

So in our education spending scenario, if the status quo is that nothing is spent at all (alternative 1), an agenda setter could make it so that any of the other three alternatives wins. If the agenda setter doesn't want to spend very much, they could propose alternative 2 (or even less), and everyone would vote for it. If they wanted to spend a lot of money, they could propose alternative 4 (or even a little bit more), and everyone would vote for it.

The voter in the middle always wins.

The choice of which policy to adopt is of course a collective choice. So if politicians vote for the policy they prefer the most, then the politician in the middle, the **median voter**, will always be on the winning side. This is because in our hypothetical, one-dimensional world, any majority must include the median voter. If the median voter likes some outcome, then everyone between the median and that outcome must also like it. In the education spending scenario, the median voter is Legislator B. There is no majority that doesn't include Legislator B. If B prefers some alternative, then either Legislator A also prefers it (because the other choice is larger than the alternative), or Legislator C also prefers it (because the other choice is smaller). There is no way for Legislators A and C to want something that Legislator B doesn't also want.

If we have a larger legislature, the idea of the median voter becomes even *more* useful. In the next figure, we have nine legislators considering gun control policies. If we want to know what alternative will succeed, we only need to look at Legislator E, who prefers background checks over the status quo, and so does everyone to E's left. Background checks beats the status quo. But Legislator E also prefers background checks to a ban on all guns, as does everyone to E's right. Background checks beats the ban on all guns.

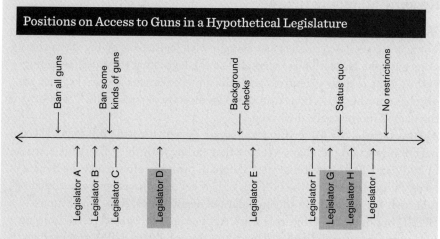

Positions on Access to Guns in a Hypothetical Legislature

Legislators D, G, and H are on the committee that will consider gun control legislation.

The median voter also wins among any other set of actors. In the U.S. Congress, bills are often referred to a committee before they move to the floor. The background checks bill is sent to a committee with Legislators D, G, and H. There, the median voter is Legislator G, who prefers the status quo. So Legislator G would never mark up any bill to be considered on the floor.

In that scenario, the committee is an agenda setter, and in this case, the agenda setter controls the agenda by not proposing anything. The other important players in Congress that the committee must think about are the median voter on the floor in each chamber, as well as the medians of the two parties.

Political scientists use the spatial model to explore many different questions. The spatial model is, however, a simplification in many cases, an oversimplification. But it does help us clarify how different legislative alternatives will influence the behavior of members, and thus how important the agenda, and those who create it, are. This model can help legislative leaders map out their best options for success, and it can be very helpful for scholars seeking to understand the influence of those leaders on their legislative colleagues.

Keeping Members in Line

How can leaders encourage members to vote the way they want them to? There are several ways. They can bargain with legislators, giving them concessions until the legislation is acceptable to the legislators they are bargaining with. They can offer incentives and punishment (carrots and sticks) that are unrelated to the legislation. And they can directly persuade the legislators that the party's interests are their own.

For example, the leadership can bargain by adjusting the bill to get the support of important members. We saw that earlier with the Affordable Care Act in 2009 and 2010. Several key legislators in both the House and the Senate were willing to support the bill, but only if certain provisions were added or removed. For instance, in the final days of negotiations, Rep. Bart Stupak (R-MI) opposed the Affordable Care Act because he wanted restrictions on federal funding for abortion. He and Rep. Joseph Pitts (R-PA) proposed an amendment to do just that, but the amendment failed. Stupak and others planned not to vote for the final bill. President Obama negotiated with Stupak and issued an executive order restricting abortion funding, which earned Stupak's vote.

Most compromises show up in the text of the bill itself, of course, and not in the inside deals like the one you just read about. The final product usually involves just enough compromise needed to get sufficient votes to pass. Again, looking at the Affordable Care Act, the final proposal jettisoned things like the public option, which would have introduced a government-run insurance option among existing insurers. While many Democrats wanted the public option, that provision likely would not have had enough support from moderate Senate Democrats; dropping that part of the bill was the compromise that won their support. More liberal Democrats in Congress were upset by the exclusion of the public option, but still saw the compromised bill as far better than the status quo, and they voted for it.

But compromise does not have to involve the text of the bill itself. A legislator might support the current bill in exchange for support on their priorities in the future. As we discussed in Chapter 2, this sort of logrolling is, in many ways, the main thing that parties help to coordinate.

POLITICAL SCIENCE TOOLKIT
The Spatial Model: Part 2

As legislators try to get a bill passed, one thing they can do is compromise on the language of the bill itself. As we noted in the text, the Affordable Care Act was not going to pass until leadership dropped the provision for the public option.

In the terms of the spatial model, compromise effectively moves the bill toward some members' ideal points. And while some other members may not be not happy with these concessions, they generally still prefer the compromise bill to doing nothing—so they support it.

The next figure shows the preferences of a hypothetical legislature with nine members who are considering the Affordable Care Act. Five are Democrats, on the left of the continuum, and the four on its right are Republicans. A bill needs five votes to pass. The ACA with the public option is too far away from the median voter, who prefers the status quo to any reform that would include the public option. But the median voter would like to see some reform. When the party leaders dropped the public option, they were able to secure the support of the median voter and pass the bill.

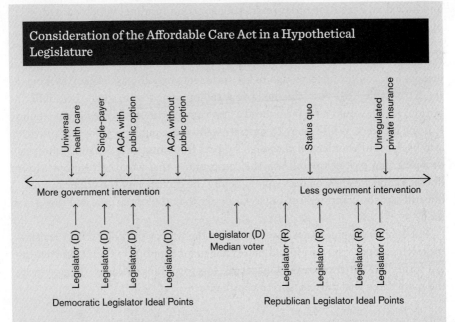

Consideration of the Affordable Care Act in a Hypothetical Legislature

The spatial model focuses on actual changes to the legislation, but leaders don't have to change the legislation to win over votes. On many issues, a legislator might have a preference, but only a weak one. Or they won't know enough about the vote's outcome to have a preference.

The ability to persuade or at least guide other legislators is an under-appreciated source of party-leader influence. Party leaders very rarely demand members vote a particular way—they don't generally have the tools to back up threats, and if they make too many demands, members may go shopping for a new leader. But party leaders do have certain advantages that make them influential in getting the votes they want, including control over campaign money, collection of information, influence over where bills get assigned, who serves on which committees, and where members' offices are. Their mastery of information is particularly impor-tant, and in many ways is similar to how party cues operate in the elector-ate (Chapter 11). Voters don't know how a policy will affect their lives, so they take cues from political elites who are often party leaders. Similarly, legislators may not know how a policy will affect their political fortunes, so they look to leadership for cues and guidance.

Legislators, of course, have some sense of what people care about in their districts. They understand local sentiment on the higher-profile issues that they ran on and that they hear about when constituents contact them. But how will a new business regulation, or a health benefit, or education proposal be received by voters when most of those voters know nothing about it today? Legislators can guess about this sort of thing or they can turn to politically connected people like lobbyists, interest group representatives, and, yes, their own party leaders. Lobbyists and interest groups provide information to members trying to figure out what the best decision would be, but they may not have the members' best interests at heart. The party leadership, on the other hand, won't remain in leadership for long if its party members are not reelected, so their interests are aligned.

Finally, party leaders do have some more blunt tools of persuasion to use. The most obvious is campaign finance. Both parties have committees in both chambers that are designed to get party members reelected: the Democratic Congressional Campaign Committee (DCCC), the Democratic Senatorial Campaign Committee (DSCC), the National Republican Congressional Committee (NRCC), and the National Republican Senatorial Committee (NRSC). These committees are tasked with helping members of their party get reelected. Such committees, and the party in general, rarely try to directly harm incumbents. However, priorities must be made. A member who is consistently out of line may find themselves with less support from their party than they would like.

That would take a lot of getting out of line, though. If voting against their party really is in the interest of the member, it may be in the interest of the party leadership to let them be free to vote that way. After all, the party leadership wants to reelect as many of its own caucus as it can. On the 2010 Affordable Care Act vote in the House, Speaker Nancy Pelosi had more than enough Democratic votes for passage, so she freed Democrats from more competitive districts to vote against it to help them in their reelection races.[20] If a vote will hurt a member's reelection chances, it's not good for the party's majority status, nor for the party leadership itself. The occasional defection isn't going to get the party upset, especially if it's not decisive.

Reelection considerations can put a real constraint on the ability of the party to pressure legislators to vote the way they want them to. However, not all legislative votes are equally important to members' reelection chances. Our discussion so far focused on what we call **substantive votes**. These are votes that are directly on the content of bills and resolutions. However, much of what a legislative body does is procedural. A **procedural vote** is a vote on how the legislature will proceed, such as whether it will allow or cut off debate on a bill, or whether it will send a bill back to its originating committee. Such votes may seem technical and arcane, but they determine how the decision can be made. For example, it's common for a legislator to move to send a bill back to committee for more deliberation. Such a "motion to recommit" at a minimum will delay the bill, and at most may end up killing it. In practice, then, procedural votes can determine which bills pass and which do not. In terms of the actual outcomes in a legislature, these procedural votes are often at least as important as substantive votes.

But legislators don't treat them the same. Several political scientists have shown that, for all their potential defections on substance, legislators are much more likely to vote with their parties on procedural votes.[21] Since voters and activists don't pay as much attention to procedural votes, legislators are freer to vote the way their party would like them to. If someone is going to make a campaign ad about a member of Congress' vote, it isn't going to be about their vote on a motion to recommit.

In some cases, this allows a member to vote against something without ever openly opposing it. In some cases, members may not want to go on record opposing a popular bill. Some Democrats, for example, didn't want to go on record opposing the Powell Civil Rights Amendment, even though they saw it as undermining school funding. In that case, those members could simply vote with their party to "recommit" the bill. A motion to recommit is almost always raised right before the vote on "final passage," or the ultimate vote on the final form of the legislation. If the motion to recommit passes, the bill goes back to committee before the floor can vote on it. Again, in terms of the actual outcome of the bill, recommitting it is functionally the same as voting it down, but it doesn't attract nearly the same level of attention, and it's easier to tell a constituent that you sent something back to committee rather than killed it.

Agenda Control

The easiest way to prevent opposing party members from voting the way their leadership wants them to is to control what they vote on in the first place. For party leaders, control of the agenda—what gets a vote and when—can be nearly as powerful as persuasion.

This can work in two ways. The most common is **negative agenda control**. This is when the party leadership keeps decisions off the agenda to prevent them from having a public vote. It is also possible to manipulate items onto the agenda, or **positive agenda control**, but this is more difficult and less common.

The notion of negative agenda control is often associated with former Speaker of the House Dennis Hastert (R-IL), who in a 2003 speech in the Capitol said, "the job of [S]peaker is not to expedite legislation that runs counter to the wishes of the majority of his majority." Note that he is not saying that he necessarily supports everything that the majority of his majority (in this case, Republicans) want to do. But he is not going to advance legislation that the majority of Republicans do not want. Observers called this "the Hastert rule." (Hastert has since said that this was never a real "rule" for him, but as Gary Cox and Mathew McCubbins argue in *Setting the Agenda*, most party leaders tend to use this strategy, and have done so since well before Hastert became Speaker.[22]) Another way of putting it is that the party leadership will only advance legislation that their party is united behind. For legislation where their party is divided— such as Democrats on civil rights in the 1950s—the party will keep those issues off the agenda. A Democratic Party exercising negative agenda control in the 1950s would never have allowed the Powell amendments to come up for a vote, and the legislation on which northern and southern Democrats agreed would have passed.

For frustrated members, there are ways around the party's control over the agenda. For instance, if the majority party leadership is unwilling to consider a bill that a majority on the floor wants to vote on, the bill's supporters can sign a **discharge petition** forcing the committee to send the bill to the floor. The discharge petition was created precisely to limit the power of the leadership. But the use of discharge petitions is rare. If the leadership wanted the bill to proceed, there would be no need for the discharge. If the leadership does not, then signing the discharge petition means going against the leadership in a public way. Most members will not want to upset their party leaders unless they care a great deal about the legislation that is bottled up in committee. A few members might be that passionate, but a majority rarely is.

Negative agenda control is effective for getting legislation passed. It also protects members of the legislature. And in the end, the leadership is interested in helping members get reelected. Sometimes that means helping them to avoid a costly vote. Just as we saw that the leadership might want to let members defect when it is in their interests, so too will the leadership want to protect members from having to choose on difficult issues.

POLITICAL SCIENCE TOOLKIT
The Spatial Model: Part 3

One way for party leaders to get what they want is to compromise, as we saw in the previous Political Science Toolkit. But negative agenda control can help them get what they want with less compromise.

The following figure illustrates the benefits of negative agenda control with a hypothetical scenario. In the model, the majority of the majority likes the status quo. But a majority of the legislature would like something else. In particular, the hypothetical proposal for more regulations on the financial industry (right at the chamber median legislator) would surely pass the legislature.

But such a bill divides the majority party. If the majority of the majority likes the status quo, they don't need to report any bill to the floor at all. In that case, the committee chair—appointed by party leadership—controls the agenda and thus would let the bill die in committee.

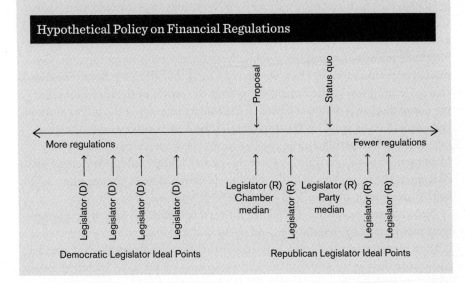

Hypothetical Policy on Financial Regulations

Control of Amendments

Agenda power is more flexible than it might appear. It's not just that the leadership can only allow votes where they will win. They can choose the content of the bills to ensure that they will pass, and avoid putting forward bills that would not pass, or would pass in a form they don't like.

Control of amendments is the key tool the majority uses to shape the content of legislation. When, in the 1950s, Democrats advanced spending bills such as the one in the story of the Powell Amendment, they allowed anyone on the floor to propose an amendment. This meant Powell could propose something that turned people against the bill. The leadership has a tool to prevent this: assigning a restrictive rule. In the House, every bill that is considered on the floor is given a rule, which dictates how long it will be debated and what amendments are allowed. The rule is assigned by the Rules Committee, which as we discussed earlier is dominated by the majority party and answers to the party leadership. A strong party leadership can choose a rule to affect the outcome of debate.

There are a variety of rules that can be assigned, but the most common distinction is between open rules and closed rules. Under an open rule, anyone can propose amendments to the bill. Under a closed rule, the bill must be voted on as is. Sometimes they will use a modified closed rule that allows only a certain number of amendments to just certain parts of the bill. These rules are very useful for the party leadership. Sometimes, the content of a bill is a delicate balance of many different competing interests within the party. Leaders may push for a closed rule to avoid any amendments that could threaten the bill's success on a final vote. At other times, the majority may allow an open rule so that many members can propose amendments to benefit their districts. Amendment rules are a vital tool the majority party uses to translate members' preferences into actual laws.

The party leadership has a hand in nearly every procedural decision made in Congress. In order to move policy toward their own preferences and away from the center of the legislature, majority party leaders can implement more and more complicated strategies with the agenda. As previously discussed, the decision to move the Affordable Care Act forward by using budget reconciliation rules was only possible because Democratic leaders controlled the agenda.

So why didn't the Democratic Party just use a restrictive rule on the Powell Amendment? As we discussed earlier, how much power the party leadership gets varies. A unified, homogeneous party will give its leadership a lot of power; the members of a divided party will want the freedom to go their own way. As we saw in Chapter 2, in the 1950s, the Democratic Party was perhaps the most divided it has ever been. So the party leadership's ability to set a restrictive rule was limited.

Obstruction

So far, most of the tactics and strategies we have described have been from the point of view of the majority. Minority leaders use most of the same tools to persuade, pressure, and encourage their members to vote the way they want them to. The minority has tools to try to achieve its goals, but because the majority sets the agenda, most of what the minority can do is reactive. Often, the minority tries to disrupt the majority party legislation, extract concessions, and sometimes simply embarrass the majority with an eye toward the next election.

The Filibuster The most obvious strategy for obstruction is in the Senate, where the institution of the filibuster means that even one senator can, in theory, prevent legislation from moving forward. Since the Senate does not limit debate, any member who can hold the floor indefinitely can prevent the body from moving to vote. It is hard for a single member to do this alone, so, in the twentieth century when filibusters became more common, most successful ones involved teams of opponents who could speak at length and then yield to an ally. Occasionally, this could be performed well by only a handful of senators in the majority committed to a cause, but a minority party, united in opposition to a bill, could also coordinate a filibuster very effectively.

The filibuster works through delay. Opponents of the bill commit to holding the floor while the bill is debated. This means that not only can the Senate never move the bill forward to a vote, they can't do anything else while they try. So the leadership has to either drop the bill or negotiate with the filibustering faction until they agree. Again, the party leadership orchestrates these negotiations.

The filibuster once involved literally speaking on the floor without interruption, but the Senate eventually realized that this was unnecessary. Anticipating how everything will play out, the potential filibusterers and the leadership negotiate in advance. In other words, merely the threat of the filibuster is enough. This has the effect of strengthening the filibuster option because it makes it easier to use.

The Senate has made other moves that weaken the filibuster. The biggest is changes to the **cloture vote**. Cloture is a procedure to cut off debate in the Senate. It used to require two-thirds of those "present and voting," which could be up to 67 members if everyone was participating in a 100-member Senate.[23] In 1975, the Senate changed this to only 60 percent of all senators "duly chosen and sworn," whether they were present or not. In 2013, the Democratic majority eliminated the filibuster for executive branch appointments and judicial nominees other than the Supreme Court. The Republican majority extended this precedent to Supreme Court nominees in 2017. In both cases, a mostly united majority was enough to limit the filibuster.

Despite elimination of the filibuster on executive branch appointments, the filibuster on legislation still stands. Why? Once eliminated, the filibuster would likely not come back (which is why this move is sometimes termed the "nuclear option"). Senators, even those deeply frustrated by filibusters, often remain loyal to Senate traditions and culture, and given how frequently the Senate has changed partisan hands in recent decades, any majority member knows they may soon be in the minority and might want to use this handy tool.

Other Strategies of Obstruction The filibuster is dramatic, but there are other ways in which members of the minority can extract concessions from the majority. Sometimes, the majority needs a few minority votes. That might be because of disagreement within the majority, or even because the majority needs to let some of its own members to vote against a bill. Particularly in recent years, when Senate control has been by just a few seats, the majority may sometimes need a few minority members for a win, and those minority members are in a good position to exact a price.

The minority may sometimes try to force votes on amendments that it knows it will lose, just to embarrass the majority party.[24] For instance, as the Senate was considering the legislation that became the Affordable Care Act in 2010, Senator Tom Coburn (R-OK) introduced an amendment that would prohibit the insurance programs being used by sex offenders to pay for Viagra. (Recall that the Affordable Care Act was passed by the reconciliation process, which required that no words be changed in the bill. Even an innocuous amendment would be a problem.) Democrats didn't want to vote against the amendment and have to explain to their constituents that they didn't prohibit coverage of Viagra for sex offenders (even though it was already barred by existing law). But they couldn't vote for the amendment because of the limitations of the reconciliation process. Democrats were between a rock and a hard place, but ultimately had to vote against the amendment to allow the larger bill to pass through the reconciliation process.

Individual members of the House have neither the filibuster nor the freedom that senators have, but there are other strategies for obstruction that House members can employ.[25] Even a small amount of delay can create a lot of inconvenience for the majority party, and sometimes this is enough to convince the majority to make modest concessions.

For example, in 1997, as the Rules Committee began to consider rules for a foreign aid bill, the Republican majority planned to allow consideration of an amendment that would have barred funding for abortion in other countries. Minority member Nancy Pelosi (D-CA) wanted to offer an alternative, pro-choice amendment. Republicans initially agreed to allow the amendment, but a trio of Republicans would be the ones allowed to offer it. Pelosi and other Democrats protested by delaying progress on a different bill. Pelosi and others called for recorded votes on procedural matters, delaying an agricultural bill until the majority conceded to let Pelosi offer an amendment on the foreign aid bill.[26] This example is typical of House obstruction. The concession was minor, and the effort was significant. But the minority believed the effort was worth it.

PARTY GOVERNMENT

It is very easy to describe how a bill becomes a law without any reference to political parties. Legislators are free to organize in almost any way, and they sometimes do. But it's misleading to describe the process that way. Legislators have, over the course of American history, organized Congress around political parties. They have chosen this system. How much power they give to party leaders can wax and wane, but the practical structure has almost always been partisan.

The reason is simple. Members of the majority party realize they will be better off if they can get someone to serve as a leader and prevent members from deviating too wildly from the party's agenda. The minority party, too, realizes they should organize to counter the majority, and to try to become a majority themselves.

There are legislatures where this doesn't happen. Notably, when legislators were able to run for office without choosing a party in California in the 1950s, they did not organize along party lines.[27] The Nebraska legislature, mentioned in the chapter opening, is explicitly nonpartisan. But these are exceptions. In most legislatures, and certainly in the United States Congress, the driving force for legislative organization is the party.

The central role of party should change how we think about legislatures. It is tempting to depict Congress as a place for deliberation. The U.S. Senate is sometimes called (usually by senators) "the world's greatest deliberative body." Deliberation does take place, but the organization of the Congress is not oriented around deliberation. It is oriented around partisan conflict, and especially in the House of Representatives, around empowering the majority party.

For this reason alone, parties become central to many other areas of politics. Which party is in the majority may matter more than whether you agree with your legislator, or even whether they are a good person. Those things matter too, of course, but party matters a lot. Observers sometimes decry this partisanship, and certainly party conflict can grind the legislature to a halt. But partisanship can also empower legislators to coordinate, compromise with one another, and thereby accomplish their goals.

Discussion Questions

1. For what reasons would a legislator want to be part of a political party? What advantages do they get from being a party member?

2. The Speaker of the House holds a position of leadership for the entire House of Representatives. Why are elections to this position almost always straight party-line votes?

3. In what ways is partisanship more relaxed in the Senate than in the House?

4. What tools do legislative leaders have to make sure that their members vote along party lines? Do they mostly use threats to enforce party-line voting or offer rewards?

5. Describe a lesson of the spatial model that might not otherwise be obvious to someone observing legislative behavior.

4

Parties and the Executive

From the middle of March 2020 until well into April, the president of the United States gave an almost daily briefing to the American people on the nation's response to the COVID-19 pandemic. As befits a national crisis, the nation's chief executive stood alongside the White House Coronavirus Task Force to inform the public about developments in the pandemic and the best practices to limit its spread.

But Donald Trump did not use these briefings only to address the pandemic and its devastating national health and economic effects. Trump and others in the White House also spent time during these televised events defending his administration's handling of the crisis;[1] claiming that he had always believed that the virus would be a pandemic;[2] suggesting that the House impeachment inquiry, which ended on February 5, 2020, had distracted the president from attending to the potential of a pandemic;[3] criticizing Democratic governors over their handling of the crisis;[4] promoting the use of malaria drugs hydroxychloroquine and chloroquine to treat COVID-19, contradicting the advice of medical professionals;[5] and accusing President Barack Obama of undermining efforts to develop a test for the virus.[6]

Throughout the COVID-19 crisis, U.S. governors also gave regular televised updates to inform the public about the number of new cases and deaths from

During the coronavirus pandemic, President Trump's response, as well as governors' responses, often took partisan tones. Here, Trump answers questions at a Coronavirus Task Force briefing.

the virus in their states and to detail the actions and policies they would implement to address the pandemic. As with the president's briefings, these state-level announcements could sometimes convey partisan aspects as well. At first, both Democratic and Republican governors were willing to implement social distancing requirements, close nonessential businesses, and enact other executive orders to address the crisis. Most of the governors, regardless of party, took executive action to try to get ahead of the virus within three weeks of the first reported case in their state.[7] Of the eight states that had not issued any COVID-19 orders by mid-April, all were led by Republican governors. And Democratic governors were particularly vocal in blaming the White House for not doing more to help get their states critical medical equipment. By midsummer, the state responses had become considerably more polarized by party, as every state with a Democratic governor had a mask law in place while most states led by Republican governors did not.

Americans often imagine their leaders being above partisan politics, especially in a crisis. And sometimes, that is possible. But presidents and governors can never stop being leaders of their party and their states. Balancing the role of unifying leader and zealous partisan is one of the biggest challenges of being an elected executive in the American political system.

- "This election will decide whether we're ruled by a corrupt political class or whether we are ruled by yourselves, the people. It is time to reject a failed political elite that has bled this country dry."

All these statements were uttered by Republicans, and the content is almost interchangeable. The words touch on the same basic theme—that an intellectual elite controls the government and is out of touch with and dismissive of the needs of average Americans. Yet these quotes come from very different speakers and eras. The first one comes from Wendell Wilkie, running against Franklin Roosevelt in 1940.[8] The second is from Ronald Reagan's "A Time for Choosing" speech in 1964.[9] The third is former Pennsylvania senator Rick Santorum, running for president in 2012.[10] The fourth is from Donald Trump, shortly before Election Day in 2016.[11] The point is that parties are quite consistent over time. This is helpful for presidents and members of Congress trying to advance an agenda.

Similarly, by sharing a party affiliation, members of Congress share a common fate with the president. Legislators recognize that an unpopular president at the top of their party's ballot can drag them down and jeopardize their chances for reelection. It's often in their interest to keep their president popular, which means providing public support that projects an image of unity with the commander in chief.

Relatedly, the whole logic of forming a legislative party in the first place (see Chapter 3) ends up including the presidency. Members of Congress want to be able to point to a record of legislative achievement when they next go before their voters seeking another term. They can't do this without the president's signature on their bills. Just as it makes sense for them to join a long coalition of other legislators, which makes it easier to pass bills, it makes sense to have the president be a part of this coalition.

All of this helps explain why Democrats such as Senator Blanche Lincoln (Arkansas) and Senator Ben Nelson (Nebraska), both from conservative states, voted for President Obama's controversial Affordable Care Act in 2009. Had they simply been representing what their constituents wanted, they almost certainly would have voted against the landmark bill. But they were also part of a larger party coalition that, based on Lincoln's and Nelson's votes, would either succeed or fail on its biggest legislative priority. And they were tied to a president whose reelection might be less secure if his biggest campaign promise failed. The party allowed for coordination across branches; it made it possible to govern in a system designed to make governing difficult.

POLITICAL SCIENCE TOOLKIT
Measuring the President's Ideology

Was President Donald Trump a conservative Republican, committed to a right-wing vision of the social and economic world? Or was he actually a moderate, tacking to the right on issues like abortion but actually trying to pull Republicans to the center? Is it possible he was a closet liberal? Political observers following his career have made all these claims, with considerable evidence in support of each, but they can't all be true.

Like any other politician, presidents have their own ideological predilections. Some are deeply ideological and committed to advancing a worldview and a set of policy goals. Some are quite pragmatic and willing to do what they see as necessary to maintain their popularity and keep their governing coalition together.

As we saw in Chapter 3, political scientists sometimes represent these ideological preferences spatially. Those who are more liberal are on the left, those who are more conservative, on the right. Every politician can be said to have an **ideal point** on that dimension, and they would prefer the policies closer to them. That model, while imperfect, can help us understand why some things happen and others do not.

That spatial model does not need to be merely a thought experiment. Political scientists have developed a number of tools for measuring the ideal points of politicians. One of the most common of these, known as DW-NOMINATE, is a computer program designed by Keith Poole and Howard Rosenthal.[12] The idea is simple—just take some publicly available decisions by the politician (such as roll call votes) and see who they vote similarly to and dissimilarly from. The program generates a number that we can treat as an estimate of the politician's ideological preferences—their location on that ideological dimension. The more decisions that get put into it, the more reliable the estimates. This is far from complete, and, importantly, it's derived from the politician's *public* behavior rather than their private thoughts or speeches. It's also based on roll call votes or opinions that the politician themself may not have wanted to be made public. But it's proven to be a pretty reliable indicator of a politician's preferences over time.

The most common application of NOMINATE scores is to members of Congress. Based on their votes in the House or the Senate, we can tell which members are more liberal and which are more conservative. For instance, based on her roll call record, the most liberal member of the U.S.

Senate in 2020 was Elizabeth Warren. Several other notable senators can be also seen in the figure below.

Political scientists can use these scores to understand politics in the Senate, but they can also apply them to politics outside of Congress. A number of the 2020 presidential candidates are included in the figure, and their ideological preferences can help us understand some of their appeal in the nomination process. Even politicians who are not in the Senate in 2020 can be fit into this space. Joe Biden, who won the 2020 Democratic presidential nomination, is not in the figure, but his NOMINATE score when he was last in the Senate was −0.314, which would put him exactly in the middle of the Democratic Party.

Techniques like NOMINATE can even be used on politicians other than legislators. Since presidents take positions on policy questions before Congress, we can treat those positions as "votes" and estimate their ideal points. The figure below shows the ideal points for every president from Franklin Roosevelt to Barack Obama. The evidence used for evaluating presidents comes when the White House issues the president's stance on pending legislation. That way, the president can be compared to members of Congress who vote on that legislation. Again, this isn't a perfect indicator, since presidents don't issue public stances on all pending bills, but it's quite reliable. As the figure shows, Republican presidents have been getting more conservative over time. Dwight Eisenhower was actually the most moderate president of the postwar era. Ronald Reagan represented a

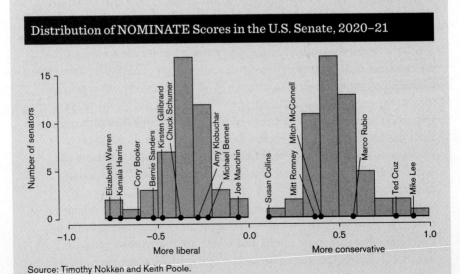

Distribution of NOMINATE Scores in the U.S. Senate, 2020–21

Source: Timothy Nokken and Keith Poole.

sharp movement rightward, and George W. Bush was about as conservative as Reagan.

The story is less clear for Democrats. Judging from these figures, Jimmy Carter would appear to be the most liberal postwar president, with Franklin Roosevelt, Lyndon Johnson, and Barack Obama among the more moderate ones. Yet this may demonstrate some of the limitations of this research method. Roosevelt, Johnson, and Obama, after all, secured significant expansions of the social welfare state through Social Security, Medicare, and the Affordable Care Act, while Carter has almost no significant liberal policy achievements to his name.

It turns out to be difficult to classify presidents neatly by their ideologies. American presidents help shape their times but are also shaped by

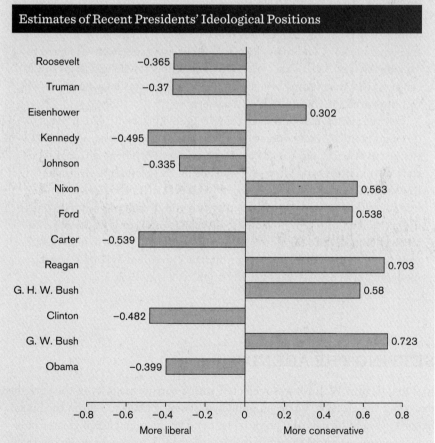

Estimates of Recent Presidents' Ideological Positions

Source: Nate Silver, "How Liberal Is President Obama?" FiveThirtyEight, April 29, 2011, https:// fivethirtyeight.com/features/how-liberal-is-president-obama/ (accessed 2/27/2020).

them. Ronald Reagan, at the time of his 1980 election, was one of the most conservative major party nominees the country had ever seen, and he remains an icon among conservative Republicans today for his stances on taxation and regulation and his fierce opposition to Soviet communism. Yet his willingness to work with fellow Democrats on budget proposals, his shoring up of Social Security, and his constructive negotiations with Mikhail Gorbachev, among other things, would make him look fairly moderate today. He was conservative for the Republican Party of the 1980s, but the party itself has moved considerably rightward since then.

Similarly, Democrats look back with pride on much of Franklin Roosevelt's policy achievements, including Social Security and many other Depression-era initiatives to increase employment and reduce poverty. But those achievements, notable as they are, came at political costs. To keep southern Democratic members of Congress on board, Roosevelt was willing to make many concessions on civil rights. He eased off on pushing anti-lynching laws, and many forms of public assistance were designed to exclude African Americans. Was Roosevelt a liberal who had to give in to conservatives to get some of his agenda passed? Or was he a moderate who was pressured into his more liberal actions?

Overall, presidents are deeply complex individuals with hundreds of different political forces operating on them at any given time. Voters, activists, party officials, old friends, family members, members of Congress, staffers, and others can all exert influence on the president's decisions. Roosevelt himself once famously said to labor leaders about a set of new initiatives they were pushing, "I agree with you, I want to do it, now make me do it." And different presidents will manage this array of pressure differently. But, despite the power of DW-NOMINATE data to help characterize a politician's ideology, to summarize a president as simply liberal, moderate, or conservative is usually hopelessly simplistic.

SETTING THE AGENDA

In 2004, George W. Bush was reelected with a narrow majority of the vote. Just days after the election, he began publicly discussing plans to reform the Social Security system by partially privatizing it and giving each citizen greater individual control over how their funds were invested. This caught many political observers off guard, as the issue had hardly been central to the 2004 presidential campaign, which had largely turned on antiterrorism and the Iraq War.

Nonetheless, said Bush, "I earned capital in this campaign, political capital, and now I intend to spend it."

While Bush's plan ultimately failed to garner sufficient support among the public and the Congress, many Republican Party leaders enthusiastically backed it, despite not having run on the issue previously. Think tanks and interest groups provided moral and economic justifications for the plan. Congressional leaders, including Senate Majority Leader Bill Frist, promised to make Bush's plan a top legislative priority for 2005.[13]

In this case, the president was *setting the agenda* for his party. As we will see in this section, executives have some ability to shape what issues their party will focus on, although this power has important constraints.

Mandate Politics

Winners of presidential elections wield great political power, but it's open to interpretation what they're supposed to do with it. Did the voters who put them in office want them to follow through on all their campaign promises, or did the candidate win for reasons totally unrelated to those promises? Electoral rules can make this even more obscure, since the Electoral College system by which the United States selects presidents can lead to a president being elected who did not win among a plurality of voters (for instance, in 2000 and 2016).

In such an environment, as political scientist Julia Azari notes, new presidents tend to claim **mandates** from the voters to enact their vision of public policy.[14] A mandate is a claim that the winning candidate or those within the winner's party make after the election about what the voters want to see from the new administration. It's not enough to have won office—the fact of their victory is supposed to ratify whatever they were arguing on the campaign trail. "When you win," George W. Bush said shortly after his 2004 reelection, "there is a feeling that the people have spoken and embraced your point of view." As in 2004, presidents sometimes use mandate claims to try to advance their party's agenda even when their own election margin wasn't particularly large.

There is no precise definition of a mandate. The Constitution doesn't grant presidents extra powers if they win by a large margin. And it's generally a mistake to assume that voters are broadly supportive of some policy idea simply because the candidate who advocated for it won office. Voters tend to have vague and weak policy commitments and don't necessarily know what their favorite candidate advocates with any real specificity. Presidents Clinton, Obama, and Trump all ran for office advocating substantial changes in the health care system—and won—but found public opinion turning swiftly against them when they actually tried to effect those changes.

Nonetheless, presidents still attempt to assert mandates, and those claims, if believed, can have an influence on that president's effectiveness in dealing with

Congress. Presidents are especially likely to claim some sort of mandate when the legitimacy of their own election is in question. Note that Donald Trump spent roughly his first month in office falsely claiming that he had the largest inauguration audience in history and one of the largest Electoral College margins of modern times. This was done, in part, to push back against his popular vote loss and to claim support from the American people. Mandate claims have also become useful in our very partisan era as a way for presidents to influence media coverage in favorable ways.

The Speech

Every January, the president delivers the State of the Union Address to a joint session of the U.S. Congress. In most states, the governor delivers a State of the State Address around the same time. The U.S. Constitution requires an annual report from the president, but over time, this speech has taken on a much greater significance.

A speech like this allows a president or governor to **go public** on an issue that's important to the party's agenda. When an executive goes public on an issue, they are attempting to use the power of their office—the strong name recognition and access to the media—to affect public opinion.[15] In theory, this improves the executive's hand in negotiations with legislators. There are some anecdotes to support this idea. For example, when Ronald Reagan found his first federal budget proposal bogged down in the Democratic-controlled House, he gave a televised Oval Office speech in which he outlined the details of his economic plan and exhorted voters to call their members of Congress. This speech is credited with increasing pressure on House Democrats and ultimately giving President Reagan much of his budget requests that year. And there's at least some evidence that presidents can get a bit more of what they want in a budget negotiation when they give a speech on the item.[16]

Yet when examined systematically, there's not much evidence that speeches actually move public opinion or force members of Congress to change their minds. Studies of State of the Union Addresses find no regular impact on public opinion—they're as likely to make presidents less liked as more liked.[17] And indeed, speeches can also have the effect of polarizing public opinion on an issue. All of Obama's speeches on health care reform only seemed to convince liberals to support the program while convincing conservatives to oppose it. Obama's relative silence on same-sex marriage during his first term may well have been an attempt to avoid polarizing an issue that was already gaining acceptance in the public at large.

One thing that such speeches can do, however, is raise the salience of an issue. When former governor Scott Walker of Wisconsin gave his first State of the

In 2011, protesters in Wisconsin staged 24-hour demonstrations in opposition to the state budget proposed by Scott Walker, which included restrictions on public employee collective bargaining. Walker remained unpopular in Wisconsin and was subject to a recall effort, which he won in 2012.

State Address in 2011, he focused on solving the state's ongoing financial challenges and included a somber warning for public employees:

> One area we will have to look at is public employee benefits. . . . However, the difficult reality is that healthcare costs and pension costs have risen dramatically and that has created a benefit system that is simply unsustainable. Government benefits have grown while so many others in the private sector have seen their benefits adjusted in order to protect jobs.
>
> Currently, most state employees pay next to nothing from their salaries toward their pension, while the state's taxpayers pay more than $190 million each year on state employees' behalf. Similarly, most state workers only pay about 6% of their premium costs for their health care plan.[18]

Political observers knew what this meant. The legislature moved ahead with a plan to restrict collective bargaining by the state's public employee unions, and those unions responded with a massive campaign of resistance. Public employee unions had been a Republican target for years, but Walker helped to elevate that issue to one of statewide importance.

As Walker's actions show, when a governor or president mentions an issue in a prominent speech, it's a signal to other political actors that this is a priority. It sends a message that this is something the executive is willing to fight for and make deals on in order to get a win. This can focus a party's and a legislature's attention on those items.[19]

This does not mean that the executive has a free hand to turn their party's attention to anything the executive wants. Even though the executive has a great deal of power, they are still constrained by longstanding party commitments to positions on various issues. The George W. Bush administration found this out in 2006 when it approved a deal allowing a security company owned by the United Arab Emirates to manage American ports and terminals. When word got out it sparked a rebellion among Republican officeholders. Rep. Sue Myrick of North Carolina wrote to President Bush, "In regards to selling American ports to the United Arab Emirates, not just NO but HELL NO!"[20]

Success Rates

Parties and partisanship have a massive impact on how successful presidents and governors are in getting their legislative priorities passed. In the modern era, the executive typically has a productive first year or so—often called the **honeymoon** period. This is usually when the executive tries to enact the agenda items on which they ran for office in the first place. It's quite common for legislative success rates to fall off significantly in subsequent years. That is, the president's or governor's priorities tend to have a harder time passing as time goes on. Even though presidents have widely ranging success rates, they almost invariably end lower than they started (see Figure 4.1).

Several factors influence the president's or governor's success rates with the legislature:

- *Party affiliation*: An executive of the same party as the legislative majority will have an easier time passing the bills they want. That doesn't mean an executive facing an opposition party legislature can't get bills passed. Republican Ronald Reagan entered office facing a U.S. House controlled by Democrats; his first-year success rate was still about as high as Democrat Jimmy Carter's was with a Democratic Congress.
- *Polarization*: As the parties move further apart ideologically, it becomes more important for legislators of the executive's party to pass the executive's agenda, and more important for the other party to stop that agenda. Thus we see a pattern where presidents are doing increasingly well with Congress when their party controls that branch and increasingly poorly in times of divided government.[21]
- *Public opinion*: The legislature will be more inclined to vote for the priorities of a popular executive. Lyndon Johnson, for example, was able to pass many substantial pieces of legislation—including Medicare, the Civil

FIGURE 4.1   Presidential Success Rates in the House, 1953–2018

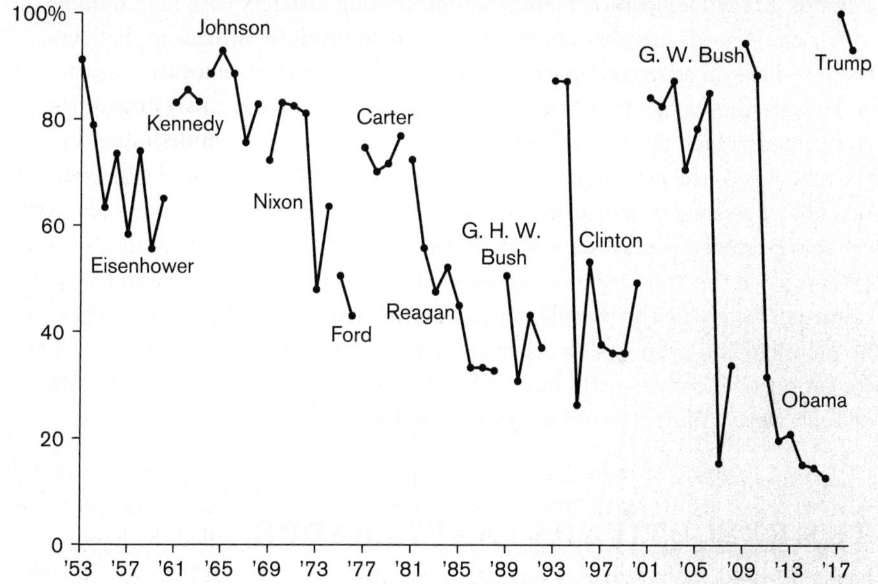

Source: Jeffrey E. Cohen, Jon R. Bond, and Richard Fleisher, "Placing Presidential-Congressional Relations in Context: A Comparison of Barack Obama and His Predecessors," *Polity* 45, no. 1 (2013): 105–26; authors' updates.

Rights Act, and the Voting Rights Act—in 1964 and 1965. The legislation crossed his desk soon after the assassination of John F. Kennedy in 1963 and after Johnson's own strong election margin in 1964, when he was highly popular. He was far less successful later in his presidency, once the Vietnam War took a toll on his approval rating.

- *Agenda size*: Researchers have found that when governors have a longer list of priorities, their overall success rate will drop. More successful executives generally have only a handful of priorities they seek to pass.[22]

It's worth recalling that legislators and the executive have different constituencies and different agendas. They are elected by different groups of people at different times, and they are being held accountable to their own promises. President Clinton found this out in 1994 when he pushed for the passage of a massive crime prevention bill known as the Violent Crime Control and Law Enforcement Act. Coming on the heels of several high-profile violent crimes and a general background of nationally high murder rates, Clinton saw this bill as a way to address campaign promises to make the nation safer. Yet the bill contained several provisions that congressional Democrats found problematic. It included a federal assault weapons ban, which irked rural-state Democrats (and Republicans) who represented many gun-owning constituents. It also included an expansion of the number of federal offenses for which the death penalty could be used, and it eliminated some education funding for federal prison inmates. Many Democratic members representing districts with high numbers of African Americans were deeply concerned about these provisions, believing them to have an adverse impact on African American communities.

Despite these objections, the Violent Crime Control and Law Enforcement Act passed, which demonstrates the importance of party membership. Given the objections, the bill might never have passed, but Clinton had signaled that this bill's passage was a priority for him, having mentioned the scourge of violent crime repeatedly in that year's State of the Union Address. And because Democrats were in the majority in Congress that year, they were in a position to be rewarded for giving the president a win on this issue. Democratic concerns could be mollified and promises on other unrelated issues could be made in exchange for support. There were still quite a few Democratic objections to the bill, but enough were willing to work with the president to assure the bill's passage.

THE EXECUTIVE AS PARTY LEADER

The Steven Spielberg film *Lincoln* (2012), based in part on historian Doris Kearns Goodwin's book *Team of Rivals*,[23] dramatizes the few months between President Lincoln's 1864 reelection and his 1865 inauguration. During this time, Lincoln was pressuring the lame-duck Congress to pass the Thirteenth Amendment to the U.S. Constitution, which would formally abolish slavery in the United States. He felt he had a mandate to enact this amendment given his reelection, and he didn't want to squander the moment.

Lincoln's amendment faced numerous obstacles. First, a secret Confederate peace envoy was offering to cease hostilities if slavery could be retained in some form; news of this could have eroded popular support for the amendment. Second, while Lincoln's fellow Republicans commanded large majorities in Congress, they didn't quite hold the two-thirds of the House necessary to pass an amendment, meaning the president had to win over some Democrats to succeed. Third, Republicans were far from united on the amendment; conservatives thought it went too far, radicals thought it didn't go far enough, and none of them liked him forcing this on a lame-duck Congress. Fourth, Lincoln's own views on slavery and the war had evolved over his first term, and many in Congress and in his own cabinet distrusted him as a result.

The film nicely portrays the limitations on the presidency. Notably, Lincoln had no direct power over Congress. He couldn't write a bill or force Congress to consider one. And just because he shared the same party as Congress' majority, that didn't mean he could tell its members what to do. In one scene, Preston Blair, one of the founders of the Republican Party, made far more demands on Lincoln than the other way around, and Lincoln basically begged U.S. Representative Thaddeus Stevens (R-PA) and the other Radical Republicans for their support.

As the film demonstrates, however, the president does have the power to make patronage appointments (which allowed Lincoln to buy the support of some vacillating members of Congress) and to control the military (which allowed him to detain the Confederate peace envoy). It wasn't remotely his most important power, but Lincoln did have some ability to persuade and negotiate with members of Congress, explaining to them the importance of that moment in history.

Lincoln shows that presidents have some partisan tools in dealing with their colleagues in Congress. Many of those tools exist today, though in modified form. The patronage system that Lincoln was able to exploit is not as much of a presidential power today as it once was. The rise of the civil service (a pool of career government employees loyal to the Constitution rather than to an individual president or party) in the late 1800s meant that federal employees couldn't be fired just for being in the wrong party, and thus presidents couldn't offer jobs to their friends or to people they wanted to buy off. But presidents can still offer people help in exchange for their support.

A prominent example of this came in 1993 when President Bill Clinton was trying to pass his first budget, which contained a tax increase on upper-income Americans. Even though Democrats controlled both the House and the Senate, a number of more conservative members from competitive districts were wavering. One such member was Marjorie Margolies-Mezvinsky, a first-term Democratic congresswoman from Philadelphia's suburbs. She expressed to the White House that while she wanted to provide the backing the president needed, she worried that the price of such support would be the loss of her seat in Congress. Clinton assured Margolies-Mezvinsky that he would make a campaign appearance in her district if he had her vote. With her support, the bill narrowly passed. Clinton followed through on his promise, but Margolies-Mezvinsky, like many other Democratic House members, lost her seat in 1994 anyway. (In an interesting but unrelated sidenote, Clinton's daughter, Chelsea, is now married to Margolies-Mezvinsky's son.)

Beyond this ability to use their office to help in such a concrete way, presidents and governors are simply the individuals most directly associated with their parties, and this makes them powerful leaders. Members of Congress recognize that there's only so much they can do to distance themselves from an unpopular president of their party, and it's in their interest to help that president be popular and successful, even if they don't fully agree with their governing agenda.

Interestingly, the presidency has actually become a more partisan institution in recent decades. Mid-twentieth-century presidents often relied on the growing nonpartisan civil service for support and governed with bipartisan support. Since Ronald Reagan's tenure, a more partisan presidency has emerged, with the White House working more closely with party organizations and ideological allies, and using an increasingly partisan press to get its message across.[24]

Running the Party from the White House

As we explored in Chapter 2, presidents used to be somewhat secondary figures in national parties in the nineteenth century. This changed in the late 1800s as innovations in campaigning styles and reoriented national party priorities made the president much more central to the party itself. Still, modern presidents have played a mixed role with regard to their parties, sometimes helping those parties and sometimes exploiting their capabilities.

As Daniel Galvin's research has shown, some presidents have worked to build up their party's capacity by devoting resources to new initiatives for voter education and candidate recruitment, while other presidents have largely let their party atrophy. A lot of the party building in the post–World War II era came during Republican presidential administrations, as they were operating in a period when they had mostly lost control of the Congress. Democratic presidents, confident in their long-term hold on the Congress, did less to create party-building strategies during this time, and sometimes even preyed upon those party resources for their own purposes.[25]

That is, Democratic presidents used party funds and personnel to assist with their own reelection efforts, sometimes at the expense of supporting their allies in Congress and elsewhere. Galvin finds that this was particularly true in the mid-twentieth century. Dwight Eisenhower repeatedly supported party development plans to make Republicans more competitive across the country, while John Kennedy was a "party predator," using Democratic resources to aid his own interests. These patterns changed in the mid-1990s when Democrats lost control of the House of Representatives for the first time in four decades. Bill Clinton devoted his second term to making the Democratic Party more competitive.

One of the innovations in national party building was the advent of the White House Office of Public Liaison (OPL) in the 1970s. As Katherine Krimmel's research shows, Richard Nixon's administration began this effort as a way to take advantage of the fragmented party system of the 1960s, in which many interest groups were not necessarily loyal to one party or the other. Indeed, despite decades of labor loyalty to Democrats, the Teamsters union endorsed Nixon in 1972, and the AFL-CIO remained neutral in the contest. The Nixon White House reached out to a number of prominent interest groups it saw as helpful to getting its message out to prospective voters.

Gerald Ford formalized this outreach approach under his presidency through the White House's Office of Public Liaison. It hosted frequent "Tuesdays at the White House," inviting an average of 70 people per event across 35 different organizations representing key demographic groups like veterans, racial minorities, religious adherents, and women's organizations. OPL also convened meetings across the country with different groups to gauge their interests in current national issues. The office served the immediate purpose of helping Ford assemble a coalition to back his 1976 election campaign; OPL also helped the GOP repair its image in the wake of the Watergate scandal. But more generally, it was becoming the center of presidential party organization.

The mission of OPL has changed somewhat under subsequent presidents, particularly as the parties have polarized. President Reagan's OPL was much more ideologically narrow than previous ones, and it helped to build conservative Christian organizations into the Republican infrastructure. President Obama modified the office somewhat and renamed it the Office of Public Engagement, appointing actor Kal Penn as one of its associate directors. President Trump renamed it the Office of Public Liaison and Intergovernmental Affairs.[26]

As we have stressed at various points in this textbook, it is difficult to pinpoint any one office or organization as *the party*. However, if you had to point to one, you could do worse than the White House Office of Public Liaison. By bringing together the various groups that constitute a party under one White House endeavor, hearing those groups' viewpoints and using those interactions to formulate and sell public policy, the OPL comes pretty close to the idea of a party. It also reflects the increasing centrality of the presidency to a modern American party. OPL would have seemed almost a comical idea in the nineteenth century, but today it's a key facet of the party and party building.

Social Movements

Social movements are vital to the life of political parties. Indeed, it's sometimes difficult to determine where a movement ends and a party begins. But there's an important, close relationship between the two. Party leaders are eager to tap the enthusiasm and energy of a social movement, while movement leaders hope to capture the allegiance of a party to ensure that their preferred policies actually become law.

Presidents have sometimes played key roles in forging relationships between movements and parties.[27] There's a longstanding debate, for example, over just how critical President Lyndon Johnson was to the civil rights movement. Many of the movement's crowning achievements, including the Civil Rights Act and the Voting Rights Act, occurred early in his presidency and with his signature. But did this happen because Johnson pushed for it, or because he was forced into it?

On the one hand, civil rights activists had targeted the Democratic nomination process as a useful locus of activity since the early 1960s. The Mississippi Freedom delegation, for example, recognized that to turn civil rights claims into law, it would need to take over enough Democratic party delegate seats to become an important player in presidential nomination contests. It wasn't enough to march in the streets; civil rights activists had to be involved in the process of picking and persuading a president. When Lyndon Johnson supported civil rights laws, he was acknowledging the increasing political power of African Americans and their influence on the Democratic Party.

Yet there's also substantial evidence that Johnson did genuinely seek out the influence of civil rights activists and was frustrated with the more moderate pace on civil rights charted by the Kennedy administration.[28] Johnson recognized that the Solid (Democratic) South was, by the 1960s, no longer very solid; increasing numbers of conservative southern Whites were voting Republican. To Johnson and other more liberal southerners, the way forward lay in wooing African American voters and making it easier for them to participate. Upon meeting Johnson for the first time, Martin Luther King Jr. assessed him this way:

> His approach to civil rights was not identical with mine—nor had I expected it to be. Yet his careful practicality was nonetheless clearly no mask to conceal indifference. His emotional and intellectual involvement was genuine and devoid of adornment. . . . [I]t was Vice President Johnson I had in mind when I wrote in *The Nation* that the White South was splitting, and that progress could be furthered by driving a wedge between the rigid segregationists and the new White elements whose love of their land was stronger than the grip of old habits and customs.[29]

The strong relationship between the Democratic Party and one of the most powerful social movements of the twentieth century paved the way for substantial accomplishments in civil rights legislation and for African American loyalty to the Democratic Party that continues to this day. This relationship is also what sparked a substantial realignment of the parties on racial issues and helped drive conservative southerners away from the Democratic fold, helping to create modern party polarization.

A similar pattern can be seen in President Ronald Reagan's relationship with the Christian Right. The evangelical community was instrumental in Reagan's rise to power. This social movement had been working since the early 1970s to become more active in elections from school boards and city councils up to the presidency. They had managed to seize control of Republican nomination processes, and they saw in Reagan a champion for their causes.

But Reagan also worked to bring the Christian Right's views into greater prominence during his presidency. He advocated for constitutional amendments protecting school prayer and abolishing abortion. He appointed prominent evangelical leaders to high-profile government positions. The fact that White evangelical Christians voted for the Republican ticket over the Democratic one by more than 50 points in 2020 and even more in 2016 stems in large part from the work Reagan and his team did back in the early 1980s.

THE EXECUTIVE AS CAMPAIGNER

It was truly the worst of times for the nation in 1932. Struggling with the Great Depression, the United States lost a quarter of its wealth in that year alone, and nearly 24 percent of Americans were out of work. The presidential election gave Americans a chance to weigh in on how they felt about the status of the country and the direction it was heading. Overwhelmingly, the nation voted for change, tossing out an incumbent president (rare then as now) and replacing him with Franklin Roosevelt, the governor of New York. Roosevelt beat Herbert Hoover by 18 points and won all but six states.

But Roosevelt wasn't the only Democrat on the ballot. Governors, members of Congress, state legislators, and many city and county officials also shared his party label and also had an unusually good year. Ninety seats in the U.S. House switched from Republican to Democratic control that year, along with nine Senate seats. This put Democrats in control of the House, the Senate, and the presidency for the first time in two decades, with large majorities in both chambers and a substantial agenda of change to enact.

The Coattail Effect

The dynamic that played out with the election of Roosevelt is what's known as the **coattail effect**. Party leaders know that if their presidential nominee is popular, that can help candidates win other offices all the way down the ballot. Conversely, putting a bad nominee on the top of the ballot can harm the party down the ballot. Republicans lost 37 House seats in 1964, the year they nominated the unpopular Barry Goldwater for president. This was a lesson many Democratic leaders allegedly ignored when they encouraged presidential nominee Walter Mondale to take a stance in favor of tax increases in 1984. The party saw this move as a way of shaking up an electoral map that looked bad for them. Instead, not only did Mondale lose by even more than expected, but he brought down many Democratic Senate and House seats with him.

The coattail effect derives from the fact that most voters don't pay very close attention to their candidates for Congress or state legislature. As Steven Rogers has shown, most voters don't even know which party is in control of their state legislature.[30] Thus their presidential vote is highly consequential. Most of the electorate will cast a presidential vote based on partisanship and the fundamental aspects of the country (like the economy), and then largely vote that same party all the way down the ballot.

As Figure 4.2 shows, the people's vote for state legislature tracks their vote for the U.S. House of Representatives almost perfectly. Voters aren't really distinguishing between different candidates and weighing how well one might do in office compared to the other. To a very large degree, they are picking a party and voting for it up and down the ballot.

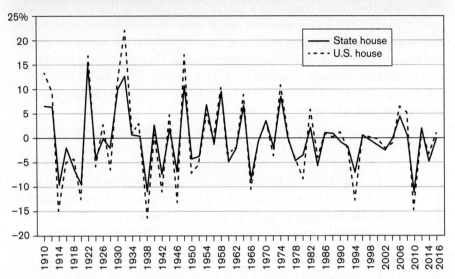

FIGURE 4.2   Percentage of Democratic Seats Gained or Lost in State House and U.S. House Elections, 1910–2016

Source: Steven Rogers, "Accountability in American Legislatures." Unpublished Manuscript.

Relatedly, Figure 4.3 plots the incumbent party's presidential vote share against the number of seats won or lost by that party in U.S. House elections. The correlation is a strong one, and it suggests that for each additional point a presidential candidate wins, their party will gain two or three more seats in the House. This pattern even holds in the modern era, when redistricting is presumed to make many seats safe. Hillary Clinton beat Donald Trump in the popular vote in 2016 by around 2 percentage points, and Democrats picked up six House seats.

We have a general tendency to think of elections as occurring independently from each other. Voters are assumed to be constantly monitoring elected officials, keeping them in office if they are doing a good job, or throwing them out if they aren't. In fact, however, the vast majority of partisan elected officials are being held accountable to the party label that appears at the end of their name on the ballot. And voters' impression of that party label is strongly determined by the occupant of the White House. If voters are angry with the president, many members of Congress and state legislators who share the president's party affiliation will lose their election, even if they themselves had nothing to do with the president's policies.

That doesn't mean that the fate of legislators is driven solely by what happens at the top of the ticket. Many will do what they can to distance themselves from an unpopular presidential candidate of their own party in an effort to maximize their own chances for reelection. Senator John McCain notably criticized and distanced himself from fellow Republican Donald Trump on numerous occasions

FIGURE 4.3   The Presidential Coattail Effect, 1952–2020

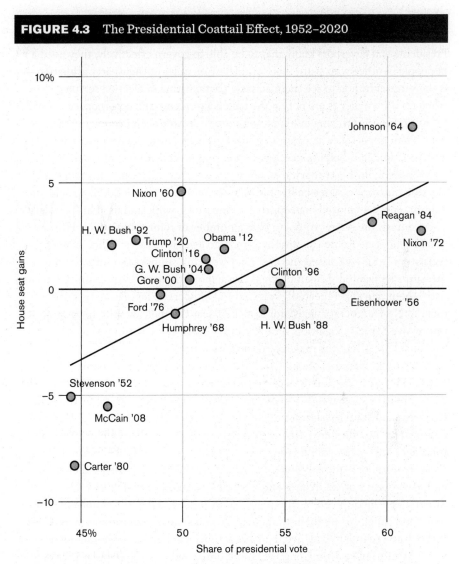

Source: U.S. House Clerk's Office, National Conference of State Legislatures.

in 2016, concerned that Trump might drag him down in the surprisingly competitive state of Arizona. In the end, Trump won the state by only 3.5 percent of the vote, while McCain managed to beat his Democratic challenger by 13 points.

Similarly, a well-funded and tightly orchestrated campaign by Colorado Democrats to target key state legislative races in 2004 pulled off an unusual coup: Republican president George W. Bush managed to win the state by 5 points that year, even though Democrats managed to take over six state house seats and one state senate seat, flipping control of the state legislature.

The Executive in Legislative Races

Presidents and governors know that to be able to govern effectively, they need a lot of people in office who share their worldview or, at least, their party affiliation. It is therefore common to see them actively participating in election seasons, even when their own names are not on the ballot. Presidents and governors can be helpful campaigners, bringing out large, supportive crowds and encouraging them to vote. Their appearance at a campaign event can also bring media coverage for legislative candidates, helping to improve their name recognition among the public.

Even with all this activity, executives aren't always effective in changing election outcomes. After he became California's governor in 2003, Arnold Schwarzenegger enjoyed high approval ratings for a while and used his popularity to encourage the state's voters to pass a number of reform initiatives. However, in 2004, he tried to use this approach in state legislative races. When Democratic legislators (who comprised the majority) wouldn't support the sorts of budget measures he wanted, he campaigned throughout the state threatening to "terminate" them. He also repeatedly referred to Democratic legislators as "girlie men."[31] No Democratic legislator lost their seat that fall. Despite his popularity, impressive name recognition, and commitment to campaigning, Schwarzenegger was unable to affect the makeup of the legislature.

In a similar example of executive powerlessness, President Obama largely failed to improve the fortunes of his fellow Democrats during the 2016 election cycle. He took substantial criticism for the decline of Democratic fortunes in Congress and state legislatures during his tenure in office. In 2016, with his approval ratings climbing, Obama sought to mitigate earlier Democratic electoral declines by campaigning extensively not only for Hillary Clinton, but for Democratic congressional candidates all across the country. He publicly endorsed dozens of candidates and cut ads for several of them in which he directly appealed to voters. He singled out those candidates' Republican opponents and sought to tie them to Donald Trump's most extreme statements. It's difficult to see much evidence that this activity paid off, though. Democrats did win a handful of seats in Congress, and Clinton did win the popular presidential vote, but a good deal of this would likely have happened without Obama's help, and it obviously fell well short of Democrats' hopes. Moreover, Democrats actually lost state legislative seats across the country.

Midterm elections—when the entire House and a third of the Senate stand for election but the president is not on the ballot—often pose a challenge for the president's party. As Figure 4.4 shows, the president's party almost always loses seats in the U.S. House of Representatives in midterm elections. This same pattern shows up in U.S. Senate races and state legislative races. This happens for several reasons. For one, voter turnout is lower in midterms than in presidential elections. Those occasional voters who showed up to elect the president often

At a rally in Pittsburgh, Pennsylvania, in September 2020, Trump shows support for Republican congressional candidate Sean Parnell (far left).

don't show up to elect legislators two years later. This leaves a voting electorate that is somewhat more hostile to the sitting president. Midterms also offer an opportunity for those bothered or even hurt by the administration's new initiatives to vote against candidates who share the president's party label.

President Bill Clinton won a stunning victory in 1992, defeating a sitting incumbent for only the fourth time in the twentieth century. But the beginning of his administration was beset by disorganization and scandal, and the public quickly turned against his health care reform proposal in 1993 and 1994. A newly energized Republican base showed up in the 1994 midterm elections and defeated 54 Democratic House incumbents, flipping the Congress to unified Republican control for the first time in four decades. That fall, eighteen state legislative chambers flipped from Democratic to Republican control as well.

It was a similar story in 2010, when Tea Party Republicans organized in opposition to several of President Barack Obama's early initiatives, especially the Affordable Care Act (ACA, or Obamacare). Republicans took 63 House seats and 21 state legislative chambers from Democrats that autumn. A study of voters in the 2010 midterm elections found that Democratic House members who had voted for the ACA were especially vulnerable because voters perceived them as more liberal and out of step with their districts. Those Democrats who voted for the bill ran about 6 points behind those who voted against it. As a

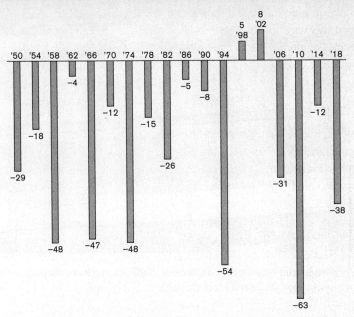

FIGURE 4.4   House Seats Gained or Lost by the President's Party in Midterm Elections, 1950–2018

Source: "Party Divisions in the House of Representatives, 1789 to Present," U.S. House of Representatives, history.house.gov.

result, around 25 Democrats lost their seats simply because they voted for the ACA, and that was enough to flip control of the House.[32]

Of course, as Figure 4.4 suggests, the president's party doesn't always lose seats in a midterm election. Those seat losses can be mitigated by a strong economy or an unusually popular president. Despite severe Democratic losses in 1994, Democrats actually gained a few House seats in Bill Clinton's second midterm in 1998. Democrats may have been helped by the late 1990s dot-com boom, Clinton's high approval ratings, and something of a public pushback against Republican efforts to impeach the president. Four years later, Republicans managed to gain a few House seats in the 2002 midterms, due in part to President George W. Bush's record high post–September 11 approval ratings. Republicans in 2018 lost 40 House seats—consistent with President Donald Trump's relative unpopularity—but picked up several Senate seats with the help of an electoral map favorable to Republicans.

Nonetheless, the data strongly suggests that the winds are against the president's party in midterm elections. Media coverage of those elections often ends up blaming the president for these outcomes, but it seems clear from modern history that there's not much a president can do to mitigate those losses.

Competitiveness

It's easy to look at the current political system—characterized by high levels of party polarization and closely competitive elections—and assume things have always been this way. In fact, America's political system is in an unusual era of competition. Divided control of the federal government, in which one party has the majority in Congress and the other holds the presidency, was once quite rare. Today it's the norm. For most of the twentieth century, the Democrats were the majority party in Congress. Today, each new election brings a realistic chance of one party flipping control of at least one chamber.

Meanwhile, the presidency is currently about as regularly competitive as it's ever been. Democrats held the White House for two terms under Clinton (1993–2001), then Republicans held it for two terms under Bush (2001–09), then the Democratic Party regained control and held it for two terms under Obama (2009–17) (this cycle was broken by Joe Biden's win in the 2020 election, beating incumbent Donald Trump). The last time we saw three successive two-term presidents was Jefferson-Madison-Monroe (1801–25). What's more, we just don't see landslide presidential elections anymore. Obama's 2008 victory over John McCain, the biggest margin in a presidential race since the 1980s, was by a mere 7 points in the popular vote, a far cry from Ronald Reagan's 18-point victory over Walter Mondale in 1984.

As political scientist Frances Lee notes, the time period since 1980 has represented the longest period of sustained competitive balance since the Civil War—and possibly ever.[33] This tight competition between the parties, somewhat surprisingly, contributes to the intensity of partisanship. Every election, presidential negotiation, or close congressional vote becomes a test of leadership. It's the reason that Republican senate minority leader Mitch McConnell in 2010 said, "The single most important thing we want to achieve is for President Obama to be a one-term president." It's the reason that roughly 94 percent of Republicans voted for Donald Trump and roughly 94 percent of Democrats voted for Joe Biden in 2020. When the political system is this competitive, even a small loss is seen as a potential tragedy. The stakes are simply so high.

POLITICAL TIME

American party systems are often associated with various presidencies. The period of dominance of the Democrats in the mid-nineteenth century is often referred to as the Jacksonian era, for example, and scholars often associate figures like Franklin Roosevelt and Ronald Reagan with party realignments. This is not simply a matter of convenience. Presidents are important both for shaping, and being shaped, by party systems. But the interplay between parties and presidents is complex and it shifts a great deal from generation to generation.

Political scientist Stephen Skowronek has come up with a useful way to think about this relationship between presidents and parties over time. In his concept of "political time," there are decades-long "regimes" that occur in American politics, during which one party is usually dominant in Congress and in the states yet doesn't win every presidential election. For example, one regime began with the election of 1860, with Abraham Lincoln winning a stunning victory and reshaping politics into a period of Republican dominance. Later Republican presidents would help articulate those themes and ideas, although some Democrats would manage to get into power and find their authority limited. That regime collapsed with the Great Depression, and then a new era of Democratic dominance began with Roosevelt's election in 1932.

As Skowronek views it, presidential political styles fall into four main types:

- *The politics of reconstruction*: A new regime takes over and sets the ideological themes for the coming years. These presidents sometimes sound almost revolutionary in their words. This includes presidents like Thomas Jefferson, Andrew Jackson, Abraham Lincoln, and Ronald Reagan. They had the good fortune to take office following a failing and unpopular regime of the other party.
- *The politics of disjunction*: This is for presidents who had the misfortune of representing a party at the end of its regime life. The party has become unpopular, and these presidents usually find themselves fighting an uphill battle, compromising many of their own beliefs, and serving just one term in office. This includes presidents like John Quincy Adams, Herbert Hoover, and Jimmy Carter.
- *The politics of articulation*: This is for presidents serving in the middle of their party's regime. They will often reassert things the regime already stands for, occasionally adding their own twist or modest additions to it. This includes presidents like James Monroe, Teddy Roosevelt, and Lyndon Johnson.
- *The politics of preemption*: This describes presidents who somehow find themselves in office while the other party is dominant. They may successfully triangulate, borrowing some ideas from the dominant party and making them their own, although they are rarely very successful in bringing their own party back into dominance. This can include presidents like Dwight Eisenhower, Richard Nixon, and Bill Clinton.

Skowronek's theory is a useful one for dividing up the presidency and giving us some idea of how different administrations will behave. It can be difficult to know, however, just where one is in these party regime cycles at any given point. If Reagan began a period of Republican dominance, is it still occurring today? Did Barack Obama exemplify the politics of reconstruction, beginning a New Democratic era, or was he preemptive, managing to secure some Democratic goals in the middle of a very Republican era? Was the passage of the Affordable

Care Act the work of a reconstructionist president or a lucky preemptive one? And where does Donald Trump fit in?

EXECUTIVES IN A PARTY SYSTEM

As a long look at the partisan presidency suggests, quite a bit of what happens to a president's party is beyond their control. Presidents may call for an end to divisive partisanship, but it will usually continue whether they want it or not. Their party will most likely lose seats in midterm elections, and it will probably end up in a worse position over the course of the administration than it was when it started. Virtually every president takes office promising an era of dominance for their party, only to see those dreams quickly dashed. We could assume that every president has been incompetent at this task, or we can accept that there are large historic and political forces operating against the president's party during their term in office.

That said, presidents and governors do have choices that can affect their party's long-term fortunes. Presidents can help build up their party's infrastructure, raising money for it and devoting their own efforts toward its future successes. They can also poach from their party, using the party's capabilities for their own immediate political needs. Most presidents do a bit of both.

Whether a party wants it or not, its reputation will often rise and fall with that of its executive. A party that nominates an irresponsible or unpopular president or governor will soon find many who share that party label losing their jobs and other potential candidates being less likely to affiliate with it. Nominating someone who develops a positive reputation can help that party for years or even decades to come. Thus picking nominees for governor and president is one of the most important tasks a party will ever undertake.

Discussion Questions

1. Describe an important consequence of having a presidential system instead of a parliamentary system. How do parties affect politicians' behavior in each?

2. What does it mean for a president to have a "mandate"? Is there a way to define a mandate that people of both parties would agree upon?

3. What sorts of things determine how successful a president is in turning the campaigning agenda into law?

4. Describe some powers a president has to enact an agenda other than trying to persuade people with oratory.

5. For what reasons does the president's party tend to lose seats in congressional midterm elections?

5

U.S. Parties in Comparative Perspective

The 2016 presidential election stands out as unusual in American politics. In the United States, we occasionally see "populist" candidates—those who run against the political order and have few ties to it and champion the vague concerns of the "average American"—but those candidacies rarely amount to much. In 2016, Donald Trump, a populist outsider, ran and won. As odd as this seemed in the United States, from a global perspective, the election did not appear unique. In the years before and after, populists were succeeding in many countries:

- In the United Kingdom, in early 2016, populist opposition to the influence of the European Union led to a vote to leave the confederation, dubbed "Brexit." By 2019, the Conservative Party had handed the reins of power to Boris Johnson, a populist and flamboyant former mayor of London.

- In the 2017 French presidential election, Marine Le Pen, the candidate of the far-right Front National (now known as the National Rally), was one of two candidates to make the second round of the country's runoff election system, where she lost to centrist Emmanuel Macron.

While the political system in the United States is mainly operated by two dominant parties, many other democracies have multiparty systems. Here, a man looks at the multitude of parties registered to be on the ballot in the 2018 Italian general election.

- In the 2018 Italian parliamentary election, the populist Movemento Cinque Stella (M5S) won the most votes, while the right-populist Lega party outpolled its coalition partner, Silvio Berlusconi's Forze Italia.

- In Germany, the far-right Alternative für Deutschland party (AfD) went from winning no seats in 2013 to gaining 94 seats in 2018, capturing 12 percent of the vote and coming in third. In subsequent polling, the AfD has replaced the Social Democrats as the second-place party.

- The right-wing Sweden Democrats, formed in 1988, had almost no traction in the country's politics, but surged in 2014, winning almost 13 percent of the vote and getting as much as a quarter of national support in polls a year later.

- In 2018, populist leader Jair Bolsonaro's far-right conservative Social Liberal Party (PSL) was top in Brazil's first round of presidential voting and then defeated the Worker's Party candidate in the second round with 55 percent of the vote. Many compared Bolsonaro's campaign style to Donald Trump's.

- In India, support for the right-wing Hindu nationalist Bharatiya Janata Party has been growing steadily since the 1990s, and the party became the leader of the government in 2014 with 30 percent of the vote. In 2019 elections, the party won an outright majority, with Prime Minister Narendra Modi again being compared to Donald Trump.

Some observers saw this pattern and declared a populist, nationalist trend in democratic politics worldwide. Were they right? Was Trump unique, or just one example of an international phenomenon?

Although they are a central feature of every democracy, political parties take on different forms and work in different ways in every political system. Every democracy has its own political rules or institutions. Those institutions shape how politics is conducted in that country. In this chapter, we explore three specific ways that politics is different in the United States than in many other democracies, focusing on how those variations shape the roles of political parties.

First, democracies follow different rules for picking leaders. In the United States, we elect our politicians through single-member districts. Many other democracies use some form of proportional representation. This is one explanation for why the United States has a two-party system.

Second, political parties in the United States are particularly permeable and institutionally weak. It is hard for American parties to prevent those outside the party from participating and even taking over. A movement that in another country might form a new party would likely only reshape an existing American party.

Third, the United States has a presidential system, with a separation of powers between the legislative and the executive branches. The head of government who implements the laws—the president—is elected separately from the legislators who craft them. Many other developed democracies have parliamentary systems, in which the head of government—the prime minister—is chosen by the legislature. Because parties are critical in both the election of politicians and in the organization of the legislature, this difference means that parties operate very differently across the two systems. In parliamentary systems, minority parties can join the government and support a prime minister of another party. In presidential systems, the formal ties between the president and the president's party in the legislature may be minimal.

The purpose of this book is to explain the role of political parties in the United States. But an important step in understanding parties in the U.S. system is to know what parties around the world look like—in other words, what the options are. We do this by examining the three major, interrelated aspects of democratic political systems, namely, electoral rules, internal democracy, and executive systems.

ELECTORAL RULES, OR, WHY DOES THE UNITED STATES HAVE A TWO-PARTY SYSTEM?

We've noted several times that political parties are often criticized in America. (They're not particularly popular in many other countries, either.) But even among those who argue that political parties *are* necessary for democracy, many complain about the "duopoly" that the Democrats and the Republicans hold in the United States. Even if parties aren't a problem, the argument goes, the two-party system is. We'll return to that argument below. But first, it's important to understand why the United States has two parties.

The United States is unusual in having just two major parties. Even other countries that are often described as having a two-party system, such as Canada and the United Kingdom, usually have more parties than the United States. What's more, the dominant parties in most other advanced democracies tend to be young compared to the Republican Party (which dates back to 1854) and the Democratic Party (which grew from Thomas Jefferson's organization at the end of the eighteenth century and was consolidated under its current name by Andrew Jackson and Martin Van Buren in the 1820s).

Why do some countries have only a few parties while others have many? We can begin to explain this by asking what incentivizes politicians, political activists, and voters to join a large coalition, and what are their incentives to stay with a smaller faction? As we've noted, all parties are coalitions. The long coalitions framework we described in Chapter 2 implies that political actors have an incentive to form larger parties so they can capture majorities and win. But not all systems require a majority to win in elections.

POLITICAL SCIENCE TOOLKIT
Counting Parties

Americans regularly observe, and sometimes lament, that the United States is a two-party system. But clearly, this is not exactly true. Minor parties are legal, and they do get votes—just not very many. In 2020, less than 2 percent of the presidential vote went to third party candidates, and in 2016, about 6 percent of the electorate voted for the Green Party, the Libertarian Party, or about 20 other minor parties.

But it would be grossly misleading to count all of those parties, or to compare the U.S. system to that of, say, Germany, which in 2017 held a federal election with a similar number of total parties, but with about six receiving a significant share of the vote. When we say the United States is a two-party system, we mean that only the Democratic Party and the Republican Party have any real probability of winning the presidency. The Libertarian and Green parties, with a tiny share of the vote, do not have such a chance.

Before political scientists can say anything about why only two parties have a chance to win the presidency, or what the consequences of such a system are, we need to be able to answer this question: How many parties does the United States have, and how many parties do other countries have? If reformers want more political parties in the United States, it makes sense to look at countries that have more parties to see how things work there. If we think a country's political institutions affect the ability of minor parties to thrive—and that they might influence politics and become major parties—we need to know how many parties thrive in countries with various institutions.

But counting parties can be tricky. One approach, which is time consuming, is to ask which parties actually "matter" in the system. Political scientist Giovanni Sartori recommended just this in his classic book *Parties and Party Systems*.[1] Sartori noted two criteria for counting parties, which he called *coalition potential* and *blackmail potential*. Coalition potential is the possibility that the party might be included in a coalition government. Blackmail potential is the possibility that the party, even though they might be too extreme to be in government, would be large enough to disrupt the government unless they are given concessions.

Coalition and blackmail potential make most sense in terms of a parliamentary system. It is harder to apply the concepts to the United States. Using this criteria also requires analysts to make judgment calls about which parties actually could affect politics, and which could not.

Another approach is to count the parties and weight them according to their vote share. This measure is cruder than Sartori's because not only does it pay attention to how much influence a party has but it allows us to update our counts with every election quickly and transparently.

In weighing vote share, most political scientists use a measure called the effective number of parties. This measure was proposed by political scientists Markku Laakso and Rein Taagepera. The approach weights each party by its size. If every party is the same size, then that weighting doesn't matter, but if some parties are much smaller than others, then they count for less. The table here shows how the measure is constructed for a number of recent elections.

We can compute the effective number of parties for the parties that compete in the election, as well as for those who win seats in a legislature or in any other place that is divided by parties. This approach allows us to compare different party systems without having to decide which parties are important on a case-by-case basis.

In the table, we compute the effective number of parties for five elections in five countries. In each election, every party that received more than one-tenth of one percent is listed. In the United States in 2016, that was 5 parties. In India in 2019, it was 34. But most of those Indian parties were tiny. How many parties should we say India really had?

Effective Number of Parties in Five Recent Elections

Country Election	Party	Party's Share of the Vote	Effective Number of Parties
United States 2016 Presidential Election	Democratic Party	48.0%	2.26
	Republican Party	45.9	
	Libertarian Party	3.3	
	Green Party	1.1	
	Independent	0.5	
Germany 2017 Federal Parliamentary Election	Christian Democratic Union	26.8	6.18
	Social Democratic Party	20.5	
	Alternative for Germany	12.6	
	Free Democratic Party	10.7	
	The Left	9.2	
	Alliance 90 / The Greens	8.9	
	Christian Social Union in Bavaria	6.2	
	Free Voters	1.0	
	Die PARTEI	1.0	
	Human Environment Animal Protection	0.8	
	National Democratic Party	0.4	
	Pirate Party Germany	0.4	
	Ecological Democratic Party	0.3	
	Basic Income Alliance	0.2	

Effective Number of Parties in Five Recent Elections (*continued*)

Country Election	Party	Party's Share of the Vote	Effective Number of Parties
France 2017 Presidential Election	La Republique En Marche	24.0	5.30
	National Front	21.3	
	Republicans	20.0	
	La France insoumise	19.6	
	Socialist Party	6.4	
	Debout la France	4.7	
	Others	2.3	
	Workers' Struggle / New Anti-capitalist Party	1.7	
Israel 2020 Knesset Election	Likud	29.6	5.19
	Blue and White	26.6	
	Joint List	12.7	
	Shas	7.7	
	United Torah Judaism	5.9	
	Labor-Gesher-Meretz	5.8	
	Yisrael Beiteinu	5.7	
	Yamina	5.2	
India 2019 Parliamentary Election	Bharatiya Janata Party	37.4	5.41
	Indian National Congress	19.5	
	All India Trinamool Congress	4.1	
	Bahujan Samaj Party	3.6	
	Samajwadi Party	2.6	
	Yuvajana Sramika Rythu Congress Party	2.5	
	Dravida Munnetra Kazhagam	2.3	
	Shiv Sena	2.1	
	Telugu Desam Party	2.0	
	Communist Party of India	1.8	
	Biju Janata Dal	1.7	
	Janata Dal (United)	1.5	
	Nationalist Congress Party	1.4	
	All India Anna Dravida Munnetra Kazhagam	1.3	
	Telangana Rashtra Samithi	1.3	
	Shiromani Akali Dal	0.6	
	Communist Party of India	0.6	
	Janata Dal (Secular)	0.6	
	Lok Janshakti Party	0.5	

Country Election	Party	Party's Share of the Vote	Effective Number of Parties
India (cont'd)	Aam Aadmi Party	0.4	
	Jharkhand Mukti Morcha	0.3	
	Indian Union Muslim League	0.3	
	All India United Democratic Front	0.2	
	All India Majlis-e-Ittehadul Muslimeen	0.2	
	Apna Dal	0.2	
	Revolutionary Socialist Party	0.1	
	All Jharkhand Students Union	0.1	
	Rashtriya Loktantrik Party	0.1	
	Nationalist Democratic Progressive Party	0.1	
	Viduthalai Chiruthaigal Katchi	0.1	
	National People's Party	0.1	
	Kerala Congress	0.1	
	Naga People's Front	0.1	
	Jammu & Kashmir National Conference	0.1	

Sources: U.S. Election Atlas, "2016 Presidential General Election Results," https://uselectionatlas.org/RESULTS/; The Federal Returning Officer, "Bundestag Election, 2017," www.bundeswahlleiter.de/en/bundestagswahlen/2017/ergebnisse/bund-99.html; Le Conseil Constitutionnel, "Décision n° 2017-169 PDR du 26 avril 2017," www.conseil-constitutionnel.fr/decision/2017/2017169PDR.htm; Elections to the 23rd Knesset, "The truthful results of the 23rd Knesset elections," https://votes23.bechirot.gov.il; One India, "Lok Sabha Elections 2019," https://www.oneindia.com/lok-sabha-election-2019.

In the table, you can see that the final number doesn't perfectly reflect how many parties there are, or even how many parties are "important." But it captures the *idea* of how many parties there are. In Germany, there were four major parties, and two more that were close in size, followed by several others, so a little more than six seems right.

Throughout this chapter, we will discuss the causes and consequences of multiparty systems. In several figures, we'll be showing how different institutions relate to the number of parties in those systems, and we'll be discussing research that makes those comparisons. In most of these cases, the scholars use the effective number of parties approach. Look back at the table. It's not that those countries have exactly that number of parties—there's no such thing as 0.26 of a party, of course—but the effective number of parties makes it easier for us to make effective comparisons across countries.

The first and most widely cited reason for the number of parties is the electoral system. Systems that require majorities to win seats in the legislature tend to encourage two major parties, while those that grant seats to significant minorities allow for multiple parties. The scholar most associated with this idea is the French social scientist Maurice Duverger, who wrote in 1954 what is generally termed **Duverger's law**, which states, "The simple-majority single-ballot system favours the two-party system." Duverger continues:

> [T]his approaches most nearly perhaps to a true sociological law. An almost complete correlation is observable between the simple-majority single-ballot system and the two-party system: dualist countries use the simple-majority vote and simple-majority vote countries are dualist. The exceptions are very rare and can generally be explained as the result of special considerations.[2]

Since the time that Duverger wrote those words, many countries with simple-majority systems have developed multiple parties, so the relationship he described isn't as strong as it used to be. But before we get to that, let's unpack Duverger's argument. We can examine the different kinds of electoral systems that a polity could have—we specifically explore what Duverger means by "the simple-majority single-ballot system"—and how each system creates incentives for more or fewer parties.

The Effects of Electoral Rules

If you grew up in the United States, your picture of democracy is probably one of majority rule. Whoever gets the most votes wins, and if there's a rare election that deviates from that, it's considered a big deal and often subject to quite a bit of criticism. But this is not the only way to run an election. Are you electing one representative from your district or several at once? Are you voting for a candidate or are you voting for a party, or both? Can you rank your choices? Divide your vote across several options? How are the votes counted? How are the districts drawn? Is there more than one round of voting? Is there an institution like the U.S. Electoral College, under which it's possible for one candidate to win more total votes but still lose the election?

With so many options, you can imagine how many different combinations we might see in the world. But broadly speaking, there are five different kinds of electoral rules, and each provides different incentives for coordination and coalition formation.

Single-Member District Plurality Rule Most elections in the United States operate under **single-member district plurality rule**. Under this system, each member of Congress, for example, represents a district, and each district is represented by only one member (hence "single-seat" or "single-member" district). In the election, each voter gets only one vote. Whichever candidate gets the most votes (a "plurality") wins, and gets the seat. Even the Senate in the United States uses this rule. There are two senators per state, but they are elected separately, so it is as if there were two districts that perfectly overlap. Plurality is sometimes called "first past the post," because whoever comes in first wins, even if they have less than a majority. A race between four candidates who win 27, 26, 24, and 23 percent respectively will go to the candidate with the highest percentage.

This is the system Duverger was talking about. What he terms "simple majority," we will call "plurality," because you can come in first without a majority. It is "single ballot" because there is no runoff or ranking or other information in the vote. Just one ballot.[3] Why does this system tend to produce just two parties? Let's look at this from the point of view of voters and from the point of view of politicians.

First past the post encourages voters to focus their attention on the top two candidates. Suppose several parties are fielding candidates for the single seat in your district, your own preferred party is Party C, and each party has the support illustrated in Table 5.1.

TABLE 5.1	Party Support in a Hypothetical Election
Party	Estimated Support
Party A	25%–35%
Party B	20–30
Party C	15–25
Party D	10–20
Party E	5–15

While you can't be certain about the support that each party has, you have a relatively good idea. Odds are slim that your preferred party, Party C, will come in first. In that case, you will probably consider Parties A and B. Do you have a preference between them? Probably. Even if neither party is what you really want, one is probably closer. So when it comes time to vote, you can vote for your preferred party (casting a "sincere" vote for Party C), but it won't affect the outcome of the election. It is no different from not voting at all. Actually, it could make your situation worse; if the vote between parties A and B is very close, and you decline to vote for one of them, you could be making it

France employs a majority runoff system in its elections, which requires multiple rounds of voting. Here, poll workers count first-round ballots in June 2017. Emmanuel Macron went on to win the presidency in the second round of voting.

In a list PR system, each party generates a ranked list of candidates it wants for the legislature. In the election, people vote for a party, and the percent of the vote is translated into seats for that party. So a party that receives 10 percent of the vote may receive 10 percent of the seats. The Netherlands' Tweede Kamer der Staten-Generaal, or House of Representatives, for example, contains 150 members. If a party received 10 percent of the vote, it would get to name 15 members (10 percent) to the chamber, going through its list of candidates in rank order.

In most list PR countries, it's a bit more complicated than that, and each party does not just use the same list for the whole nation. Rather, they break the country into multimember districts, each with several seats available, and the elections and lists are managed at that level. The number of seats in the district is called the **district magnitude**. Around the world, the average district magnitude is about seven.

Most countries modify this basic system in one way or another. To begin with, if a district has only five seats, for example, then how many of those seats should a party with 16 percent of the vote get? Different systems use different counting rules to allocate seats. These rules vary slightly in how much they favor large parties versus small parties. Some countries also have a threshold requirement, so a party will not receive any seats unless they have some minimum share of the vote.[5] For example, in Germany, a party must reach 5 percent of the vote nationwide to win any seats, even if the party does better regionally. In Turkey, that threshold is 10 percent.

Importantly, countries often introduce rules for how parties select and order list candidates. These rules give voters more or less influence over the list. Under the simplest system, which is called a **closed list**, the party determines who is on the lists for each constituency, as well as their rank order. If the party wins two seats, the top two candidates on the list get those seats. If the party wins three, the top three candidates get seats, and so on. But there are also ways to give voters some say over the order of the candidates on the list. These are called **open list** systems. Voters are given a preference vote, which they can use for a specific candidate. Those with more votes can move up the list.

Regardless of whether the list is open or closed, however, the proportional results from list PR systems mean that minor parties can succeed with only minor support. In our hypothetical example in Table 5.1, suppose that the five parties are competing for seats in a district with 10 seats and no minimum vote threshold, or in a district with five seats and no threshold. Table 5.2 lays out those scenarios.

TABLE 5.2 Hypothetical Allocation of Seats in List Proportional Representation System

Party	Vote Share (%)	Seat Allocation (10-seat district)	Seat Allocation (5-seat district)
Party A	30	3	2
Party B	25	2	1
Party C	20	2	1
Party D	16	2	1
Party E	9	1	0

Note: These results are allocated using the Hare system with the largest remainder, one of the simplest systems to allocate seats proportionally. The system begins with a quota based on the number of seats. With 10 seats, each seat is worth 10 percent of the vote. Party A easily gets 3 seats. Party B gets 2, and so on. After initial seats are allocated, there are 2 left, and the two parties that are closest to getting the quota are Parties E and D, so they get the remaining seats. With 5 seats, the quota is 16.67 percent, and similar calculations get us to the results in that column.

Table 5.2 shows that district magnitude (the number of seats allocated to each district) greatly affects how close to proportional the ultimate allocation is. In the larger district, the result is closer to proportional. In the smaller district, the smaller parties don't do as well.

List PR gets proportional results in a fairly straightforward manner. But there is another way to get proportional representation. The **single-transferable vote** (STV)—sometimes referred to as ranked-choice voting or instant-runoff voting—also gives proportional results with multimember districts. With STV, voters rank-order parties or candidates. Each party or candidate needs to reach some threshold of votes to get a seat—determined by how many seats are available. In a simple five-seat district, you need 20 percent of the vote to get a seat. Any first-place votes that are not needed—either because they are over the quota or because the party can't reach a quota—are reallocated to voters' second choices. The process continues until all the seats are allocated.

To apply STV to the preferences in our hypothetical election, we just need to know the voters' references for other parties. Figure 5.3 shows how the process might play out.

There are efforts to enact STV in the United States, and several cities, including San Francisco, Minneapolis, and Santa Fe, already run their elections this way. But the key for proportional results, and thus for more parties, is the district magnitude. Ranked-choice voting with single-member districts may allow voters to express their full preferences, but small parties still don't win many seats. And larger parties that attempt to appeal to broader constituencies will do better than smaller parties with narrower goals. To get proportional results, multimember districts are needed.

One important distinction between list PR and STV is that STV doesn't require parties at all. Some people see this as an advantage. It limits the power

FIGURE 5.3 How Seats Are Assigned in a Single Transferable Vote System

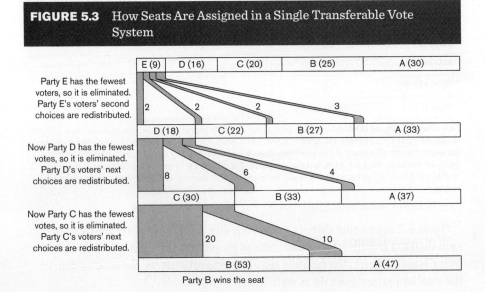

Party B wins the seat

of possibly corrupt and out-of-touch parties, instead allowing voters to express preferences for candidates directly. But as we've noted in this book, parties serve an important role in organizing politics. Once in office, like-minded legislators will form coalitions with one another. That is, they'll form parties. But if party labels are missing from the ballot, then voters have little say in what happens once the politicians are elected. STV has some promising features, but the fact that it potentially divorces the choices voters make from the governing decisions that politicians make once they are in office is, for many, a flaw, not a feature.

Mixed Systems If you want to maximize proportionality and the number of parties, the best system is probably proportional with districts containing a large number of seats. But there are advantages to single-member districts. For one, a single-member district means that each citizen can identify a single representative in the legislature that is *theirs*, representing their district's interests. Several countries have devised hybrid systems to try to accomplish both proportionality and representation, called **mixed systems**. These countries elect some legislators using plurality voting in single-member districts, and others using list proportional representation. There are two ways to combine these electoral rules.

One approach just lets the two systems play out independently, so one part of the legislature is selected using a system that encourages few parties and another part is selected using a system that encourages more parties. This is described as **parallel** elections, or **mixed-member majoritarian**. As expected, with these systems countries have more parties than do strictly majoritarian systems, but fewer than they would likely have if they had only a proportional system. Japan uses this system and has an average of about 3.6 parties.

Another approach, called **compensatory** or **mixed-member proportional**, uses the proportional part of the legislature to counteract the majoritarian tendencies of the single-member-district part. So a party with a smaller proportion of seats than votes in the single-member districts will get even more seats in the other part, to balance out the distortion. Germany uses this system, and they have about six parties.

Evaluating Duverger

Duverger's law is simple, but as we have seen, its logic can be applied to a variety of systems. Broadly speaking, the law says: the more proportional the electoral system, the more parties it will support. Single-member districts with plurality rule (which can be very disproportional) tend toward only two parties. Is this true?

Not quite. Duverger himself employed a few qualifiers when he coined his law, writing that "this *approaches* the *most nearly perhaps* to a true sociological law."[6] Of the countries that use first past the post, only the United States is truly a two-party system (and even the United States has additional minor parties). Canada, Great Britain, and India all have three or more major parties despite having single-member districts with plurality rule. This has led many political scientists to claim that Duverger's law is simply false.[7] However, what is true is that countries with majoritarian systems tend to have fewer parties, even if they don't have the strict two-party dominance that we see in the United States. Figure 5.4 shows the effective number of parties in several developed democracies, organized by their electoral system. While few countries have exactly two parties, the tendency toward two major parties is strongest in majoritarian systems.

Duverger's law is thus not an ironclad law, but it does describe a significant factor in limiting the number of parties in a political system. Later in this chapter we'll discuss two major features of the U.S. system: its presidential system, with its unique Electoral College, and its relatively weak and open political parties. These features have significant implications beyond how they affect the number of parties, so we will discuss them later. That being said, they do play a factor in limiting the number of parties in the United States.

First we will discuss two additional, yet minor, factors that contribute to our two-party system. The first relates to how much potential political conflict there

FIGURE 5.4 Effective Number of Parties by Electoral Rules

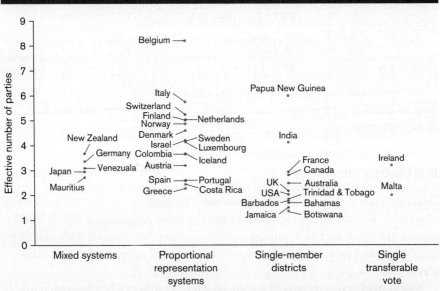

Source: Arend Lijphart, *Patterns of Democracy: Government and Performance in Thirty-Six Countries.* 2nd ed. (New Haven, CT: Yale University Press, 2012); Adrian Vatter, "Lijphart expanded: three dimensions of democracy in advanced OECD countries?" *European Political Science Review* 1, no. 1 (2009): 125-54.

is in a country. The more social cleavages there are, the more parties may form to reflect them. The second involves barriers to new parties' attempts to compete with established parties.

Social Cleavages The effect of national divisions on the number of parties can be seen in Figure 5.4. A handful of countries stand out as having an unusually large number of parties despite their electoral system. Papua New Guinea, India, Belgium, Switzerland, and Italy all have more parties than other countries with similar electoral systems. What do these countries have in common?

All five are particularly ethnically and culturally diverse. Papua New Guinea, India, Belgium, and Switzerland are all multilingual countries. Italy also has significant language minorities, but more importantly, it is divided by a long-standing cultural division between the north and the south. (Italy has also changed its electoral system several times in the past few decades, in ways that have both encouraged and discouraged more parties, so it's likely its system is still adjusting to changes in the incentives for politicians.)

Papua New Guinea has the largest number of languages of any country in the world—more than 850. Papua New Guinea uses a single-transferable vote, and as many as six or seven parties receive first-choice votes in parliamentary elections.

India is both religiously and linguistically diverse. Before the 1980s, the Congress Party was consistently the largest, but it was challenged by many other parties around the country. More recently, the Bharatiya Janata Party has replaced Congress as the dominant party, but many others continue to compete, particularly on the local level.

Belgium has two dominant language groups, the Dutch-speaking Flemish and the French-speaking Walloons. In many cases, this leads to two parallel parties, one Flemish and one Walloon, which advance similar goals and ally together in the legislature. Switzerland's territory is divided between French, German, and Italian-speaking regions.

This sort of diversity can make it hard for politicians and voters to coordinate the way that Duverger's law imagines they will. A party that offers exactly the policies you want but is dominated by another language group might be hard to support. Another party that offers a similar platform, but in your language, might be appealing.

Making things even more complicated is the fact that these ethnic and religious differences are usually geographic as well. Duverger's logic applies at the level of the single-member district itself. If parties A and B are the two top parties in one district, but C and D are the top two in another, all four parties should survive. For a long time, party competition in India was between the dominant Congress Party, which competed across the country, and a number of smaller parties that had only regional appeal. This kind of ethnic or linguistic

The prime minister of India, Narendra Modi, is the leader of the Bharatiya Janata Party. While the party has found nationwide success, the party's (and Modi's) actions have been heavily criticized at the local level where other parties dominate. Here, demonstrators from the All India Trinamool Congress Party protest Modi's alleged misuse of the nation's intelligence agencies.

concentration also explains the success of the Bloc Quebecois in Canada and the Scottish Nationalist Party and Sinn Fein in the United Kingdom.

We're emphasizing linguistic and geographic differences in countries like India and Belgium in part because they are easy to measure. But what we are really after are what we would call "social cleavages" of any kind. Political scientists Seymour Martin Lipset and Stein Rokkan noted that there can be many different types of social cleavages—between workers and employers, between religious leaders and government, or between cities and rural areas. They argued that the way cleavages divide up a country drives the number of social groups in the country, and in turn the number of political parties. Where the cleavages create many different groups that are alienated from one another, you get many parties. It's simply harder to get very divergent groups into the same coalition. But where there are fewer cleavages, or the cleavages line up with each other (so that most people with the same language also live in the same part of the country and have the same religious beliefs), or the cleavages are not particularly deep, fewer parties may be needed to reflect those groups.

Perhaps the best way to think about this is that the groups defined by social cleavages are the building blocks of party divisions, but institutions either encourage or discourage them to overcome their differences.[8] When the electoral system is less permissive of minor parties, even diverse societies will tend to have fewer parties than they would if the system was more permissive. And when the electoral system is more permissive, such as with proportional representation, a society that has few differences may have fewer parties. This argument implies that the only way to get many parties is with many social cleavages *and* proportional representation.

We can of course think of examples where a system has many parties despite its restrictive electoral system. But across the numerous electoral systems in the world, the social cleavages pattern is mostly borne out. It's worth noting that while the electoral system has not constrained India to only two parties, it does have far fewer major parties than we might expect from a country as large, diverse, and internally divided as it is.

Barriers to New Parties

Separate from any effects of institutions, advocates of third parties in the United States often blame the existing parties for putting up barriers to meaningful competition. There is some truth to this. New parties do face hurdles to get on the ballot. Debates usually don't invite third-party candidates. Media coverage tends to focus on the major party candidates. And advocates for the Republican and Democratic parties do prefer to keep those hurdles in place.

At the same time, these barriers are not insurmountable. They also are generally secondary to the institutional disadvantages that minor parties have. Without those institutional disadvantages, the other hurdles would not be as significant, and might not exist at all.

The Democratic and Republican parties enjoy automatic access to the ballots in most cases, because they have established themselves as viable parties. New parties can and do get the same access after minimal success. In 2020, the Libertarian, Green, and Constitution parties each had automatic ballot access in a significant number of states, despite remaining minor parties everywhere. Where parties are not automatically granted a line on the ballot, most states allow access through petitions or through running independent candidates.

Third-party candidates who have almost no chance of winning the election are still given extensive media attention and are sometimes invited to debates. Ross Perot was on the debate stage in 1992, and he went on to win only 1 out of 5 votes in the general election, and no Electoral College votes. What hurt Perot was not a lack of attention, but the electoral system. Similarly, Jill Stein and Gary Johnson got considerable attention in the 2016 election. The attention was nowhere near what the major party nominees received, but it was well in excess of their chances of actually winning the election.

Even in multi-party democracies, there are disadvantages for minor parties. Many democracies with public financing and media access rules make the receipt of resources conditional on past electoral success. In such a system, a party that does poorly is given less financing and media attention than one that performs well. It is hard for a new party to break through in any system.

Some of the barriers that minor parties or independent candidates face arise because political actors are actively trying to prevent those minor parties from playing a spoiler role. If debate organizers think a minor party cannot win, but might pull votes away from the two major parties, they might want to help frame the race in terms of the two leading candidates. The two major parties may both want to go along with that framing as well.

Similarly, all but a few U.S. states have "sore loser" laws, which bar a candidate who ran and lost in a party's primary from running as an independent in the general election. These rules acknowledge that an independent may serve as a spoiler in the general election (see, for instance, the discussion of the election of 1912 in Chapter 9).

Nevertheless, the barriers to third parties are real. Well-organized, well-funded political parties with long histories in the political system—like the Democrats and the Republicans in the United States—have an advantage over newcomers. The barriers to entry for minor parties thus reinforce the effects of the institutions on the party system.

INTERNAL DEMOCRACY, OR, WHY DO OUTSIDERS SOMETIMES SUCCEED IN U.S. POLITICAL PARTIES?

In February 2020, as six candidates met on a Las Vegas debate stage in their bids to become the Democratic Party's nominee for president, one of those candidates jabbed two of his rivals. "Let's put forward somebody who's actually a Democrat," Pete Buttigieg, the former mayor of South Bend, Indiana, said. "We shouldn't have to choose between one candidate who wants to burn this party down and another candidate who wants to buy this party out."

Buttigieg was referring to two standouts in the race: Bernie Sanders, Independent senator from Vermont (and the front-runner at the time), and billionaire Mike Bloomberg, who had served as mayor of New York, first as a Republican and later as an independent. While Sanders had long worked with Democrats in

Congress, he and his supporters had taken aim at the party itself as a major obstacle to change. Bloomberg had sat out the early part of the nomination process, but had gained support through an expensive, self-financed national advertising blitz in the previous weeks. While both Sanders and, especially, Bloomberg were dealt a serious blow a few weeks later on Super Tuesday, both seemed to be in strong positions at the time of the debate.

The 2016 presidential race also featured party outsiders. Eventual Republican nominee Donald Trump had been, through the course of his career, registered as an independent and a Democrat—as well as a Republican, and he had told CNN's Wolf Blitzer in 2004 that "In many cases, I probably identify more as Democrat." Sanders ran in 2016 as well.

In 2016, both Trump and Sanders, and especially their supporters, at times complained that the parties whose nominations they were contesting were being unfair. When Colorado's Republican delegates pledged for Ted Cruz in 2016, Trump complained "The system is rigged, it's crooked."[9] Sanders, meanwhile, claimed that he was "entitled" to the support of unpledged Democratic delegates in states where he did well, and that the calls for him to drop out of the race when Clinton's victory appeared certain were "outrageously undemocratic."[10] In a 2019 interview, Sanders said, "Maybe if the system was not rigged against me [in 2016], I would have won the nomination."[11] Internal DNC communications, hacked and released to the public through WikiLeaks in the summer of 2016, suggested that party staffers held some animus toward Sanders, which further fueled claims by Sanders' supporters that the party was not truly open to his candidacy and had rigged events in Clinton's favor. A protester at the Democratic National Convention in the summer of 2016 said he would "rather watch the DNC burn" than see Clinton nominated.[12] In light of these sentiments, it may surprise you to learn that the American political parties—especially their presidential nominations—are possibly the most open to outside nominees of any political parties in the world.

Political scientists call the group that chooses party nominees and leaders the **selectorate**. In the United States, the selectorate is technically the delegates at the national convention, but since they are ultimately chosen by voters in state party primaries and caucuses, the voters are effectively the selectorate. In other countries, the voters rarely comprise the selectorate. Recall the 2017 French election discussed in the previous section. Before the candidates competed in even the first round, the parties had to choose their nominees. The French system requires that any candidate for the presidency get 400 signatures from elected officials. Voters played no role at all. In many countries, the system is different among the various parties. In the United Kingdom, the Labour Party chooses its leader through an election in which only those who are registered members and supporters of the party can vote. That's about 1 percent of the

The degree of internal democracy in U.S. parties sets them apart from the rest of the world. For all the frustration that many have with the major American parties, they are among the most (small "d") democratic in the world.

Internal Democracy and the United States' Two-Party System

The openness of the U.S. party system to outsiders is significant in its own right, but it also contributes to the tendency for the United States to be a two-party system. As we saw earlier in this chapter, Duverger's law highlights the incentives for politicians to join one of the two major parties rather than go it alone, but other factors also go into that decision. One is whether or not the major parties are accommodating of new politicians joining them.[15]

Suppose that, in 2020, the Democratic Party picked a presidential nominee the way that German political parties choose their leaders—at a convention where long-standing party figures choose, from among themselves, who will be their leader. There would be no way for Bernie Sanders to run the sort of grassroots campaign he ran. To have any chance at the nomination, he would have to join the Democratic Party first and win over its influential members. No amount of grassroots support, by itself, would do anything for him. Indeed, Sanders and his supporters might choose another path, like forming a separate political party. That effort might have little or no chance of winning, but for ideologues not willing to accept the Democratic leadership, it might seem like their only option.

Bernie Sanders' 2016 presidential campaign shows how unlikely and probably counterproductive starting a new party would be. Sanders and his supporters believed that the Democratic Party was not especially open to them. And once the primaries were over, there was nothing stopping Sanders from forming a third party to contest the presidency. But this didn't happen. Sanders' own reason for not taking this step was very Duvergerian. Speaking at the 2016 Democratic National Convention, Sanders acknowledged the ways in which he and his movement had pushed Hillary Clinton. "I am happy to tell you that at the Democratic Platform Committee there was a significant coming together between the two campaigns, and we produced, by far, the most progressive platform in the history of the Democratic Party," he crowed. But he also added that the best thing for him and his supporters to do was to work for Clinton's victory, because Donald Trump's winning would be worse for his supporters. "Our job now," he said, "is to see that platform implemented by a Democratic Senate, a Democratic House, and a Hillary Clinton presidency—and I am going to do everything I can to make that happen."[16]

The fact that American parties will accommodate outsiders who disagree with their platforms reduces some of the pressure to form third parties, and thus makes the two major parties that much stronger. The Democratic and Republican parties have each changed significantly since the Civil War, but their names and organizational structures have endured. The last major change in the parties in the United States—the rise of the Republican Party to replace the Whigs as the primary alternative to the Democrats (see Chapter 2)—occurred when the parties were less capable of absorbing such outside pressure. It is thus likely that vibrant internal democracy actually contributes to the two-party system.

EXECUTIVE SYSTEMS, OR, WHY DO OTHER COUNTRIES HAVE FEWER BARRIERS TO PARTIES?

The previous two sections have focused on features of parties that affect their roles in getting politicians into office. Internal openness affects who the party puts forward as candidates, and electoral rules affect who wins elections. Institutions also affect how parties function once their candidates are in office.

The United States has a **presidential system**, while many other democracies have a **parliamentary system**. The two systems differ in many important ways, but we highlight three structural differences here. We will explore how power is distributed within the executive branch, the constituency to which the head of government is beholden, and the flexibility—or lack thereof—in scheduling elections.

A Divided Executive

Parliamentary systems split the roles of head of state and head of government, while in presidential systems the same person takes both roles. The **head of government** is the person who runs the executive branch of the country. This individual typically heads up a cabinet of officials. In a parliamentary system, the term "government" is reserved for the ministers who run the country, including the prime minister. When the government does something, whether it's enacting a new health policy initiative or entering a war or providing disaster relief after a pandemic, the head of government is in charge of it. The **head of state** is the person who represents a sovereign nation. In many countries, this is a monarch, like a queen or king, who embodies the nation.

The United Kingdom is perhaps the best-known parliamentary system. The head of the government is the prime minister. (In 2020, that was Boris Johnson,

No Independent Constituency

In a presidential system, the president is selected independently of the legislature; in most presidential systems, this means a direct vote of the people. (In the United States, the Electoral College is an intermediate step, but we don't expect the electors to do anything but vote the way their states instruct them to. So the Electoral College amounts to a complicated way of translating the vote of the people—so complicated that the popular vote winner might not even win. But the electors play no independent role. They do not exercise their own judgment. And even if the members of the Electoral College did exercise their own judgment, this would still be considered an independent constituency, separate from that of the legislature.)

By contrast, in parliamentary systems, the head of the government is the prime minster or premier. In a parliamentary system, the power to name the prime minister is ultimately held by the parliament and only indirectly by the people. After an election, the head of state invites the largest party to form a government. The largest party in the legislature (the parliament) then selects the prime minister, either alone or with the support of other parties.

This indirect selection is akin to the way in which U.S. senators used to be chosen by state legislatures, rather than by the people of the state. One reason the United States ended this practice in the early 1900s was that voters were selecting state legislators based on who they preferred for U.S. Senate. In a parliamentary system, this is the whole point; voters choose legislators based on which party they are in, which in turn means which prime minister they back. So voters still have a say, but that say has to go through the parliament.

In other words, the president's constituency is the people (in the United States, as aggregated by the Electoral College). This is a different constituency from that of the legislature, which is elected by states or by congressional districts. While all eligible voters vote for president and for Congress, which ones vote for which are different.[19] The president and Congress have separate constituencies.

But a prime minister's constituency is the parliament, or by extension, the people who elected the parliament. Unsurprisingly then, the prime minister is not accountable to the people directly, but to the parliament. Because of this, it is rare to have something like divided government, as we often have in the United States, where one party controls the legislature and another controls the executive branch. In a parliamentary system, the parliament will not select a leader from an opposing party. It is possible that, if no party controls a majority of seats in Parliament, a minority government, or coalition government built on agreements among minority parties, will form. But these arrangements don't create the kind of confrontational gridlock that we are used to in the United States.

No Fixed Elections

If the prime minister is accountable to the parliament, what happens when Parliament changes its mind about the prime minister? In the United States, the Congress can often disagree with the president, even a Congress controlled by the president's party. When the differences are political, not much can be done about that. Everyone must just wait for new elections to see if there is a change in who is in power. (The obvious exception is impeachment, which is meant to be used for abuse of power rather than disagreements over policy.) In a parliamentary system, if tensions between the chief executive and the parliament grow too significant, the country can directly move to new elections.

Who has the power to dissolve the parliament? It varies. If members of the parliament want to remove the government, they can call for a **vote of no confidence**, which means that the parliament no longer supports (has confidence in) the government. Sometimes, the parliament is then given the chance to form a new government. If that fails, new elections are held and the new parliament gets a chance to choose a government. The government itself can sometimes call new elections. If the government cannot get approval for its policies from Parliament, they can dissolve the parliament and perhaps get a more favorable legislature.

This power to call elections means that strategic politicians can time elections to their favor. If public opinion suggests that the party in power is gaining popularity, that would be a good time to hold new elections. And if the party in power is becoming less popular, the government may not want to hold new elections, but the opposition in Parliament might.

The challenge is that it can be hard to predict the outcome of elections. For example, British prime minister Theresa May, who was set to negotiate the United Kingdom's exit from the European Union (as mandated in the 2016 Brexit election), called for new elections in 2017 with the hope of increasing the Conservative Party's share of seats in Parliament. But the Conservatives did not capture a clear majority, and her position did not get stronger. Two years later, the new prime minister, Boris Johnson, gambled on an election to bolster the Conservative Party's numbers to support his push for Britain to leave the European Union. The gamble paid off when Conservatives picked up 48 seats and an outright majority in the House of Commons.

Accountability to Parties

These three structural differences between presidential and parliamentary systems—with parliamentary systems having a divided executive, no independent constituency, and no fixed elections—have important consequences for political parties. Together, these factors mean parties in a parliamentary system have more influence over the government than they have in a presidential system. The government—the prime minister and all the other ministers, as opposed to the head of state—is accountable to the legislature, which means the government has to acquiesce to the parliament's constituency, and when that relationship breaks down, the parliament may need to be dissolved. So the government's fate is bound to that of the parliament. And because parties, particularly the governing party or parties, are in control of the parliament, they are more influential than they would be in a presidential system.

Under a presidential system, the president builds their own electoral coalition. The president can rely on party loyalty from voters and can use the party to coordinate with the legislature. But the president also has personal loyalties and personal connections. Parties are important, but presidents have independent paths that can work around the parties.

That is harder to do in a parliamentary system. There, the government is put in place by the party or parties that select it. Thus the party exerts influence not unlike the way the party chooses the Speaker of the House in the United States. If the government is supported by a coalition, then the parties that make up that coalition all have to be satisfied. Everything works through the parliamentary parties. If the party or parties that support the government doesn't like what the chief executive is doing, that person can be removed.

This happened to British prime minister May after her continued efforts to navigate the country's exit from the EU broke down. As repeated efforts to find a plan with support in Parliament failed, Conservative Party members began to call for May to resign, which she did at the end of May 2019. The Conservative Party members in Parliament then went about choosing a new prime minister, and they chose Boris Johnson by the end of July. The head of government in the United Kingdom changed, not through elections, but with a vote of Parliament.

Compare this with the conflicts that President Trump had with Congress when he took office in 2017. The Republican majority in both the House and the Senate often wanted something different from what the president himself wanted. In some cases, they outmaneuvered him.[20] Despite repeated campaign promises to build a border wall between the United States and Mexico, Trump was unable to persuade Republicans in Congress to fund the wall. Trump's proposed health care reform bill also didn't pass a Republican-controlled Congress. In other cases, however, the president's independent support was enough to keep Republicans in line. Republican legislators didn't want to challenge the president and risk a primary challenge or loss of the support of their own partisans. Republicans who consistently opposed the president were likely to resign before the 2018 election. Even after the president's electoral loss in 2020, Republicans who continued to serve in government did not want to make an enemy of the former president, who would likely continue to be influential in the party.

In a parliamentary system, this would not be possible. The voters who put the prime minister in office do so through electing members of Parliament. If those members lose, so does the prime minister. That doesn't mean there is never tension between the prime minister's government and those in their party. We saw intense conflict between Teresa May and members of her Conservative Party in the UK. And members who are not in the government themselves (sometimes termed "back-benchers" because they do not sit in the front benches with the government ministers) can cause trouble for the government. But the party and its government share a fate more than they do in a presidential system.

After the 2018 elections in the United States, when Democrats took control of the House of Representatives, the president's relationship with the legislature became even more fraught. Now, not only did the members of Trump's party at times want something the president didn't want, but they no longer controlled an important part of the legislature. Indeed, without that election, Donald Trump almost surely would not have been impeached in 2019.

This kind of divided government is not generally possible in a parliamentary system. However, if no majority can be formed, it is possible that a minority of the legislature will form a government. Thus the parties who are not in government will be a majority of the parliament. But in such a situation, the party not in government will generally not be very cohesive or disciplined (or else they could have formed a government of their own).

Coalition Government   In a parliamentary system, it is not generally possible to have the kind of "divided government" in which different parties control the legislature and the executive, as described in the previous section. Whichever party or parties control the parliament will control the executive. But it is possible that no one party is large enough to control the parliament by itself. So more than one party will have to join together to form the government. The government then has divisions. This is called a **coalition government**.

A coalition government is not really possible in a presidential system, where a single president is selected. In multiparty presidential systems, multiple parties do often enter in a pre-electoral coalition to back the same candidate, but that president, once elected, may be relatively free to govern without constraint from those parties. In a parliamentary coalition government, the government continues to rely on the support of parliament.

Does it matter that a government is a coalition government? It might. We think that the way to approach this question is to think about how the groups in politics are organized into the government. Recall that we have described parties as coalitions of different groups. In a two-party system, you have two large parties made up of many smaller groups. In a multiparty system, larger parties will include many groups, but smaller parties may have only a few groups or just one group. A single-party government and a coalition government might both be made up of the same smaller groups, but in the coalition government, those groups were first organized into smaller parties before being organized into the large governing coalition. In the single-party government, they were organized directly into the large party.

Political scientists Kathleen Bawn and Frances Rosenbluth described the difference by distinguishing between a "party coalition"—a large party with many subgroups, as in a two-party system—and a "coalition of parties"—a coalition government with many parties.[21] In a coalition of parties, the groups are bound together into many parties, which in turn form the coalition.

Bawn and Rosenbluth's framework puts the focus on forming a governing coalition. Because government formation involves getting a majority, or close to it, it is not enough to only think about the number of parties in the election. How they form governing coalitions *after* the election matters too. Advocates for multiparty democracy often focus on the limited choices that voters have with only two major parties in the United States. Major big-tent parties compromise on issues important to many voters, and this is frustrating for multiparty advocates. But when it comes time to form a government, the parties in that government also compromise. Even minor parties need to ally with major ones if they want to join the government. They just make those compromises at a different stage.

Does it matter whether the governing coalition is formed as a single party, before the election, or among many parties, after the election? We think it does, for several reasons. First, coalition governments make parties even more central to parliamentary politics. When parties are brought together to form a government, it means that those parties and their leaders are central to the negotiations. Second, forming a coalition government also tends to give more power to the groups in the minor parties. A small party whose support is necessary to form a government may have as much leverage as a large party. A classic example is in Israeli politics, where one of the larger parties, often Labor or Likud, tends to need the support of several minor parties to form a government. Several minor parties in Israel are religious, the largest of which is Shas. The religious parties naturally care a lot about religion, and so the Israeli minister for religious affairs is often a member of Shas or another religious party. Influence over policy in this area is the price for support from that party.

This power for minor parties is so important that Giovanni Sartori thought it was the main criteria for whether a party should be counted. If the party has the potential to join a governing coalition, it should be counted. (See the Political Science Toolkit in this chapter for more on counting parties.)

Bawn and Rosenbluth looked for broader evidence of this bargaining advantage for minor parties. Let's imagine an environmental group, which seeks more regulation of industry, and a rural group, which seeks more aid to farmers, in the context of two-party and multiparty systems. In a two-party system, we might see the environmental interests and the farming interests as groups within one major party. Each group is important, but neither of them would typically be willing to bolt the party to get what it wants. This might limit each party's bargaining power. In a multiparty coalition, however, the governing coalition may have to promise more, in terms of government spending, to win the support of the crucial minor parties and keep them in the coalition. Bawn and Rosenbluth tested this idea and found that government spending tends to be higher in multiparty coalition governments. This suggests that groups represented by small parties in a multiparty coalition have greater leverage than they would if they were represented by a big-tent party in a two-party system.

It is not obvious to us whether this bargaining advantage for smaller groups is a good thing or not. Minor parties today represent environmentalists, libertarians, ethnic and religious minorities, socialists, communists, neo-fascists, right-wing nationalists, and so on. Some of those groups have important values that might be overlooked in a big-tent party. Others are small for very good reasons.

The advantage to small groups aside, it is also not obvious whether it is more democratic or more representative in general to form a governing coalition before or after the election. In the multiparty model, voters have little direct say over the governing coalition. They can back a party, only to find it joining a coalition with another party they disagree with. (This nearly happened in 2018 in Italy, when the Democratic Party and the Five-Star Movement considered a coalition, despite some supporters of each party significantly disliking the other party. A year later, those two parties did end up forming a coalition.) But while voters have little say over what kind of coalition ultimately forms, they have more of a say in the relative strength of the different subgroups within the coalition. In addition, agreements between those groups—in this case, separate parties—are more transparent and thus easier for voters to understand.

In the two-party model, voters get to choose between two possible governing coalitions. They know going in which compromises are likely to be made, because they were already determined when the party was being formed. But if they don't like either coalition, voters must get involved earlier—in the nomination process or within the party—to shape the coalition that will go into power.

DIFFERENT INSTITUTIONS; DIFFERENT PARTIES

In the opening of this chapter, we asked whether the election of populist, nationalist Donald Trump in 2016 was part of a global pattern or not. Reasonable observers can reach different conclusions about that, but any attempt to understand American politics in a global context requires thinking about the ways the rules differ from one country to the next, and how those rules affect party politics.

But the United States has a two-party system. So part of what makes Trump notable is not just that he is in power, but that he is the head of one of the two large parties that has the support of about half the electorate. Populist parties in many countries have gotten attention with a smaller share of the vote, because having a smaller share matters in those systems. Support for the populists in Sweden and Germany, for instance, can be traced in the slow growth of their share of the vote, which is still far from a majority. Meanwhile, the populist, antiestablishment appeal of Trump has been around in the United States for a long time, but it wasn't represented by a single political party.

The United States has particularly open parties. Trump didn't just win in the electorate. He first won in a presidential primary against a score of other contenders. Many Republican leaders opposed him. In another system, he might never have been nominated.

But the United States has a presidential system. Thus Trump's support can be seen directly in the vote for president (and its distribution across states in the Electoral College). In a parliamentary system, a populist leader might work their way to power more indirectly. In Italy, populist Matteo Salvini became the deputy prime minister after his Lega party came in second in the election. But he has been able to have a large role in Italian policy making from that position.

The fact that populism has been expressed in many different systems suggests that perhaps it is surging today. But it also suggests that it is hard to find a common benchmark for such a surge. The question of whether or not populism and nationalism are on the rise illustrates the importance of the comparative perspective. Even if all we care about is politics in the United States, it is hard to judge the system without thinking about what would happen if the system were different. And among the world's democracies, differences abound.

Discussion Questions

1. For what reasons does the United States tend to have a two-party system while many other democracies have far more parties?

2. What is Duverger's Law? How well does it describe differences in the numbers of parties across different democracies?

3. Describe a "list proportional representation" party system. How does this differ from the system in the United States? Do you think adopting such a system in the United States would be an improvement? Why or why not?

4. Who is the "selectorate" in American party nominations? Is this selectorate generally bigger or smaller than that of other countries? What are the consequences of having a selectorate of this size?

5. In multiparty nations, parties typically have to negotiate a governing coalition after the election. In the United States, these negotiations occur within a party before the election. Does it matter whether such negotiations occur before or after elections? How?

6

Party Machines

A visitor to the Cook County Building in Chicago in the 1950s might have been greeted by a police sergeant known around the building as The Hawk. In many ways, he wasn't much of a police officer. He had little law enforcement training and poor vision; he was terrified of guns, and his primary job was supervising the man who ran the building's freight elevator. He later held a job as a uniformed officer for the County Treasurer's office, providing directions to visitors to the building, and after that wore the uniform of a state highway inspector.

The Hawk, as described in journalist Mike Royko's landmark book *Boss*,[1] had not exactly risen through the ranks of Illinois law enforcement as a result of his law enforcement prowess or physical skills. Rather, The Hawk, so nicknamed due to his early work as a lookout man for a gambling organization, had earned his distinguished résumé by winning the favor of county and state Democratic officials, who had appointed him to his various jobs. And they did that because The Hawk was good at his most important job: supporting the local Democratic machine. He knocked on doors as a precinct worker, turning out the Democratic vote in Chicago neighborhoods every Election Day. He frequently attended local fundraising dinners for the

Mayor Richard J. Daley, considered one of the last "big city bosses," was mayor of Chicago from 1953 to 1976. Here, Mayor Daley thanks his supporters on the night of his sixth election to the office of mayor.

party and paid regular dues to his local ward leaders. He was one of tens of thousands of people who helped keep Chicago's mayor Richard J. Daley and his allies in power and was rewarded for it with a regular string of easy government jobs.

This is the essence of the power of party machines. They can be corrupt or brutal, but they need not be. Sometimes a well-run machine is simply a series of tacit exchanges; party leaders offer benefits to people who work to keep them in power. It is a power relationship that goes back millennia, but it has taken on a particular form in the political development of the United States. Moreover, it is an entity that continues to thrive today, even while formal machines of the type that Mayor Daley ran no longer exist.

In this chapter, we will examine the nature of party machines, looking at several examples of their organizational styles in history. We will explore their particular role in American party politics and come to know the logic of machine organization. We will also examine efforts to undermine and destroy political machines in the United States and see what can be learned from those successes and failures.

MACHINES: A BYGONE MODEL WITH AN ENDURING LEGACY

As the story of The Hawk suggests, party machines are something of a relic. They thrived at an earlier time in our nation's political history. But even though the traditional, patronage-based machines are no longer seen in American cities, they cast a long shadow on modern American politics. As it turns out, much of the way Americans think about politics stems from that era, and the language of political reform, so commonly heard today among journalists, activists, and even officeholders, is steeped in and organized against machine politics.

As we'll discuss in this chapter, corruption remains a strong concern among observers of American politics, even while that term's meaning is hopelessly vague. Reform-minded U.S. politicians like John McCain and Russ Feingold, multiple newspaper editorialists, and satirists like Jon Stewart have all railed against the corruption of America's parties and media created by big money. They decry the party machinery that turns hacks into elected officials and bribes into legal contributions; they worry that our party system needlessly creates controversies where none exist and that parties function solely for their own perpetuation. Corruption became a major topic in the 2020 presidential election and in the impeachment of Donald Trump, who called on political allies overseas to address the alleged corruption of his opponents.

References to corruption fuel political reform movements across the nation today, from campaign finance reform to top-two election systems to nonpartisan redistricting commissions. It is also the same type of language that was used over a century ago to attack the party machines that dominated the political systems of dozens of American cities. Many people claim that machines are dead, but if they are, why are so many reformers today pointing out the same ills in modern politics?

It might be that reports of the death of party machines are greatly exaggerated. The type of organization that Mayor Daley ran in Chicago in the mid-twentieth century (effective in getting its favored candidates elected but criticized for allegedly strong-arm tactics) really isn't around anymore, but the system it stemmed from—networks of supporters, favoritism, loyalty, trust, delegation— is at the basis of all party organizations, including those that exist today.

Some modern complaints about "corrupt" politicians do aim at the parts of machines that are now dead. But in many ways, we're still having the same argument we were having a century ago or more: some people are organizing parties to advance ideas or advantage their friends, and others perceive those very purposes as corrupt. If we want to understand this argument and the basis for party organization as well as the opposition to it, it's helpful to understand the party machines of the nineteenth and twentieth centuries that involved so much creativity and productivity and engendered such vehement pushback.

Patronage

The word "machine" is often thrown around rather loosely in American politics. When a political observer refers to the "Clinton machine" or the "Byrd machine," they're usually just referring to a well-run, well-financed political organization, usually built around a politically successful individual or family. A "party machine," however, is something much more specific. It is an organization operating with loyalty to a political party, run by leaders who are often party officers, elected officials, or both. Such an organization centralizes resources that candidates need to successfully run for office—particularly money, volunteers, expertise, and endorsements—and doles out these assets to those candidates it determines to be worthy of its support. The party often rewards individuals who have provided those resources with public resources, such as government jobs, lucrative contracts, preferential treatment, or even just cash. The party machine's primary task is to ensure that its preferred candidates are nominated for office and that those nominees obtain office.

The Patron-Client Relationship Party machines are rooted in the concept of patronage, a form of organization that dates back to the earliest civilizations. In the patronage system, a *patron*—usually a person of some wealth and status in society—forms a mutual relationship with one or more *clients*—usually people who are poorer and in a lower class. A patron might provide things that typical clients usually cannot obtain on their own, such as legal representation, money, access to certain jobs, influence in a political decision, and so forth. In exchange, the clients provide the patron with other forms of support, such as political backing should the patron seek public office. Such relationships were rife in ancient Rome, for example, fueling the political ambitions of numerous senators.

An example of patronage familiar to many Americans might be the relationships depicted in the classic 1972 film *The Godfather.* At the film's opening, we see a client (Amerigo Bonasera, a modest mortician) asking a favor from his patron (Don Vito Corleone, a powerful local Mafia leader in New York). Bonasera's daughter has been physically assaulted, but the justice system has failed to punish the attackers, so he is seeking retribution. Corleone, as godfather to Bonasera's children and employer of many men who can deliver this retribution, has a patron's obligation to help his client. Notably, Corleone repeatedly refuses to accept money in exchange for his help; this is not a one-time business exchange but a traditional and lifelong relationship between a patron and a client. The patron will grant the favor, in exchange for some vague future favor from the client further down the road. Each helps the other.

In this exchange, we see the essence of the patron-client relationship, which we can call **clientelism**. A client has tried to navigate the legal and political

The Godfather provides a classic example of the patron-client relationship. On the right, Don Vito Corleone holds his hand out to his client, to whom he has just granted a favor. The client kisses his hand, signaling his loyalty and promise of future service to Corleone.

world but has failed to do so. So they turn to their patron—a man with substantial reserves of friends, political influence, and physical muscle—and receives the needed support. In exchange, the client pledges lifelong support and the willingness to perform future services. The exchange enhances the patron's reach while improving the client's power position.

The Corleone family (or the real families on which it was based) was not, of course, a party machine. It sought political influence when needed but did not work closely with a political party and was not regularly involved in selecting candidates for office or trying to elect them. Criminal organizations are also, it goes without saying, criminal. Vito Corleone acquired the power and influence to be a patron through violence and intimidation (depicted in detail in the 1974 movie *The Godfather, Part II*).[2] We are not suggesting at all that party machines were inherently criminal or violent, although many did have ties to organized crime. Yet party machines and the Mafia are built around the same sort of relationship. As in the example of The Hawk, a small-time client in the movie pledges his ongoing support to a powerful patron. In return, the patron provides the client with something the patron has in rich supply—government jobs—and both are enhanced by the exchange.

American politics has been host to party machines essentially since before the nation's founding, but their heyday was in the late nineteenth and early twentieth centuries. The market for *clientelistic* (based on a relationship between a patron and a client) politics was at its peak then. Rapid industrialization and immigration in the mid-1800s created a boom in the populations of many cities in the northern United States, including New York, Chicago, Boston, Cincinnati, and Philadelphia. The poorest areas of these cities were suddenly filled with unassimilated immigrants, many of whom did not speak English and were regarded as culturally, religiously, or biologically inferior by societal elites. These immigrants nonetheless had basic everyday needs; they sought access to jobs, housing, education for their children, financial assistance after misfortunes, or resolutions to disputes with neighbors. As they quickly found, American government *could* provide some help with their struggles, but obtaining such relief required the successful navigation of an extremely complicated government structure. There were members of Congress, state legislators, aldermen and city council members, school boards, and other officials, each loyal to their own particular level of government. James Walsh describes the American government of that era as a "decapitated monster whose ever extended extremities might otherwise flay unknowing bystanders with total unpredictability."[3]

In a famous exchange, reformer journalist Lincoln Steffens asked Richard Croker, a New York City Democratic Party boss of the late nineteenth century, "Why should there be bosses when cities had mayors, a council, and judges?" Croker responded, "It's because there's a mayor *and* counsel *and* judges *and*—a hundred other men to deal with. . . . A business man wants to do business with one man, and one who is always there to remember and carry out the business." These businesspeople were, in short, prospective clients for would-be patrons. They had many needs but had little with which to repay other than their loyalty and their numbers.

Patronage Jobs The term "patronage" has a specific definition within American political history, referring to government jobs and contracts that could be given out to people in exchange for political support. For much of the nation's history, it was common for newly elected officials to hire those who had supported their campaigns, regardless of their qualifications for the job. This is sometimes called the **spoils system**, referring to U.S. senator William Marcy's 1832 phrase, "To the victor belong the spoils." The offices of legislators, governors, even presidents were regularly lined with people justifying their past work for the officeholder and asking for some sort of public job. Public employees expected to lose their jobs as soon as their boss left office, so they worked tirelessly to delay that event.

The ability to hand out jobs to supporters was an extremely valuable commodity, allowing a candidate or a party to essentially purchase political support with the public's money. Thus party organizations sought to control parts of the government that contained large numbers of government jobs. Public works projects, customs houses, and post offices, among other offices, were considered plum prizes, and the organization that could control such places could all but guarantee itself a long period in power. Richard J. Daley became one of the preeminent party bosses of the twentieth century by becoming simultaneously the mayor of Chicago and the chairman of the Cook County Democratic Party. This gave him access to thousands of public jobs that he could hand out to supporters of his longstanding regime.

THE LOGIC OF THE PARTY MACHINE

As is stressed throughout this text, we view parties as coalitions of policy demanders who work together to win elections and control government. This definition works well for helping us understand just what party machines are and how they function.

Policy Demanders

When looking at party machines, we can think of the *policy demanders* as the party bosses, big-city mayors, and influential industry leaders who are trying to get the government to do something that would benefit them or to work in their best interests. They could simply want the government to be passive—to let industries operate free from regulation or anticorruption probes, to keep their business taxes low, and generally to help them maximize profits. They could also want the government to do something very active, such as providing funds for research and development, protecting patented inventions, insuring investments, keeping labor costs low by cracking down on unions, and so forth. They could also be looking for the government to either open or close borders to new immigrants, to provide city infrastructure projects or leave them to the private sector, to hire or fire certain employees. Every decision the government makes (at the federal, state, or local level) affects people and creates winners and losers. Policy demanders are simply those people who organize so that they can be on the winning side more often than not.

A major priority for the policy demanders is to recruit the right slate of candidates to run for office, from city council and school board on up to the presidency. We'll discuss later in this chapter and in Chapter 9 just what makes a good candidate, but the brief version is that policy demanders want people who can both deliver the policies they want and also get elected. Those goals may conflict with each other. Voters might not want the kind of loyal foot soldiers that machine leaders like—especially if those candidates are seen as lapdogs or very strong partisans. Party leaders are continually navigating this puzzle, trying to nominate people who will do what the party wants, but also being mindful of the need to not alienate the majority of voters.

Loyal Party People

Loyal candidates may be easy to identify—perhaps they're current officeholders or loyal party-machine workers like The Hawk. Then again, they might not be that obvious. Party leaders may need to actively recruit people to run for office. This could involve plucking someone from obscurity, giving them nice clothes and telling them what to say, and then hoping for the best. That usually does not happen, but it has on a few occasions. Famed California lobbyist Artie Samish (a boss of sorts, although not really affiliated with a party) bragged of grabbing an educated but indigent man off the streets of Los Angeles when he needed someone to run for the California State Assembly; that man, John Pelletier, went on to serve five terms in Sacramento.[4]

More often, though, party leaders recruit among people who have already demonstrated some useful political skills. Perhaps they are good at fundraising, have solid public speaking abilities, are involved in labor unions or church groups or other organizations active in elections, and so forth. Or they may simply choose candidates who have demonstrated loyalty to the party organization, either by working on campaigns or publicly advocating for candidates. From the party leaders' perspective, the ideal candidate is someone with many of the skills necessary to run for office but lacking the ability to do it on their own. This creates a system of dependency, whereby the candidate still relies on the party leaders for election and reelection. If it costs $100,000 to run for office, the ideal candidate is the one who can raise $50,000: having the ability to bring money to the table but still needing to stay in party leaders' good graces in order to win and maintain office. This helps ensure that the candidate will still work for whatever it is that party leaders want.[5]

The relationship between party leaders and candidates tends to be one whereby the party occasionally makes some policy demands on the candidate, assuming they win office. This doesn't need to be an antagonistic relationship; often both the officeholder and the party are working toward similar ends. But in general, party leaders are working to advance some sort of policy agenda, and officeholders are working to perpetuate their stay in office. Thus those elected end up working to advance the goals of the party leaders. This might create conflict on only a few issues per year. Assuming the party leaders have recruited well, the officeholder may already largely agree with them on a great many things. But once in a while, conflicts will occur, as we will see.

In the age of the traditional party machines, nominating and electing the desired party candidate wasn't necessarily a difficult job. The bulk of nominations prior to 1915 occurred at party conventions. Such meetings were often dominated by loyal party machine employees, handpicked by their party boss. It was certainly possible for rival factions to pack their supporters into the convention hall and seize control from the bosses, but it was very difficult to do so. The bosses were usually both better organized and funded, and if they got wind of a conspiracy, they might close the doors or move the event. Delegates, knowing that their path to a successful political career was keeping the boss happy, eagerly voted as the boss instructed.

Given their access to the levers of power, party machines may also attract those in search of more craven rewards. George Washington Plunkitt, a late-nineteenth-century Tammany Hall member (see the next section), who worked his way up from local organizer to state legislator, contributed the concept of "honest graft" to the American lexicon in describing his lengthy and profitable career. As he described it, access to power gives one the ability to make substantial sums of money, often quite legally. In one such example, Plunkitt described his process of learning about the future locations of city public expenditures, such as parks or schools, and then buying up the land inexpensively and selling it to the city at a substantial markup. (Today this would likely be considered criminal, or at least unethical, although moves like this were rampant a century ago.)

Accounts of party bosses are rife with examples of leaders plundering public treasuries through the normal transactions of politics. A city councilor may shape public laws to benefit his particular business interests. A mayor may hire people for city jobs with the implicit requirement that they give a percentage of their salary back to finance the mayor's political campaigns. A legislator may ensure that relatives are kept on the public payroll regardless of qualifications. In the 1880s, San Francisco (then under the control of its own Democratic boss, Christopher Buckley) created an "inspecting teacher" position, the holder of which was responsible for reviewing public schoolteachers' performance and hiring and firing them as necessary. The position conveniently turned out to be held by a string of local party leaders' wives and girlfriends.[6]

These public plunderers may be considered policy demanders, broadly defined. After all, they are attempting to steer public policy in a way that is preferable to them, even if it is in a nonideological direction. And in order to achieve their aims, they attempt to nominate and elect candidates who will remain loyal to them once in office. The same logic of today's party organization applies; the goals and rewards just tend to be different in the case of the traditional party machines. Besides, plunder and good public policy need not be mutually exclusive, and the definition of each is often in the eye of the beholder. Many of the party bosses who profited off city construction in the nineteenth and twentieth centuries are the same ones who helped develop the social welfare state, advance public education and sanitation, and bring the voting franchise to many new immigrants. And those corrupt city construction contracts of the nineteenth century defined the beloved city skylines of the twentieth century.

A LOOK INSIDE A MACHINE: TAMMANY HALL

The archetype of the American political machine is that of Tammany Hall, an organization affiliated with Democratic Party politics in New York City across two centuries. This section examines the machine that grew from modest origins to become the organization that ran the largest city and state in the United States and would exert a heavy hand in the selection of legislators, governors, and presidents. Its evolution and functioning help us understand what a party machine is and how it can survive for so long.

Origins

The Society of St. Tammany, or the Columbian Order, was founded in New York City in 1788. It bore the name of two key historical figures: Tamanend, a Lenni-Lenapi chief who had greeted European immigrants in friendship in the 1600s, and Columbus, the New World's first visitor from the European mainland. This legacy of welcoming Europeans and incorporating them into the American fold would define the Tammany Society, as it came to be called. (Its meetings were held in Tammany Hall, and soon the order would be referenced by that name alone.) While originally a largely fraternal order, one of its early members, Aaron Burr, saw its potential as a political tool and got Tammany members involved in organizing and turning out votes on behalf of the Democratic-Republican Party in 1800. Tammany's influence in that election may have been enough to swing New York's 12 electoral votes to Thomas Jefferson, tipping the result of the entire election (and giving Burr the vice presidency).

One of the key issues that would define Tammany throughout its existence was its attitude toward new immigrants. At least for European immigrants (who would form the bulk of New York City's new residents during the nineteenth century), Tammany's attitude was almost invariably one of welcoming them, making them citizens, and getting them voting privileges as soon as possible. This attitude naturally earned them the derision of many "good government" advocates in the city, who dismissed Tammany's supporters as a "noisy rabble." "Would you admit the populace, that patroon's footman, to vote?" asked a writer in the 1820s. Indeed, that was the source of Tammany's strength.[7]

the leader would be out of a job. If the vote was strong and remained that way, the leader might find himself moving up the ranks and even becoming an advisor to the boss of Tammany Hall. Barbara Porges, a district leader long before women were granted the right to vote, explained, "I can't make a speech, but I get to the individual, and I get the vote."[11]

Tammany also had a general committee, consisting of thousands of members elected by party primary voters or convention attendees. They sometimes struggled against the rule of Tammany's executive committee, which consisted of all the assembly district leaders.

At the top of the organization was an individual sometimes with the official title of "Grand Sachem," but usually referred to as simply "the boss." Assembly district leaders reported directly to him. This boss held a great deal of power and often served for many years. Tammany bosses tended to have big personalities and were treated as top political officials—even as celebrities—in New York City. Boss Tweed's face was so famous, thanks to many years of being lampooned by cartoonist Thomas Nast, that police were able to identify him to arrest him after his 1875 prison escape by looking at the cartoons. Richard Croker, who led the organization in the 1880s, first caught party leaders' attention as a successful street fighter at a Tammany picnic event. He was also one of Tammany's most reliable "repeaters," in other words, one of those who would regularly cast multiple ballots in an election.

Corruption

Corruption is typically a problem in any party machine, and Tammany was no exception. But it's worth thinking about just what we mean when we label a political organization "corrupt." This charge has been leveled at nearly every powerful political group but without a very precise definition. A recent report by Transparency International finds that 3 out of 4 Americans consider our party system to be corrupt, ranking it as the most corrupt political institution in the country. But that probably just means that people don't like parties. They may object to partisan obstruction, to poor representation of citizens' wishes, or to advocating solely for the needs of the powerful few, but those aren't the same thing as being actually corrupt. Corruption traditionally refers to a public figure resorting to dishonest or illegal actions for personal (usually financial) rewards. We will rely upon this more traditional definition here, and yes, Tammany more than fits within this mold.

Tammany's electoral strength relied upon its ability to provide services and social welfare to poor potential voters. Throughout the 1800s, it established a series of neighborhood clubhouses all over the city, serving as local clearinghouses for citizens in need. Long before the American government was in the

Tammany Hall, the physical location and name of New York City's Democratic Party machine of the nineteenth and twentieth centuries, was located on 14th Street in Manhattan.

habit of providing aid for the destitute, Tammany was providing needy citizens with rent money, coal, help in filling out citizenship papers, jobs, peddler's licenses, a friendly word to a judge, and other things a struggling family might need. They also funded a network of Catholic orphanages, asylums, schools, and homes for unwed mothers. These were all legitimate services, provided under Tammany leader "Big Tim" Sullivan's motto: "I never ask a hungry man about his past. I feed him not because he is good, but because he needs food." "If we go down in the gutter," Boss Croker echoed, "it is because there are men in the gutter, and you have to go down where they are if you are going to do anything with them."[12] To be sure, these forms of civic generosity were usually repaid many times over by votes, but whether they were or not, the aid kept coming.

Yet the flip side of this generosity was often very serious corruption. Tammany assisted with the promotion of loyal police officer candidates who had failed their required exam. They bent city laws on taxes and alcohol prohibitions on behalf of friendly business owners. Tammany leaders skimmed a tremendous amount of money from city contracts using Plunkitt's "honest graft." They made sure that businesses owned by their friends and families, or even themselves, received key municipal contracts. Boss Tweed and his close "ring" of friends owned a number of buildings and office spaces in town and ended up charging the city exorbitant rents for the use of them. Tweed was also, through his alliances with the many city and state officials he had helped to elect, in charge of the city's public works projects, which gave him an enormous ability to steer hundreds of patronage jobs and millions of dollars to those who had been loyal to him.

In a famous later example of Tammany corruption, Tammany leaders worked to allow only one ice supplier, the American Ice Company, access to the city's docks in the late 1890s, creating an effective monopoly on ice in the era before electrical refrigeration. This drove up prices of essential ice for everyone. The company rewarded city and Tammany leaders with stock in the company. As this scandal came to light, many sympathetic voters and local leaders soured on the organization.

What's more, Tammany members were quite brazen about their activities, questionable or not. In a state inquiry about Tammany corruption led by Republican state legislators, an attorney asked Boss Croker whether he was working for his own profit. "All the time," responded Croker. "Same as you." The Croker-inspired slogan "I am working for my pocket all the time" became an oft-repeated election quote around the turn of the twentieth century, and Tammany supporters quoted it with pride.

Tammany and Ideology

While Tammany was primarily concerned with obtaining and keeping control of government, it would occasionally use that control for explicitly ideological purposes. In the wake of the Triangle Shirtwaist Factory fire of 1911, which resulted in the deaths of 146 garment workers, mostly young women, the city created the Factory Investigating Commission (FIC) to determine the causes of the fire and make recommendations for reforms. Tammany leaders used the results of the FIC report not just to recommend fire safety laws, but to go well beyond that and dramatically expand city and state social welfare systems. Under Tammany's direction, and with the strong hand of Boss Charlie Murphy, the state legislature introduced a mandatory workers' compensation bill, a ban on child labor, a minimum wage, a Sunday day off, and more. It approved the building of new state-controlled energy plants, and even pushed to bring the New York Stock Exchange under the control of state banking regulators.

In 1924, when Tammany sought to have New York's mayor (and Tammany loyalist), Al Smith, installed as the Democratic nominee for president, it also pushed to have the party adopt a plank in its platform condemning the Ku Klux

Klan as un-American. This plank lost on the convention floor by a single vote, but by pushing both a Catholic candidate and a civil rights measure, Tammany established itself as a fighter for racial and ethnic tolerance.

Decline

Some of the seeds of Tammany's demise lay in the passage of New York's direct primary law in 1913. Tammany boss Charlie Murphy had fought bitterly to prevent its passage, and those struggles became personal between Murphy and Democratic governor William Sulzer, a Tammany politician who had basically renounced the machine (and pushed for the direct primary) as soon as he took office. The law was widely seen at the time as the chief threat to party boss control. If voters, rather than convention delegates, had the power to nominate candidates, that meant bosses could no longer handpick their party's nominees. Sulzer refused to compromise on the bill and campaigned for it in a series of blistering attacks on the machine. Murphy and his Tammany allies in the state legislature helped kill the bill in its first round, and after it died, Murphy made sure Sulzer's political career would follow suit. Tammany led an investigation into Sulzer's life, found some financial irregularities, and used those to successfully impeach and remove Sulzer from office. Yet the legislature passed the direct primary bill the next year, and the new governor signed it.

Tammany nonetheless persisted into the 1920s, but it fell into decline in the 1930s, arguably at the peak of its influence—the president of the United States, Franklin Roosevelt, was a Tammany Democrat, albeit not the most loyal one. Yet the rise of direct aid provided by the federal government during the Great Depression undermined the less formal forms of assistance that had been Tammany's lifeblood for over a century. Several losses by Tammany-backed candidates to Republican reformer Fiorello La Guardia, New York's charismatic mayor in the 1930s, similarly meant a loss of many patronage jobs, and Roosevelt gave out federal spending projects to many non-Tammany officials. Tammany men would remain somewhat influential, choosing, for example, Harry Truman for the vice presidency in 1944 (a decision with many long-term consequences), but by then they had largely closed up shop as an official organization in New York City.

CANDIDATES

What sorts of candidates did party bosses—Tammany members and beyond— want? As with modern politics, parties want two things. First, party leaders want a candidate who will do well by the party in office—that is, a candidate who will protect friends within the party and seek policy goals that the party considers important—and second, they want a candidate who can win office.

However, what constitutes doing well by the party for a machine is different from what a modern party might want. In previous generations, there was little expectation that candidates be good orators or debaters, that they be especially attractive or relatable, or that they be smart or experienced. San Francisco's boss Abraham Ruef famously told a prospective mayoral candidate:

> You have as much experience and information as many men who have been nominated . . . and more than some who have filled the office. What you lack can easily be supplied. The speeches and the funds we can take care of.[13]

There's a broad sense that a good party boss could turn anyone into a candidate. In the film *Mr. Smith Goes to Washington* (1939), an established senator complains when a party boss tells him how to vote. The party boss responds, "My methods have been all right for the past twenty years, Joe, since I picked you out of a fly-specked hole in the wall and blew you up to look like a senator."

Bolters and Muldoons

Despite the real and fictionalized examples we've talked about here, party bosses never spent much time picking people from complete obscurity and running them for high office. That's an enormous waste of a party's resources and engenders a great deal of risk. The candidate could turn out to be terrible, costing the party influence or electoral control. Instead, the party chooses from among ambitious politicians those that satisfy the two aforementioned goals: What does the party want from the job? Who can get elected to that job?

We will discuss these potentially conflicting goals at greater length in Chapter 9, but parties want candidates who can be expected to bring them the benefits that they want—in policy, patronage, or anything else. At the same time, they need candidates who have the campaign skills and personal appeal to actually win elections. Since voters might not want a candidate who gives too much to his party, these goals can conflict. For the party machine, this conflict is mostly one of loyalty. The party boss wants someone who is loyal, but not so obsequiously loyal as to raise suspicion. This means avoiding both "bolters" and "muldoons."

As powerful as party bosses may be, an incumbent officeholder always poses a risk. Officeholders can pass laws and press policies that result in undercutting patronage, allowing the investigation of **graft** (illicit practices), undermining boss control of nominations, and so forth. As we saw earlier, helping to put Franklin Roosevelt in the White House was a mixed blessing for Tammany Hall. Many politicians inherently resist the control of others and are eager to demonstrate their own independence. These people are called **bolters**.

The "stooge" or the **muldoon** refers to excessively loyal party people. Loyalty is valued, but people who appear to be lapdogs may ultimately be viewed with suspicion by voters. Nominating such a person could be seen as a sign of corruption and invite pushback, perhaps costing the party an election.

Writing in the 1920s, journalist Frank Kent, who had covered Baltimore politics for years, penned a profile of party boss control and tried to describe what a boss was looking for in candidates. And here he nicely captures the tension between finding someone who will be loyal but will not cost the party much. "First," he explained, "get a man who, after he is elected, will not prove a 'kicker' or a 'bolter,' but will train with the organization, take advice from the executive, and 'go along.' In other words, a man whom he can 'deliver,' when needed. . . . Second—get a man with whom he can win in the general election."[14]

Kent also explains how the party boss would organize the candidates for an election. Remember, a boss doesn't just care about the presidency or the governor's mansion; he's trying to control as much of government at as many different levels as possible. Thus figuring out the **slate**—the list of candidates running for various offices—is a challenging and precise art. "What [the boss] does," explains Kent, "is to try so to load the ticket in the primary with the precise proportion of 'Muldoons' that can get by in the general election—but no more." This is key: a slate full of muldoons will be sure to deliver the policies you want but could so anger voters as to cost your party in the election. The trick is to balance control of government with electability. Sometimes it may make sense to nominate one or two independent-minded candidates just to make the rest of the slate appear less corrupt.

Assembling the Slate

Mayor Daley, the famous boss of Chicago Democratic politics in the mid-1900s, famously spent a great deal of time working on his candidate slate. With a remarkably diverse coalition of Italians, Jews, Poles, and Germans, he needed to decide how many candidates of each ethnic group to put on his slate and which offices to run them for, all in an effort to keep the ticket electable and to keep the coalition happy.[15] In *Candidate*, Joseph Lyford, a candidate for Congress in Connecticut in 1958, offered a revealing account of his efforts to seek Democratic machine approval and nomination. Lyford was a White Anglo-Saxon Protestant, or a "Yankee" in local parlance, and there could be only so many of those on the slate. In one early meeting with party officials, Lyford explains, "He discussed my problem in competing for a nomination which usually went to someone of Polish extraction. He said the nomination of [Thomas] Dodd, an Irish Catholic, for the Senate would improve my chances for Congressman at large: there would then have to be at least one 'Yankee' on the ticket. If, on the other hand, [Chester] Bowles or [William] Benton (both 'Yankees') were nominated, he felt this would damage my prospects."[16]

Artie Samish, the "super lobbyist" in mid-1900s California, operated as a sort of boss in state politics, using a vast operation to help elect legislators favorable to his clients and to defeat those who might oppose them. From his own autobiography, we know that he wasn't necessarily interested in controlling the candidates he helped on every issue. For the most part, he just elected good candidates and let them behave as they wanted. "I had nothing but contempt," he explains, "for any legislator who could be influenced by a few drinks and a steak dinner. . . . I selected the candidates that I thought would be agreeable to my clients, and I saw that they got elected. And if they didn't behave, I saw that they got unelected."[17]

Once in a while, however, Samish would need to call in a favor. A bank or an oil refinery or a movie studio he represented would want a vote to go a certain way, and he needed to make sure it did. This would happen just a handful of times per session. Legislators could otherwise build up a solid reputation of representing their district other than these few key votes, and for the most part, voters would never learn about them. Few paid close attention to state political coverage, and these solicited votes were largely on pretty obscure, nonideological issues. Thus the legislators could serve as good muldoons, doing what the boss wanted while still getting reelected.

Marketable Goods: Votes, the Currency of the Machine

Tammany's poet/politician George Washington Plunkitt penned a short essay on just what one needed to do to succeed in politics in the era of the party machine. As he described it, one needed "marketable goods"—specifically, votes.[18] He got his start, he explained, with the help of his cousin Tommy, a person who didn't follow politics much but agreed to vote however Plunkitt told him to vote. So Plunkitt went to his district leader and told him he could promise two votes, Tommy's and his own. The district leader took him seriously and encouraged him to keep at it.

Plunkitt then got some neighbors to agree to vote his way, then some others, to the point where he had 60 people who would vote how he told them to. As Plunkitt explains, "What did the district leader say then when I called at headquarters? I didn't have to call at headquarters. He came after me and said: 'George, what do you want? If you don't see what you want, ask for it.

Wouldn't you like to have a job or two in the departments for your friends?' I said: 'I'll think it over; I haven't yet decided what the George Washington Plunkitt Association will do in the next campaign.'" Plunkitt was able to write his ticket in politics after that, becoming a city leader and eventually a state legislator. He had the one thing that the machine valued most—the ability to deliver votes.

Plunkitt's advice to prospective candidates was to do as he did:

> Get a followin', if it's only one man, and then go to the district leader and say: "I want to join the organization. I've got one man who'll follow me through thick and thin." The leader won't laugh at your one-man followin'. He'll shake your hand warmly, offer to propose you for membership in his club, take you down to the corner for a drink and ask you to call again. But go to him and say: "I took first prize at college in Aristotle; I can recite all Shakespeare forwards and backwards; there ain't nothin' in science that ain't as familiar to me as blockades on the elevated roads and I'm the real thing in the way of silver-tongued orators." What will he answer? He'll probably say: "I guess you are not to blame for your misfortunes, but we have no use for you here."

REFORMERS, OR THE ANTI-MACHINE MACHINE

In virtually any political system with a vibrant party machine, there will be an opposing coalition describing itself as a "reform" movement. We can think of the reformers in a number of ways.

Reformers, Clean Government, and Nativism

In their nineteenth- and twentieth-century manifestations, reformers presented themselves as advocates of "good government." They highlighted examples of corruption within the machines they opposed, arguing that party machines were essentially blights on the political system. Machines represented cronyism and a system where backroom deals supplanted the rule of law and ignorant voters were bribed and driven like cattle by the bosses. The reformers, meanwhile, offered a cleaner vision of politics, one in which enlightened voters made educated choices based on candidates' ideas for the future and in which political decisions were made in the open and subject to scrutiny by an objective media. To many disgusted by accounts of vice within the political system, these reformers offered an attractive alternative.

We can similarly see such reform coalitions as simply another organized group of policy demanders. They're trying to do the same thing that the party machine is—control government by installing as many sympathetic officeholders as possible and using that control to create the policies that benefit themselves and their allies. It's not really that one coalition is corrupt and another is clean; they're just different coalitions operating roughly the same way. A coalition of laborers working together to enact policies sympathetic to unions is no more or less pure than one of realtors working together to enact policies favorable to land development.

It's also difficult to look at these struggles between "machines" and "reformers" and not notice the distinct demographic profiles. As we saw earlier, urban party machines tended to embrace ethnic minorities and poorer groups of European immigrants. The reformers who opposed machine tactics tended to oppose the sorts of voters who benefited from them. The nativist movement of the mid-1800s tended to oppose urban Democratic machines in large part because they opposed the rising influence of Catholics and those of non-Anglo ancestry. In 1856, U.S. Representative Thomas Whitney insisted on the House floor that most "of the Papists—I do not say Catholics—in this country are foreign-born, and . . . they carry with them to the ballot-box the anti-American influences, prejudices, and superstitions of their church." Horace Greeley's *New York Tribune* warned in 1858 about a "Catholic conspiracy" by Irish American schoolteachers.[19] Alcohol was a particular concern of these reformers, who saw whiskey as a peculiarly Irish vice and beer as a German one. Limiting access to alcohol, particularly on election days, was a way to stifle the machine vote.

Such divisions live on today, even if not quite so explicitly. In many cities, a longstanding "machine" exists, consisting often of a coalition of African Americans, Latinos, and others, and is predominantly working class. And they are often opposed by a reform coalition that tends to include more White people and be more concentrated in the professions. The language of inclusion and exclusion isn't nearly so explicit as it was a century ago, but the divisions remain real.

Political scientist Jessica Trounstine offers us a helpful way to think about the various distinctions between machines and reform movements.[20] Both machines and reform movements are essentially different forms of **political monopolies**—organizations designed to control access to political power in a local area. They each establish this control by the use of what Trounstine calls **electoral bias**—the systematic disenfranchisement of voters hostile to their efforts. That is, whenever one of these groups is in power, they will manipulate election laws to make it harder for their opponent's supporters to vote and influence the political system. For example, when machines are in power, they will seek to make it easier for poorer people to vote by prolonging polling hours, simplifying voting procedures, and offering work holidays. When reform groups are in power, they will tend to enact voting restrictions such as voter ID laws, voter registration rules, and restricted polling times. Then only those who can take time off of work and have the time and energy to navigate complicated rules will be able to vote. Indeed, nineteenth-century machines often made it easy for people to vote many times in one election; early-twentieth-century reformers created voter registration laws to stop this practice but ended up reducing turnout from greater than 80 percent to below 60 percent in presidential elections, largely at the expense of working-class voters.

Trounstine compares the classic party machine of mid-twentieth-century Chicago with the modern reform machines in place in San Jose, California, and San Antonio, Texas. While each resorts to similar methods to retain and use power, there are some notable differences. Reformers usually have the backing of the business community and tend to be White and Protestant; machine politicians tend to be more working class and backed by a coalition of racial and ethnic groups.

POLITICAL SCIENCE TOOLKIT
Identifying Party Machines

You might think the existence of party machines would be obvious, but outside of a few celebrated historical cases, it can be tricky to identify and categorize them. Political scientist David Mayhew attempted to do that with a team of researchers in the late 1960s and early 1970s.[21] His team conducted extensive journalistic investigations and in-person interviews with key actors in each state, endeavoring to report just how organized the parties were at the state level. He ultimately rated each state on a 1-to-5 scale of "traditional party organizations," or TPOs, with 5 being the most organized or "machine-like." Most of the states, he found, had fairly disorganized, non-machine party systems. Machine states were clustered on the top right of the national map, stretching from Missouri and Illinois to Rhode Island and New York.

Interestingly, some of the most polarized state governments today (places like California, Colorado, and Wisconsin) exist in places with the weakest history of party machines, while those states where machines once dominated (Illinois, Massachusetts, and Maryland) now see relatively less polarized legislatures. It may well be that the strong party machines election. There would be no more municipal employees like The Hawk (profiled at the beginning of this chapter). People would get city jobs based on their abilities to perform certain office tasks and they would lose them if they couldn't perform those tasks. Their support for the mayor's candidates—through voting, door-knocking, or donations—was no longer related to their employment. Party bosses had lost their primary means of rewarding and punishing people. They'd lost their main supply of labor. Who would go to work to elect a party slate now, and why?

It seems clear that the classic party machine, the sort of organization that dominated nineteenth-century New York and twentieth-century Chicago, simply no longer exists in the United States. Without patronage jobs to fuel them, these organizations have largely disintegrated within the past few decades.

A New Source of Party Labor

If machines do not exist, that does not mean that parties never use machine-like strategies. There are no longer the patron-client relationships of the machine variety, but that's because in the modern era, what would-be clients want is not jobs or favors but policy. In his book *The Amateur Democrat*, James Wilson noted the rise of a new form of political labor in the 1960s: the amateur.[22] A phenomenon of post–World War II American social life was leisure time. Middle-class people suddenly had more leisure time thanks to rising incomes and the advent of labor-saving home devices. People joined social clubs, bowling leagues, and charities, and some started volunteering in politics. This presented campaigns and parties with a new source of labor to replace the one that was dying in the wake of civil service reforms.

This new population of political laborers was very different from the previous one. The old laborers expected city jobs for their efforts; the new ones wanted ideological policies. That is, the thing that most motivated these new party workers was not an expectation of steady public income (they already had jobs) but a chance to reshape America. Some wanted the federal government to recognize the rights of African Americans and women. Some wanted a ban on nuclear tests. Some wanted a repeal of the social-welfare-state architecture of the New Deal. Whatever they wanted, they were more than willing to do the hard labor of politics—such as walking precincts, calling voters, posting leaflets, and giving speeches—but they demanded ideological purity from the parties and candidates they backed.

This shift gave party organizations an entirely new set of incentives. It no longer made sense to control every public works division or other job-heavy areas of government activity; there just wasn't the political payoff for it anymore. It did make sense, however, to nominate increasingly ideological candidates and to advocate publicly for more extreme issues.

The New Machines

Today, a variety of informal political organizations exist across the United States. One of the pioneering areas of this form of organization is California, a state with a modest history of formal party machines. A modern Republican machine of sorts exists in Orange County, where a group of wealthy conservatives band together in an organization known as the Lincoln Club to review candidates, issue endorsements, and make donations in races at the city, county, state, and federal level. They do not have access to patronage jobs the way an early machine might have, but they do maintain tight control over the resources candidates need to be competitive in Republican Party primaries: money, endorsements, and expertise. Candidates who take stances that please the Lincoln Club have a decent shot at getting the Republican nomination; those who don't are likely to lose.

A little north of Orange County, we can find this new form of machine operating in Democratic circles, where people like Rep. Maxine Waters and Los Angeles County Supervisor Gloria Molina exert control over their party's nominations for local, state, and federal offices. They maintain ties to labor unions, wealthy donors, church groups, and other organizations that can help turn out the vote in a primary. Candidates appeal to them through their ideological commitments and personal loyalty; they can reward this loyalty with the guarantee of a steady political career through many levels of government.[23]

There have even been attempts to organize informal political machines at the national level. In the 1990s, U.S. House Majority Whip Tom DeLay and anti-tax activist Grover Norquist organized what became known as the K Street Project. They informed many D.C. lobbying firms that they should only hire Republican staff; in exchange, they would be offered access to high-ranking Republican officials in the White House and Congress. This was a modern version of a party machine, with ideology and access, rather than patronage, being the main assets traded.

This ideologically motivated party system might not sound particularly clientelistic, but it certainly can be. In many political communities, there are just a handful of people (patrons) who maintain control over access to office. Through their influence and their control over the resources needed to run for office, they get to determine who can compete for a party's nomination and who can't. And they are in a position to demand a price for their support and to deliver policy goods to clients who don't know the system as well as they do.

7

Formal Party Organizations

Every presidential nomination cycle unfolds with unique issues and peculiarities, many that are difficult to predict. The presidential primaries and caucuses of the 2020 election cycle certainly had their own unusual features, but some of the most notable were direct consequences of decisions made by the parties, especially the Democratic Party.

Early on, Democratic Party leaders were concerned about a potential problem: the enormous number of candidates interested in running for office. By some estimates, more than 30 or 40 known public figures had expressed interest in running for the Democratic presidential nomination that cycle. The Democratic National Committee, concerned that such a large number of candidates could lead to the nomination of an unqualified or unelectable candidate, sought to steer the winnowing of candidates by setting specific rules for participation in the primary debates of 2019 and early 2020. Past primary debates had usually been organized by media organizations, candidates, or local parties; now, the national party was setting specific thresholds for polling and fundraising for candidates to participate in party-approved debates, and those thresholds became even more stringent as the contest went on. Candidates who didn't have enough polling support or donors would be excluded from the

The 2020 Democratic presidential primary saw an enormous number of candidates, and the Democratic Party implemented restrictions on which candidates qualified for the many debates that were held.

debates and thus be deprived of media attention at a time when primary voters were seeking information about the candidates and making decisions about which ones they might support.

Naturally, the candidates who failed to meet those thresholds were upset with the system and objected to the party's heavy-handed steering of the nomination contest. Colorado senator Michael Bennet, who failed to meet the qualification for all but the first two debates, complained, "If we wanted to be the party that excluded people, we'd be Republicans."[1] Spiritual author Marianne Williamson complained, "Our establishment politics is run by elites within elites. DNC poll requirements are a perfect example, a situation with no transparency but with power to block candidates not anointed by a gatekeeper class."[2] According to *Politico*'s Bill Scher, Montana governor Steve Bullock's presidential campaign "was undercut by the DNC's awful debate rules."[3] New Jersey senator Cory Booker, who circulated a petition calling for the DNC to loosen its debate qualification rules, said, "Candidates who have proven both their viability and their commitment to the Democratic Party are being prematurely cut out of the nominating contest before many voters have even tuned in."[4]

This intervention into the 2020 presidential nomination cycle was a reminder of the kind of power that **formal parties**—those state and national organizations that are the official structures of America's party system—have in guiding the parties' most significant decisions. The roles of formal parties have fluctuated substantially over time in the United States, and they vary considerably depending on who the chair is, who comprises the rest of the organization, what rules govern their behavior and deliberations, and what the formal party's relationship with party-affiliated elected officials is. Sometimes formal party groups guide a party's direction; other times they seem to exist to serve the immediate needs of politicians. Today, formal parties are enjoying a period of considerable and growing influence.

In this chapter, we'll look at how formal parties are structured at the national, state, and local levels and how the way they are put together varies substantially from place to place. We'll begin with how these party structures developed over the eighteenth and nineteenth centuries, declined somewhat in significance in the twentieth century, and then later resurged. Then we'll discuss the activities formal party organizations engage in during campaigns, including fundraising, coordination, and recruitment. Because parties tend to lose about half the time, we'll focus on how organizations adapt to party losses and interpret those losses to pave the way to future victories. Finally, we'll examine the complex relationship these party groups have with presidents and other party leaders.

THE FORMATION OF PARTY ORGANIZATIONS

Where did America's formal party organizations come from? They weren't just invented by scheming politicians in George Washington's cabinet. Their history is surprisingly longer and more interesting. The further one goes back, the more difficult it is to distinguish between formal and informal parties. But understanding a bit about their formation helps us understand more about how they function today.

Colonial Organization

The formal national party organizations that we would vaguely recognize today as the Democratic and Republican national committees didn't emerge until the mid-nineteenth century, but their antecedents began well before that. American party organizations of one sort or another predate the formation of the United States. And they began with an informal structure—they had no stable headquarters, budgets, or known officers. Indeed, American parties have an unusual origin story: they began as anti-government conspiracies that sought to resist or undermine English rule during the colonial period. Their organizers were eager to not draw attention to themselves, as their activities were somewhere between unpopular and seditious. Even if they could have had more-formal institutional support like modern parties have, they probably would have avoided it.

As has been widely noted, the U.S. Constitution contains no reference to political parties. The Founders spoke of them critically—Madison warned about the "mischiefs of faction" in *Federalist* No. 10, and Washington rued "the baneful effects of the Spirit of Party" in his farewell address (see Appendix). Although many of the Founders would quickly be involved in creating parties after the Constitution's adoption, it seems that they had hoped to create a federal government without them.

It is curious that the Founders thought that a government without parties was possible. After all, it wasn't as though they hadn't seen a functioning democracy before. Britain, although still a monarchy, had a thriving parliamentary system rife with partisanship. What's more, the Founders knew from personal experience about the influence of parties in colonial legislatures prior to the American Revolution.

In many colonies, a locally elected legislature competed for control with a governor, who served at the pleasure of the king of Great Britain and represented his interests. These legislatures were typically under the control of something we might recognize today as an informal party organization (see Chapter 8), usually referred to as a **junto** (a rough appropriation of the Spanish word for "together"). New York's junto had, by the mid-1700s, managed to seize control of spending appropriations and could even withhold the salaries of colonial administrators as a tool for leverage. In 1751, New York's colonial governor George Clinton complained in a letter that "the Faction in this Province continue resolute in pursuing their scheme of assuming the whole executive powers into their hands, and that they are willing to risk the ruin of their country, in order to carry out their purposes."[5]

The New York junto consisted of people both inside and outside the legislature. A report by colonial governor Cadwallader Colden explained that it involved owners of large estates, lawyers, merchants, and small farmers. The lawyers, it seems, were particularly well organized, as they were familiar with the craft of lawmaking and had close ties to nearly all the most prominent families in the colony. Through such influence, the junto not only steered the function of the legislature and limited the authority of the governor, but also served as a kind of cabinet for legislative leaders.

North Carolina's junto functioned in a similar way, with leaders asserting control over the payment of administrators and thus ensuring compliance, and also setting such stringent qualifications for judicial appointments that only their closest allies could serve. As in New York, North Carolina's colonial governor complained to London about "the few mischievous, but too successful Demagogues who have hitherto governed the Assembly."[6]

We see another instructive example of junto-like activity in the Massachusetts Colony in 1766. The recent Stamp Act had produced an uproar and several riots in Boston, and the colonial governor demanded that the statehouse investigate to find out who was responsible for the destruction of property. The statehouse, under the control of the Boston junto of brewer/patriot Sam Adams, John Hancock, and others, appointed five investigators from outside Boston who knew nothing of the city, of committee work, or of the riots. Those investigators were completely out of their element and didn't have the ability to find, much less prosecute, the rebels. But the statehouse leaders gave the impression that they had done their job—it was just that the investigation came up with results that British leaders found useless. This sort of party activity helped to undermine British rule and to nurture the colonial rebellion. The relationship between colonial juntos and the colonial governors provided the framework for the party system that would develop in the next century.

Early-Nineteenth-Century Organization

The parties that formed following the adoption of the Constitution in 1789 largely stemmed from factional disputes within President George Washington's cabinet. Treasury secretary Alexander Hamilton and his allies tended to favor a stronger role for the federal government in the regulation of business and trade and the management of public money. His group would soon be known as the Federalists. Meanwhile, Representative James Madison and Secretary of State Thomas Jefferson would organize a group that resisted the growing power of the central government and sought to preserve a more agrarian vision of the nation that honored the rights of states. This group would generally be referred to as the Democratic-Republicans.

Those two early parties functioned largely as legislative coalitions in the Congress (see Chapter 2) and even played a role in recruiting and backing candidates for office. But the parties developed little in the way of national organization. This was not for want of ideas so much as interest. Alexander Hamilton actually had bigger plans for his Federalist Party. In 1802, he proposed creating a "Christian Constitutional Society," which would have looked something more like the type of national party organization we are familiar with today. The Society would have a president and a 12-member national council, and it would have subcouncils for each state and local branch below that. It would assess annual dues from members and use those funds to work for the election of "fit" men by campaigning for them in newspapers, pamphlets, and meetings. The Society would also organize philanthropic activities aimed at helping immigrants and workers in the cities. Hamilton's vision was at least half a century ahead of its time, though, and his Federalist colleagues ignored it.[7]

Had Hamilton had his way, the Federalists might well have established a national organization early in the nineteenth century and avoided or at least delayed their party's demise. As it was, what organization existed tended to be at the state and local level. Richmond, Virginia, had a junto, while the Albany Regency controlled the New York state capital, and Tammany Hall was already steering New York City elections by the early 1800s (see Chapter 6). But national party organizations wouldn't develop until the 1840s.

The first permanent national party organization belonged to the Democrats. To understand why and how it developed, it is helpful to understand the presidential election of 1824 (for more, see Chapter 2). This election marked the end of the "Era of Good Feelings"—that period in the 1810s and early 1820s when the Federalists had collapsed and little partisanship existed within Congress. Several high-profile national leaders ran in the 1824 election, including General Andrew Jackson, Senator Henry Clay, and John Quincy Adams, the son of the nation's second president. Jackson waged a highly populist campaign (see Chapter 2 for more on populism), seeking to win mass electoral support at a time when only some of the states chose their presidential electors through mass elections. Jackson actually won the popular vote that year, but no candidate had a majority of Electoral College votes, which sent the contest to the U.S. House of Representatives. There, a bargain was struck among members that installed John Quincy Adams as president.

Jackson and his associate Martin Van Buren responded to this loss by immediately working to build a campaign for 1828 based on the argument that the people's choice had been railroaded by a "corrupt bargain." They built their campaign atop that structure developed by Thomas Jefferson and the Democratic-Republicans a generation earlier, now calling the party the Democratic Party, and sought a broad national coalition of farmers opposed to wealthy elites and banks. This relatively new form of campaigning proved successful in 1828, installing Jackson for two terms as president and Van Buren as his vice president. This marked the end of the "King Caucus" period in which Congress functionally chose presidents; this power now transitioned to a vast and growing electorate. The new party group—the Democrats—held the first national party convention in 1832, where they overwhelmingly chose to send Jackson back to the White House. The convention established a rule by which two-thirds of delegates were necessary to nominate a presidential candidate; this rule would endure for roughly a century.

During his presidency, without the close congressional alliances that many of his predecessors had enjoyed, Jackson relied heavily on his "Kitchen Cabinet," a rotating group of informal advisors. These advisors would soon form the core of a new national Democratic organization. He also developed a great many new federal jobs that he could staff with employees personally loyal to him. Known as patronage or the "spoils system" (see Chapter 6), this form of partisan hiring would be a signature feature of American parties for the next century and would provide much of their labor force.[8]

In 1844, with the Democrats now out of power and Whig John Tyler in the White House, the Democrats formed a central committee with the hope of guiding the party as an opposition group. The first Democratic National Committee (DNC) followed in 1848, becoming a permanent organization in 1852.

The DNC at that point contained representatives from all the state Democratic organizations. It was not yet the strong centralized organization we think of today. Rather, the DNC of the mid-nineteenth century allowed the exchange of information and ideas among the much stronger state groups. Rather than dictate how national campaigns would be run, the DNC deferred to state organizations on the best way to sell a candidacy to their residents. They generally believed that local politicians knew best how to appeal to partisan actors in their districts.[9] This was a model largely mirrored by the Republicans when they organized as a national antislavery party in 1854. Even though Republicans had a common national message, they were still a parochial party. In the words of historian Robert Wiebe, the parties of that era "lacked a central nervous system."[10]

The Transition to Stronger Twentieth-Century Party Organizations

The late nineteenth century saw important rhetorical and organizational shifts in the style of the national party organizations. If there is any clear event marking this shift, it is President Grover Cleveland's 1887 campaign against a tariff on imported goods, a move that he saw as demanding national party leadership. "If this involves the surrender or postponement of private interests and the abandonment of local advantages," Cleveland explained, "compensation will be found in the assurance that thus the common interest is subserved and the general welfare advanced."[11] In other words, locally elected politicians might have interests at odds with the party—a pattern we've mentioned several times already—but the president, in an effort to bring local politicians in line with his agenda, was promising to reward their loyalty in backing him against the tariff.

A decade later, Republican political organizer Marcus Hanna helped orient his party on a more national scale when he helped run William McKinley's successful 1896 presidential campaign. The Republican National Committee took control of the party's state-level infrastructure in service of McKinley's election.[12] With Hanna in charge, the national committee efforts constituted the "first major public relations campaign in modern American politics."[13] Hanna himself referred to the effort as a "campaign of instruction" or a "campaign of education." Through his leadership, the party generated and distributed McKinley campaign materials directly to voters, bypassing the state and local party organizations.

While Cleveland's expansion of the national party was in the service of policy making, Hanna's strategy concerned elections. As we have noted, these two goals go hand in hand, and the party organization was starting to build connections across different campaigns, on behalf of the party.

The party organizations of the twentieth century would look and behave very differently from those of the earlier era. Between 1828 and 1884, for example, only four sitting presidents were renominated by their party. Between 1888 and 1944, however, sitting presidents were renominated 11 times.[14] As this suggests, the president and those immediately around him had become much more critical to the organization and messaging of the national parties. By the dawn of the twentieth century, the centrality of the president to these parties would herald the parties' true national orientation.

Decline and Resurgence of the Modern Party Organization

As we saw in Chapter 6, urban party machines dominated many American cities in the nineteenth and early twentieth centuries. Their power to recruit candidates, control election outcomes, extract benefits from government to line their pockets, and pay off their own supporters was legendary. But the reaction to them, when it came, was swift and severe. The progressive reforms of the early twentieth century were designed, in large part, to drive these party organizations from power. Wisconsin progressive reformer Robert La Follette, who would later serve as governor and senator, highlighted the case against party machines in a famous 1897 address:

> This is the modern political machine. It is impersonal, irresponsible, extra-legal. The courts offer no redress for rights it violates, the wrongs it inflicts. It is without conscience and without remorse. It has come to be enthroned in American politics. It rules caucuses, names delegates, appoints committees, dominates the councils of the party, dictates nominations, makes platforms, dispenses patronage, directs state administrations, controls legislatures, stifles opposition, punishes independence, and elects United States senators. In the states where it is supreme, the edict of the machine is the only sound heard, and outside is easily mistaken for the voice of the people.[15]

Reformers achieved control of many state governments in the early 1900s and pushed through several pieces of legislation designed to drive party machines out of American politics. Among these reforms were such things as

- The Australian (or secret) ballot, which meant that party leaders couldn't know which voters were supporting their candidates.
- The direct primary, which took party nominations out of the hands of bosses and convention delegates and gave them to voters, who were theoretically more independent and harder to control.
- Nonpartisan local government, which meant that party bosses could not as easily control city and county governments.
- Establishment of a nonpartisan commissioner and manager-commissioner city government, which was a substantial change from strong partisan mayors who could hold sway over a city council.

A series of mid-twentieth-century changes in the law and court rulings served to undermine the patronage system, by which party leaders could reward supporters with jobs (see Chapter 6). Most government employees are now protected by civil service laws and can't be fired for their political allegiances.

Formal party organizations at the local and state level, which were no longer able to use patronage jobs to compensate their loyal workers, saw the mid-twentieth century as a low point in their history. Many political observers at the time saw the formal parties as dying out. Perhaps they had served their purpose and just weren't needed anymore. After all, one important thing parties did was help candidates become better known; thanks to television, candidates could now do this by themselves. This decreased party activity came at a time when voter partisanship was low as well. Columnist David Broder famously suggested "The Party's Over" in 1972. Maybe the parties would simply wither away.

They didn't. By the late 1970s, the state parties had begun staffing up again. Over the next few decades, they became more institutionalized: hiring specialized staff; establishing permanent headquarters; and becoming more reliable and professional organizations that could recruit, train, and support candidates.[16] This mirrored growth in the national party organizations' capacities, as well. This growth continues today, even at the local level. In 1996, only about a third of county party organizations even had a phone number associated with them; by 2008, half had their own website.[17] Indeed, local parties are far more likely today than they were just a few years ago to have complete sets of officers, written bylaws, formal budgets, and year-round offices. Formal parties are growing and becoming more institutionalized at all levels.[18]

It's difficult to come up with a reliable measure of the strength of formal parties. In Chapter 6, we mentioned political scientist David Mayhew's effort to categorize party organizations in all 50 states. This helped indicate the things we associate with party machines, or Traditional Party Organizations (TPOs).

However, many of the most polarized party systems in the country exist in states with some of the weakest TPOs. California, Wisconsin, and Colorado have little history with traditional party machines but have some of the most polarized state legislatures in the country today—far more polarized than the U.S. Congress. When we think about what a "strong" party looks like, we need to be cognizant of several factors, including organizational style and party discipline.

PARTY STRUCTURE

Today's formal parties have developed highly professionalized and specialized organizations. The central committees (the DNC and RNC) consist of representatives from each state who make formal decisions about the direction of the party and the rules and structures for the national party conventions. In this way, both parties mirror the structure of the United States government, in which each state is represented in the government in Washington.

Basic Structures

The two parties comprise their committees differently. The DNC contains hundreds of members, including the chair and vice chair of each state Democratic Committee and over 200 others elected by conventions in the 50 states and territories. More populous states get to send more committee members to the DNC. By contrast, the RNC consists of one chair, committeeman, and committeewoman from each of the states and territories. In other words, the DNC is more like the House of Representatives, giving more representation to larger and thus more urban and liberal states, while the RNC is more like the Senate, with disproportionate representation from rural and conservative states.

Electoral Committees

Each national party also maintains committees organized around congressional elections. The Democratic Congressional Campaign Committee (DCCC) and the National Republican Congressional Committee (NRCC) are devoted to elections to the U.S. House of Representatives, while the Democratic Senatorial Campaign Committee (DSCC) and the National Republican Senatorial Committee (NRSC) focus on Senate elections. These "Hill committees" consist of incumbent members of those parties. Incumbents are expected to contribute substantial sums to their relevant committee. Each House Democrat in 2008 was expected to give $125,000 to the DCCC and then pledge to raise even more during the next term. These figures were even higher for committee chairs and chamber leaders.[19] This adds to the fundraising burdens of members of Congress, who are already spending a substantial portion of their free time raising money for their own reelections. The Hill committees generally allocate these funds to other incumbents facing challenging reelection campaigns.

There are varying opinions on what roles Hill committees should play. Few object to their activities in general elections, but they can create a great deal of controversy when they get involved in internal party decisions and have a mixed track record in this area. In early 2016, the DSCC intervened in a Pennsylvania primary to back Katie McGinty over former Rep. Joe Sestak in a hotly contested Senate race. Although the Hill committees tend to try to avoid getting involved locally, this race was seen as sufficiently important to warrant intervention. The general election was predicted to be close, as incumbent Republican senator Pat Toomey was considered unpopular and McGinty was viewed as not only a stronger candidate than Sestak but also a more reliable Democrat on many key issues.[20] With the DSCC's financial assistance, McGinty prevailed in the close primary election. Several liberal groups expressed anger at this intervention, given Sestak's strong electoral history and McGinty's relative inexperience. McGinty went on to lose the general election by less than two percentage points.

Early in the 2018 congressional election cycle, the DCCC made clear that it was supporting Jason Crow, a former army ranger, to run as the Democratic nominee against Republican incumbent Rep. Mike Coffman in Colorado's Sixth Congressional District outside Denver. Levi Tillemann, a former Obama administration staffer, objected to the DCCC's presence in the race and sought the Democratic nomination as a progressive challenger. The DCCC pushed back. Steny Hoyer, then the House minority whip and one of the most prominent national Democratic officeholders, spoke directly to Tillemann and encouraged him to drop out of the race, telling him that the party had already settled on Crow. Tillemann recorded the conversation and then released it to stoke outrage against the formal party.[21] Tillemann stayed in the race but still lost in the primary to Crow by over 30 points. Crow went on to defeat the Republican incumbent that fall.

In 2010, the NRSC intervened in a Florida primary on behalf of Republican governor Charlie Crist, who was running for U.S. Senate.[22] The Republican incumbent had decided to resign, and Republicans wanted to hold control of the seat in this competitive state, so support for the moderate Crist seemed a safe move. However, statehouse Speaker Marco Rubio also wanted the Republican nomination for this Senate seat. Crist's support for President Obama's stimulus plan in 2009 undermined his support among conservatives and Tea Party activists, who rallied to Rubio's campaign instead. His support flagging, Crist withdrew from competing for the Republican nomination and

While national party organizations are usually the best known, party organizing often takes place at the hyperlocal or state level. In Anderson County, Texas, where Republicans hold the majority of seats in local government, a Democratic Party organization advocates for local Democratic candidates.

decided to seek the Senate seat as an independent. The NRSC then withdrew its endorsement of him and demanded he refund their financial support. Rubio went on to beat Crist and Democrat Kendrick Meek by a substantial margin in the general election.

Similar committees exist for the national parties to assist their colleagues in state politics. The Democratic Governors Association (DGA) and the Republican Governors Association (RGA) help raise money and recruit candidates for gubernatorial elections and also serve as policy-generating platforms for state politics. The Democratic and Republican Legislative Campaign Committees (DLCC and RLCC) similarly exist to help channel money and ideas for state legislative campaigns.

State party committees vary significantly in their structure and composition. Most state parties have some sort of state central committee, as well as congressional district committees, county committees, and ward or precinct organizations. This can create a great many overlapping and even conflicting jurisdictions and loyalties. For example, California's Democratic State Central Committee consists of state and congressional elected officials, delegates selected at Assembly district committee meetings, Democratic club members,

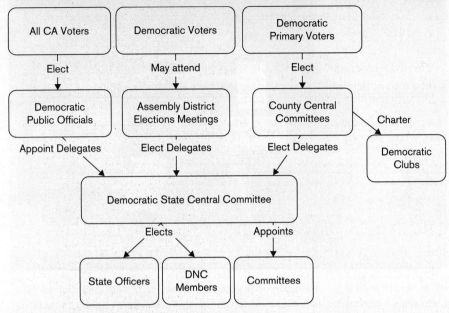

FIGURE 7.1 California State Democratic Party Organizational Chart

Source: California Democratic Party, www.ardems.org/tag/cadems/ (accessed 6/2/2020).

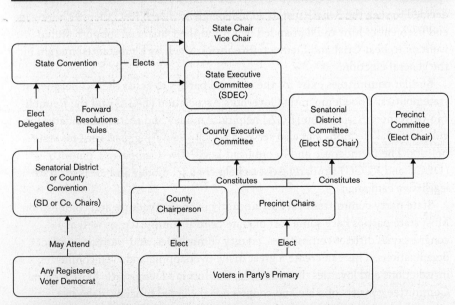

FIGURE 7.2 Texas State Democratic Party Organizational Chart

Source: Collin County Democratic Party, www.collindemocrats.org/texas-democratic-state-and-county
-structure/ (accessed 4/2/2020).

county committee members, and party staffers (Figure 7.1). These people don't often see eye to eye. Club members, for example, are usually very ideologically committed and want to push their party to the left, while officeholders may be worried about reelection and want their party to maintain more of a centrist image.

Texas' Democratic Party (Figure 7.2) is organized somewhat differently from California's. There's no reference to clubs or other outside organizations. But it does contain similar sorts of tensions, with primary voters selecting county chairs and precinct chairs, while all registered Democrats pick state convention delegates.

POLITICAL SCIENCE TOOLKIT
Analyzing the Relationship between Campaign Spending Limits and Partisanship

States impose vastly divergent rules on how party organizations can both raise and spend money, and these rules may have an important effect on partisanship. As the table below shows, in 22 states parties may contribute below unlimited amounts of money to their nominees. In many other states, there are very low ceilings placed on party support for candidates. Montana's political parties may contribute no more than $1,400 to a state senate candidate and no more than $850 to a state house candidate. In Maine, the cap is $375 for both chambers. Most states have somewhat higher limits. National party organizations can donate up to $5,000 to a congressional candidate in a given year.

Annual Limit on State Party Donations to Lower Chamber (House or Assembly) Candidates, 2019–2020				
Less than $1,000	$1,000–$4,999	$5,000–$9,999	$10,000–$100,000	Unlimited
ME, MT	AR, DE, GA, HI, ID, MA, MO, NH, WV	AZ, CT, MD, NM, NV, SC	AK, CO, FL, IL, MI, MN, OH, OK, RI, TN, WA, WI	AL, CA, IN, IA, KS, KY, LA, MD, MS, NE, NJ, NY, NC, ND, OR, PA, SD, TX, UT, VT, VA, WY

Note: Nebraska has nonpartisan legislative elections.

Source: www.ncsl.org/Portals/1/Documents/Elections/Contribution-Limits-to-Candidates-2019-2020.pdf.

Fundraising and Spending

Raising and spending money is a critical part of a party's job profile. As we have noted elsewhere, spending is not necessarily determinative of election outcomes. It's not uncommon for the candidate who spent less to win—in 2016, Hillary Clinton outspent Donald Trump by a margin of nearly two to one, but Trump won. And even when the candidate who spends more wins, it's not necessarily the case that the spending made the difference. That said, money is clearly important in politics. Candidates do need to get their name in front of voters, to run advertisements, to travel to different areas to meet people, and to hire competent staff. All that requires a lot of money.

The formal parties generally spend little or nothing on candidates in nomination contests—they usually prefer to remain professionally neutral. But they do spend a great deal in general elections. The Republican and Democratic national committees, including the congressional committees, spent a combined $3.4 billion on federal campaigns in 2020, including congressional and presidential races. However, as Figure 7.3 shows, this was only about a quarter of all the spending on federal races that year. The campaigns themselves, along with political action committees and other groups, spent nearly $14 billion. Interestingly, formal party spending on campaigns has been pretty flat since 2000, although it's declining as a percentage of overall spending, which has been rising substantially.

Professionalized Staff

The party typically has employees and contractors who have expertise in training new campaign staff, advising candidates, writing speeches, and managing campaigns from day to day. Just what sorts of people end up staffing or running party organizations? To help illustrate, we offer a few profiles of party officers who served at different levels of government in recent years.

Reince Priebus was the chair of the Republican National Committee from 2011 to 2017. Priebus grew up in Wisconsin. He majored in political science at the University of Wisconsin–Whitewater, and was president of the College Republicans there. He later worked as a lawyer and ran, unsuccessfully, for the Wisconsin senate. But he was elected chair of the Wisconsin Republican Party in 2007 and led it during the strong Republican election year of 2010, which resulted in the election of Governor Scott Walker and Republicans seizing control of the state legislature. He chaired the RNC during its 2012 presidential loss and led it in some frank introspection afterward. He presided during the party's successful 2014 cycle and its surprising presidential win in 2016. Priebus left the RNC in 2017 to become President Donald Trump's first chief of staff.

FIGURE 7.3 Spending in Federal Elections

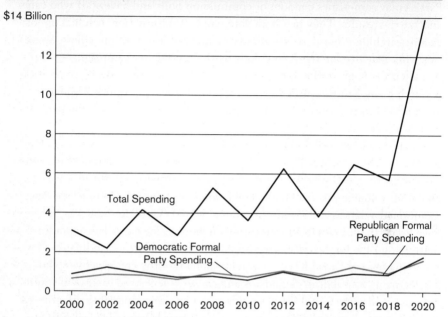

Source: Center for Responsive Politics, "Political Parties" and "Cost of Elections," www.opensecrets.org /elections-overview/cost-of-election (accessed 12/15/20).

Rick Palacio was the chair of the Colorado Democratic Party from 2011 to 2017. He grew up in Pueblo, Colorado, and graduated from Regis University in Denver. He has worked much of his adult life in politics, staffing for the state-house majority leader and then for the state party during the 2006 election cycle. He then served as a legislative aide to U.S. Rep. John Salazar and House Majority Leader Steny Hoyer. He is openly gay and is the first Latino to chair the Colorado Democratic Party.

Carol Donovan became chair of the Democratic Party of Dallas County, Texas, in 2015. Donovan was the first female student body president at the University of Texas at Austin. She has worked with the party for three decades as an attorney, fundraiser, and campaign consultant, and she ran once, unsuccessfully, for state house. She was a staffer for U.S. Rep. Jake Pickle.

These are just a few examples of the sorts of people that work for and run formal parties at the national, state, and local levels. They have some commonalities—all spent their professional lives in politics—but took different paths to get where they are. Formal party organizations vary widely in their size and capabilities. Many county-level parties have no paid staff at all, and only 20 percent even have a permanent office, although this number is increasing.[25]

Research and Analysis

Parties may sometimes conduct or commission polls and have staff who can analyze the results. They maintain voter contact information, conduct opposition research on other parties' candidates, and publish position papers. Some of this work may overlap that being done by the candidates' campaigns—a campaign with enough staff and funding can usually assemble a strong opposition research team. But the voter contact lists require years of research and a substantial infrastructure to update and maintain. In this regard, the party is indispensable.

Today, both national party organizations maintain their own voter contact databases, which include basic demographic information on voters, their voter turnout history, estimates of the likelihood of their voting in future contests, and other valuable pieces of data. The Democrats, since the last decade, have maintained a database through the company NGP VAN. Republicans, however, have found themselves in an interesting quandary. The party has maintained a master voter file for years, making it available to Republican candidates. However, Charles and David Koch—two extremely wealthy conservatives who funded many Republican candidates and causes—generated their own voter database, and some Republican candidates find it easier and more effective to use.[26] Yet as private individuals, the Koch brothers (David died in 2019) are under no obligation to make their data available to all Republican candidates; they can pick and choose those they wish to help based on the candidates' ideological stances. This has led to legal struggles between these private individuals and the formal party and some soul searching about who really controls the Republican Party.

Communications

Parties conduct their own advertising campaigns and reach out to voters through an extensive network of field offices. Here, the parties are rather different from each other. At least since the 2008 Barack Obama campaign, the Democratic presidential candidate has largely run his or her own field operation. National and state parties support these efforts, but the candidate campaign itself has mainly been in charge. Constructing a field organization is expensive, so congressional and state-level campaigns usually rely upon existing party infrastructure or presidential field offices to aid them in their quest for election. But some well-funded sub-presidential Democratic campaigns, including Senator Michael Bennet's 2010 senatorial campaign in Colorado and Rep. Jim Himes's 2008 campaign in Connecticut, have developed their own ground-game efforts.[27]

On the Republican side, however, the national and state parties have largely taken on the role of running and staffing field offices. "The Romney campaign doesn't do the ground game," explained RNC political director Rick Wiley in 2012. "They have essentially ceded that responsibility to the RNC. They understand this is our role."[28] The Trump team largely followed this model in 2016. However, the Trump team also benefited from substantial turnout efforts conducted by aligned organizations such as evangelical Christian groups and police fraternal orders.[29] Such efforts may have given the Trump team a key edge in upper midwestern states that year.

Why the differences between the two parties' communication strategies? Part of this comes from different beliefs about the value and purpose of field offices. Republican efforts have largely focused on conversion of voters, making sure that conservative-leaning voters stay with the party's nominee even if torn on some key issues. Democrats have focused a great deal on voter turnout and registration. They'll often place many offices in strongly Democratic areas not necessarily to convince voters that their candidate is better than the Republican, but to make sure that more liberal voters register as Democrats and show up to vote on Election Day. The situation largely reversed during 2020. In response to the COVID-19 pandemic, the Biden campaign pretty much abandoned traditional Democratic ground game efforts, concerned that it was unsafe and possibly intimidating to send volunteers to people's doors. The Trump team, however, expanded its ground game. While there are usually far more Democratic field offices than Republican ones, Trump had 300 such offices in 2020 while Biden had none.[30] The difference in 2020 may be explained, in part, by different partisan attitudes toward the virus, with Democrats generally perceiving it as more of a threat. It's hard to know how much difference this made in the end—field offices usually only make a small impact—but it helped produce an unusually high turnout election.

Why Join the Party?

As the previous examples suggest, there's quite a bit that a party can do for a candidate. But more generally, there's a persuasive logic for anyone seeking office to affiliate with a party. The major parties maintain duopoly control over the American electoral system. As of 2016 (apart from nonpartisan Nebraska), Republicans or Democrats held 99 percent of state legislative seats in the United States. The same was true for 98 of 100 U.S. Senate seats and all 435 U.S. House seats. Every president elected since 1852 has been either a Democrat or a Republican. Yes, on very rare occasions, third-party or independent candidates will get elected—former Minnesota governor Jesse Ventura remains an inspirational example for many third-party advocates—but the odds are long against such successes. If you want to obtain office, by far the most reliable strategy is to go through one of the two major parties to do it. Even Donald Trump, who was far from a perfect fit ideologically with the Republican Party, chose to work through that party's nomination system in order to obtain office.

Being part of the party conveys a great many advantages for a candidate. Candidates receive an automatic base of supporters by winning a party's nomination. (Trump, despite his disagreements with many longstanding party stances and his unorthodox and sometimes offensive campaign behavior, got the support of 90 percent of Republican identifiers in 2016.) A party will help increase awareness of a candidate, raise money for them, secure ballot access for them, and coordinate a campaign for them across 50 different states with very different election rules and procedures. Even a very wealthy and famous person would have great difficulty running without the technical expertise made available by a political party.

DEFEAT AND RESPONSE

The formal party organizations are notoriously self-improving. Particularly at the national level, the parties often make adjustments in their membership, leadership, and practices to make their party more representative of its voters and more competitive in elections. This is especially true of parties that have just lost a presidential election. After a defeat, party organizational leaders have a somewhat freer hand to make changes to their party. As former DNC chair Robert Strauss said, "When the party's out of office, you're the head; when a Democrat is president, you're a goddamned clerk."[31]

This, of course, doesn't mean that the formal party organization can "fix" their party so that it wins in the next election. For one thing, as we'll discuss further in Chapter 12, aspects of the political environment like the economy and the candidates' own advertising and spending patterns will have a far greater effect than anything the formal party does. Also, as we've argued throughout this book, the formal organizations are only one of many moving parts within a modern American political party, but they are important parts and can influence others, particularly in matters concerning the selection of nominees. In this section, we review several attempts by formal parties to adjust from a recent loss to make their party more competitive.

The Post-1968 Reforms: Making the Party More Representative

Many modern presidential nomination practices flow from the reforms enacted by the Democratic Party following its loss in the 1968 presidential election. We'll go over this in more detail in Chapter 9. But understanding how the formal party changed its shape at that point is valuable for understanding formal party organizations.

Nineteen sixty-eight was a divisive year in the United States and a difficult moment for the Democratic Party. Its national convention in Chicago that summer is one of the most memorable party conventions in history because of the ugliness surrounding it. Anti–Vietnam War activists were protesting outside the convention hall, and Chicago police, under the direction of Mayor Richard Daley, were filmed by news crews savagely beating the protesters and arresting them. When news of the violence filtered onto the convention floor, many delegates rose to criticize Daley, who was hosting the convention. Senator Abe Ribicoff of Connecticut, during his remarks, singled out Daley for his use of "gestapo tactics" and moved for the convention to be suspended and reconvened in another city.

The convention ultimately ended with the nomination of Vice President Hubert Humphrey for president. This met with great dissatisfaction by the antiwar wing of the party, as Humphrey had largely supported U.S. actions in Vietnam. Further angering antiwar activists, Humphrey had entered no primary contests at all, while delegates pledged to antiwar candidates like Eugene McCarthy and the recently slain Robert Kennedy were essentially ignored. Fronting a demoralized party, Humphrey went on to lose to Republican Richard Nixon.

The DNC convened a commission to address several of the issues associated with 1968. Chaired by South Dakota senator George McGovern and Rep. Fred Harris, the Commission on Party Structure and Delegate Selection sought to address one of the difficult lingering legacies of 1968: many key activist groups had felt excluded. Antiwar activists, women, African Americans, and other strong Democratic supporters were not well represented among national convention delegates.

The Commission's recommendations focused on changing delegate selection procedures. It established quotas for gender, racial, and ethnic groups among the state delegates and eliminated many restrictions on prospective delegates. The Commission also called for an end to the **unit rule**, by which state delegations could be bound to vote as a single uniform group. These recommendations were adopted by the party as rules for their 1972 national convention.

The new rules radically changed the process of winning the Democratic nomination, the face of Democratic Party delegates, and the sorts of candidates they preferred. Within a few years, the party became worried that it had opened up the nomination system too much. George McGovern, its presidential nominee in 1972 (and conveniently one of the architects of the reforms), had few ties to the formal party structure. He ran a poor, error-ridden campaign, was painted as an extremist by incumbent president Nixon, and went on to suffer one of the largest electoral defeats in history.

The Hunt Commission: The Party Strikes Back

In 1980, Democrats suffered a rare occurrence: the defeat of an incumbent president. Jimmy Carter had been nominated in 1976 after running the same sort of outsider campaign McGovern had run four years earlier. Carter's presidency was generally considered an unsuccessful one for Democrats—they had few policy achievements to point to, and several economic and international crises had steadily undermined his popularity. Perhaps if the party could reassert some control over the nomination system, they could get better presidential candidates who could work well with Congress.

In 1982, Democrats convened a Commission on Presidential Nominations, chaired by Governor James Hunt of North Carolina, with an aim toward reforming the nomination system. Following the commission's recommendations, the party established "superdelegates" for the 1984 convention. **Superdelegates**, or "unpledged party leaders and elected officials" (PLEOs), consist of governors, senators, House members, elected party committee members, and other distinguished party leaders. Superdelegates are granted votes as delegates in the convention but, unlike those delegates selected through primaries and caucuses, they are not formally pledged to any candidate.[32] They would comprise about 14 percent of the floor votes in the 1984 convention. This would give party elites an edge in nomination contests. The delegates selected through primaries and caucuses would always have more votes, but in theory, insiders would have some ability to prevent the nomination of someone popular with activists but whom insiders saw as unelectable or otherwise a poor choice. Indeed, the superdelegates proved helpful in 1984, giving former vice-president Walter Mondale an edge over "insurgent" candidates Gary Hart and Jesse Jackson.

In the years since, superdelegates have not proven to be a very formidable barrier to nomination. When Hillary Clinton ran for president in 2008, she had the backing of a considerable number of superdelegates. However, when Barack Obama began winning the bulk of pledged delegates in primaries and caucuses, many superdelegates switched their support to him. After all, many of these superdelegates are elected officials, and they're not eager to anger their most engaged supporters by voting against their wishes on such a high profile nomination. It's possible they would have continued to stand by Clinton if she had been running against a candidate seen as more threatening to longstanding party goals or who might run a weaker general election campaign.

Superdelegates were a source of a great deal of contention within the Democratic Party during the 2016 presidential nomination, as most were strong supporters of Hillary Clinton but were portrayed as a symbol of internal party corruption by some of Bernie Sanders' supporters. In 2018, the Democratic National Committee voted to reduce superdelegates' powers by prohibiting them from participating in the first floor vote in presidential nominating conventions. They would only have a direct say in picking a nominee if the presidential nomination vote went to multiple ballots. This didn't happen in 2020, as Joe Biden accrued a majority of pledged delegates months before the convention began. Indeed, there hasn't been a multi-ballot convention since the 1950s. But superdelegates still have the potential to be influential under a pretty narrow set of circumstances.

The GOP Growth and Opportunity Project: Trying to Manage the Chaos

For the Republican Party the 2012 election results were mixed. Their presidential nominee, former Massachusetts governor Mitt Romney, had fallen a few points short of defeating incumbent president Barack Obama, and their party didn't win control of the U.S. Senate as they had hoped. Nonetheless, they still maintained a strong position of control over the House and most state legislatures. The party had some considerable strengths but kept coming up short in presidential elections, having lost the popular vote in every presidential election since 1992 (except one: 2004). Party leaders were worried that the composition of their party—in particular, a Whiter, older, and more conservative set of voters—was preventing them from forming a winning coalition in an increasingly diverse country.

Republican National Committee Chair Reince Priebus called for the creation of the Growth and Opportunity Project, which became known as the "postmortem" analysis of the party after its 2012 losses. The report produced by this commission was blunt and self-critical:

> Public perception of the Party is at record lows. Young voters are increasingly rolling their eyes at what the Party represents, and many minorities wrongly think that Republicans do not like them or want them in the country. When someone rolls their eyes at us, they are not likely to open their ears to us.[33]

After the 2012 elections, in which the Republicans lost the presidency and were unable to win back the Senate, the chair of the party, Reince Priebus (right), commissioned a "postmortem" that reflected on the party's losses and proposed modes of change.

Part of what the commission proposed was a change in messaging and a greater attempt to reach out to new voters:

> The Republican Party needs to stop talking to itself. We have become expert in how to provide ideological reinforcement to like-minded people, but devastatingly we have lost the ability to be persuasive with, or welcoming to, those who do not agree with us on every issue.[34]

The commission's report further advised the party to be more welcoming to a more diverse set of voters. It encouraged a serious commitment to immigration reform, and it called for a program to reach out to communities of color at the local level to enhance the racial diversity of the party.

It also called for several changes to the nomination system. In particular, commission members felt that the presidential debate system had become too chaotic, particularly as the number of candidates seeking the presidential nomination had grown. Recent cycles had featured an unwieldy number of debates—twenty-one in 2008 and twenty in 2012, respectively, whereas there'd been only thirteen in 2000 and never more than seven prior to that. What's more, the schedule for these debates was arranged haphazardly, usually as a result of decisions by the hosting media organizations, and occasionally in conjunction with state parties. Just prior to the 2012 New Hampshire primary, for example, ABC News hosted a candidate debate on the night of Saturday, January 7, in Goffstown, and NBC News hosted one the very next morning in Concord. The dates, times, and locations of such debates might be announced with as little as 48 hours' notice.

Beyond the issues raised in the report, party leaders perceived an additional problem with the 2012 debate cycle, in that moderators were seen as having an agenda substantially different from those of candidates and viewers. They perceived moderators as appealing to a national audience and sometimes trying to embarrass candidates for their conservative stances, even though the purpose of the event was seen as providing Republican primary voters with information needed to cast a party vote.[35]

Taken together, the issues with the 2012 debates were generally perceived as creating several problems. First, they aided former House Speaker Newt Gingrich, whom Republican leaders saw as a poor general election candidate who would not represent the party well and whose candidacy was already functionally dead. Second, they undermined and needlessly tarnished eventual nominee Mitt Romney, with whom party elites were generally comfortable. Third, to the extent insiders were not comfortable with Romney, they were looking for candidates like Tim Pawlenty or Rick Perry, accomplished governors with solid conservative credentials. The debates essentially destroyed those candidates' chances based on just a handful of incidents. A better primary debate system, according to the report and other critics, would be one that allows candidates to get their messages to primary voters but doesn't necessarily undermine strong candidates in favor of demagogues.

In the wake of the Growth and Opportunity Project, the RNC asserted some control over primary debates in three specific ways:

1. It limited the number of party-sanctioned debates and required ample intervals between them.
2. It prescribed the geographic locations of those debates.
3. It insisted on conservative panelists joining other network moderators.

Those new controls were evident in the 2016 cycle, which saw only 12 Republican debates, most of which had conservative voices like political commentator Hugh Hewitt on the panel of questioners. Somewhat surprisingly, though, those debates only ended up boosting the candidacy of Donald Trump, who was hardly the preferred candidate of party insiders. Trump's presidential victory in November 2016 will likely tamp further calls for nomination reform for a while within the RNC, but eventually the party will likely seek further changes. As we saw at the beginning of this chapter, Democrats responded to their loss in 2016 by tinkering with their primary debates, tightly prescribing qualification rules for each debate in 2019 and 2020 in order to winnow the large field of candidates.

Though every party responds to defeat, there is no one standard response. At least in the second half of the twentieth century, Republicans tended to adjust to losses through organizational changes. These are primarily improvements in efficiency, upgrades in technology, new approaches to data analysis, and fundraising. Democrats, meanwhile, have tended to adapt to losses through procedural reforms, often making adjustments in ways their party seats delegates, nominates candidates, and conducts conventions.[36] The examples discussed are consistent with this idea, although the Republicans' post-2012 reforms contain aspects of both organizational and procedural changes.

One thing party organizations tend not to do after a loss is to make major policy changes. That is, they generally don't betray core beliefs in an effort to achieve victory in the next cycle. It's not clear they could even do this if they wanted to. Parties' ideological positions are determined by a sophisticated inter-play of the various individuals and groups who support it. A determination by the DNC that they need to, for example, soften their support for abortion rights or abandon environmental protection as a goal simply wouldn't be accepted by the broader party and could well result in those DNC leaders losing power. For-mal party leaders must generally accept that they cannot determine who is in the party or what it stands for, but they still have some leeway in governing the party.

WHOM DO THE FORMAL PARTY ORGANIZATIONS SERVE?

One of the themes of this book is that parties exist to solve problems. That is, political actors will use them to achieve their political goals, even though some-times parties may end up controlling those same political actors. In this section, we look at how political actors have structured formal party organizations to serve their own ends. In many cases, those individuals have been politicians, especially presidents. But other political actors outside the government have their own agendas for parties. In addition, party organizations have developed their own agendas over time, and their needs sometimes conflict with those of officeholders.

Presidents as Party Builders

Presidents don't always have the best reputations within their formal party organizations. Formal party leaders invest a great deal in their presidential nominees and are happy to align themselves with a successful and popular president, but that relationship is not always reciprocal. Presidents are sometimes perceived as using the formal party to help get them elected but then viewed as effectively distancing themselves from or even dismissing the party once they're in power.

Political scientist Daniel Galvin has noted an interesting divergence across the parties in this regard: Republican presidents tend to build up their party, while Democrats tend to let theirs atrophy.[37] Dwight Eisenhower, for example, took office at a time when the Republican Party was facing a challenging internal struggle between moderates like him and the party's increasingly conservative and southern members. Eisenhower worked to build up his party's capacities and outreach, and to staff any new party committees with people who adhered to his worldview and his vision of an ideologically broad party coalition. He created new party initiatives to recruit and train candidates, mobilize voters, and enhance fundraising abilities. As president, Richard Nixon expanded on these efforts, furthering efforts to register voters in the South, to identify and appeal to them through various databases, and to raise money for the party. Presidents Ford, Reagan, and G. H. W. Bush operated along similar lines during their administrations.

The story has been different for the Democrats, though. John Kennedy initiated some party-building activities, but also poached several party functions to serve his own (unused) reelection campaign. Subsequent Democratic presidents (Johnson, Carter, and Clinton) similarly undermined Democratic Party initiatives and concentrated mostly on their own reelection campaigns. Galvin considers Democratic postwar presidents to be "party predators," although Clinton did make some party-building efforts in his second term.

Why the difference between parties? The most likely story is that the parties' electoral situations were very different. During much of the second half of the twentieth century, Democrats held a majority in the U.S. House and often controlled the Senate, along with most state legislatures. Democrats had the luxury of not worrying about building their party; it was large enough to maintain control. Republicans were trying to grow from an unpopular minority party in the wake of the New Deal into one that could compete for control of government. Indeed, once Republicans took control of the Congress in the mid-1990s, Clinton started devoting more effort to party building.

Barack Obama's legacy of party building was somewhat mixed. He did make some effort, campaigning heavily for Democrats in congressional races in

2016 and creating the Organizing for Action (OFA) outreach group—an outgrowth of his 2008 presidential campaign—within the DNC.[38] But many party needs still went unmet, and the party failed to recruit candidates for several districts in 2016. Trump's legacy for his party appears mixed. He was a successful fundraiser for Republican organizations and candidates, and Republican voters turned out in high numbers when he was on the ballot. What's more, Trump proved to be highly influential in party primaries, often overtly picking favorite congressional and state candidates in a way that presidents usually shy away from. Yet he was also unpopular as a president, leading to large House losses for his party in the 2018 midterms and his own failure to secure a second term in 2020. The post-Trump Republican Party is one that has yet to chart a course independent of him and is struggling with its identity.

Parties as Service Organizations

It's certainly fair to focus on the presidency when examining the behavior of formal parties. The presidency is far from the only office that parties are focused on, but it's the biggest prize and can have the greatest impact on whether a party is able to enact its vision of public policy.

It is also fair to depict modern party organizations as being "in service" to their candidates. Yet parties also have their own agendas. The parties did build up their capacities during the twentieth century, with greater budgets and abilities to serve their various candidates, but they did not do so evenly. Republicans began many of their twentieth-century developments in the 1930s, largely in response to the collapse of their majority in the beginning of that decade in the midst of the Great Depression. The RNC's then chair John Hamilton set his goal as a "return to a majority position," saying, "I don't intend that the next Republican chairman should have to build from the ground up, such as I did." He built up the party's national headquarters such that it would function year-round, even in nonelection years, which was new. He created a database of major party donors and boosted party fundraising. The party continued these efforts for decades, but they began not simply because presidents or other politicians requested them. The party itself was adapting to a new electoral system in which it was facing long-term minority status. Democrats undertook a similar boost in development in the 1980s when they were seeking to make themselves more competitive nationally after several losses at the presidential level.[39]

Additionally, formal party organizations have a good deal of authority in deciding just what sorts of initiatives to undertake and what sorts of candidates to help. In the 1960s, for example, the Republican Party struggled with how best to deal with its minority position, and an internal battle raged within the RNC about whether to embrace White southerners, who had traditionally been Democrats, or to woo African American voters, who had previously been staunch Republican supporters thanks to the legacy of Abraham Lincoln. Either direction would have important consequences for the party and its brand, but the party couldn't credibly move in both directions at once.[40]

An RNC commission run by Ray Bliss in 1962 determined that the party had lost the presidency in 1960 because Republicans were "outmanned, outorganized, outspent and outworked"[41] in the big cities. While the Bliss Commission argued for increased outreach among urban African Americans, the RNC's chair, William Miller, pushed the party to largely write off any plans to expand the urban vote and instead concentrate on building its voter base in the rural South. It built on an earlier party initiative called Operation Dixie, aiding many state Republican organizations throughout the South. It sent a regular newsletter to southern voters and ran ads criticizing the Democrats in the South throughout 1962.

Republicans attacking Democrats in the South may not seem particularly daring today, but it was a striking departure in the early 1960s, when the southern states were reliable Democratic supporters. (Democratic Massachusetts senator John F. Kennedy won almost all the states in the Deep South in 1960.) The Republican strategy seemed to pay off, as they made substantial gains in the 1962 congressional elections in the South.

The early successes of this southern strategy, and the defeat of many Republican moderates in the 1964 election, helped steer the party in a decidedly more conservative direction. Given the strength of the Republican Party in the South today, it's easy to see this path as inevitable in hindsight, but it wasn't necessarily so at the time. The Republicans' path toward becoming a more southern, more White, and more conservative party was determined to a considerable degree by RNC leaders in the 1960s. To say that the party was in service to its candidates is not quite accurate or complete; it helped some candidates while turning away from others. And it had profound consequences for the country that resonate still.

When Parties Pick Favorites

The 2016 presidential election was marked by several embarrassing revelations for Democrats. In particular, hundreds of e-mails among staff of the Democratic National Committee were hacked and made public during the campaign. Some of these e-mails portrayed the nomination contest between Hillary Clinton and Bernie Sanders in a new light, showing that many DNC staffers were dismissive or even hostile to Sanders' campaign. While the e-mails didn't offer any evidence of party officers actually harming the Sanders campaign, they raised questions about just how neutral staff were or could be expected to be.

As discussed in Chapter 9, party insiders or elites are rarely neutral in presidential campaigns. They often take sides early, rallying behind a favorite candidate and providing that candidate with endorsements, funding, expertise, and other advantages that can prove pivotal in primaries and caucuses. And few would expect formal party staff to be truly uninterested in the outcome of a nomination contest. After all, these individuals became involved with their party presumably because they wanted it to move in a certain direction and wanted it to win more elections—their party's choice of nominees can obviously bear heavily on these goals.

Yet party staff are also expected to behave in a neutral manner when dealing with the candidates. As mentioned earlier, the DNC contracts with NGP VAN to maintain key voter contact list files. The presidential campaigns actually work against each other using these huge databases of voter. At one point in late 2015, a computer error left the Clinton voter files available to the Sanders campaign. The DNC responded by temporarily cutting off the Sanders campaign's access to the files right before the early primaries and caucuses. Access was quickly restored after the Sanders campaign sought legal action. Even if the problem stemmed from a misunderstanding, the controversy fed the perception that the DNC favored Clinton over Sanders.

THE MOST TRANSPARENT AND ACCOUNTABLE PART OF THE PARTY

The formal parties are regularly regarded in the political discourse as some sort of relic from the 1800s. They are seen as an old and inferior model of political organization, one that is bloated, sometimes corrupt, and inefficient in the vital modern skills of spreading information, changing voters' minds, and encouraging them to turn out on Election Day.

Yet repeated efforts to undermine the formal parties has not seemed to kill them off. They don't quite wield the power they did in earlier eras, but they are still vibrant and important parts of the larger party system. It's difficult for candidates to ignore the formal parties and get anywhere in politics. Formal parties are one of the healthier components of the party systems. They're much more transparent and accountable conduits of money, power, and influence than almost any other organization in politics, and they serve as a moderating and stabilizing force within the political system.

Discussion Questions

1. The chapter opens with quotations from some 2020 Democratic presidential candidates complaining that their party's debate rules were excluding them and making it harder for them to compete. Are the party's debate rules as described here similar to or different from other examples of party strength discussed in this chapter? How new was the manipulation of debate rules as a party power?

2. Many of the nation's Founders seemed to want a country without formal political parties. Why did they want this, and how realistic was this vision at the time?

3. What sorts of reforms were passed in the early twentieth century to limit the power of political parties? To what extent did they work?

4. This chapter offers several examples of national party organizations involving themselves in congressional primaries to help a preferred candidate. Just how powerful are the national parties in these examples? Can they force a candidate to drop out of a primary? What happens if a candidate whom a party organization wants to drop out refuses to do so?

5. This chapter describes parties as trying to learn from election losses, such as the Democrats after 1968 and 1980, or the Republicans after 2012. What do you see the Republicans learning from their 2020 loss? How do you think what they learn will affect their activities going into 2024?

8

Party Activists

Rich Carlson and Tom Swenor grew up together in Petoskey, Michigan, and had been good friends for nearly 40 years without either taking much of an interest in politics. The economic crash in 2008 took a substantial toll on both of their professional lives, and the federal government's responses to it—including a financial sector bailout and a large proposed stimulus bill—angered them greatly. Sitting on the sidelines and letting other people make decisions on their behalf was no longer an option for them. According to Swenor, "Sometime in March, I said, 'We've got to do something.' Even if it's just three guys, you know, go do something, protest, something. Something. Because I was tired of yelling at my TV."

In a short time, Swenor and Carlson had organized a Tea Party rally in Petoskey with some national political figures. They'd become well-known members in a local Tea Party chapter and were playing prominent roles in an upcoming congressional race. In 2010, they'd find themselves backing different candidates for Congress, arguing over whether to support a traditional Republican or a more conservative third-party candidate. Politics ultimately tore their 40-year friendship apart. In less than two years, two old friends without any interest in politics had become activists,

Activists angry with President Barack Obama's policies organized protests against his administration, including one, pictured here, on September 12, 2010, on the West Lawn of the U.S. Capitol. These protests were not directly orchestrated by the Republican Party, but Tea Party activists were largely either already active in the Republican Party or became active in the party, ultimately shaping its direction. Note that the quotation on the sign on the right is falsely attributed to Thomas Jefferson—the source of the quote is actually unknown.

and their beliefs had become strong enough to undermine their lifelong relationship.[1]

Ana Maria Archila and Maria Gallagher had known each other for only a few hours before they made history together in the fall of 2018. Archila, a political activist from New York City, traveled to Washington, D.C., to protest the nomination of Brett Kavanaugh to the U.S. Supreme Court after Christine Blasey Ford accused him of sexual assault. Gallagher, a recent college graduate from Virginia, went to the Capitol for the same purpose as Archila, and the two met there. They walked to the office of Senator Jeff Flake (R-AZ), one of the last Republicans to declare his support for Kavanaugh's appointment.

Gallagher and Archila followed Senator Flake from his office and cornered him at a Senate elevator, preventing the door from closing, while they demanded to know why he was supporting Kavanaugh. Gallagher volunteered that she'd been a victim of sexual assault, apparently the first time she'd told anyone publicly. "Don't look away from me," Gallagher said to Flake. "Look at me and tell me that it doesn't matter what happened to me, that you will let people like that go into the highest court of the land."

The deeply personal exchange, caught live on news cameras, apparently affected Senator Flake, who called for a weeklong delay in the confirmation vote so that the FBI could conduct an inquiry into the charges against Kavanaugh. Gallagher and Archila, through their organization and courage, affected the behavior of a U.S. senator and nearly derailed a Supreme Court justice's confirmation.[2]

What is it that turns people like Carlson, Swenor, Gallagher, and Archila into political activists? Why are they willing to devote so much time, energy, and emotion into organizing rallies, tracking down elected officials, walking precincts, and licking envelopes, knowing full well that their efforts will usually have only a tiny impact—if any—on the issues that they care about? This chapter focuses on activists, who provide much of the labor that allows parties to function. We hope to give you an understanding of what sorts of people become political activists and what motivates them. We'll also look at the key roles that activists serve in modern political parties, how they shape and sustain those parties. In particular, we'll examine how activists can affect the behavior of elected officials and keep them from breaking their promises, and what happens when activists themselves run for office.

POLITICAL ACTIVISTS AND THEIR MOTIVATIONS

The examples of activists Carlson, Swenor, Gallagher, and Archila show just some of the forms of political activism we see in American politics today. People who participate in strikes and marches are activists, as are those who walk through precincts or make preelection phone calls to encourage people to vote; those who write blog posts, tweets, and letters to newspaper editors to advance causes they care about; and those who organize boycotts against companies in an effort to change those companies' political stances.

In general, we can define **political activists** as people who contribute time or labor to advance a candidacy, group, or cause. But just how common are such people? As we can see in Figure 8.1, different forms of political activism are more or less popular. A full half of Americans reported having talked to people about voting for a particular candidate or party during 2016, although far fewer attended rallies or speeches or wore campaign buttons. Only 12 percent donated to a candidate that year. This should hardly be shocking. After all, even in competitive presidential elections, only roughly two in three Americans actually vote, and voting requires far less time or effort than political activism.

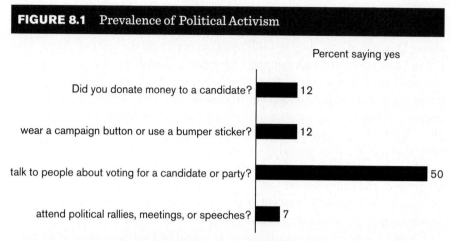

FIGURE 8.1   Prevalence of Political Activism

Percent saying yes

Source: American National Election Studies, University of Michigan, and Stanford University. ANES 2016 Time Series Study. Ann Arbor, MI: Inter-university Consortium for Political and Social Research [distributor], 2017-09-19, https://doi.org/10.3886/ICPSR36824.v2.

The Logic of Activism

Some economists and political scientists question whether voting is a "rational" act. After all, the chances that our one vote will affect the outcome of an election, even in a close race, is infinitesimally small; we have a better chance of getting injured on our way to the polls.

To understand the logic we are talking about, it's helpful to look at a simple formula often thought to explain the logic behind voting:

$$P \times B + D > C$$

where:

P is the probability that your vote will determine the outcome of the election.

B is the benefit you'll receive from your preferred candidate's election compared to the other candidate's.

D is a sense of civic duty or fulfillment you feel from participating.

C is the cost of voting (learning about the candidates, going to the polls, waiting in line, etc.).[3]

P, the probability that your vote is the decisive one, is functionally zero; aside from very small "elections" (such as you and two of your friends deciding where to go for dinner), it's virtually impossible for you to be the one vote that determines the outcome. This means it doesn't matter how big the B term (benefit) is,[4] since it's multiplied by effectively zero. So you have to have a fairly strong D (sense of civic duty or fulfillment) to overcome the costs of voting. The D can be increased through campaign advertising; friends, family members, or teachers instilling in you the idea that voting is important; or a charismatic politician or campaign volunteer convincing you to vote. And we generally experience higher voter turnout in close presidential elections, which see literally billions of dollars spent convincing people to vote. But even in the most contested modern presidential elections, only two-thirds of eligible voters show up. Congressional midterm elections typically see voter turnout below 50 percent, and primaries see well below that. City elections may experience turnout in the range of 10 percent. Without a powerful sense of civic duty or fulfillment, the rational calculus leading citizens not to vote is strong.

If a purely cost-benefit calculating voter would find voting somewhat irrational, imagine how they would view activism. The costs of engaging in political activism are much higher than for simply voting. Activism requires far more time, physical work, and disruption of one's life. As a result, people who engage in political activism are, in some ways, different from other Americans. Some, of course, simply have more resources, time, and money to dedicate to politics. They have the means to surmount those higher costs. And many activists are driven to activism in part because of how the activism itself makes them feel. This can serve a similar function as the D term in the voting calculus.

But activists also perceive differences between candidates and parties that others do not and they see those differences in more dire terms. The benefit of electing the right person over the wrong one feels much greater for activists. And activists have a higher sense of their own efficacy. They evaluate their own contribution to the political system at a much higher level than do others. In short, activists care more about the outcome of an election and think they can have more influence over it.[5]

Similarly, activists tend to have stronger and more polarized opinions about political issues than do non-activists. Figure 8.2 compares the attitudes of activists (defined as those who reported donating to a candidate or attending a rally in 2016) across the political spectrum with non-activists on the issue of legal restrictions on abortion. As can be seen, activists have more polarized opinions than non-activists across the board. For example, the strong Republican non-activists are about twice as likely to be pro-life as the strong Democratic non-activists. Among activists, however, the strong Republicans are about three times as pro-life as the Democrats.

There are several reasons for the greater ideological intensity of activists. For one, as suggested, only those who perceive great costs and benefits to be associated with the victory of one party or candidate over another will have the motivation to get involved as activists. Second, people who are activists tend to be those who

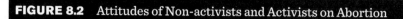

FIGURE 8.2   Attitudes of Non-activists and Activists on Abortion

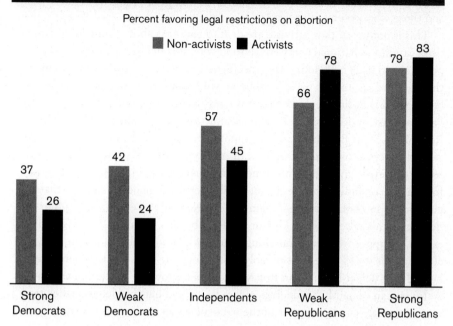

Source: American National Election Studies, University of Michigan, and Stanford University. ANES 2016 Time Series Study. Ann Arbor, MI: Inter-university Consortium for Political and Social Research [distributor], 2017-09-19, https://doi.org/10.3886/ICPSR36824.v2.

have paid attention to, thought about, and argued over political questions for some time. In doing so, they are more likely than others to have come to some conclusions about issues and candidates. Third, as political scientist John Zaller has shown, politically interested people tend to filter the information they receive. They are more likely to acknowledge information that conforms to their previously held positions while ignoring information that challenges them.[6] Thus being involved as an activist tends to produce its own polarization.

Political scientist John May suggested that political activists tend to be more ideologically motivated than either rank-and-file voters or the party leadership.[7] Voters, after all, tend to pay attention to politics only sporadically—usually right before an election. Party leaders obviously follow politics constantly, but they are preoccupied with matters of electability, that is, nominating candidates who are moderate enough to win office and protecting party majorities. Activists, however, are more often motivated by the idea of advancing an ideological agenda. For an activist, a majority isn't to be protected so much as exploited. Majorities allow you to actually enact the agenda that motivated your supporters in the first place. Yes, enacting such an agenda may put the majority in jeopardy, but for an activist, it is far better to follow through on longstanding promises and lose than to hold on to a majority but gain nothing from it. And activists follow politics closely and remember the politicians who were there for them—and those who weren't—for years.

This is not to say that activists are deaf to concerns about political pragmatism. Studies of national party convention delegates (who consist mainly of political activists) have found that electability is a serious concern for them, and that they are hesitant to back a candidate who stands for much of what they believe in if they do not think they have any chance of winning.[8] Similarly, Tea Party activists in Massachusetts and nationwide strongly supported moderate Republican Scott Brown when he competed in a special election to replace the recently deceased senator Edward M. Kennedy in 2010. They were willing to tolerate or even ignore Brown's stances on many issues of importance to them for the sake of ending the Democrats' filibuster-proof majority in the Senate, and for the symbolic victory of claiming Ted Kennedy's Senate seat—a four-decade Democratic stronghold—for the Republicans. In late 2017, progressives rallied in support of Democrat Doug Jones' bid for an Alabama Senate seat, although his views were considerably more moderate than theirs. Their support helped him defeat Republican Roy Moore by a narrow 1.5 percent of the vote. Activists can certainly be ideologically extreme and hardheaded, but they may also be flexible in their stances in the name of achieving larger movement goals.

The Rewards of the Activist

So what motivates activists? Political scientists tend to group activist motivations into three different categories: material, social, and ideological.

Material rewards are tangible rewards offered in exchange for political activity, including income or some form of benefit or discount. The loyal party workers of the mid-twentieth-century political machines generally provided their labor in exchange for a stable city job and a chance to climb a professional ladder. Rank-and-file party activists may put in their service at a young age simply for a chance of getting a summer job as a lifeguard. Some may volunteer just for the promise of a campaign lawn sign or a candidate's button. All of these activists may be considered to be motivated by material incentives.

Social rewards tend to work in relatively small environments where members know one another and fear the social repercussions of not participating in a group effort. As such, they are helpful in avoiding collective-action dilemmas. A union strike, for example, can be difficult to arrange, since it is in each worker's individual interest to continue to work and draw a paycheck, even if they would be better off in the long run if they and all their colleagues stayed on strike together and obtained concessions from their employer. The fear of being ostracized by colleagues or being jeered while crossing a picket line, as well as the positive motivation of continued friendship with colleagues, are considered social motivations. Campaigns are known to play on people's desire for social rewards by informing voters how many of their neighbors have voted or signed a petition to motivate them to do the same. Social media outlets such as Facebook may have a strong role here. People are more likely to vote if they see that a friend in their Facebook feed has already voted, and it helps if they see a picture.[9]

Sometimes activists may be motivated by a chance to take a political stance or change some aspect of public policy. These benefits are called **ideological rewards**. The activist who wishes to prevent women from obtaining abortions, to restrict access to handguns, or to protect the environment can be said to be motivated by ideological incentives. Even an activist whose chances for policy success are extremely remote, such as an antiwar protester demanding an end to U.S. involvement in the Middle East or a Tea Party activist decrying the income tax as slavery, is acting on the promise of an ideological reward. For some, it is enough to simply to take a stance and be heard.

As should be clear, parties are increasingly dependent upon ideological rewards to ensure a supply of activist labor and money. For one thing, parties no longer have many direct material rewards to offer. The decline of the formal party machines in the late twentieth century (see Chapter 6) meant that most government jobs were now protected by civil service laws (people could no longer be hired or fired due to their loyalty to a particular party regime). Second, while social rewards certainly do exist in some scenarios, they are somewhat meager as our society has grown and become less personal. Thus if parties are going to attract activists to their cause and motivate them to help get out the vote come election season, they need to offer ideological incentives. This need for ideological motivations is considered by some to be a cause of the ongoing polarization of the parties. They need to continually offer ideological "red meat" to their activist corps; evidence of compromise only serves to demobilize activists.

Journalist Frank Kent expressed concern about American politics becoming increasingly polarized back in the 1920s. In a book he wrote in defense of political machines, he lamented the situation that might result if machines lost their power:

> If the machines did not work and pull and haul to get enough voters out in the primaries to put over the machine candidates, the present state of indifference and ignorance of the average citizen would permit our candidates to be chosen for us by the freaks and fanatics who abound in every community, and are constantly and zealously stirred to political activity on behalf of their half-baked schemes for saving the world.[10]

Arguably, this is precisely what has happened. Political machines are largely gone. Voters remain largely uninterested in and uninformed about politics. It is

Kent's "freaks and fanatics"—those whom we would today call "activists"—who now provide the key labor in political parties and do much of the selection of candidates for us.

Kent's pejorative terms aside, political activists really do not act or think like the vast majority of voters. Most voters simply don't pay close attention to politics except in the few weeks before a major election; activists care about these things passionately, basically all year round. This can make it hard for activists and non-activists to communicate with each other, with activists sometimes outraged that non-activists don't care more, and non-activists sometimes terrified by the activists' passion. And yet campaigns tend to rely on activists for their voter outreach efforts; they are the only ones willing to uproot their lives and speak passionately to locals about a candidacy in the months before primary day or Election Day.

WHAT IS THE ROLE OF ACTIVISTS IN THE MODERN PARTY?

Not every activist is part of a political party. Indeed, many strongly consider themselves independent of the major parties. Many Tea Party and Black Lives Matter activists, for example, have displayed strong disdain toward both major parties, even while they may lean ideologically toward one or the other. Many of these activists feel that the parties are corrupt institutions that protect office-holders while ignoring the most important issues of the day. Yet many activist efforts end up closely related to party activities.

We can think of activists as facing a choice when they get involved in an issue. They can, first of all, work within a political party. Parties are well funded and organized and hold sway over existing and future officeholders. But activists may have to compromise their goals a great deal to work within the party framework. It's also quite possible the activist cares about an issue that just isn't on the party's radar or that the party is actively avoiding. In this case, a second option would be to work for an established interest group. This offers a network of allies and connections to policy makers. It also might allow for more ideological purity and less compromise than working within a party. But that might limit effectiveness, and compromises might still be demanded as that interest group seeks to work with others to affect a policy change. An activist frustrated by these options may then seek to go it alone, but this would certainly limit how successful that individual would be in their efforts. Difficulties lie along any path.

The American antiwar movement offers an interesting case study. Starting in 2002, American cities began to see a rise in antiwar protests, motivated by outrage toward military actions in Afghanistan and the threat of military involvement in Iraq. By the middle of the decade, hundreds of thousands of activists were participating in antiwar rallies across the country. A 2007 rally on the National Mall in Washington, D.C., brought tens of thousands of protesters and a variety of high-profile speakers, including actors Sean Penn, Jane Fonda, and Danny Glover.

By late 2008 and early 2009, however, the streets had gone almost silent. Attendance at antiwar rallies plummeted, even though American involvement had remained constant in Iraq and had even increased in Afghanistan. What changed? The answer is pretty simple: Democrat Barack Obama won the presidency. A study by Michael Heaney and Fabio Rojas shows that self-identified Democrats made up between 40–50 percent of antiwar protesters prior to 2009. After Obama's election, that percentage dropped to about 20 percent. Democrats simply stopped attending the rallies. The antiwar movement had been a way for many Democratic activists to register their disapproval of President Bush. With him gone, they lost their primary reason for participating, even while the ostensible reason for the movement—two wars—raged on.[11]

This does not mean that activists are hypocrites—far from it. Many of those rally attendees no doubt felt confident that Obama was going to draw down U.S. involvement in Iraq in short order (and that George Bush or Obama's rival for the presidency, Republican senator John McCain, would not), and thus Obama's election was to them a strong indicator that things were about to change. But the drop in Democratic antiwar activism does suggest that a great many activists are closely tied, either organizationally or ideologically, to a major political party. Indeed, activists have become central to the work of political parties in recent decades. It would be difficult to imagine a modern American party helping its candidates in a meaningful way if it could not rely on activist labor to knock on doors, address envelopes, write letters to editors, and raise money.

Activists in the Informal Party

As discussed earlier, modern parties generally don't adhere well to the more hierarchical models that were prevalent a hundred years ago. The idea that there was a mayor or party chairman at the top, with ward bosses below him and precinct captains below them, certainly made some sense when the party that was being described was the Tammany organization in 1800s New York City or the machines that emerged in places like Boston, Baltimore, and Chicago in the early 1900s. Those organizations are out of the picture today, but strong parties clearly are not. Parties are still able to help their preferred candidates win in primaries and give them huge advantages in elections. These organizations are still able to put people in office who will carry out party policy priorities. The parties are about as polarized as they've ever been, even while their formal organizations seem about as weak as they've ever been.

The unions and church leaders with whom Waters is aligned will dispatch their lay members throughout the precincts to make sure that the right people vote on the primary election day. As a result, Waters' support of a candidate has proven to be highly valuable to their primary success; a Democrat who doesn't have her backing has little shot at the nomination.

A similar pattern emerges an hour to the south in Orange County, where a group of entrepreneurs works with business leaders and some officeholders to ensure that only conservative, business-friendly Republicans get that party's nomination. They do so, again, through the use of endorsements, funding, and campaign expertise—and sometimes with hardball politicking. These sorts of informal party organizations appear throughout California, a state known to have weak formal parties but a highly partisan state government. But this model is hardly limited to California. There is evidence of informal organizations operating at the local level in places like Wisconsin, Nebraska, and other states with formal parties that are constrained by state law.[14]

One could describe the "K-Street Organization" run by Republican Party operatives in the early years of the twenty-first century in similar terms. This was essentially a collaboration of conservative lobbying firms in Washington, D.C. Several Republican elected officials and organizers simply instructed Republican-leaning lobbying firms that they would only be granted access to congressional offices if they hired Republican staffers. In this way, an informal Republican machine was built, ensuring a steady source of jobs for regime supporters and a willing audience for conservative governing ideas.[15]

These informal party groups have many different roles. First and foremost, they seek to control party nominations. That is, they have a particular vision of what the ideal public policy should look like, and they are trying to secure the nomination of those who can bring these policies about—within reason. (After all, these groups do recognize the limitations of electability, knowing that someone who explicitly advocates for all their policy preferences may well lose the general election because of it.) They seek to nominate those who can come close to effecting what they desire without alienating too many voters in the process.[16]

Informal party groups do more than influence the nomination process. They are also involved in pressuring elected officials to enact their agenda once in office. This activity can come in many forms. Informal party groups may lobby elected officials directly, sending their members to speak with the politicians and persuade them of the rightness of their cause. Also, they may directly threaten those politicians by suggesting that they may back another more faithful candidate for the nomination in the next election cycle. Sometimes such threats may be communicated obliquely, via a public meeting or with a check sent to a promising candidate. Or these groups may state in the media something to the effect of "We're considering several candidates for next year and haven't yet made up our minds."

When an informal Democratic organization run by Los Angeles County Supervisor Gloria Molina grew tired of U.S. Rep. Marty Martinez's string of conservative votes on handguns and labor issues, they found a promising state legislator named Hilda Solis to run against him, devoting a vast range of funds and endorsements in the Democratic primary in 1998. This enabled her to overwhelm a sitting incumbent in the Democratic primary by a 2-to-1 vote. Few incumbents are taken down in such a dramatic fashion, but then few need to be. The rest get the message that they have only so much leeway in their voting behavior. Ignoring the informal party groups that are active in primaries can be the last mistake a politician makes.

An informal party organization may have other less direct impacts on political dialogue. For example, it may seek to affect the framing of a political story to influence the way voters perceive the information. Shortly after Senator John McCain tapped Alaska governor Sarah Palin to be his vice-presidential running mate in 2008, Republican operatives saw some potential risks due to her relative lack of political experience and her unmarried teen daughter's pregnancy. Republicans thus sought to define her quickly before reporters and Democrats defined her in their terms. Their approach seemed to come from every direction at once, and it involved a heavy use of **surrogates**—people designated by a party or campaign to speak on behalf of a candidate. Bill O'Reilly took to the Fox News airwaves to explain that an out-of-wedlock pregnancy was a private family matter, Karl Rove played up Palin's executive experience as a governor and a mayor (compared with Obama's lack of executive experience), while other consultants appeared on TV and in newspaper op-eds to portray Palin's critics as sexist and elitist. This was a highly coordinated party effort on behalf of one of its nominees, even though it was difficult to pinpoint just who was orchestrating it. But as we have seen, simply because we can't easily identify who is pulling the party's strings doesn't mean that there are no string-pullers. These informal party networks can be just as effective as the older boss-run party hierarchies, despite the different mechanisms.

Activists and Campaign Finance

Activists can also transfer campaign funds within a party group. Before the development of modern campaign finance regulations beginning in the 1970s, donating money to a campaign was a relatively straightforward task, if not a very well regulated one. An individual would write a check to a candidate's campaign, the transaction would (or should) be reported to the federal government, and that was that. Several decades of campaign finance reforms, combined with a dramatic increase in the cost of running campaigns (thanks in part to television advertising), have made financing a campaign a dramatically more complex enterprise. Most offices now have fairly low limits on campaign donations

There are a number of ways for activists to reshape the party. It may involve simply occupying formal party offices. Prior to 1964, conservative activists ran for local party positions all across the country in an attempt to make the party safe for delegates who would nominate a far-right candidate for president, Barry Goldwater. Christian conservatives backed candidates for party offices and local governments in the late 1970s in an attempt to steer the Republican Party further rightward and enable the election of Ronald Reagan in 1980. It could mean running for office themselves. Most often, though, reshaping the party involves dominating its processes for nominating candidates, whether that's done through primaries, conventions, or less formal means.

Different Goals for Activists and Politicians

It's worth pausing to recognize the differences between the typical activist and the typical officeholder, although these are, to some extent, simplified caricatures. Activists can be thought of as "policy demanders." That is, they want something out of government. They want taxes to be higher or lower, they want abortions or handguns to be easier or harder to obtain, they want more or less government involvement in health care, and so forth. They may also be motivated by more-tangible rewards, such as tax breaks for people in their income bracket or government contracts for the labor union of which they are members. Regardless of the specific policy goal, to get what they want, activists seek to get people who agree with them nominated for office.

Officeholders' objectives can be somewhat different. Presumably, they want to remain in office—David Mayhew memorably characterized officeholders as "single-minded seekers of reelection."[18] And even while most officeholders enjoy high reelection rates, they know that the next election could be their last and want to minimize the risk of running afoul of voters. To quote Mayhew again, "Congressman Smith is unbeatable as long as he continues to do the things he is doing."[19] So the officeholder's instinct is to hew quite closely to what the typical voter in their district wants.

This puts activists and officeholders on a collision course. The officeholder usually wants to stick to the safe center of the district, while the activist wants to pull the officeholder toward more extreme positions. The main way activists can achieve their goal is through activity in the party's nomination process. As we saw in the example of the Club for Growth backing of Pat Toomey over Arlen Specter in Pennsylvania, involvement in primaries can achieve results. Even though officeholders know most voters are only marginally attentive to politics, they still don't want to alienate the general electorate. They also know that those who do become active in nomination contests are highly attentive to politics and will devote money and labor to candidates they like and will withhold support from those they find insufficiently committed to their cause.

It should also be noted that activists are usually playing a long game, while officeholders tend to be focused on the next election cycle. (This isn't always true, of course; sometimes activists are impatient while politicians insist they need to win reelection to effect change. But more often than not, it's the activist who possesses the longer perspective.) Those conservatives who engineered the nomination of Barry Goldwater in 1964 were no doubt greatly disappointed in his landslide loss to President Lyndon Johnson that November. Nonetheless, they had succeeded in taking over the Republican Party's infrastructure. Ronald Reagan's strong primary showing in 1976, his nomination in 1980, and his enactment of tax cuts, increased military spending, and limitations on the welfare state during his presidency were the long-term payoff for the many years of laboring those conservative activists had done.

ACTIVISTS AS POLITICIANS

Alexandria Ocasio-Cortez was sworn into Congress in January 2019. Just a few months earlier, she was a bartender living in the Bronx. She was also a political activist. She had worked for the nonprofit National Hispanic Institute, for Bernie Sanders' 2016 presidential campaign, and then at the Standing Rock Reservation in North Dakota protesting the construction of a new oil pipeline. Shortly after the 2016 presidential election, a new political action committee, Brand New Congress, consisting mainly of former Sanders staffers, called Ocasio-Cortez to recruit her to run in 2018 as a progressive challenger to veteran Democratic Rep. Joe Crowley, the chair of the House Democratic Caucus. Defying expectations, she beat the powerful incumbent by 15 points, and went on to win the fall election, becoming a member of the House of Representatives at the age of 29. In Congress, she has been a consistent advocate for many progressive causes, including "Medicare for All," the Green New Deal, canceling student debt, and abolishing ICE (Immigration and Customs Enforcement).

As Ocasio-Cortez's experiences suggest, pressuring officeholders is not the only way for activists to affect policy making. Another way is to recruit other activists to run for office. After all, constantly policing officeholders and issuing threats to ensure they stick with your agenda is tiring and expensive work. This is the perennial problem of any principal (an activist, in this case) who hires or elects an agent (the officeholder) to perform a task. There is always concern about **agency loss**: the difference between what the principal wants and what the agent provides. One solution is to simply hire better agents—those who are already on board with the principals' objectives.

Indeed, many candidates today come from the ranks of activists. To party leaders, some activists make ideal candidates, as they come with ties to hundreds of other activists who can devote their money and labor toward getting them

Bill Clinton (left) was a campaign worker and activist before becoming Governor of Arkansas and President of the United States. Here Clinton is seen meeting with Senator George McGovern (center) at the Little Rock Airport in early 1972. McGovern was in Arkansas campaigning for the Democratic presidential nomination.

elected. What's more, should they become elected, their behavior is relatively predictable and usually consistent with party preferences. Most activists have a long history on some range of issues and a well-defined set of issue stances. Compared to a wealthy celebrity who hasn't thought much about specific issues, or to many other sorts of candidates, an activist may be a relatively good choice for the next candidate for office.[20]

Many of our recent U.S. presidents have histories of political activism. Barack Obama got his start in politics as a community organizer, helping to set up a job training program and a tenants' rights organization on Chicago's South Side. Bill Clinton worked on George McGovern's 1972 presidential campaign (as did his future wife and eventual senator, Secretary of State, and presidential candidate Hillary Rodham Clinton). George W. Bush's work on his father's presidential campaigns could be considered a form of activism. Ronald Reagan, after a successful career in film, turned his attention to political activism in the early 1960s as an outspoken advocate for presidential candidate

Barry Goldwater and more generally for limited government. These examples may seem extreme—few activists-turned-politicians become president—but these individuals exemplify that activist experience can be helpful when running for office. Their involvement in activism gave other activists the confidence to support them when they sought political office.

There are undoubtedly drawbacks to recruiting an activist, however. For one thing, while their views on one set of issues may be well defined, they might not translate easily to another set of issues. For example, can a labor union activist from Detroit be counted on to vote consistently with the traditional Democratic positions on reducing auto pollution restrictions or allowing undocumented immigrants a path to citizenship? There may be considerable uncertainty there. Activists may also be too ideologically purist for party leaders, refusing compromises even among others within their own party.

How the Parties Differ in Their Approach to Activists

Thus far, we have largely described activists as being similar across parties. And they do share a focus on the same basic activities: putting pressure on politicians to advance certain policies and using their control over nominations to exert this pressure. Yet activists on the left and right may differ from each other in some important ways.

In his studies of political activists in the 1950s and 1960s, James Q. Wilson discerned these distinctions across coalitional lines: "The chief resource the conservative brings to civic—or to political—action is economic: money, corporate power, and the personal contacts flowing from business position. The liberal, lacking money, brings numbers and personal contributions of time and effort."[21] Jo Freeman echoed these impressions in her 1986 examination of party political cultures, noting a distinct group orientation among those rising through the Democratic Party's ranks that simply wasn't present among Republican activists. One gained power in the Democratic Party by organizing an interest group, she wrote, while one gained power in the GOP through one's social status.[22]

It is possible that these liberal and conservative activist roles have evolved over the years. The rise of the Tea Party movement in 2009 revealed a more grassroots-oriented version of modern conservatism, with activists meeting in urban areas to attend large rallies and marches the way liberal activists did a generation earlier. And abortion opponents and gun rights activists, while certainly no strangers to money, have taken on increasingly confrontational roles in recent years, even to the point of civil disobedience in some cases. In January 2020, thousands of gun owners brandished their weapons in a march through the streets of Richmond, Virginia, to resist state consideration of gun regulations. Marchers specifically cited the more-liberal marchers of half a century earlier: "Today was the civil rights march of my life," said one armed protester.[23]

HOW ACTIVISTS POLARIZE THE PARTIES

As described, activists are often trying to monitor the behavior of members of Congress, state legislatures, and city and county governments to make sure those elected stick to the agenda they care about. Officeholders may well tend toward the ideological center, but we also know that officeholders are more interested in politics and thus more polarized than the typical voter is. So how can we tell what kind of influence activists are having over politics? Perhaps we'd see the same sort of polarized behavior in our legislatures even if activists did nothing.

We actually have a useful natural experiment on this topic. From 1913 to 1952, California had an unusual election system that had the effect of driving activists out of the political system.[24] Under California's election rules, candidates for any partisan office could *cross-file*—that is, they could run in as many different party primaries as they wanted for the same office in the same year. A Republican member of the state assembly could run in the Republican primary, the Democratic primary, and the Socialist primary simultaneously, and only had to pay a nominal filing fee to do so. What's more, that candidate's party affiliation did not appear on the primary ballot. Voters had very little idea for whom they were voting, and incumbents (usually with the only vaguely recognizable names) won in record numbers, usually in all the different primaries. They faced no opposition in the general election. In such a political environment, there was little point in activist efforts in primaries. It was basically impossible to coordinate a threat against a disloyal incumbent if there were so many unrecognizable names on the ballot from so many different parties. Activist groups largely fell silent during this period.

So what happened to legislative partisanship in the absence of activists? It bottomed out. Republicans and Democrats in the statehouse began voting in all sorts of different directions. Party became a poor predictor of the way members would vote. Instead, members seemed to form unstable voting coalitions built around candidates for Speaker, regions of the state, even lobbying groups. Corruption and lobbyist control reached epic proportions.

In 1952, California voters passed an initiative that required party labels to appear on primary ballots. Few candidates were able to cross-file after that, since voters now could see which candidates were members of their party in primary elections. And quickly, activist groups formed to put pressure on candidates in primaries. The legislature began to polarize shortly after that, and within a few decades the California legislature would emerge as the most polarized in the country.

The lesson from this is clear: activists drive legislative polarization. Take them out of the equation, and parties fall apart quite quickly.

Social Media and Activism

Political activism saw a revolution in tactics in the first decade of the twenty-first century with the widespread use of the Internet. Entrepreneurial political activists began using websites to raise money and share information about candidates and causes. Some of these "netroots" pioneers soon had the power to influence party nominations. The 2007 Netroots Nation convention, founded by blogger Markos Moulitsas, drew not only a large number of attendees, but nearly every major Democratic candidate for president, including John Edwards, Hillary Clinton, and Barack Obama. These conventions are far from simple Democratic rallies; attendees at the 2013 convention booed former House Speaker Nancy Pelosi when she defended President Obama's domestic surveillance program.

Today, social media technologies are facilitating all sorts of political activism. Activist groups coordinate activities, organize events, and raise money with the help of Facebook, Twitter, Instagram, and other online services. Companies like WinRed and ActBlue perform a key role that political parties have traditionally performed—allocating donors' money to the races where it's most needed. Other new organizations like MagnifyYourVoice help people find causes they care about in their communities and help them determine the best way to support those efforts.

But these technologies carry some dangers with them as well. For one thing, recent events suggest that social media activism is "hackable." According to a U.S. Senate report, much of Russian interference in the 2016 U.S. presidential election involved advertising on social media sites, targeting conservatives with messages about immigration, race, and guns, and targeting African Americans with false claims about voting processes.

Even when such activism comes from within the country, it may be contributing to or even misrepresenting polarization. Brian Schaffner and Laurel Bliss examined Democratic primary voters in 2018 and found that those who regularly post on Twitter and other social media about political issues were far further left than those that didn't.[25] If Twitter interactions seem angrier than those in real life, it's in part because the people online are more polarized to begin with. To the extent that journalists, politicians, and party leaders look to Twitter and other social media to learn what issues Americans care about and how they are being argued, they are getting a skewed presentation of the political discourse.

Donald Trump became the first sitting president to address the annual March for Life in Washington, D.C., which he did on January 24, 2020. Trump, who is on his third marriage and does not have a history of religious piety, has nevertheless been very popular with conservative religious groups, in large part because of his consistent appeal to their interests, including opposition to legal abortion.

Politicians, to the extent they can, want to keep online activists satisfied. Doing so ensures that those activists will continue to volunteer their labor, send their money, and educate their friends and allies in their service—all things that are vital in primary and general elections. Displeasing the activists, meanwhile, often means losing many of those valuable resources to another candidate. Keeping the activists happy, however, generally means moving toward the ideological extremes, both in words and in deeds. There's risk in that for the politicians, as they well know; the same things that make online activists happy may also make moderate voters squirm. But this is a risk that politicians are increasingly willing to take. After all, moderate voters tend not to pay close attention to individual politicians' behavior and don't always show up to vote, while online activists seem to be getting better and better at their work. The rewards provided by these activists may well be enough to compensate for any angering of the moderates. Thus activists help pull politicians further and further to the extremes.

In fairness, we should note that these activists, like the Tea Party volunteers and Kavanaugh protesters we discussed at the beginning of the chapter, don't get involved in politics because they want the parties to move further apart. Polarization isn't usually anyone's policy goal. They get involved in politics because they don't like the way things are going and they want the government to do something different. And increasingly, they're closely aligning themselves with major parties to try to get what they want, almost as if they are organizing themselves into party teams. Polarization is just the result of people working this way in different parties.

MAKING THEM DO IT: THE FRUSTRATIONS OF ACTIVISM

Earlier in this chapter, we described activists as being, in a sense, "irrational." This is not meant to be in any way pejorative. Rather, it's a way of describing behavior in which an individual voluntarily pays considerable costs without receiving any personal benefit. Activists, that is, do a great deal of organizing and provide their own money and labor on behalf of a cause that rarely yields a measurable payoff. Beyond that, even when activism is going well, it's incredibly frustrating. Max Weber famously described politics as "a strong and slow boring of hard boards."[26] What makes it frustrating is that the parts that many activists find pleasurable—such as attending rallies, speaking publicly, and marching—create pressure on politicians but rarely directly yield the desired results. Those results only come, if they come at all, after months, years, or even decades of practicing coalitional politics—forming alliances with other groups of activists and party members and balancing each other's priorities. This can be extremely delicate work; activists will disagree as to the best time to publicly pressure or rally behind a politician. At what point does an activist stop advancing a party's goal and start undermining it? There's no clear answer, but figuring that out is a key part of working in a coalition.

All of this is a reminder of just how challenging political activism can be, even when it's going well. As political journalist Jonathan Bernstein wrote about the passage of the Affordable Care Act in 2010:

> If you're a supporter of health care reform, you don't get to just work with Ron Wyden, and Sherrod Brown, and Chris Dodd, and Barbara Mikulski. You have to work with the Senator who just won't go along unless his constituents in the drug industry are taken care of. You have to work with the Senator who really, truly, is pro-life. And the Senator who has no policy convictions, or even substantive needs for his state, but is deathly afraid of casting a vote that will be perceived as liberal. And then you start to realize that even your allies, the people that you think are all on your side, are different, too. To be active—to really engage—in democratic politics means constantly being confronted with just how different everyone is, and how much that feels right and important and necessary to you is going to be threatened. And to be active in politics means that you,

yourself, have to collaborate in threatening those things that feel right and important and necessary to you, at least if you are going to get anything done. It's painful. It's painful when you win . . . in some ways, more painful than when you lose.[27]

POLITICAL SCIENCE TOOLKIT
Is Your Movement Succeeding?

If political activism is such a slow and frustrating process, how can we know if a movement is succeeding? Political scientist Erica Chenoweth has extensively researched protest movements around the world in an attempt to understand why some succeed while others do not.[28] Following are some of the traits of successful movements.

1. *Size*: Successful movements consist of large coalitions. Just how large a movement must be can vary; sometimes fairly small movements have been quite effective. The Women's March in protest of the Trump administration on January 21, 2017, saw between 1 percent and 1.6 percent of the U.S. population take to the streets in protest, according to Chenoweth's research—one of the largest protest movements in American history and one that garnered significant media attention. Research around the world suggests that any protest movement involving 3.5 percent of the population is going to succeed in seriously changing public policy or even changing the regime.

2. *Diversity*: It's not enough to have only your friends organizing with you; successful movements require diverse coalitions from many sectors of society. There's an old expression that if you look around your coalition meeting and don't see someone with whom you disagree strongly, you're not in a coalition. This is what makes such efforts both successful and frustrating.

3. *Nonviolence*: Violent resistance to government actions can drive away potential supporters, while nonviolent movements tend to have more staying power and are better organized.

4. *Innovation*: Successful movements are flexible in their approaches to activism and don't just follow the same path consistently.

5. *Loyalty shifts*: Activists are doing their job if they can get their opponent's allies to shift sides or at least stay silent instead of defending their friend.

Party Activists in Action: Passing Obamacare

The Patient Protection and Affordable Care Act, also known as Obamacare, offers an example of the difficult work and long time frame activists must face. Congress' passage and President Obama's signing of the ACA in 2010 was the culmination of a century-long effort to make health insurance a responsibility of the federal government. Over the decades, activists concerned with guaranteeing health care access to Americans worked both inside and outside government and were heavily involved in party nomination politics. Medicare and Medicaid (signed into law by President Lyndon Johnson in 1965) and President Bill Clinton's failures with comprehensive health insurance reform in 1994 and success with SCHIP (State Children's Health Insurance Program) in 1997 are all stepping stones in this lengthy effort to ensure Americans' access to health care.

A variety of interest groups and activist umbrella organizations have pushed for comprehensive health care reform for decades. Families USA, for example, has been assembling health coverage statistics and a database of hard luck stories for many years in an attempt to steer media coverage of health reform in a sympathetic light. Health Care for America NOW! is an umbrella organization of dozens of different activist groups, from labor unions to racial and ethnic organizations to children's advocates, who coordinated across many different agendas to promote health care reform among presidential candidates in 2008. Various think tanks across the ideological spectrum, including the Brookings Institution, the Kaiser Family Foundation, and even the Heritage Foundation, have been conducting research, writing reports, and offering testimony and articles about health care reform over the years.

While many are tempted to refer to the Affordable Care Act as "Obamacare" (and even President Obama has embraced that label on occasion), that name is misleading in a number of ways. The ACA was hardly just a notion Obama dreamed up one night. Indeed, the ultimate version of that law was similar to that which was embraced by all the major Democratic Party presidential candidates in 2008, including Obama, Hillary Clinton, and John Edwards. And the reason these different candidates were all embracing it was because those advocates who had been pushing health reform for so many years had fundamentally taken over the Democratic Party's nomination process. By 2008, it was difficult to imagine anyone having a realistic chance of becoming the party's presidential nominee without comprehensive health insurance reform as a main component of his or her platform. Even as John Edwards' campaign prospects faded in the primaries and caucuses that year, his wife Elizabeth, then battling the cancer that would soon take her life, played an activist's role in pushing universal coverage among the remaining candidates.

The version of health care reform that President Obama finally signed was a product of decades of activity and negotiations among activists to find a

9

Nominations

On June 22, 1912, former Republican president Theodore Roosevelt and most of his progressive Republican supporters ditched the Republican National Convention at the Chicago Coliseum and convened for a speech a few blocks away at Orchestra Hall. Roosevelt, with one foot in the Republican Party and one foot outside, asked his supporters to find out whether a third-party run for the presidency would be viable. Thus began Roosevelt's nomination as the Progressive Party candidate for president. At that moment, Democrat Woodrow Wilson was effectively handed the U.S. presidency.

Roosevelt and his supporters bolted the Republican convention because incumbent president William Howard Taft was about to win renomination. Everything about the convention was contested, from the seating of delegates to the selection of the presidential nominee. But the Taft forces were winning. Roosevelt claimed that Taft's success came from dishonest tactics, and so the former president asked his supporters not to vote for a presidential candidate at all. Instead, they would form the Progressive Party, also called the Bull Moose Party, and Roosevelt ran as their nominee.[1] This meant that in the general election, there were two Republicans on the ballot—the current Republican incumbent in Taft, and the party's former president in Roosevelt.

After William Howard Taft was named the presidential nominee at the Republican National Convention of 1912, former president Teddy Roosevelt (center, standing) urged his supporters to form the Progressive Party. They nominated him as the Progressive Party nominee in August 1912 and effectively handed Woodrow Wilson the presidency in November.

In the general election, Taft and Roosevelt split the Republican vote, and Wilson won the presidency with only 42 percent of the popular vote. Had everyone who voted for Taft or for Roosevelt voted for the same candidate, that candidate would have easily won the election.

While the Progressives never won the White House, Progressive Party candidates did later win some congressional seats, and at the time, they may have believed their third party had the potential to supplant one of the two major parties. From the point of view of Progressive Party activists, therefore, Roosevelt's defection from his party may have made sense. From the point of view of the Republican Party, an institution concerned with winning elections, the defection was a spectacular failure.

More than a century later, in early 2020, Democratic voters and leaders became worried that the presidential field was hopelessly crowded and that the nomination might be contested and get handed to Vermont senator Bernie Sanders, whom many believed would cost the party the election as well as control of the House of Representatives. Indeed, that might have happened had the field remained crowded, with nearly a dozen candidates competing in the Iowa caucuses and the New Hampshire primary. Yet something stunning happened a

221

few weeks later, right after the South Carolina primary: party insiders coordinated. They began endorsing former vice president Joe Biden in large numbers.

Following Biden's strong win in South Carolina, other prominent candidates, including Minnesota senator Amy Klobuchar and former South Bend, Indiana, mayor Pete Buttigieg, dropped out and endorsed Biden. Suddenly, the vote wasn't so split anymore. During the Super Tuesday contests, held just three days after South Carolina's primary, Sanders was expected to do well given his split opposition. Instead, Biden dominated the night, winning the bulk of contests and delegates. Within a few days, nearly all the remaining candidates had dropped out of the contest, and Biden was the presumptive nominee. The party had escaped what it saw as a potentially catastrophic election outcome by coordinating around one candidate and pushing others out of the race, avoiding the sort of internal divisiveness that doomed the Republicans of 1912.

This chapter and the next concern nominations. This one analyzes the nomination decision at all levels, from the presidency to Congress to state and local offices. Chapter 10 focuses on the special nature of the rules for presidential nominations. As we have noted, the power to nominate candidates is central to the purpose of a party, specifically, to win elections and thereby put like-minded politicians into office. We'll look at the goals parties have and how they must trade and compromise some of those goals in the nomination process. We'll also focus on the tools parties use to pick nominees and enforce their choices once they've made them.

THE QUESTIONS PARTIES TRY TO ANSWER WHEN NOMINATING CANDIDATES

The nomination battles of 1912 and 2020 illustrate the two intertwined questions that a party must answer when choosing a nominee:

1. Whom shall we nominate?
2. How shall we ensure that the party unites behind our nominee?

Republicans had a path to winning the 1912 election. Figure 9.1 compares the hypothetical situation of a single Republican candidate with what actually happened, and Figure 9.2 shows how Taft and Roosevelt together won about the same number of votes in 1912 as Taft alone did in 1908. That was enough for Taft to win in 1908, but when the two Republicans split the vote, Woodrow Wilson ended up winning a lot of states in which the two Republicans together outpolled him. Figure 9.1 shows the states the Republican would have won if all the votes for Taft and Roosevelt in those states had gone to one Republican. Instead, Wilson won because the opposition was divided.

But would all Republican voters have voted for Taft, who was unpopular with many progressive Republicans? Would more-conservative Republican voters have

FIGURE 9.1 Actual and Hypothetical Results of the 1912 Election

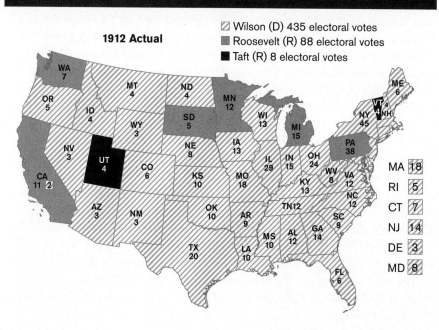

1912 Actual

Wilson (D) 435 electoral votes
Roosevelt (R) 88 electoral votes
Taft (R) 8 electoral votes

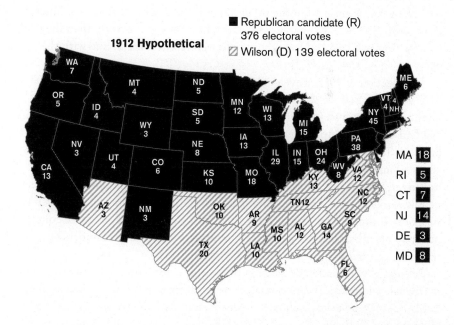

1912 Hypothetical

Republican candidate (R)
376 electoral votes
Wilson (D) 139 electoral votes

supported Roosevelt, had he won the party nomination? Many Republican voters, no doubt, would have voted for their party's candidate regardless of who it was, because party labels are a very useful shortcut (or "cue") for most voters, telling them how a politician will behave in office (see Chapter 12). Either Taft or Roosevelt likely would have beaten Wilson, and it's hard to know which Republican would have done better in those cases. But we know that both of them running produced a major loss for the party.

Even if Roosevelt and his backers believed Taft was more likely to beat Wilson in the general election, it's possible that they would have still wanted to bolt the party. Winning elections is one purpose of a political party, but as we have noted, it is not the only purpose. Partisans want to win elections so that they can enact policy. And the policies that Taft would have supported were not progressive enough for the progressives. The ideological cleavage in the Republican Party in 1912 was unusually large by modern standards. The current-day differences between, say, progressive Democrats like Alexandria Ocasio-Cortez and more-moderate Democrats like Joe Biden in 2020 are nothing compared to the differences between Taft and Roosevelt a century earlier.

The trade-off between the two considerations of electability and enacting policy is at the heart of the first question parties face: *Whom shall we nominate?* On the one hand, since the party cares about holding office, winning the general election is important. The party should choose the candidate who has the best chance of winning. On the other hand, if the candidate does win office, they get to govern. If the party cares about how they will govern, then they will want to nominate a candidate whose policy preferences are in line with the party's.

The election of 1912 is even more illustrative of the second question: *How shall we ensure that the party unites behind our nominee?* Even before Taft was nominated, Roosevelt instructed his supporters to bolt the party. Indeed, Roosevelt had been contemplating a third-party run for some time. The battle between Taft and Roosevelt leading up to the convention had been fierce. The convention, we shall see, is designed to resolve those conflicts, with the party uniting behind its one nominee. But institutions, like conventions, require that people respect them. The convention lacked the ability to prevent Roosevelt's supporters from leaving and forming their own party. Indeed, in a free country, informal organizations like parties will never be able to force members to remain loyal, and so other incentives are needed.

Posing the nomination decision in this way is a departure from the way many journalists and political commentators treat nominations. Rather than asking, "what does it take for a candidate to get the nomination?" we ask, "what kind of nominee will the party choose?" Both perspectives are valid. Ambitious politicians who want gain higher office must win a party's nomination, and it is reasonable to think about what they can do to win it. But we think it is

FIGURE 9.2 Taft and Roosevelt Split the Republican Vote

This figure compares the Republican vote in 1908, when Taft was the only Republican running (horizontal axis), with the vote for Taft and Roosevelt in 1912 (vertical axis). If Taft and Roosevelt together got the same share of the vote in 1912 that Taft got in 1908, then the lines would all come up to the 45-degree line, which they mostly do. In short, the Taft vote in 1912, added to the Roosevelt vote in1912, would have equaled the Taft vote in 1908.

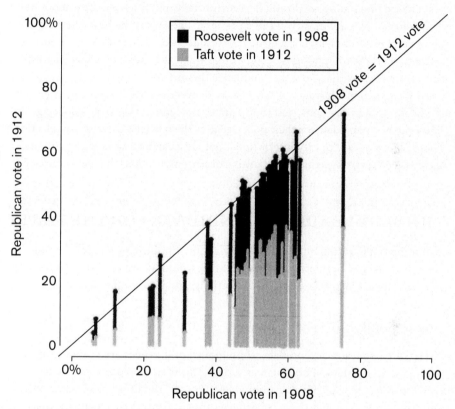

Source: *Dave Leip's Atlas of U.S. Presidential Elections* (https://uselectionatlas.org).

important to put the emphasis on the party that is doing the choosing, rather than on the candidates who are being chosen.

Once we make this shift, all of the strategies candidates use to win nominations are reframed in terms of what the parties are looking for. Commentators sometimes describe primary elections like the early rounds in a sports competition—candidates face off in the primaries, and the two best campaigners emerge for the final showdown. But this is misleading. The party creates political institutions to choose a nominee with the general election in mind. Where there are primaries, the form of the game may look a lot like the general election, but the goals of the players are not the same. Party leaders care about who will be the best representative of the party. Imagine if Major League Baseball let the National League and the American League choose whichever team they wanted to play in the World Series. The two leagues might set up an internal playoff, but the leagues' leaders might also try to influence the outcomes of those games to favor the team that best represented the values of the league, and who was believed to have the best chance of winning the World Series. Similarly, party leaders care about more than who can win the most votes in a primary. They want the best candidate for the general election, which is a different consideration. Many apparently puzzling features of nomination politics become clear when they are viewed by what the party wants rather than how the candidates themselves behave.

As we argued in Chapter 1, a party has two objectives. Party members want their candidates to win elections, and they want to implement the party's policy goals. Thus, the best candidate for their policy goals is the one who can also win election. These objectives are tightly intertwined, but they can also be at odds with one another. Let's start by examining how parties attempt to find the ideal nominee.

THE BEST LEADER: A CANDIDATE FOR THE PARTY

Assuming the party didn't need to worry about winning the general election, whom would they nominate? In general, they would want the person to be ideologically correct, acceptable to all factions, and loyal to the party.

Ideologically Correct

First, the party wants a candidate whose policy preferences are in line with the party's. In an ideological era (such as today), this is an ideological test. Conservative Republicans who complain about "RINOs," or "Republicans in name only," are making the case that these copartisans are not conservative enough; that they aren't true Republicans. Why work to elect a candidate who doesn't agree with you?

But party coalitions are about more than just ideology. Even in a less polarized era, party leaders cared about the policy positions of the candidates. The parties and the candidates were more ideologically diverse, and each party had its share of liberals and conservatives, civil rights advocates, and white supremacists. So, it was just a lot more complicated to balance such a range of policy positions. Figuring out who was the best candidate to speak for all the ideological factions within a party was no small feat. And there were quite a few candidates who wanted to take no stance on anything at all to avoid making enemies. This is why, as we noted in Chapter 8, so many candidates are drawn from the ranks of activists.

Activists are effectively choosing one of their own to be nominated, and they know they can count on such people to fight for the policies the party supports.

The problem can be more difficult when the party is more ideologically diverse. The House Progressive Caucus wants ideologically pure candidates, but many in the Democratic Party would prefer more moderates. But even establishment Democrats generally want liberal candidates, just not as liberal as many activists would like. Nearly all Democrats would agree that they would like people who are more liberal than any Republican.

Compare the conflicts Republicans face today to those endured in the party when Roosevelt and Taft were competing. Roosevelt was championing a **progressive** agenda, which would include increased government involvement in the economy, particularly to break up business monopolies. This progressive ideology didn't have a party, and in fact had support in both major parties. Taft himself was often allied with progressives on trade policy, and he had been instrumental in bringing about the progressive policy goal of an income tax with the Sixteenth Amendment. Still, few would disagree that the Taft wing of the party was the more conservative wing, while Roosevelt supporters wanted to move the party in a more progressive direction. On a dimension of most to least progressive, Roosevelt and Taft were far enough apart that their Democratic opponent, Wilson, was surely in the middle between them. In such a case, it's not hard to see why Republican party activists, wanting an ideologically ideal candidate, would disagree deeply over Taft versus Roosevelt.

Modern ideological divisions within political parties pale in comparison. In 2008, Barack Obama and Hillary Clinton both sought the Democratic Party's nomination. Policy differences between the two frontrunners were so minimal that the debates turned on matters of style and personality.[2] The key difference in their constituencies in the primaries came down to their personal characteristics. Clinton's voters were older and more likely to be women. Obama's were younger and more likely to be Black. In 2016, the policy differences between Hillary Clinton and Vermont senator Bernie Sanders were greater than those between Clinton and Obama in 2008, but they were still relatively minimal. In almost all cases, the more moderate Clinton sought to move policy in the same direction as Sanders, just not necessarily as far or as fast. The biggest difference between them was in their priorities and strategies rather than in their goals. Even in 2020, nearly all the Democratic presidential candidates agreed on basic goals, such as Donald Trump's impeachment, the expansion of health insurance, and the enactment of strong environmental regulations. Their largest disagreements were about the speed with which to pursue those goals, the willingness to compromise to achieve them, and how far to take reforms.

We do not wish to dismiss these differences—they are real—but they are minor compared to the divisions that both parties have faced historically. And yet even these relatively minor divisions play a significant role in dividing the party today.

Acceptable to All Factions

Nominating one of your own is an excellent way to ensure that candidates believe what you believe. But it is not always possible, especially when party coalitions are complicated. Parties usually consist of many different factions who don't always see eye to eye on candidates or policies. So in addition to being ideologically correct, parties also want to nominate candidates who are acceptable to all factions.

Abraham Lincoln articulated this consideration in a letter he wrote to supporter Samuel Galloway in 1860, when he was strategizing his campaign for the Republican nomination. Lincoln recognized that he was probably "not the first choice of a great many," but he thought that he would be acceptable to most factions, so long as he and his supporters would "give offense to no one":

> CHICAGO, March 24, 1860.
>
> *My dear Sir*: If I have any chance, it consists mainly in the fact that the whole opposition would vote for me, if nominated. (I don't mean to include the pro slavery opposition of the South, of course.) My name is new in the field, and I suppose I am not the first choice of a very great many. Our policy, then, is to give no offense to others—leave them in a mood to come to us if they shall be compelled to give up their first love. This, too, is dealing justly with all, and leaving us in a mood to support heartily whoever shall be nominated. I believe I have once before told you that I especially wish to do no ungenerous thing toward Governor Chase, because he gave us his sympathy in 1858 when scarcely any other distinguished man did. Whatever you may do for me, consistently with these suggestions, will be appreciated and gratefully remembered. Please write me again.
>
> Yours very truly,
>
> A. LINCOLN.[3]

Lincoln's strategy has been employed again and again. In the middle of the twentieth century, when the New Deal coalition of the Democratic Party included southern conservatives and northern liberals, candidates had to be acceptable to both factions. The New Deal coalition was held together largely by the commitment of southern Democrats to acquiesce on labor and economic issues, and the agreement from northern Democrats not to press for civil rights. This tension required presidential candidates to have appeal in both parts of the country. Even as late as the 1990s, the Democrats have often nominated southerners for president. When they didn't, the vice-presidential nominee has often been a southern Democrat.

This consideration helps explain why so many presidential hopefuls visit various organizations, especially those that they might not otherwise be that

Candidates often meet with skeptical factions of their party in order to drum up support among key demographics. In 2020, Joe Biden met with members of the NAACP to reach African American voters.

related to. Since about 2010, likely Republican presidential candidates have made appearances at the Conservative Political Action Conference (CPAC) every year. Republicans also appear before the Faith and Freedom Coalition and at the Family Research Council's "Values Voters' Summit." These events are especially important for candidates who worry that they are perceived as too moderate as they need to demonstrate that they are acceptable to all the factions of the party—in this case, the more conservative factions. Democrats, too, make the rounds of important groups within their party. But instead of appearing at annual meetings of conservative, religious, and business groups, they address groups affiliated with the Democratic Party, such as labor unions, environmental groups, civil rights organizations, and gun control advocates.

Candidates also make speeches or public appearances that are targeted to skeptical factions. Early in the 2012 nomination cycle, Mitt Romney gave a much-hyped speech at the University of Michigan on health care. When he was governor of Massachusetts (2003–07), Romney enacted a health care plan that is now widely seen as the model for the Affordable Care Act passed by Democrats and signed by President Obama in 2010. Republicans who wanted to make the attack on Obamacare a centerpiece of the 2012 election, and who wanted to

beat the other party's candidate. They should not and will not naively nominate a favorite without considering **electability**. This, too, involves multiple factors.

Not Too Extreme

The simplest expectation for an electable candidate is that they be ideologically moderate enough to appeal to the general electorate. As we discussed in Chapter 3, political scientists sometimes use a spatial model to understand election dynamics. In elections, the model suggests that parties will want to run moderate candidates, close to the preferences of the median voter. The simple version of the spatial model does not account for parties having preferences over policy, however. A candidate who just wants to win will appeal to the median voter, but a candidate who also cares about policy may not want to move that close to the center. But even if parties care about policy, they will still need to think about the median. The result is a compromise candidate, not as moderate as the median voter, but not as extreme as the typical activist.[6] This tension creates a potential conflict within the party. Some activists, especially those who want more extreme policies, will put more weight on ideological purity than other activists and candidates themselves who are more concerned about electability.

This consideration was likely a big part of the appeal of Bill Clinton when the Arkansas governor considered running for the presidential nomination. Clinton had a history with the centrist Democratic Leadership Council, staking himself out as a moderate. He actually spent a good bit of time trying to convince Democrats that he was not too moderate, acknowledging party leaders' desire to nominate someone who is ideologically correct. But once they knew he was still on their ideological side, a lot of party leaders found Clinton's moderation appealing because they thought that made him more electable.

Compared to Tom Harkin, for instance, Clinton was less liberal, particularly on labor union issues. But many labor unions favored Clinton over Harkin. One leader of the AFSCME union told political scientist Taylor E. Dark, "We believe that we need to be about winning in 1992. . . . If we went for Harkin we probably could get 90% of our agenda. If we went for Clinton we probably could get 85% of our agenda. But it's Clinton who, in my opinion, can get us to the White House."[7]

The dynamic was also evident in the 2012 election. Republican Mitt Romney, a former governor of the relatively liberal state of Massachusetts, had spent several years convincing Republicans that he was a true conservative. Having held positions in line with Massachusetts voters on abortion and health care, he was pushing back against his "flip-flopper" label. And he had largely succeeded. Going into the first debate against incumbent Barack Obama, Romney was viewed as a conservative. In the debate, however, he quickly tacked back to the middle, so much that he even seemed to throw Obama off. And indeed, while Romney had managed to convince many conservatives that he was ideologically acceptable, he had not taken extreme positions on many issues. It is not possible for a candidate to be completely flexible ideologically, but Romney showed that it is possible to find a balance.

We saw these dynamics clearly in the intense Democratic nomination contest of 2020. Democratic voters were unusually fixated on electability that year, according to surveys, and many were willing to nominate a presidential candidate with whom they strongly disagreed if it meant that person would defeat Donald Trump in November. Throughout the contest, Joe Biden's most effective selling point was polling that showed him as the strongest challenger to Trump. Ultimately many prominent Democrats—including those who had strong policy disagreements with Biden—endorsed him as the best chance for the party to retake the White House.

Another example that illustrates how parties recalculate the balance of ideology and electability comes from the state of Colorado, which has recently shifted from a safe Republican state to a competitive one that leans Democratic in presidential years. In 2006, the Democratic Party believed it could win the governor's office only with a moderate nominee. Party insiders rallied behind Bill Ritter, the former district attorney for Denver, who had solid Democratic credentials but a pro-life stance on abortion. Democrats largely perceived Ritter to be about as liberal a Democrat as they could nominate yet still win a statewide election. Ritter, however, ended up beating his Republican opponent by a solid 15-point margin in 2006, and Democrats made further gains in their control of the state legislature. This convinced party activists that they could nominate somewhat more extreme candidates and still win statewide. When Ritter declined to run for reelection in 2010, the party nominated John Hickenlooper for governor and Michael Bennet for a full term as U.S. senator. Both had more traditional Democratic stances, including pro-choice beliefs, and both won. In 2018, Colorado Democrats nominated Jared Polis for governor, who was not only well to Hickenlooper's left but would also become the state's first openly gay chief executive.

POLITICAL SCIENCE TOOLKIT
The Spatial Model: Part 4—Elections

In Chapter 3, we introduced the spatial model, a tool political scientists use to understand how changes in the policies offered can affect outcomes. There, we discussed how different legislators might choose different policies in a legislature. The same tool can be applied to elections. There, the party and the voters are both choosing among candidates.

In this figure, we treat the "dimension" as simply liberalism versus conservatism. Each party needs to choose a nominee. Both want to win. Both also want a candidate who will give them what they want if they do win. Then the voters choose from those two candidates.

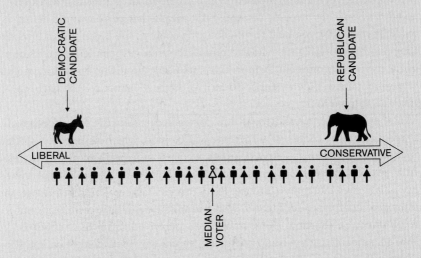

The choice of candidate includes the choice of where the candidate is in the space. Each party can choose a moderate, an extremist, or someone in between. And the outcome of the election depends not only on their choice, but on the choice of the other party. In the example below, the Democrats choose someone who is very liberal, and the Republicans choose someone only somewhat conservative. The result is that the Republican wins.

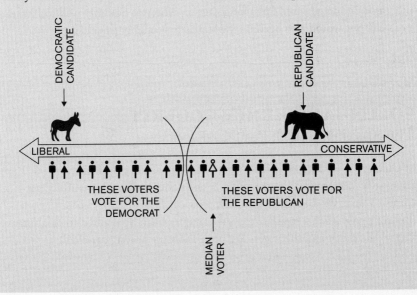

If, however, the Democrats choose someone who is very moderate, while the Republicans continue to hold that somewhat conservative position, then the Democrats would win.

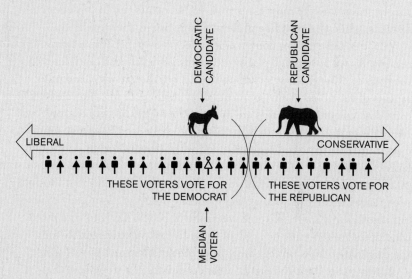

In both of the above examples, notice that the median voter votes for the winner. Just as in Chapter 3, the median voter is central in this framework. This logic suggests that both parties should nominate someone who is centrist and compete for the median voter's vote.

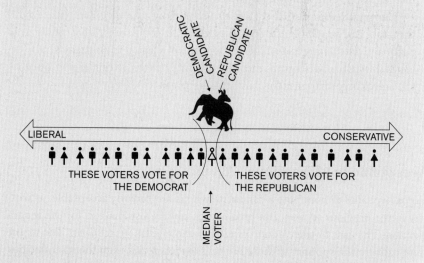

Economist Anthony Downs explained this outcome, in which both parties nominate moderates, in his classic 1954 book *An Economic Theory of*

Democracy, which applies the spatial model to elections. In the real world, this basically never happens, as even Downs acknowledged. Nevertheless, this does explain why the parties tend to avoid nominating extremists. It also explains why the most conservative Democrats run in conservative districts, while the most liberal Republicans run in liberal districts.

Why don't the parties nominate a perfect moderate? There a number of reasons. As we have noted elsewhere, many voters choose candidates on the basis of other factors, including the state of the economy and other aspects of the political environment. They might vote for a more extreme candidate when other factors are in play. Ronald Reagan, for example, was likely the more extreme candidate when he challenged President Jimmy Carter in 1980, but the flagging economy and several foreign policy challenges weighed heavier in voters' minds, leading them to deny Carter a second term. It is also possible that voters may be misinformed about the policy preferences of the candidates. And moderate voters are less likely to vote, but ideologically more-extreme voters might be less likely to vote if the candidates are too moderate. All of these factors make it possible for the candidate who is further away from the median voter to still win.

But there are limits on just how far candidates can stray from the median voter. When parties have nominated truly extreme candidates, such as Republican Barry Goldwater in 1964 and Democrat George McGovern in 1972, they have lost big. So it is probably still true that the probability of a win increases as the party's candidate gets closer to the median voter. Why don't parties maximize those chances?

The main reason is that parties also care about *who* they win with. And that, too, can be seen in the spatial model. The problem is, what makes party activists happy is usually the opposite of what gets politicians elected. Most activists want more ideologically extreme candidates. So as the activists get happier, the candidate becomes less likely to win.

Acceptable to All Factions—Again

No party wants to nominate a candidate who is not broadly acceptable, as we saw in the previous section. But broad acceptability also matters for the general election. The case of the election of 1912 is the nightmare scenario. The winner can't capture the support of those backing the loser, and then the loser decides to run as an independent. This hasn't happened at the presidential level since 1912, but it does happen from time to time for other offices.

One high profile case came in 2006, when Connecticut senator Joe Lieber-
man lost the Democratic primary for his seat. Lieberman had alienated many
Democrats by voting for several conservative policies and choosing sides with
Republican president George W. Bush over his fellow Democrats. This is exactly
the sort of disloyalty that a party wants to avoid in its nominee, and so liberal
Democrat Ned Lamont challenged Lieberman in his primary.

A successful primary challenge against an incumbent is rare, but Lamont
won, depriving Lieberman of the Democratic nomination. Lieberman then ran
in the general election as an independent and won. Unlike in the 1912 presidential example, the voters in Connecticut are sufficiently Democratic that the
Republican nominee, Alan Schlesinger, never really had a chance. But Lieberman's defection still had consequences. Lieberman had been a Democrat. The
tools the Democratic Party had to ensure his loyalty were blunted now that he
had proven he could win the seat even without the help of the party.

True defections like Lieberman's are rare, however. This is because, even
when there is potential for defection, parties manage to nominate candidates
who can unite the party. Indeed, scholars have found only mixed evidence of
"divisive primaries" hurting a candidate in the general election. A divisive primary might indicate a divided party, and the losing faction may sit on their
hands in the general election. Then again, a divisive primary might indicate a
robust party filled with good candidates and vibrant ideas. What should matter
is whether the party can unite after the nomination process.

It is easy to think of cases in which a party lost an election because of lack of
support from their own party. President Carter faced an organized primary
challenge in 1980, a rare thing for a sitting president. He went on to lose to
Ronald Reagan by almost 10 percentage points. It is tempting to say this loss
was due to the failure of Democrats to unite behind their candidate. However,
Carter's loss is more than accounted for by an economic recession in 1980. His
primary challenge was more likely the result of his apparent weaknesses going into
the fall election than the cause of them. Gerald Ford and George H. W. Bush
both faced serious primary challengers when they ran in 1976 and 1992,
respectively, but their general election losses those years are better explained
by other factors, such as a weak economy and, in Ford's case, an unpopular
pardon of Richard Nixon. Meanwhile, some bitterly contested nominees go on
to win big, as Barack Obama did in 2008, after a close primary contest against
Hillary Clinton. Overall, there is no strong, consistent evidence that facing a
primary challenge hurts you in the general election.

What matters is whether the party pulls together to form a united front
behind their nominee. And they usually do. After the hard-fought and sometimes acrimonious contest between Hillary Clinton and Barack Obama in 2008,
the party took deliberate steps to unify behind the nominee. The party orchestrated a moment for Clinton be the one to call for Obama's nomination. As the

convention worked its way through the roll call of states, it came time to recognize New York, where Clinton stood. Rather than announce New York's votes, Clinton called for Obama to be nominated "by acclamation," thus very publicly supporting her former adversary. Clinton's husband also spoke in favor of Obama. Even when the primary battle does not come down to the wire, the parties seek to demonstrate unity. In 2020, when Joe Biden had secured the nomination earlier in the process, the party still offered a prime speaking spot to his primary rival, Bernie Sanders, who used his platform to make the case for Biden to his supporters.

If a party does fail to hold together, the threat of what happened in 1912 looms. The breakdown in 1912 was extremely unusual. It only happened after many efforts to hold the party together failed. The risk is greatest in contests with lower stakes than the presidency. For that reason, many states have "sore loser laws," which prevent a candidate who ran for a party's nomination from running as an independent in the general election.

Good Candidate Qualities

The ideal candidate is the living embodiment of what the party stands for. Their job is to get themselves elected. Whatever else that entails, the party needs someone who is capable of running a good campaign. Running for office is grueling, with day after day of public appearances and humbling fundraising. Campaigning puts a strain on relationships. Some people are cut out for it and others are not. And some people have more natural charisma, a more compelling personal story, or other features that make them appealing to voters.

In general, we think too much is often made of these personal characteristics. At the presidential level especially, almost everyone who throws their hat in the ring has the skills needed to run for the office. Terrible candidates don't get much consideration. Commentators in the media love to talk about how one or another candidate is dull or has some other fatal flaw. After the fact, it is easy to subscribe to that kind of explanation: John Kerry lost in 2004 because he was a long-winded, overeducated elitist; John McCain lost in 2008 because he was too old and out of touch; Hillary Clinton lost in 2016 because she was "over-prepared."[8] The Donald Trump who won in 2016 is the same person who lost in 2020. We find these narratives flawed. As we have noted repeatedly, presidential elections are largely decided on the basis of the fundamentals, such as the state of the economy. Had he been elected, John McCain would have been less than three years older than Ronald Reagan was when he won. And to his detractors at least, Barack Obama is every bit the elitist John Kerry was.

Even if we don't think that campaign skill is the most decisive candidate trait, it is important. At the presidential level, pretty much everyone is a good campaigner. For lower office, it is important to nominate candidates who can compete well. Probably the first consideration is fundraising ability. For local candidates attempting to get their party's support, demonstrating the ability to raise money independently can show that they have the skills to run for office and will use party money wisely.[9] But parties will also prefer candidates who are comfortable in campaign settings.

SOLVING THE SECOND NOMINATION QUESTION: UNITING BEHIND A NOMINEE

The previous sections outlined the kind of candidate a party would want. But as we saw, some of the qualities a party would like to maximize are at odds with other qualities—for example, someone who is ideologically correct might not be acceptable to all factions. Thus, different activists within the party will favor different candidates. We saw this in the election of 1824 (see Chapter 2). Four candidates ran as Democratic-Republicans, each chosen through a separate mechanism.

To avoid chaos and the resulting electoral losses, parties need what Nelson Polsby called "coalition-forcing institutions" to help them come to a conclusion on which nominee they will support.[10] The party has a number of options in the institutions it uses to choose a nominee. As E. E. Schattschneider puts it, what matters is whether the nomination is "binding, whether it effectively commits the whole party to support it. . . . The nomination may be made by a congressional caucus, a delegate convention, a mass meeting, a cabal, an individual, or a party election. The test is, does it bind? Not how was it done?"[11] Next, we look at some of the different ways American political parties nominate candidates for office.

Party Leaders and Party Committees

The most efficient way for a party to choose its nominees is for the party leadership to meet, discuss likely candidates, and then choose among them. Especially in local contexts, the party leadership might gather to draw up a **slate** of candidates for the next election. They would not confer with voters in the process.

In some cases, a single party leader might have the final say. In Mayor Richard J. Daley's Chicago in the 1960s, a committee of Democratic ward leaders would put together slates, but, as journalist Mike Royko put it in his account of Daley's machine, *Boss*, "even the slate-makers do not kid themselves into thinking they are deciding who the candidates will be. They listen to the applicants, push their favorites . . . and wait for Chairman Daley to make up his mind."[12]

The advantage of a centralized decision-making process, be it a select committee or one powerful leader, is in coordinating many offices. In its effort to appeal to all factions, the party leader might work out a logroll across multiple offices: a Latino politician for this position, a business leader for that one, a Christian conservative for another one. A central committee or boss can also ensure that some inexperienced candidates are groomed for future success. As one Chicago ward boss told Royko,

> [Daley] moves us around like a bunch of chess pieces. . . . I think his idea is to slate people who aren't going to try to rival him or add to someone else's strength. Look at how Cullerton got to be assessor. First he was a nothing alderman. He was a real nothing. But Daley put him in as finance chairman so he could have somebody who wouldn't get out of line. Then he put him in as assessor. Keane wanted assessor for his brother George. George would have loved it. Funny how people love to be assessor, haw! But Daley wasn't about to give Tom Keane the assessor's office, so he looked around and there was faithful Parky Cullerton.[13]

This kind of control comes with costs, of course. For one, it takes a particularly brilliant political mind to play multidimensional chess like Daley was doing. Systems that are open to more people permit more people to share their knowledge and wisdom. For another, politicians who are locked out of the candidate-choosing process may get frustrated. If a system does not allow ambitious politicians an opportunity to try to break in, those ambitious politicians may start looking for other ways to advance their cause. If the party leaders themselves don't consider reforms to accommodate them, they may find reforms thrust upon them.

The Legislative Caucus

Since political parties do much of their activity in the legislature, it is natural to think of the party members in the legislature as representing the party more broadly. Early in U.S. history, a caucus of party members in the Congress would meet to decide who would represent their party in the general election.[14] As we saw in Chapter 2, the election of 1796 was the first real two-party election for president. The nascent anti-Federalist faction had already decided informally to back Thomas Jefferson for president. They decided on Aaron Burr as their vice presidential candidate at a meeting of members of their party in the Congress. Meanwhile, the Federalists settled on John Adams and Thomas Pinckney in the same way. Both parties used that method until the election of 1824, when the system broke down.

The congressional caucus is a flawed method of party nomination because it is restricted to those who are in the legislature. If a party lost big in earlier elections, there may be few members of that party to meet in the caucus. The officeholders in the legislature may also be a poor representation of all the factions of the party. Officeholders also tend to be more interested in holding office than in achieving policy goals. Thus the caucus may not satisfy some of the party's criteria that we have described.

This was the problem in 1824. Many Democrat-Republicans felt that the congressional caucus didn't represent the rest of the party. Only members of Congress could participate, and even many in that body felt it was inappropriate for that reason. A minority of congressional Democrat-Republicans in Congress did meet as a caucus to nominate William Crawford. Meanwhile, *state* legislative caucuses in Massachusetts, Kentucky, and Tennessee nominated favorite-son candidates John Quincy Adams, Henry Clay, and Andrew Jackson, respectively. That outcome was clearly unsatisfactory, and so the national **legislative caucus** was abandoned as a way to nominate candidates.

Conventions

After the 1824 election, the supporters of Andrew Jackson realized that part of their problem was a failure to coordinate on nominations. In 1825, the Tennessee legislature nominated Jackson for the presidency for the 1828 election, and the shadow of the failure to coordinate in 1824 kept other candidates out of the race. Jackson won. For 1832, the supporters of Jackson, now coalescing as the Democratic Party, formally organized a **convention** to renominate Jackson and nominate a vice president.

Conventions have many similarities to legislative caucuses. A select group of party loyalists gather and deliberate. The difference is that the convention is made up of party members who were not elected to Congress, and who may have no interest in holding office themselves.

From 1832 to 1968, the national party conventions developed a format that we would find quite familiar nowadays, although the proceedings of those conventions were a good deal more consequential than those of today. Delegates from across the country would meet every four years to argue about the strengths and weaknesses of various candidates, hold a series of votes, and ultimately pick a presidential and vice-presidential nominee. Importantly, during that era, the presidential nominee was chosen at the convention. It was quite common for attendees and outside observers to have no idea whom the party would nominate before the convention began.

As we discuss in Chapters 7 and 10, however, the party nomination system changed after 1968, and now the choice of nominees is a foregone conclusion by the opening day of party conventions. The major parties' national conventions typically take place after the primaries and caucuses and last four days in the late summer of the election year. Their primary purpose is to nominate a candidate for president and for vice president. The conventions also craft and vote on a platform—a statement of what the party stands for—and activists have an opportunity to meet and network with other politicos from around the country. Since conventions are televised, they provide an opportunity to promote the party and its nominee to the country.

The parties in the states also hold conventions, which do similar things, including nominating candidates for state-level office. State conventions also sometimes choose delegates for the national convention. While the results of the national convention are usually predetermined, the state conventions are not.

States use conventions because, as a tool for nominating candidates, conventions are very effective. All the stakeholders in the party could be present, and they can negotiate directly with one another. So if a candidate who is acceptable to all factions exists, they have a good chance to emerge. The trade-off between ideological purity and electability-enhancing moderation can be hashed out face to face. In their discussion of national party conventions of the 1960s, political scientists Nelson Polsby and Aaron Wildavsky describe the drama that played out between "pragmatists," who were more interested in a candidate who can win, and "purists," who were more interested in policy.

Most conflicts are not resolved, though, on the convention floor. Important party leaders, those whose advice and instruction will be heeded by other delegates, can strategize and coordinate in private. In 1920, a reporter used the term "smoke-filled room" to describe the room in the Blackstone Hotel where Republican power brokers negotiated their party's nomination during the convention in Chicago. They settled on Warren G. Harding. These smoke-filled rooms are no longer the setting of important decisions at the national conventions, as we will show in Chapter 10. But such bargaining remains important at state conventions.

The advantage of a convention over a legislative caucus is that it can be open to all elements of the party, even those who might not have won election to the legislature. This opens new ground for party factions to compete, yet important questions remain, like "Who gets to come to the convention?" Convention delegates are selected in a variety of ways, almost as varied as the ways in which candidates are nominated. A faction, especially one interested in nominating its own candidates, can coordinate to send delegates from across the state.

The institution of the convention enabled the nomination of Tea Party Republican Ken Cuccinelli for governor of Virginia in 2013. Cuccinelli planned to run against incumbent lieutenant governor Bill Bolling for the gubernatorial nomination in a primary. Bolling had expected to run for the nomination unopposed. The State Central Committee decided to switch to a convention, on the grounds that Democrats couldn't participate in the convention, but could vote in the primary. The convention was then filled with more conservative Republicans, many self-identifying with the Tea Party. Anticipating the outcome of the convention, Bolling dropped out and Cuccinelli became the nominee (though he lost the general election to Democrat Terry McAuliffe).

Primaries and Caucuses

Probably the most common method for a party to select a nominee today is a **primary**. Candidates register to compete in the primary, and then voters affiliated with that party vote. The candidate with a plurality of the vote will represent that party in the general election.

Progressive reformers of the early twentieth century advocated primaries because they wanted to keep the choice of candidates out of the hands of party leaders. The compromises that we have described in the previous section as central to the party's decision—such as ideological correctness, acceptability to different factions—were exactly the sort of thing progressives didn't like. At the same time, some party leaders found primaries appealing, since they were a route around the intraparty conflict that could bubble up at a convention.[15]

In many ways, progressive reformers got their way. Primaries do take the decision of who to nominate out of the hands of party leaders and put it in the hands of voters. But which voters? Exactly how primaries work depends a great deal on how they are implemented. There are at least five different kinds of primaries, each with their own consequences. Political scientists do not agree on the precise definitions of these different kinds of primaries, but they do agree that there is a range in how restrictive the primary is as to whom it allows to participate.

Closed Primaries The most restrictive model of a primary is a **closed primary**, meaning the contest is limited to those who are registered members of the party. Voters must typically register to vote as members of a party long before the primary itself. Closed primaries are thought to be preferred by party leaders, because only party-loyal voters participate. The primary is thus not vulnerable to meddling voters from another party, or those who are otherwise not interested in helping the party elect the best candidate who can win.

Semi-Closed Primaries While closed primaries are restricted to registered voters, some states have primaries where unaffiliated voters can choose on Election Day which party's primary to vote in; but those already registered with a party cannot change that status on Election Day. These primaries are called **semi-closed primaries**. So a registered Democrat cannot cross over to meddle with the Republican nomination, but an independent voter can easily switch allegiances. Typically, the voter must register with their new party and thus will remain registered with that party for the future, unless they later make the effort to change their registration.

Open Primaries An **open primary** is open to any registered voter, but typically a voter may still only vote in one primary at a time. So a registered Republican can decide to vote in the Democratic primary, but if they do, they will have to choose among the Democrats for every office. An open primary is in theory subject to strategic crossover voting (or "party raiding"), where voters from the other party try to sabotage their opponent by voting for a weak candidate. While this is technically possible, there is little evidence that it happens often, or that it actually affects the outcome.[16]

Blanket Primaries The least restrictive form of primary is the **blanket primary**, in which a voter may choose which primary to participate in. Each primary still pits candidates of the same party against one another, and each party then has a single candidate. For example, in a blanket primary a voter can vote for a Republican candidate for one office and a Democratic candidate for another.

Political parties are particularly frustrated with the blanket primary. In 1996, after California imposed the system through a referendum, the parties sued the state, claiming that allowing anyone access to the party's nominee infringed upon the party's right to association. The U.S. Supreme Court agreed. In *California Democratic Party v. Jones*, the Court ruled that the state could not force the parties to let nonmembers choose their nominee for them. California would later adopt a top-two, or jungle, primary.

Top-Two, or Jungle, Primaries A special form of blanket primary, called the **top-two primary** or the **jungle primary**, is used in Washington State, California, and Louisiana. It essentially does away with party primaries altogether, thus avoiding the issue in *California Democratic Party v. Jones*. Instead, all candidates across all parties run against one another in a state-run primary election. The top two candidates then face each other in the general election. So after a top-two, or jungle, primary, the general election could have two Democrats (or two Republicans) running against each other. In a famous example, U.S. Representatives Howard Berman and Brad Sherman, both Democrats who had been redistricted into the same district in the San Fernando Valley in Los Angeles, ended up in a November runoff after winning the top two slots in the June 2012 primary. The runoff campaign was intense and nasty, pitting Democratic activist groups in different geographical regions against each other and nearly driving the two longtime Democratic allies to a physical fight. Sherman ultimately prevailed.

Institutions like the top-two primary are explicitly designed to take the choice of candidates out of the hands of parties. They are introduced by those who think that closed primaries are not good for democracy, and so should be circumvented. However, parties maintain influence, even in places with top-two primaries. In California's first election under the top-two system (2012), only 16 percent of state house and congressional races saw candidates from the same party meet in the general election. In most races, the parties still coordinated around a single candidate. They do this in part through endorsements, which

In 2013, Lt. Governor Bill Bolling faced Tea Party candidate Ken Cuccinelli in the Virginia Republican primary for governor of the state. Bolling dropped out of the race, anticipating strong Tea Party turnout and unfavorable changes to the state convention rules. Here, delegates show support for Cuccinelli at the Virginia Republican Convention in May 2013.

signal which candidate with a party label is the *real* candidate from that party. Candidates endorsed by the major parties are more likely to win nomination.[17]

Caucuses Some candidates are selected in **caucuses,** which are technically different from primaries, but serve similar purposes. They are mostly used for the selection of delegates to national conventions, although some caucuses also choose other nominees.

A caucus is a lot like a mini-convention, but at the local level. It is scheduled for a specific time, and everyone is expected to arrive at that time to take part in the discussion. The caucus might be scheduled for 7 P.M. on a Tuesday, and then voters arrive and come together in one room. How much deliberation actually takes place will vary, but typically after a few hours, the participants have registered their choices for nominees and selected delegates for conventions. We describe the most famous caucus, Iowa's presidential caucuses, in Chapter 10.

Does the Process Matter?

One reason that reformers want to open the primary system to people beyond just registered party members is to combat polarization. Since one of the criteria that parties have is to nominate someone who is ideologically correct on policy, it is thought that relaxing their hold on the nomination would lead to more moderate nominees. This does not seem to have been the case, however.

10

Presidential Nominations

Incumbent presidents don't usually face serious challengers from within their party when running for reelection. They typically sail easily to their party's nomination for a second term, and the nominating convention is little more than a coronation scripted for television. Only when they are looking like dangerously weak candidates for the fall reelection do sitting presidents face challenges for their own party's nomination. Senator Ted Kennedy challenged President Jimmy Carter, and conservative leader Patrick Buchanan challenged President George H. W. Bush, for this precise reason in 1980 and 1992, respectively.

So, given his weak polling position heading into reelection, perhaps it was not that surprising to see President Donald Trump facing three high-quality challengers from within the Republican Party in 2019—former U.S. representative Joe Walsh of Illinois, former Massachusetts senator Bill Weld, and former South Carolina governor Mark Sanford. What *was* surprising was how the Republican Party handled these challenges. Republican organizations in five states—Alaska, Arizona, Kansas, Nevada, and South Carolina—decided to cancel their primary elections for 2020 and simply pledge their support for Trump's renomination rather than hold a primary in which Trump could be embarrassed or his candidacy derailed.

There are a number of ways to think about this move by the five state parties. In one sense, it is perfectly legitimate for a party to pick a nominee and act to

The qualifications for candidates to attend the Democratic debates winnowed the field from 20 candidates to seven by December 2019. Here, the remaining candidates are pictured in February 2020 at a debate in New Hampshire: (from left to right) Andrew Yang, Mayor Pete Buttigieg, Senator Elizabeth Warren, Vice President Joe Biden, Senator Bernie Sanders, Senator Amy Klobuchar, and Tom Steyer.

remove any barriers in their way. As we've shown in other chapters, party members and primary voters do not always determine a party's path, and the idea that rank-and-file partisans have a "right" to pick their nominees is a fairly new and novel one. The party organizations in these states simply chose a way to protect the candidate they wanted to win the nomination.

On the other hand, the cancellation of these primaries potentially made the party look weak, as though it was hiding a damaged candidate from a serious challenge. The three challengers wrote an opinion piece for the *Washington Post* urging the state parties to change their minds and hold primary elections. "Cowards run from fights," they wrote. "Warriors stand and fight for what they believe. The United States respects warriors. Only the weak fear competition."[1]

The 2020 presidential nominations cycle looked different on the Democratic side, but we still saw the party playing an active role in shaping the race. In particular, the Democratic National Committee announced in early 2019 a set of rules for deciding which candidates would qualify for the various primary debates that would occur in 2019 and 2020. Candidates had to have at least 1 percent support in a series of DNC-approved polls, or donations from at least 65,000 unique donors, in order to participate in the first few debates.[2] Twenty candidates qualified for that event. But for later debates, those thresholds were higher. By the

December 2019 debate, participants needed support of at least 4 percent in polls *and* donations from at least 200,000 donors; only seven candidates qualified.

These moves by the Republicans and Democrats in 2019 demonstrate something often overlooked in media accounts. Party leaders do not generally sit back and let the presidential nomination system play out. If party leaders have a strong preference that's consistent with what voters want, they can let the voters decide. If they have a strong preference that conflicts with what voters want, they can sometimes make sure voters don't have much of a say in the matter. If they're concerned about the field being too large, they can take steps to winnow that field down and shape who can compete.

Chapter 9 discussed the logic of candidate choice and the strategies party leaders use to enforce their choices. We noted that party leaders want the candidate who is both best for the party's goals and capable of winning. We also noted that the party needs some sort of mechanism for enforcing their choice, be it a caucus, a convention, a primary, or something else. This chapter will outline how those particular options are organized for the unique task of selecting a presidential nominee. We'll describe the "mixed system" of primaries, caucuses, and conventions that American political parties have developed for nominating presidential candidates. And we'll examine just what that mixed system was expected to achieve and assess how well it operates today and whose interests it serves.

HOW THE MIXED SYSTEM WORKS

It is common to describe the quest for the presidential nomination as competing in "the primaries," or even "the primary," but this is misleading. The parties' nominees for president in the United States are not chosen by primaries alone, but by a **mixed system** made up of various primaries, caucuses, and state conventions, all organized to select delegates to the national party conventions.

The major party nominees are still chosen at the national convention, as they have been since 1832. However, the selection of delegates to those conventions is through means that are open to rank-and-file voters. In most states, most of the time, that means a primary. So candidates compete in those primaries, ensuring the selection of delegates pledged to vote for them. When the candidates get to the convention, the balloting for the nominee is predictable. If one candidate has a majority of pledged delegates, as is usually the case, that candidate is assured of victory at the convention. While the convention is where the decision is formally made, the primaries are where the real contest is won or lost.

As we've noted, the mixed system combines a national party convention with state contests that determine both who gets sent to the convention and how they are supposed to vote. Nearly every state party has its own way of selecting and instructing delegates, and rules sometimes differ between the two parties in the same state.

Different States, Different Rules

State parties use various ways to involve voters in the selection of delegates to the national convention. The simplest way is through primaries. However, when voting in presidential primaries, voters are technically selecting *delegates* rather than candidates. On most ballots, the delegates themselves are not listed. Instead, it is the candidate those delegates are pledged to support who is listed, and voters vote for that candidate.

Another method the state parties can use for selecting delegates is the caucus. This is a face-to-face meeting of party-loyal citizens conducted at the precinct level, often with just a few dozen attendees or even fewer. These caucuses are often held in a party activist's home, a local school auditorium, or some other small meeting place. Attendees debate the merits of each candidate before voting. The results of all the caucuses are then aggregated. The caucus method appeals to party leaders because it might limit candidates with small followings. Those caucus-goers who support minor candidates might be persuaded to switch to a more popular choice. And even if they are not, some caucus states have threshold rules. If a candidate does not have, for example, 15 percent of the support in the individual caucus, they will receive no votes and be awarded no delegates. This means that only candidates with significant support win delegates.

Caucuses also tend to favor candidates with stronger organizations. Participating in a caucus is more time-consuming than voting, often requiring several hours of commitment. Turnout is lower in caucuses—while 20 to 30 percent of eligible voters may turn out for a primary, only 5 percent or so will likely participate in a caucus. More-attentive and engaged party activists are most likely to attend a caucus. Campaigns can also directly mobilize potential participants, reminding them to attend and even transporting them to the events. This kind of environment can be favorable to "factional" candidates— those with the passionate support of just a portion of the party, rather than those with broad, but perhaps less enthusiastic, support. Bernie Sanders would generally meet the definition of such a factional candidate, and in both 2016 and 2020, he performed considerably better in caucuses than he did in primaries.

Additional delegates are awarded at state party conventions. County and state conventions are often used in conjunction with caucuses or primaries, with some national delegates reserved to be awarded at the state convention.

Many states use some combination of these methods, often in convoluted ways. For example, in Iowa, the first-in-the nation caucuses select delegates for the county conventions, which are held later. The county conventions select delegates to the state convention, and the state convention selects the delegates to the national convention. In neither party are the delegates strictly bound to support the candidate they were selected for. Presumably, delegates are chosen because they are loyal to a particular candidate, and so we can learn something from the results of the caucuses themselves. But technically, once the process plays out, the delegates from the state might end up with a different set of candidate preferences than looked to be probable on caucus night.

The parties vary in how they allocate delegates after the voters have participated in caucuses or primaries. Democrats allocate delegates in proportion to the votes won. This is called *proportional allocation*. Candidates who received at least 15 percent of the vote will win delegates in proportion to their vote share, both within a congressional district and statewide. (This mirrors how legislators themselves are elected in some countries—see Chapter 5.) Republicans award delegates proportionally in some states, but in others the candidate with the most votes is awarded all of the delegates—a system called "winner-take-all." Some states have used proportional systems, but then also awarded bonus delegates to the top vote-getter (sometimes called "winner-take-more").

Since there is so much variety in the primary and caucus methods and in the conventions that follow them, it is not possible to fully describe how every state works. But the first two states—Iowa and New Hampshire—are largely representative of many of the features of the two respective types. Since the Iowa caucuses and the New Hampshire primary are also unusually important in the system, it makes sense to take a closer look at them.

The Iowa Caucuses The caucuses in Iowa illustrate just how intricate the rules can get—and since Iowa plays an outsized role in the media coverage of the nomination process, it is worth paying attention to. Iowa has traditionally been the first state to begin the process of selecting convention delegates, and now Iowa law requires the state to move its caucuses up if it is not scheduled to be the first in the country.[3]

Democrats and Republicans do things differently in Iowa, but the process for both parties begins with the Iowa caucuses, usually in January or February. As in other states, Iowans are technically not choosing a presidential candidate. The state will ultimately only choose delegates to the national convention, to be held that summer. And they aren't even doing that when they caucus in January or February. The event that the media converges on is the **precinct caucus**, which is the mechanism for selecting delegates to the county conventions. Those attending the county conventions, held a month or two later, will choose delegates to the Iowa state convention as well as to the congressional district conventions. Those conventions then choose the national delegates. By that time, most other states have selected their delegates, making Iowa one of the last to actually select its delegates. Even though delegates will be selected at each stage, the precinct caucus-goers can select delegates who are expected to vote for a particular candidate. Or, more precisely, they can select delegates (to the county convention) who are expected to vote for delegates (to the state and congressional district conventions) who are expected to vote for delegates (to the national convention) who are expected to vote for a particular candidate.

The precinct caucuses begin at 7 P.M. central standard time on caucus day. Voters gather with others of their party in roughly 1,700 precinct meetings, held in church basements, public meeting spaces, even in people's homes. The procedures are a little different between the parties (and the exact rules can change from year to year).[4] The caucuses are open to registered party members in Iowa. While this is theoretically the same group who might vote in a primary, participating in a caucus is more time-consuming and has a rigid schedule, so it takes a more dedicated voter. Primary voters tend to be more politically engaged than general election voters, and caucus-goers even more engaged than primary voters.

At the Democratic caucuses, someone generally makes the case for each potential presidential candidate, and then the participants physically move to one part of the room or another to join with the others who support their candidate. Once the groups form, their members are counted. Then, any candidate who has less than 15 percent of the support is dropped, and the supporters of that candidate choose a new candidate. This is designed to ensure that those who support candidates who are not "viable" have a chance to express their preference among those who are viable. Supporters of the remaining candidates may then appeal to these available caucus-goers by giving speeches, having personal discussions, or even offering baked goods. Often the most important thing that can be offered to supporters of an eliminated candidate, however, is a guaranteed delegate position for the county conventions. For example, supporters of Vice President Joe Biden might offer supporters of Senator Amy Klobuchar one of their delegate positions at the next convention, on the condition that they support Biden on caucus night. When the supporters of the eliminated candidates vote a second time, this might change the results.

Republicans also listen to advocates for different candidates, but they do not use the Democrats' intricate counting system, and they use a secret ballot. The presidential preferences of the caucus are recorded, but each participant's vote remains secret. It's essentially a straw poll. There is no formal system relating those preferences to delegates, but the participants can—and often do—decide to link the allocation of delegates to the results on caucus night.

Delegates selected in both parties' precinct caucuses then go on to the county conventions, while the media attention goes on to other states. At this point, the media tends to make estimates of the final delegate counts, but these are only estimates. Iowa still has a long way to go before its delegates are chosen. At the county conventions, delegates are selected for the state conventions, as well as for congressional district conventions. The Democrats again apply the 15 percent rule, asking delegates who support a candidate with less than 15 percent support to realign themselves. Those that switch sign pledges that they now support a new candidate. Republicans again have no formal mechanism to tie results on caucus night to the allocation of delegates, but party leaders can instruct delegates to support a candidate.

There are two more sets of conventions in each party: the congressional district conventions and the state convention. Both of these conventions select representatives to the party's national convention. The Democrats continue with their 15 percent rule at each stage. Republicans continue to only informally tie delegates to candidates.

In Iowa the delegates to the national conventions are thus selected in June, long after the media have moved on to other things. Why, then, do we pay so much attention to what happens in the Iowa caucuses if there are so many steps between that day and the final allocation?

Part of the explanation is that many people, including many journalists, do not quite understand how complicated the process is. But it's not irrational to focus on the first stage, when rank-and-file members of the party have their say. This is the part of the process that is most open to campaigning efforts by the candidates. What happens on caucus night is a challenging test not only of the candidates' appeal but also of the campaigns' ability to turn interested citizens into caucus-goers.

But Iowa is not unique in having an intricate process that follows the high-profile event that is reported in the national media. Nearly every state has some process that links voter or caucus-goer decisions to delegate selection, and the path is rarely simple.

The New Hampshire Primary Iowa is the first-in-the-nation caucus, but New Hampshire is the first-in-the-nation primary. And voting in a primary is much more straightforward than participating in a caucus. Just like in the general election, primary voters go to the polls and vote for a candidate.

For both parties, New Hampshire is a *semi-closed* primary. Independent voters can vote in any party's primary, but voters registered in another party cannot switch on Election Day. So a registered Democrat cannot vote in the Republican primary, but an independent can. This can have an effect on the results if one party's contest is considered more competitive than the other's. In 2000, for example, most political observers correctly saw Al Gore as having the Democratic presidential nomination sewn up, but the Republican contest between George W. Bush and John McCain was fiercely competitive. Independent voters helped tip New Hampshire to McCain, despite the unlikelihood that all of these voters considered themselves Republicans.[5]

Vote counts determine the number of delegates each candidate gets, but, as in Iowa, each party tabulates the results very differently. For the Republicans, delegates are all allocated proportionally. A candidate who wins 20 percent of the vote should get 20 percent of the delegates. However, candidates must get at least 10 percent of the vote to get any delegates. And since there are a finite number of delegates, there must be some rounding. When all of the delegates are allocated, if there are any left over (votes that had been awarded to candidates who didn't get at least 10 percent), those delegates go to whoever came in first.

In 2016, for example, New Hampshire Republicans had 23 delegates at stake (see Table 10.1). With this allocation, three delegates were left over, and they went to Trump as the first-place winner.[6]

TABLE 10.1 Percent of the Vote versus Share of Delegates in the 2016 New Hampshire Republican Primary

	Candidate				
	Donald Trump	John Kasich	Ted Cruz	Jeb Bush	Marco Rubio
Percent of the Vote	35.2	15.7	11.6	11.0	10.5
Share of Delegates	8	4	3	3	2

New Hampshire's Democratic delegate allocation is similar. However, in addition to awarding delegates based on how candidates do statewide, New Hampshire also awards some delegates based on how those candidates do within each congressional district. New Hampshire has two congressional districts. Each gets a third of the pledged delegates awarded in the primary, and the other third is allocated statewide. Some of those statewide (or at-large) delegates are from lists chosen by the candidates, while some are party leaders and elected officials (PLEOs) who are instructed by the party to vote in a particular way. Both of those groups of delegates are selected using the statewide popular vote. New Hampshire also sends some unpledged "superdelegates" to the convention, who are also PLEOs. The Democrats use a 15 percent threshold, rather than the Republicans' 10 percent.

In 2020, the Democrats had 24 delegates from New Hampshire (see Table 10.2). Though every state is different, these sorts of delegate calculations are quite common.

Campaigning in Early States The most significant thing about Iowa and New Hampshire, however, is that since they are the first nominating contests, the candidates can spend a great deal of time there engaging in **retail politics**, which refers to the way in which candidates appeal directly to voters, often

TABLE 10.2 Percent of the Vote versus Share of Delegates in the 2020 New Hampshire Democratic Primary

		Candidate		
		Bernie Sanders	Pete Buttigieg	Amy Klobuchar
Congressional District 1	Percent of Vote	36.3	35.0	28.7
	Share of 8 delegates	2.904	2.801	2.295
	Rounded	3	3	2
Congressional District 2	Percent of Vote	37.3	34.8	27.9
	Share of 8 delegates	2.984	2.784	2.232
	Rounded	3	3	2
Party Leaders & Election Officials	Percent of Vote	36.8	34.9	28.3
	Share of 8 delegates	1.104	1.047	0.849
	Rounded	1	1	1
At-Large	Percent of Vote	36.8	34.9	28.3
	Share of 8 delegates	1.84	1.745	1.414
	Rounded	2	2	1

in one-on-one interactions. But some have pointed out that Iowa and New Hampshire are not representative of the country in terms of race (Iowa and New Hampshire are about 90 percent and 93 percent non-Hispanic White respectively, while the rest of the country is 62 percent non-Hispanic White, according to the 2010 census), proportion of urban population (Iowa and New Hampshire are about 64 percent and 60 percent urban respectively, while the rest of the country is about 81 percent urban, according to the 2010 census), and other measurements. In response to this, both the Republican and the Democratic parties have in recent cycles scheduled Nevada's and South Carolina's contests earlier in the sequence. This helps voters in those more diverse states spend a fair share of time directly with the candidates. In larger turnout elections, or when many primaries are held on the same day, the kind of close interaction that is common in early states is much harder to achieve.

In states with early primaries and caucuses, retail politics becomes incredibly important. Candidates visit local restaurants, schools, and community centers to speak directly with voters. Here, Sen. Elizabeth Warren speaks to customers in the restaurant Milk & Honey in Harlan, Iowa.

Why is retail politics so important in these early states? In a general election, a candidate's party affiliation is critical for voters deciding between candidates. People who generally know what Democrats and Republicans stand for can make some sort of decision about a candidate without knowing much about them. But primary voters don't have the same obvious cues for whom they should vote for, because everyone they can vote for is in the same party. This lack of cues opens up opportunities for candidates who can mount serious direct appeals to voters. In the early contests, candidates crisscross the states, holding rallies, town halls, and other events. Iowa and New Hampshire voters have opportunities to see the candidates up close, which those in most of the rest of the country never will.

At a typical campaign event, held in a school or meeting hall or hotel ballroom, the candidate will deliver a "stump speech," possibly after other local politicians or those traveling with the candidate have also spoken. They usually take questions and stay to take pictures with the voters. The candidate and their team will then board their bus and move on to the next event. Candidates also visit coffee shops and other places, in what is called a "retail stop." Here, candidates shake hands, take questions, and pose for photos but do not give speeches.

Journalists at these events and who often travel with the candidate will write stories covering all of this, but they will have heard the stump speech many times. They will also have heard the candidates' well-worn answers to typical questions. So their coverage will often focus on whatever is new, which may or may not be what the candidates or even the voters are most interested in.

Thus the rallies themselves provide the candidates an opportunity to reach the voters without the filter of the media. A large percentage of interested voters in Iowa and New Hampshire have chances to see presidential candidates in person, or even meet them, take a selfie, and share a few words. That's just not plausible in bigger, more-populous states. By evaluating candidates, learning their strengths and weaknesses, and helping to decide who will survive to face the voters in other states, the voters in early states serve as a kind of representative for the rest of the country.

How Many Delegates Does Each State Get?

After New Hampshire, the process moves to Nevada and South Carolina, and then on to the rest of the country. States determine how they will send their delegates to the convention, but the national party determines how many delegates each state will be able to send.

The simplest way to allocate delegates to each state might be to make each state delegation the same size as (or at least proportional to) the states' congressional delegations, or to the states' number of Electoral College votes. And in fact, in the early days, both parties did something like this. But this method creates a problem. Some states are overwhelmingly Democratic or Republican, regardless of size. In the general election, the Democratic nominee has little hope of winning Oklahoma, and the Republican similarly won't win in Hawaii. If the party wants a candidate who can win in the general election, why let those out-of-reach states have a big say in choosing the nominee?

Candidates who lose in those states don't hesitate to point this out. In 2020, Joe Biden's victory run was set off by a big win in South Carolina's Democratic primary, which had voted almost 55 percent for Trump in the general election four years earlier. Biden's Super Tuesday was punctuated by big wins in Alabama (62 percent Trump in 2016), Arkansas (60 percent), Oklahoma (65 percent), Tennessee (60 percent) and Texas (52 percent). Bernie Sanders supporters complained that those primary victories came in states that the nominee was unlikely to win in the general election. This echoed Sanders camp complaints in 2016 about Hillary Clinton's success in red states.[7] Likewise, some Clinton supporters had complained about Obama winning in red states in 2008.

On the other hand, the primary may be the only place where partisans in deep red or blue states ever get any input into the presidency. African American voters in states like South Carolina are steadfast Democrats,[8] but their state's electoral votes will almost surely go to the Republican candidate. Both parties balance these considerations by giving some but fewer delegates in states they are unlikely to win.

The parties use slightly different formulas to reach the same goal. The Republicans start with proportionality: Each state gets 10 at-large delegates, and then 3 delegates for every seat in the U.S. House of Representatives. The GOP then gives states bonus delegates if they voted Republican in the last presidential election and have Republican-elected officials and state legislatures. The Democrats use a formula based on the state's Democratic vote in the last three election years, weighted by the number of Electoral College votes in those years. In the end, both parties' delegations are larger from large states and from states that tend to vote for the party.

HOW DID THE MIXED SYSTEM DEVELOP?

If this mix of primaries, caucuses, and conventions seems complicated, that's because it is. If it doesn't look like the sort of system that someone would consciously design, that's because it isn't. It has evolved over many decades, usually through different groups within each party seeking to tilt nominations procedures in their direction and other groups trying to counter those tactics.

Before the Mixed System

Before 1968, the Democratic and Republican delegates went to their national conventions with the outcome at least somewhat uncertain; the nominations were typically not yet locked up, and delegates made their choices public there. Those conventions, as we discussed in Chapter 9, evolved as an improvement on letting the party's legislative caucus select the candidate. By the middle of the nineteenth century, both parties had robust national conventions. There, the drama of presidential candidate selection was played out over a few days in large convention halls.

In some years, the decision was fairly straightforward. But in other years, party factions might compete for a long time before a compromise could be found. For example, in 1880, the Republican Party was divided between the two factions called the Stalwarts and the Half-Breeds. The Stalwarts favored a patronage system (by which presidents and other officeholders could reward supporters with government jobs and other benefits), and they wanted former president Ulysses S. Grant as their presidential nominee. The Half-Breeds wanted civil service reform and an end to patronage. Their candidate was James G. Blaine. On the convention's first ballot to select a nominee, Grant received 304 votes to Blaine's 284, with another 167 votes going to four other candidates. Since no candidate had an outright majority (379 votes), no one won. Delegates argued and negotiated, and then they voted again. And again. And again. Over the course of two days, the delegates voted 36 times, with Grant

National conventions can be venues for parties to work out internal conflicts. During the 1880 Republican National Convention (pictured here), with the Republican party split between two candidates, a compromise candidate emerged in James A. Garfield, who went on to be the party's nominee.

usually receiving just over 300 votes and Blaine slightly fewer. Early on the second day, a number of delegates started voting for compromise candidate James A. Garfield. Garfield won the party's nomination on the thirty-sixth ballot.

In some ways, a convention is an ideal battleground for an internal party conflict. The Stalwarts and the Half-Breeds had two days to convince each other of their candidate's merits, and eventually, a compromise was found. But numbers matter. The side with the most delegates will have an upper hand. Both parties generally allow the state party organizations to decide how they would determine who gets to be sent to the national convention. When there are disputes, they are settled at the convention. An argument over whether someone deserves to be a delegate or not is a **credentials fight**. Several state delegations supporting Grant were turned away in disputes over credentials, and rival delegates were seated instead, costing Grant 90 votes.[9] Recall that such decisions by the credentials committee were critical in 1912 as well.

Such politicking increasingly included primaries, but not in the way they are used now. Some delegates were chosen by primaries, but never enough to tip the scales. Most delegates were party officials or were chosen in state party conventions or some other out-of-the-spotlight method. In 1952, for example, Democratic state parties in 14 states selected delegates in a way that was not even nominally open to ordinary rank-and-file partisans. Many states had some mechanisms through which the rank and file could participate, but they were mitigated in some way by party leaders. Often, delegates were chosen more than a year before the convention, long before many supporters of a particular candidate may have thought about getting involved. Only 10 states in 1952 had binding, meaningful primaries that selected pledged delegates for the convention.[10]

Though primary-selected delegates were a minority, primaries still played an important role in the selection process. Candidates would compete in primaries to demonstrate to party leaders their campaign skill and appeal to the party. Then as well as now, party leaders want to know who best represents the party's coalition and who is most electable (see Chapter 9). How the candidates compete in a primary can provide useful information about that question. The few delegates they might pick up in the contest are less important than the signal their victory will send to party leaders and voters around the country. Some states even have primaries that award no delegates. So-called **beauty contest** primaries serve this informational role.

An oft-cited example of the beauty-contest approach came in 1960, when John F. Kennedy was running for the Democratic nomination. Party leaders liked Kennedy, but many were concerned that his Roman Catholicism would scare off voters. Kennedy then won the primary in West Virginia, a state with few Catholics. The small number of delegates he won in West Virginia were of less value than the signal he sent to party leaders that he could win over Protestant voters.

The Origins of the Mixed System

The 1968 Democratic National Convention in Chicago is infamous for the violence that took place outside the meeting hall, but the conflict inside also had far-reaching consequences. In 1968, a number of states selected delegates through primaries, but the majority of those delegates were *ex officio*, meaning that they were local bosses and other party officials who were delegates by virtue of the offices they held.

New York senator Robert F. Kennedy sought to use the primaries in 1968 the way his brother had in 1960—to make a statement. Kennedy and Minnesota senator Eugene McCarthy both ran on opposition to the war in Vietnam. By winning primaries, they could convince party leaders that opposition to the war was a viable position for the party. Between the two of them, an antiwar platform won almost 70 percent of the vote in 15 primaries across the country. This might have indicated that opposition to the war was popular in the party.

But neither Kennedy nor McCarthy was nominated by the party. Robert F. Kennedy was assassinated after winning the California primary in June. Even if he had lived, it is unlikely he would have been nominated.[11] While Kennedy and McCarthy were competing for delegates in primaries, Vice President Hubert H. Humphrey was shoring up support from party leaders and the delegates they had selected outside of the primaries. At the convention in Chicago in the summer of 1968, Humphrey's victory was almost certain.

Neither the protesters outside the convention nor the antiwar politicians inside could do much about Humphrey's nomination. But they were furious that the party had nominated a pro-war candidate who had done so little to win public support, while other candidates had dominated primaries. Their anger and frustration were even more palpable after Humphrey's narrow loss that fall in the general election to Richard Nixon. At that point, worries about the party splitting got the attention of the party leadership.

One task of a national convention is to set the rules for future conventions, and in response to the frustrations with Humphrey's nomination, the party appointed a commission to reform those rules. The Commission on Party Structure and Delegate Selection was chaired first by South Dakota senator George McGovern and then by Minnesota congressman Donald Fraser. The reforms that the commission created are called the **McGovern-Fraser reforms**.

The commission created guidelines designed to make the delegate selection process more open to ordinary party members. Delegates could no longer be simply appointed by party bosses. And delegates could not be required to vote by unit rule, where all the delegates in one state would follow the instructions of a party leader. The commission ended *ex officio* delegates; party leaders would no longer be sent to the convention just because they held a local or state office. The goal was to shift the power away from the party bosses and to the rest of the party. This is different, however, from a shift to the public as a whole. The McGovern-Fraser Commission still imagined that it would be loyal party members participating in the process. They simply wanted to be as inclusive as possible about what it meant to be a party member. Today's debate about open and closed primaries (that is, whether to allow independents or even members of other parties to participate in a party primary) would have been foreign to them, as they most certainly thought that the question was how to include party members, not just anyone.

The commission did not define the precise reforms that each state would implement to address these problems; such decisions were left up to the Democratic parties in each state. Many party leaders believed that the ideal model would be to make party conventions more open to a wider range of participants, and also to create party caucuses.[12] Such a caucus would amount to face-to-face meetings among local party-loyal activists. Party leaders also hoped that these caucuses would select a more diverse set of convention delegates. But such caucuses can be expensive to organize. The easiest and cheapest way to satisfy the requirements was through primaries, especially if conducted by the state government. In the early 1970s, most state legislatures were controlled by Democrats. When the Democrats moved to create primaries, they did so through the state legislatures. As a result, the new rules initiated by the McGovern-Fraser reforms applied to Republicans and third parties as well. Thus the presidential nomination system was transformed for both major parties, even though the changes were largely designed to address the experiences of the Democrats between 1968 and 1972.

The consequences of these reforms were surprising. In 1972, George McGovern, who obviously knew what the reforms required, won his party's nomination. But by 1976, many Democrats still didn't completely understand the new rules. Most candidates still competed only where they expected to do well and bowed out of states where they thought they might suffer an embarrassing loss. Only Georgia governor Jimmy Carter competed in every primary that year. What's more, Carter focused his preconvention campaign in Iowa, before the caucuses there. Carter didn't win the Iowa caucuses, "uncommitted" did. But Carter did better than any other candidate, and he did much better than anyone thought he would.

Carter's unexpected victory brought a shower of media attention and a similar shower of campaign donations, which Carter leveraged into a narrow victory in the first primary of the season, in New Hampshire. Carter went on to parlay that victory into more attention, and since he was competing in every primary, he was picking up delegates at every chance. He went to the convention with a majority and was nominated, eventually defeating Republican incumbent Gerald Ford to win the presidency in November.

Political scientists and journalists sometimes call the phenomenon Carter experienced **momentum**.[13] A candidate does well in early contests and is rewarded with media attention and increased fund-raising ability, which makes it easier to win the next contests. Those wins lead to still more attention. As the contest goes on, it gets easier and easier for them. Morris Udall, one of Carter's rivals in 1976, famously complained about the dynamic:

> It's like a football game in which you say to the first team that makes a first down with ten yards: Hereafter your team has a special rule. Your first downs are five yards. And if you make three of those you get a two-yard first down. And we're going to let your first touchdown count twenty-one points. Now the rest of you bastards play catch-up under the regular rules.

Carter rode momentum to the nomination in 1976, but no presidential candidate has had it quite that easy since. Carter was not part of the Washington establishment and didn't even have many ties to it, and it didn't take long for party insiders to worry about a system that nominated someone like Carter. In 1980, President Carter faced a primary challenge from Edward Kennedy, and before 1984, the Democrats revisited their new rules. A commission headed by North Carolina governor James Hunt reintroduced *ex officio* delegates, calling them **superdelegates**.

Superdelegates were meant to solve two problems. First and most importantly, the party aimed to avoid having a candidate who could win by virtue of momentum—and thus be able to win the nomination unchecked. Democratic party leaders felt that in a close contest, allowing some of their own to weigh in could correct a nomination cycle that had gone astray. But in no year have superdelegates overturned the result of the primaries. In 1984, 2008, and 2016, they could have, as the race was close enough that their numbers would have mattered. But in all three years, they went along with the choice of the primary process. Superdelegates are, after all, mostly politicians, and few of them are willing to vote against what primary voters—their most active partisans—clearly want. Doing so is a recipe for a short political career.

Superdelegates did, however, solve the problem of elected officials having to compete to become delegates. If all delegates are chosen by voters, elected officeholders and party officials would also need to stand for election in order to go to the convention. Presumably, most would be able to win, but it put them in the awkward position of competing against constituents. Allowing leaders to go to the convention as superdelegates untied to a candidate eliminated that problem.

As the rationale for superdelegates faded into history, though, their role in the nomination process appeared increasingly undemocratic. The clear message from the voters is what should matter, not decisions by party elites. In the 2016 presidential nomination, losing candidate Senator Bernie Sanders (D-VT) complained that the existence of the superdelegates helped create an air of inevitability around his opponent, contributing to Clinton's decisive convention victory. While Clinton would have won the nomination without superdelegates, party leaders decided to address the perception that superdelegates could undermine the outcome of the primaries. Some activists wanted the party to get rid of superdelegates altogether, while others pointed to the problems they were meant to solve. As a compromise, the party stripped superdelegates of their first vote in the process. They would only have a formal say if no candidate could win on the first ballot. In 2020 Joe Biden had enough delegates to win on the first ballot, so superdelegates played no formal role in the selection of Biden as the Democratic nominee.

This sort of tinkering has been the norm for both parties. Today, the states have a mix of institutions for selecting delegates, but that mix leans more heavily on primaries and other methods open to ordinary voters.

The Consequences of Reform The parties regularly adjust their rules when they lose an election or experience a divisive nomination battle—leaders are always trying to learn the lesson of the most recent election. The system emerging from the McGovern-Fraser reforms of the early 1970s has been thought to actually undermine the ability of the party to choose a candidate according to the criteria we described in Chapter 9. This was not exactly what reformers intended. They expected more input from rank-and-file party members, but they did not expect the rest of the party to become marginalized. But the conventional wisdom has been that it was. Why?

First, the reformed system shifts the decision away from the party leaders to ordinary party voters. Party leaders will naturally prefer not to lose power. We will address this consequence below. But regardless of who is in power, some observers worry that a system that allows candidates to pick up momentum from an early victory and ride it to the nomination favors the wrong kinds of candidates.

Second, the outcome of the race might hinge on a lucky win early in the primary season. Even if voters don't care about the party's criteria for choosing a nominee, most of them probably want a candidate who has been vetted in some way. An unknown candidate who can win an early contest and then leap to an insurmountable lead would be a problem. An early win usually means a win in Iowa or New Hampshire, which are, as we noted earlier, unlike the rest of the country. Neither state has many non-White voters, and neither has a large metropolitan city, though some political scientists argue that these states are more like the rest of the country than many believe.[14]

Third, the system might be especially bad for finding a candidate who is broadly acceptable within the party. Political scientist Nelson Polsby, in his book *Consequences of Party Reform* (1983), predicted that the post-reform system would favor a narrowly factional candidate with enthusiastic supporters. Early contests tend to feature many candidates, since few have yet dropped out due to their lack of success. When there are many candidates, one only needs a small but loyal fraction of the party to "win." The first-place candidate in a field of a half-dozen candidates might have less than 30 percent of the vote. And while such a narrow win might not garner the candidate many delegates in that state, the increased media attention and fund-raising ability will help them in later primaries. Thus a candidate with relatively narrow initial appeal may end up being nominated. That's not a candidate who is acceptable to all factions. It's a candidate who is loved by just one or a few.[15]

Finally, although leaders in both parties worried about whether candidates in this new system could appeal to all factions, leaders were more troubled about the nature of primary contests. A candidate in a primary can appeal directly to voters. Some were concerned this meant candidates could win delegates early without ever building good relationships with party leaders. Again, Carter was a warning sign for the Democratic Party on this. He was not well known by party leaders, and once elected, he was not well loved by them. Some believe that the reason Carter struggled in his relationship with the Democrat-controlled Congress and had so few legislative accomplishments during his term was that he had little experience working with his national party before being elected.

Not all of the fears and predictions of scholars like Polsby have come to pass. Since 1980, candidates nominated for president by both parties have not generally been factional candidates supported by a narrow but passionate minority. Instead, they have looked very much like the kinds of candidates that might have been selected in the pre-reform system. But there have been exceptions, the most obvious being 2016 Republican nominee Donald Trump.

Momentum, too, has rarely been as dramatic as it was for Carter. Even when a candidate wins a surprise victory in the Iowa caucuses, such as John Kerry in 2004 and Barack Obama in 2008, they have generally not seen a huge surge in support beyond their showing in Iowa. In 2008, Obama stunned Hillary Clinton in Iowa, only to lose to Clinton in the New Hampshire primary five days later. The two candidates seesawed all the way up to the convention. Few would say that Obama had it easy because of his win in Iowa. In 2020, Bernie Sanders tied or won the first three contests, but no momentum developed for him, and Joe Biden secured the nomination after winning in South Carolina and then most Super Tuesday states. If there is momentum, it is rare. In most contests, the candidate expected to win before the primaries and caucuses begin ends up winning.[16]

FEATURES OF THE MIXED SYSTEM

Reflecting on the history of the nomination process reminds us of what many commentators overlook: the nomination is ultimately made at the convention, and that means what matters is who is sent to the convention, not who wins the most votes in the primaries. The current mixed system now has several features, some of which were not necessarily imagined by the reformers who put the system in place.

The Invisible Primary

From the point of view of an ambitious politician, the quest to become the president begins long before the Iowa caucuses. Politicians begin lining up support from key party leaders and donors years before the contest begins. From the point of view of party leaders and activists trying to choose a nominee, the job is to sort through the various potential candidates, perhaps encouraging some to run and discouraging others.

This process is called the **invisible primary**. The start and end dates of the invisible primary are vague, but it generally begins right after the previous presidential election and ends just before the Iowa caucuses, when voters and caucus-goers begin to weigh in. It's said to be invisible because it is not formally scheduled and contains no actual voting, but in fact, it takes place in plain view. Candidates visit potential party leaders, hold fund-raisers, and announce exploratory committees, allowing them to raise money and attract media attention (see Figure 10.1). They attend state fairs and party fund-raisers in attempts to get the attention and consideration of active party members. Eventually, they formally announce their candidacy and begin participating in debates. For the 2012 nomination, Republican presidential hopefuls participated in 13 debates in 2011, before the Iowa caucuses. Democrats participated in seven debates prior to the 2020 Iowa caucuses.

Local party leaders also attempt to influence voters directly through campaign appearances and endorsements, and there is evidence that this kind of influence works. Primary electorates are made up of voters who identify with the party, but they also include many independent voters, who, in several states, can participate in primary elections if they wish. The authors of *The Party Decides* compared the voting choices of party-loyal voters with those of independent voters.[17] Independent voters' choices were unrelated to party elite preferences, but party-loyal voters followed the elites. Since primaries consist mostly of party-loyal voters, the elite preferences get expressed in the primary. The authors also controlled for other possible explanations of primary voter choices, such as media coverage and fund-raising, and even early popularity and name recognition, as reflected in early poll results. The impact of endorsements remained important.

Still, it is possible that party leaders are just really good at jumping on the bandwagon of candidates who would win anyway. Endorsements do not appear to be driven by early polls, media coverage, or fund-raising, but party leaders may still be able to anticipate who will become popular.

The invisible primary shapes the contest before it even begins. This tends to blunt the effects of momentum. Since 1980, the candidate leading in endorsements before the Iowa caucuses has tended to win. Even when a candidate with few endorsements has won Iowa, they have not received the kind of boost that Carter did in 1976 (Democrat Pete Buttigieg in 2020, for example). The candidate who wins the invisible primary and garners the most endorsements usually does very well in the more visible state primaries and caucuses.

Front-Loading

Another reason that momentum has been blunted recently is that there is less time for it to play out. Over the last four decades, the primary calendar has gradually compressed. This compression is typically referred to as **front-loading**. In 1976, when Carter won by competing in every contest, only one primary was held as early as February, and most were held after the end of March. In

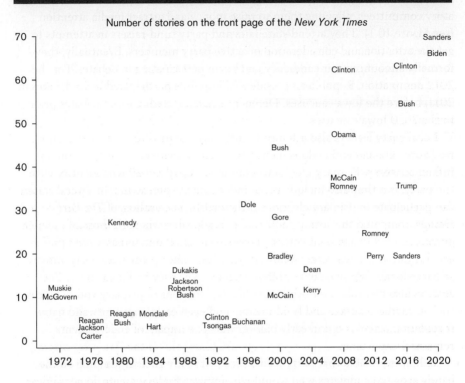

FIGURE 10.1   News Stories and Fundraising During the Invisible Primary

Number of stories on the front page of the *New York Times*

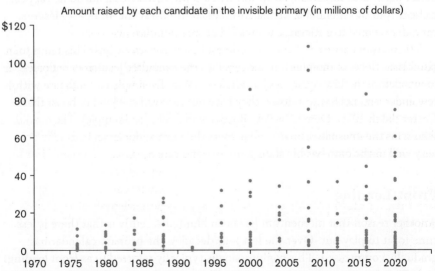

Amount raised by each candidate in the invisible primary (in millions of dollars)

Source: Martin Cohen, David Karol, Hans Noel and John Zaller, "The Party No Longer Decides." *Politico.* Feb. 20, 2020. www.politico.com/interactives/2020/the-new-rules-of-campaigning-in-2020; Marty Cohen, David Karol, Hans Noel, and John Zaller, "Party Versus Faction in the Reformed Presidential Nominating System," *PS: Political Science & Politics* 49 (Special Issue 4): 701-08, 2015. Reproduced with permission.

contrast, in 2020, thirty-two states held a primary or caucus before the end of March.

Front-loading occurs in part because the party is concerned about momentum. Since early delegate contests are thought to matter more than late ones, each state wants to hold its contest earlier and earlier, in order to shape that momentum. Even laying aside momentum itself, primaries held late in the season often do not matter, because by then a candidate will have secured enough delegates to win the nomination. A state's influence on the race decreases the later it holds its primary or caucus. Since each state organizes its own primary, each state also gets to decide (with some constraints) when to hold its primary. The consequence has been the pattern you see in Figure 10.2.

Figure 10.2 shows the compression that has generally taken place since the 1980s, but the peak of front-loading actually occurred in 2008. Some party leaders have become concerned about front-loading, and so have worked to push the calendar back. Parties have set rules protecting the status of Iowa and New Hampshire as first in the nation. In 2008, Florida and Michigan scheduled their primaries earlier than the Democratic Party would allow, and the party punished those states by stripping them of their delegates. They later compromised and seated the delegates, but allowed each of them only half a vote on the convention floor.[18]

The consequences of front-loading are not clear. Some scholars believe that front-loading means that the candidates are not properly vetted by voters. The compression also means that many primaries are held on the same day, forcing candidates to travel over a variety of states. (This can actually mean that *more* voters play a role in vetting the candidates.)[19] Simultaneous primaries favor candidates who can spend lots of money in lots of places at the same time—that is, candidates who have already raised a lot of money or are just wealthy.

While state parties are eager to influence momentum early, front-loading can also blunt momentum. The rush to primaries has resulted in a crowded calendar in which no one state has much of an effect. There is simply less time to capitalize on early surprise victories before the next contests. In 1976, when Jimmy Carter shocked the country with his surprise showing in Iowa, New Hampshire's first-in-the-nation primary was more than a month later. In 2020, there were only eight days between them. Front-loading also makes the invisible primary more important, because party leaders and voters alike have less time to change their preferences after the results of early contests are known. Part of why the contests can be so predictable is precisely because they are over so quickly.

FIGURE 10.2   Front-Loading in State Primaries

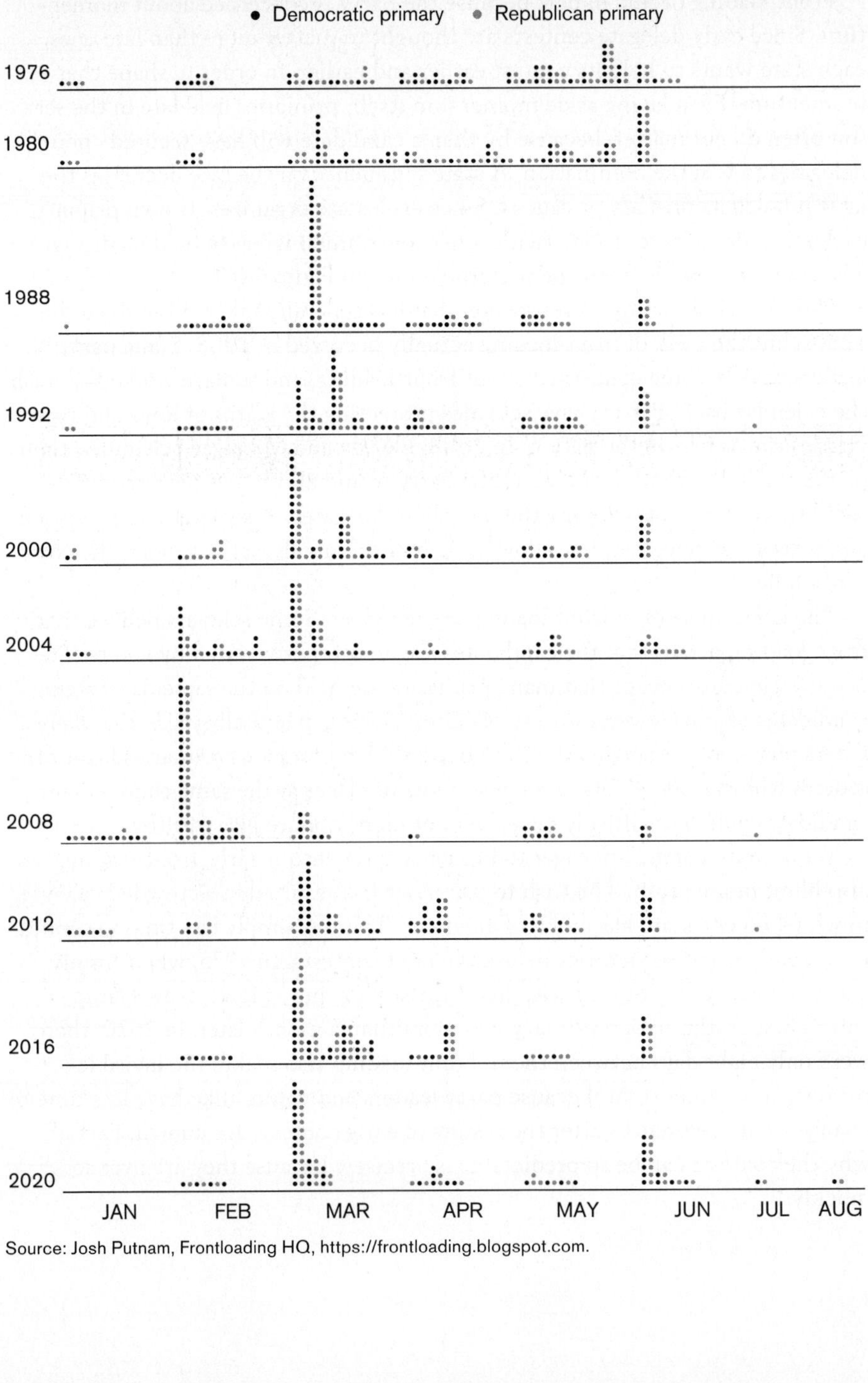

Source: Josh Putnam, Frontloading HQ, https://frontloading.blogspot.com.

POLITICAL SCIENCE TOOLKIT
Measuring Party Support in the Invisible Primary

During the invisible primary, candidates attract donors and campaign staff. They also attract the support of party leaders. Those leaders no longer choose the nominee outright at the convention, but they still matter. In their book *The Party Decides: Presidential Nominations Before and After Reform*, political scientists Marty Cohen, David Karol, Hans Noel, and John Zaller show that candidates who win the support of party leaders do better in the primaries than those who do not. The figures below show the breakdown of party leader endorsements from year to year, with the eventual winner in black.

Party Leader Endorsements and Eventual Winners

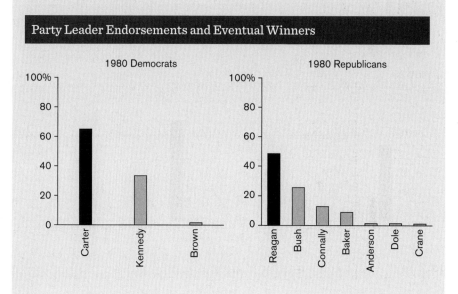

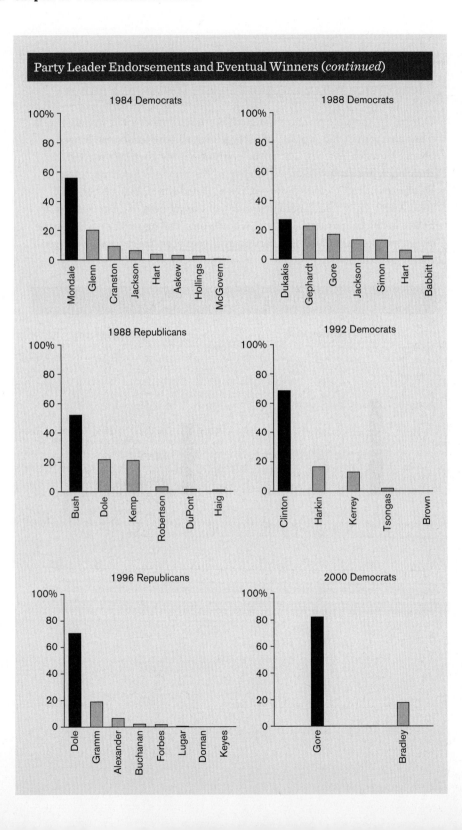

Party Leader Endorsements and Eventual Winners (*continued*)

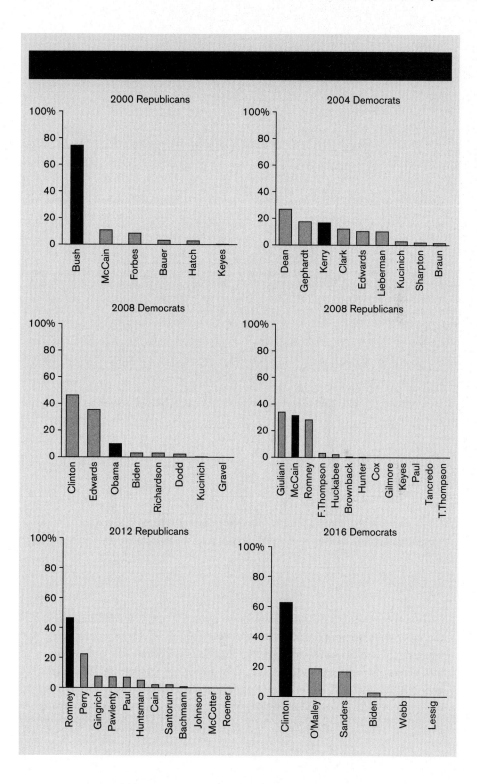

2000 Republicans

2004 Democrats

2008 Democrats

2008 Republicans

2012 Republicans

2016 Democrats

Party Leader Endorsements and Eventual Winners (*continued*)

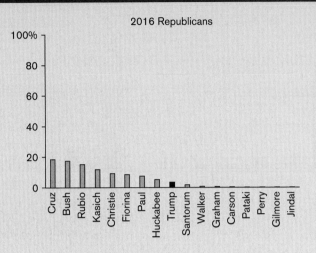

2016 Republicans

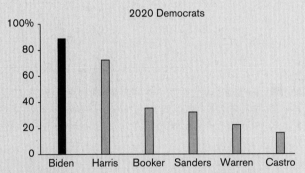

2020 Democrats

Source: Martin Cohen, David Karol, Hans Noel, and John Zaller, *The Party Decides: Presidential Nominations Before and After Reform* (Chicago: University of Chicago Press. 2008). Authors' calculations.

Two things should be clear from these figures. First, the candidate with the most endorsements usually wins. Aside from the first few contests, when party leaders were still figuring out the new system, the only examples where this was not the case are 2004 and 2008 among the Democrats and in 2008 and 2016 among the Republicans. In each of those four cases, the party was divided, and many party leaders were hesitant to participate at all. Second, in most years, the candidate who received the most endorsements shows an overwhelming advantage. Contests like the 1988 Democratic race, where support was spread across a number of candidates, are rare.

Since many of the contests in which the party has failed to decide have been in recent years, it is possible that the influence party leaders once held is eroding. For every success that party insiders have like the nomination of Hillary Clinton in 2016, there is a failure like the nomination of Trump in the same year.

In addition to there being simple irreconcilable differences among different party factions, a variety of other factors may make it harder for the party to coordinate.[20] There are many more debates, especially before the voting occurs, than there were in the past. And due to heavy media coverage of the invisible primary, increased party and campaign visibility actually makes it harder for party leaders to coordinate and allows primary voters more influence in the process.

There have been other important changes to American elections in recent years that make party coordination challenging. For one thing, campaign finance rules have evolved rapidly. Candidates can now create independent Super PACs (a type of political action committee with unlimited fundraising and spending abilities, which we describe further in Chapter 11) that can keep them funded throughout the race. Party leaders may wish to persuade a candidate to step aside, but if a candidate has independent funding and an independent following generated by media attention and success in the debates, they may not listen. Candidates who compete in the primaries today are precisely those who thrive under that kind of attention.

Cohen and his coauthors argue that the unity behind a candidate reflects an attempt to find a nominee who is acceptable to all factions in the party. When the party is unable to do that, then the party's support is of less value. But when the party can coordinate, they can help their candidate win. In this way, the party leaders seize back some of the influence they once had at the convention.

Party leaders also need to exert that influence through the primaries and caucuses. To do that, they need ways of affecting the voters. Some of that is through campaign resources. To win in state after state, a candidate needs to build a campaign organization in each state. That is easier when local party leaders are on the candidate's side.

Changing Rules

How front-loaded the system is changes from cycle to cycle, as the party leaders make adjustments to the rules in the hopes of making it easier for the kind of candidates they want to win. Party leaders try to influence the outcome, and different groups within the party can compete over rules that they think will advantage their faction.

For example, a series of winner-take-all states at the beginning of the primaries will quickly tilt the result in favor of the early winner, who is likely to have been the pre-Iowa front-runner. In 2008, the Republican Party used winner-take-all in many states and nominated John McCain, who lost in the general election. Some party leaders felt that the process yielded a victor too quickly, and noted that the Democratic contest that year between Clinton and Obama endured all throughout the spring and still produced a winning ticket and an engaged and unified party base. The Republican National Committee decided that any state holding a primary or caucus before April 1 would need to use proportional representation (PR) in 2012, to slow things down. That worked—perhaps too well. In 2012, Mitt Romney began as the insider choice, but his rivals were able to stay in the race much longer, due to the PR rules in many states. Eventually, Romney secured the Republican nomination, but party leaders felt that decision took too long. They responded by scheduling the 2016 Republican National Convention earlier in the summer, to compress the schedule from the end. But in 2016, party outsider Donald Trump was in the lead when the race reached the end of the proportional representation states and started the winner-take-all states. This switch worked as intended, pushing the leader to victory, but Trump was not the candidate party leaders had expected to be in that position.

WHO IS IN CHARGE OF PRESIDENTIAL NOMINATIONS?

As we have seen, the process by which the major parties choose their nominees for the presidency in the United States has undergone a number of changes. Some of these have been driven by a desire to make the process more effective at meeting the criteria of the party, while other changes have been driven by pressure to make the system more open to people other than party leaders.

This conflict deserves attention. It is a different sort of conflict from what we usually think about when we think about presidential nominations. Typically, we think about presidential nominations from the point of view of ambitious politicians angling for the office. Did Sanders in 2020 build on his position from 2016? How did Trump best a field of established Republicans in

2016? But in this chapter, we have focused instead on the point of view of the party. Whom does the Democratic Party want? Whom does the Republican Party want? But the party, we have to remember, has many components. It has party leaders, who are concerned about policy but perhaps more concerned about winning office. And the party has activists, who may care more about policy than about electability. Changes in the nomination rules shift the balance of power among these groups.

Changes in the rules also bring in other voters, including those "less active" activists who can participate in primaries and caucuses but tend not to become involved in all the other activities discussed in Chapter 8. It brings in voters who are not strongly loyal to the parties. Their participation can make it harder for party leaders and party activists to sort out the different goals we discussed in Chapter 9. It is difficult enough for seasoned party actors to balance electability and policy goals. On the other hand, it is hard to argue that involving more people in the selection of the presidential candidates is not more democratic.

Involving more people could also influence the outcome. The post-reform system became more open to activists who were further outside the party. Before the reforms, labor unions had a huge say in the Democratic Party. After the reforms, ideological activists who had little history in the party had a way to express their opinions. Byron Shafer, chronicler of the reforms, notes that this change in the people who can participate has meant that a candidate who appeals to ideological activists has a better shot than one who appeals to union leaders.[21]

Too much influence from party insiders and too much influence from unaffiliated voters both have pitfalls, as the 2016 nominations highlighted. The Republican Party nominated someone disliked by party leaders—Donald Trump. The Democratic Party nominated someone favored by party leaders—Hillary Clinton. And yet reaction from many in the country was dissatisfaction with the process and with the nominee on both sides.

Republicans got a candidate who not only was widely viewed as inexperienced and temperamentally unfit, but also did not support many key party principles. If the party wants the most loyal, most ideologically agreeable candidate who can also win, Trump was neither, or so it seemed at the time of his nomination. It is hard to argue that a party with more control over its nomination process would have nominated Trump.

Hillary Clinton, on the other hand, was just about perfect as a loyal, ideologically agreeable Democratic politician, and most Democrats felt she had a better shot at winning than any of the other candidates running for the nomination. Her preferences and allegiances put her squarely within the Democratic Party. But that is a party that many left-leaning activists were—and continue to be—frustrated with. As ideological activists made huge gains within the Republican

Party, liberal Democrats felt left behind by a compromising Democratic president. Clinton was squarely within the Democratic Party, but she had to be pulled along as the party shifted to the left. For some, she had not moved far enough.

Influencing the party from within like this can be the best way for activists who do not like either party to have their say in our two-party system. They cannot easily create a new third party, but they can join one of the existing parties and begin trying to change it. Pressuring the Democratic Party is really the only option liberals have. And since nominations are one of the places that are most open to influence from rank-and-file activists, nominations are where that conflict will most likely play out. It is no surprise, then, that nominations became the focus of debate again in 2020, when Bernie Sanders again competed for the nomination, this time against a larger field of candidates representing a wider range of positions from within the party. We expect the same in both parties in 2024 and beyond.

Discussion Questions

1. This chapter describes the different methods that state parties use to select delegates for presidential nominations, including primaries, caucuses, and conventions. Which do you think tends to produce the best nominees? Why?

2. The Iowa caucuses traditionally receive a great deal of media attention, with hundreds of national reporters spending weeks in Iowa prior to the event itself. Is this attention justified in your opinion? Why or why not?

3. Why do some object to the Iowa caucuses and New Hampshire primary going first in the selection of presidential nominees? What might be a good argument in favor of such a system?

4. What is the "mixed system" of presidential nominations that emerged after 1968? How has that mixture changed in the past half century?

5. In 2020, Joe Biden came in fourth in the Iowa caucuses and fifth in the New Hampshire primary, yet he arguably won the "invisible primary," and he went on to become the Democratic nominee. To what extent did the party leaders pick him in advance, or did the party's voters do that?

11

The Party in General Elections

After the November 2020 presidential election, most political attention in the United States moved to Donald Trump's attempts to overturn his loss to Joe Biden. Trump and his allies claimed there was voter fraud in several states that Trump lost, including Georgia.

But there was another reason the major political parties had Georgia on their minds. On January 5, 2021, Georgians were voting in high-profile elections for two U.S. Senate seats, the result of an odd set of circumstances.

It's rare for a state to have two simultaneous Senate elections. Each state has two senators, but their six-year terms are staggered so that they stand for reelection in different years. Republican senator Kelly Loeffler had been appointed to the position in 2019 by Governor Brian Kemp after the previous incumbent, Johnny Isakson, had resigned for health reasons. That meant Loeffler had to stand for reelection at the next general election if she wanted to continue in office. Meanwhile, Georgia's other senator, Republican David Perdue, had come to the end of his six-year term in 2020 and was running again.

Georgia also has unusual election laws. If no candidate receives a majority of the vote, the top two vote-getters go to a runoff election. As it happened, both Georgia Senate races in 2020 had other candidates in the November election

HEALTH. JOBS. JUSTICE.
WARNOCK × OSSOFF

After the 2020 elections, control of the United States Senate was up in the air as both Senate seat races in Georgia headed to runoff elections. A contentious election in early January amid unrest over the outcome of the presidential election saw both Democratic candidates, Jon Ossoff (left) and Raphael Warnock (right), elected to the Senate from Georgia.

who drew just enough votes to keep the major party candidate under 50 percent. Both races went to a runoff.

Most critically, the two Georgia races would determine the balance of power for the new Senate. Should both contests go to the Democrats, there would be 50 Democrats and 50 Republicans, and with Vice President Kamala Harris casting tie-breaking votes, Democrats would functionally be the majority party in the Senate (as well as controlling the House and the Presidency). Should Republicans retain just one of these Senate seats, however, they would maintain control of the Senate and thus would maintain a substantial check on any Democratic agenda for Biden's first term.

The November elections had kept the major parties busy across the country, with funding and personnel and effort scattered in multiple congressional, state, and local campaigns, as well as the presidential contest. But with those other contests resolved after November 3 (and the presidential contest being called on November 7), the parties trained their efforts on the Georgia runoffs, scheduled for January 5.

Throughout the runoff period, the contests looked extremely close. Loeffler's Democratic opponent was Raphael Warnock, the senior pastor of the Ebenezer Baptist Church in Atlanta since 2005. Perdue, meanwhile, drew as his opponent Jon Ossoff, a young journalist who had run for U.S. Representative in a 2017 special election and come within a few points of winning. Polls consistently showed these races tied right up until the day of the runoffs. And Biden had defeated Trump in the state by only about 12,000 votes. The once reliably Republican state had become a tossup.

All these factors conspired to make these the most expensive Senate races in history. Between candidates and party-affiliated groups, some $470 million was spent on the Perdue-Ossoff race, and another $363 million on the Loeffler-Warnock race. The national parties themselves, including the Democratic Senatorial Campaign Committee, the Republican National Senatorial Committee, the DNC, the RNC, and other organizations devoted tens of millions of dollars to these contests. And the contests themselves turned heavily on major national issues, including the COVID-19 pandemic and relief efforts, Trump's efforts to overturn his loss to Biden, a presidential veto of a major defense bill, and the competing visions of the parties for governance.

For all the reasons outlined above, elections like these are not typical. Still, the two Georgia Senate runoffs provide numerous examples of the sorts of things parties typically do in a general election.

This chapter will examine these sorts of activities and the influence they have—and don't have—over election outcomes. We'll talk about the difference between candidate-centered and party-centered campaigns, as well as the resources candidates need to be competitive in elections and the role parties have often played in providing those resources. We'll look at the importance of campaign finance and the fundraising tools candidates and parties use today. We'll also examine the contributions of parties by looking at some side-by-side examples of elections with parties and elections without them. The final section of the chapter will go through some modern examples of campaigns that illustrate the various roles, both subtle and unsubtle, that parties play.

CANDIDATE-CENTERED VERSUS PARTY-CENTERED POLITICS

In the example of the Georgia Senate runoffs described above, who do you think was in charge of the events in the campaign? Did the parties structure the events, determining who got to run in the election and what sorts of resources they had? Or were the candidates basically in charge of their own fates?

Whether American politics is candidate- or party-driven is a long-standing debate in American political science. Political scientists and historians generally agree that the nineteenth and early twentieth centuries saw a more party-centered version of American politics than we see today. At that time, as we've discussed in other chapters, state and local party organizations were quite strong and would recruit candidates to run for office and often provide the staff and funding those candidates needed. Candidates weren't unimportant, and presidential candidates could certainly be influential if they had some national name recognition, but generally it was parties doing the organizing.

By the middle of the twentieth century, as we saw in Chapter 6, urban party machines were in substantial decline and didn't have the budgets or personnel to be as influential as they had been previously. What's more, this time period saw the advent of television, which had two important effects. First, TV created a more intimate style of campaigning, allowing candidates to appeal directly to voters without them having to leave their homes and dramatically increasing candidates' name recognition. Candidates became far less reliant upon intermediaries, like party bosses, to campaign for them and arrange venues for campaigning. Second, television dramatically increased the costs of campaigning due to the price of TV advertising time. With party funds contracting, candidates were now dependent on donors for this support, and they began to cultivate this support themselves.

The era also saw the rise of political consulting. To be sure, the world had seen political consultants and campaign managers before the 1950s—one could count James Farley (who engineered Franklin Roosevelt's nomination in 1932), Marcus Hanna (who ran William McKinley's campaign in 1896), or even Niccolò Machiavelli (who advised Florentine rulers during the Renaissance) as campaign consultants. Some consider Quintus Cicero, who wrote a book on electioneering in 63 B.C.E. to help get his brother Marcus elected as a Roman consul, to be the very first political consultant. But by the mid–twentieth century, the consultant role had become a formal position. Its modern incarnation emerged in 1930s California, which had a historically weak formal party structure and a reliable stream of initiative and referendum votes.[1]

Professional political consulting expanded its legitimacy during the 1952 presidential campaign when Republicans hired Madison Avenue advertising executives to sell Dwight Eisenhower as a presidential candidate.[2] Consulting grew substantially in the 1950s, with one study showing that, by 1957, some 60 percent of public relations firms had a political account, and many of those had essentially complete control over their contracted campaigns.[3] By 1969, there were enough full-time professionals in the field—consulting on general campaign goals or working in more specific areas such as media management and fundraising—to organize the American Association of Political Consultants. Today, that organization has over 1,300 members.[4]

Political observers at midcentury tended to describe the American political system as candidate-centered rather than party-centered. Parties no longer seemed to have the ability to control events. If candidates could just raise money through their own independent sources and use that money to buy all the exposure, voter contact, and expertise they needed, then maybe candidates really could control the system.

As we have argued at several points in this textbook, the strength that parties convey really depends a lot on how you define a party. In our view, a lot of the actors normally considered "independent" are really parts of the informal party. Political consultants, in particular, are highly partisan creatures. Although they are sometimes depicted in fiction and news accounts as just going where the money is, they tend to be highly loyal to one political party, even if they'll work for multiple candidates within that party.[5] (Dick Morris, who worked for Bill Clinton in the 1990s and later became a Republican consultant, is a very rare exception.) Consultants can thus connect candidates in the same way that a formal party might, allowing them to share ideas and campaign tactics within a party coalition. Donors also tend to be very party loyal, as do the interest groups that often help candidates.

If we view parties as expanded networks of political actors, including interest groups, donors, and political consultants who are highly party loyal, we see that parties are actually intensely involved in modern electoral campaigns and play prominent roles in running them. Candidates certainly have some choices, but most campaigning takes place within a framework that has been established and is largely mapped out by political parties.

THE ROLE OF MONEY IN CAMPAIGNS

Late-nineteenth-century political guru Marcus Hanna is credited with saying, "There are two things that are important in politics. The first is money, and I can't remember what the second one is."[6] Indeed, it's difficult to ignore the political importance of money; campaigns without it rarely go anywhere, while campaigns with it are at least taken seriously. And one of the ways parties have exerted control over nominations and politicians' careers over the centuries is through their consolidation, centralization, and allocation of campaign money.

We discussed the role of money in campaigns in Chapter 7 ("Formal Party Organizations"). Campaign finance is obviously an issue of vital importance. However, people both overestimate and underestimate its role in politics. They overestimate it because the amount of money spent on campaigns seems so large, it's hard to believe it's not a major factor. Table 11.1 shows expenditures in federal elections over the past two decades. In 2020, $7.6 billion was spent on federal elections, with around $4 billion of that going to the presidential race. House and Senate races can vary a great deal in expense because races in some states and districts simply aren't very competitive and thus don't cost as much to run. But the most competitive elections can see an enormous amount of spending. Over $37 million was spent in New Mexico's 2nd district, and another $34 million in Texas's 22nd.

It's good to keep these numbers in context. For example, Coca-Cola—just one company—spent $4 billion worldwide on advertising in 2020, about the same amount as all congressional candidates for office combined spent that year. That said, a large sum of money is spent on campaigns every election cycle. The

TABLE 11.1	Expenditures in Federal Elections since 1998 (in billions of dollars)

Year	Total Cost	Congressional Races	Presidential Race
2020	7.6	3.7	3.9
2018	5.7	5.7	
2016	6.5	4.1	2.4
2014	3.8	3.8	
2012	6.3	3.7	2.6
2010	3.6	3.6	
2008	5.3	2.5	2.8
2006	2.9	2.9	
2004	4.1	2.2	1.9
2002	2.2	2.2	
2000	3.1	1.7	1.4
1998	1.6	1.6	

Source: Center for Responsive Politics, "Cost of Elections," www.opensecrets.org/elections-overview/cost-of -election (accessed 1/6/20).

magnitude of these numbers can lead people to believe that money is the most important thing in a campaign. But is it? The biggest spenders don't necessarily win. Donald Trump defeated Hillary Clinton in 2016 despite being massively outspent by her. Michael Bloomberg spent roughly a billion dollars during the early primaries of the 2020 Democratic presidential race—far more than any other candidate—and the only contest he won was the American Samoa caucuses. Nor did Tom Steyer's hundreds of millions of dollars in advertising garner him many votes in 2020. As noted, a lot of money is spent in congressional campaigns as well, but most of it by incumbents facing tough reelections; they tend to lose or win by slender margins despite the huge expenditures. Generally, while political scientists recognize the importance of money in elections, they have a difficult time proving that money *causes* an election to go a certain way.

But we can also underestimate the importance of money. While money doesn't necessarily determine the winner, money is necessary to run in the election in the first place. Spending creates name recognition, which is vitally important for a candidate starting out in politics. The ability to raise money is also an important signal to party leaders and other political actors that a candidate has some political skills. A candidate needn't be a millionaire to be taken seriously, but it certainly helps to be able to raise money.

What forms does campaign finance take? This is an increasingly complex area of the campaign world, as new laws have brought about innovative ways for money to travel from donors to candidates. Below, we outline some financial tools available to candidates for office.

Campaign finance tools can seem complicated because they have evolved in response to a number of political reforms emanating from both the courts and the legislatures. These reforms have often been designed to prevent some kinds of groups from acting politically, or to limit the influence of money in politics. Before the 1960s, for example, it was possible for a party organization to largely fund and staff a candidacy on its own. However, a series of civil service reforms deprived formal parties of the ability to do this. Campaign finance reforms enacted in the 1970s limited the abilities of a few wealthy individuals or groups to finance a campaign, so these jobs had to be outsourced further. The Bipartisan Campaign Finance Reform Act of 2002 and several other near-simultaneous state-level reforms limited the abilities of parties and donors to directly support campaigns, and the system evolved further in response to that, developing new financing organizations.

Nearly all these reforms have been done with the intent of reducing corruption—limiting the ability of a group or individual to directly support a campaign in a way that the candidate would feel obligated to repay that group or individual once in office. They've also been structured with the intent of limiting money or driving it out of politics altogether. Yet money has proven very adaptive. Decades of reform haven't reduced the role of money or political favors—they've just made it harder to track.

Political Action Committees (PACs)

The Federal Elections Campaign Act, passed in 1971 and later amended in 1974, is the first modern federal campaign legislation, and it is the backbone of the campaign regulation structure in the United States today. The law set limits for how much individuals could donate to congressional and presidential candidates, and it also set rules for the organizations known as **Political Action Committees**, or **PACs**.

The original legislation set a limit of $1,000 that individuals could donate to a federal candidate per election cycle. PACs, however, could donate $5,000 to a candidate, and $15,000 to a political party. PACs are simply organizations that exist for the sole purpose of raising and spending money to help or defeat candidates. They have to register with the Federal Elections Commission and report all donations received and contributions made.

Most PACs represent business groups, individual companies, unions, or ideological interest groups. The National Association of Realtors, AT&T, the International Brotherhood of Electrical Workers, and the National Beer Wholesalers Association all have PACs that regularly contribute several million dollars to federal candidates. Today there are over 4,000 PACs registered nationwide.

Super PACs

Super PACs emerged from the federal court decision *Speechnow.org v. Federal Elections Commission* (2010). In that case, a U.S. Court of Appeals ruled that contribution limits on what individuals could give to an independent group were unconstitutional. The organizations that operate as Super PACs are known as independent expenditure-only groups. They can raise unlimited sums from individuals, corporations, unions, and other groups, and they can spend unlimited sums advocating for or against the election of a specific candidate.

The main limitation on Super PACs is that they cannot donate directly to a candidate's campaign. They are not permitted to coordinate directly with the candidates for whom they are advocating, although this has proven to be a difficult rule to police. It's generally not difficult for a Super PAC to learn what kind of advertisements a campaign wants and where it wants them aired, even if there are few direct conversations about it.

In 2012, comedy show host Stephen Colbert registered an actual Super PAC called Americans for a Better Tomorrow, Tomorrow, to support his own satirical political campaign. In several shows, he revealed some of the limitations of the laws against coordination, especially when he placed his friend and fellow show host Jon Stewart in charge of the Super PAC. Stewart would ask Colbert questions about how to allocate the money, and Colbert would claim he couldn't coordinate—while strongly indicating his preferences with facial expressions and hand gestures. A campaign finance lawyer brought onto the show confirmed that this was perfectly legal.[7]

Restrictions on coordination can be a challenge to some candidates. As much as a candidate might appreciate an independent group running ads on their behalf, those ads may feature subjects and language with which the candidate is not comfortable. Prior to a March 2016 Republican caucus, the Super PAC Make America Awesome, run by Liz Mair, ran an ad in Utah using nude photos of Melania Trump. The intent was to create moral panic among the state's conservative Mormon caucus-goers and turn their support away from Donald Trump and toward his main rival, Senator Ted Cruz. It's difficult to know how effective the ad campaign was—Trump did lose the Utah contest—but the advertisement drew some negative press for its misogynistic tone.[8]

527s

Organizations that we call "five twenty-sevens" (**527s**) get their name from the section of the Internal Revenue Code that describes them. While many organizations can fall under this category, this term usually applies to groups that can raise and spend unlimited amounts of money in elections but are forbidden to specifically advocate for the election or defeat of a candidate.

In an ad produced by Swift Boat Veterans for Truth, which ran during the 2004 presidential campaign, several veterans spoke about their service with John Kerry, claiming he had exaggerated his valor or his injuries.

A famous early example of a 527 was called Swift Boat Veterans for Truth, which organized in opposition to Democrat John Kerry's presidential run in 2004. Kerry had campaigned in part on his record of service on a navy "swift boat" during the Vietnam War, for which he had received the Purple Heart for wounds he sustained in combat. A group of veterans who served with or simultaneous to Kerry organized to raise questions about Kerry's service record, suggesting he had embellished his valor and his injuries or even fabricated them. At no point do these ads specifically tell people not to vote for John Kerry. Instead, they end with lines like, "If we couldn't trust John Kerry then, how could we trust him now?"

501(c)(4)s

Yet another group defined by the tax code, a **501(c)(4)** is a type of nonprofit organization that the IRS refers to as a "social welfare" group. It is an organization that is allowed to participate in election communications as long as its primary purpose isn't politics. Both the National Rifle Association and the Sierra Club are 501(c)(4)s.

What distinguishes the rules for this type of organization is that it is not required to disclose its donors to the public. This enables such an organization to disguise whose interests it serves or what its goals are. A 501(c)(4) may call itself a grassroots organization even if it is funded solely by one billionaire; or one may call itself a moderate organization even if it's backed solely by liberals or conservatives. This makes it hard for voters to know how to interpret its advertisements and activities.

What's more, such organizations end up masking campaign funds. Increasingly, "dark money"—the donations that are largely unrecorded and unattributed to donors—makes up a substantial portion of campaign spending. It is getting increasingly difficult to know who is funding a particular campaign and to what ends.

All these different organizations and funding mechanisms make it sound like campaign finance is hopelessly fragmented, in terms of both how it is regulated and how it is used in actual campaigns. How are candidates and parties supposed to craft a winning message if money is being spent in different directions and by different actors, all with their own agendas?

Surprisingly, the formal party's legal disconnection from these independent spending groups doesn't tend to undermine the party's efforts or create chaos. For one thing, even if candidates can't legally coordinate their campaign messages with outside spending organizations, they don't necessarily need to. In an era of strong party polarization and ideologically homogeneous party coalitions, the risks of developing an off-brand party message are relatively low. In the past, a Democratic campaign that appealed to northern liberals with a pro–civil rights message might have alienated southern Democrats. Thanks to the greater ideological distinctiveness of the parties, this is less of an issue today.

For another thing, outside spending organizations aren't nearly as separated from the formal parties as they are often portrayed to be. In fact, many of the people who run these organizations have long-standing ties to the formal parties and some of the key party candidates.[9] To cite a few examples:

- EMILY's List maintained one of the biggest 527s in the 2020 election cycle, spending more than $37 million to help elect female candidates across various races. Its president is Stephanie Schriock, who was the finance director for Howard Dean's 2004 presidential campaign. (Dean went on to become DNC chair.) Schriock also ran a senate campaign for John Tester of Montana in 2006, and senate Democratic leaders sent her to Minnesota to help get Al Franken elected in 2008.[10]
- GOPAC donated $3.5 million in the 2016 cycle to help elect conservatives. It was run for many years by Republican Newt Gingrich when he was a House member and later Speaker of the House. It has been run by a variety of other Republican elected officials in Washington and operates in many ways as a training camp for promising young conservative candidates.[11]
- When Wisconsin governor Scott Walker announced he was running for president in 2015, a new 527, Our American Revival, organized to support his efforts. IRS records showed that the organization had only two employees, Molly Weininger (custodian) and Andrew Hitt (contact person). Hitt had years of personal and professional ties to Walker. Weininger

had interned and worked for the Republican Party of Wisconsin for several years before Walker became governor.[12]

- As we explored in our chapter on formal party organizations, the Koch brothers (Charles and his late brother David) built something like a shadow Republican Party, having in some years spent approximately as much on conservative candidates as a major party would. There have certainly been conflicts between the Kochs and some formal GOP party leaders, but on the vast range of issues they have agreed, and candidates have eagerly accepted the Koch's money.

As these examples suggest, outside groups and funding sources clearly don't undermine the parties. Indeed, such groups often complement party work. We think it more useful to describe these groups as *part of* the party. The formal party itself can't do everything and fund everyone, and the formal parties of many states are often sharply limited or even prevented from directly aiding candidates in general elections. These outside groups thus serve as part of the larger party network, retaining fierce loyalty to the party and helping the formal party organizations do things they cannot do themselves.

Nonmonetary Resources The above examples focus on a particular type of assistance that formal and informal party groups provide for candidates—money. This is obviously not the only sort of support parties provide, however. As we discussed in Chapter 7, on formal parties, party organizations can play a substantial role in coordinating and staffing get-out-the-vote (GOTV) efforts. The different parties approach this task in their own ways. For the past few cycles, Democratic presidential candidates have largely developed their own network of field offices, usually building off previous work and drawing on the expertise, experience, and volunteer efforts of state and local party groups. Presidential campaign volunteers will sometimes knock on the doors of voters and urge not only a vote for the Democratic candidate, but also one for Democrats farther down the ballot.

By contrast, the ground game of Republican presidential candidates largely defers to Republican state and local organizations. Republican-aligned groups, including pro-life organizations and other issue advocacy groups, often run their own ground games that help boost Republican turnout. On both sides, though, there is clear work by the broader party to assist their candidates by identifying likely supporters and making sure they show up to vote.

It is not immediately obvious which party has the better approach. Studies from 2008 and 2012 suggest that the Democratic voter turnout efforts are more effective.[13] However, Republicans generally begin from a position of higher voter turnout, and it's harder to measure GOP ground-game efforts if they outsource them to affiliated groups.

Additionally, there's the matter of retaining that level of organization and knowledge from one election season to the next. Barack Obama's 2008 campaign organization, Obama for America (OFA), transformed itself into an advocacy organization called Organizing for America that was supposed to help convert Obama's many campaign promises into substantial policy gains. The organization quickly waned in strength and size after the election and came under considerable criticism for failing to adequately use the massive and enthusiastic support Obama had received as a candidate.[14]

POLITICAL SCIENCE TOOLKIT
Measuring Parties' Effect on Elections

During general election campaigns, political parties are active in many direct and indirect ways, making it difficult to state with any clarity exactly what the party's contribution is. But one way to address this question is to imagine how elections would go if parties weren't involved in them. Luckily, we don't have to imagine—the vast majority of elections held in the United States, from city councils and school districts to county boards and one state legislature (Nebraska), are nonpartisan. We can compare these elections to partisan ones to get some sense of what parties bring to the table.

In 2001, political scientists Brian Schaffner, Matthew Streb, and Gerald Wright set out to measure the effect of parties in elections. They did this by conducting a series of comparisons between states and cities that were similar to each other except that one had partisan elections and the other did not.[15] For example, they compared mayoral contests in nonpartisan Champaign, Illinois, with mayoral contests in the neighboring, and partisan, town of Urbana. They also looked at Asheville, North Carolina, which had nonpartisan elections for decades but then switched to partisan ones in the 1990s. They also compared nonpartisan Nebraska with partisan Kansas and looked at Minnesota's switch from nonpartisanship to partisanship in the early 1970s.

The results? Voter turnout appears to be substantially higher in partisan elections. Indeed, turnout was about 10 percent higher in Urbana than it was in Champaign in the late 1980s. When Minnesota had nonpartisan state legislative elections, there was greater ballot **rolloff**—a lot of people who voted for president and Congress decided to not cast a vote for state legislature. This rolloff effect is particularly stark in Kansas and Nebraska, as the table on the next page shows. There was only a 6 percentage point drop in voter turnout between congressional and state house races in partisan Kansas, but a 39 point drop in nonpartisan Nebraska.

Rolloff in Kansas and Nebraska Elections, 1984–90

	Average Number of Voters	
Race	Kansas	Nebraska
U.S. House	23,374	16,962
State Senate	21,944	10,371
Rolloff	6%	39%

Source: Schaffner, Streb, and White, 2001.

There's a good reason for this. Voters start off not knowing very much about state and local elections, but party labels provide them with a good deal of information. Just knowing a candidate's partisanship can tell voters a lot about how that candidate will vote or lead on issues like reproductive rights, taxation, marriage, guns, public works, and many other things. If voters know more about candidates, they're generally more likely to vote. Additionally, parties themselves play a direct role in encouraging voter turnout, both through advertising and canvassing neighborhoods. When they're not involved, turnout tends to drop.

What's more, without partisan influence, voters rely on other information cues to make decisions about the candidates. As this and other studies have found, nonpartisan elections tend to see voters relying more on racial/ethnic voting (casting votes for candidates of their own perceived race or ethnicity), incumbency (reelection rates tend to be higher), and ballot order (candidates whose names appear toward the top of the ballot tend to do better).

It's difficult to separate out which effects are due to the simple presence of a party label on the ballot and which are due to concerted campaign activities by the parties. But the overall effects of partisanship seem to be important. Simply put, parties provide voters with information. They allow voters to make more informed decisions than they'd otherwise be able to make.

Sometimes parties can be influential in local elections in very subtle ways. Political scientist Sarah Anzia's research looked at the differences between on-cycle elections (local elections that occur at the same time as congressional and presidential elections) and off-cycle elections (those that occur during different months or odd-numbered years). She found that off-cycle elections, which receive much less media attention and can't take advantage of the kind of turnout efforts that accompany federal elections, tend to have much lower voter turnout. What's more, because of the lower turnout, those elections are often dominated by interest group members with a strong financial stake in the outcome. For example, if local school board elections or school initiative elections are held separate from federal elections, turnout will be low, and teachers, teachers' unions, and their close allies will likely prevail. As a result, teachers, police officers, and fire-fighters tend to be better paid in communities that hold off-cycle elections.

The parties seem to be aware of the advantages interest groups can gain in off-cycle elections. The interest groups that usually do well in such elections also tend to lean Democratic, and Democrats, in turn, have sought to protect off-cycle elections within their state legislatures, even while the party advocates for higher voter turnout in other avenues. Conversely, Republican state legislators, who generally don't press heavily for voter turnout, tend to advocate for making more local elections on-cycle, knowing it will reduce the influence of Democratic-leaning special interest groups.[16]

PARTY ACTIVITY IN MODERN ELECTIONS

In this section, we examine campaigns at various levels of government over the past few decades to illustrate the roles that parties have played in helping or hurting candidates. We use the examples below to help explain some of the party activities we've been describing above.

1972: A Fragmented Party Stands Down

In the 1972 presidential election, Richard Nixon was seeking a second term during a period of modest economic growth, amid a substantial decline in American military deaths in Vietnam, and with a decent record of moderate first-term policy achievements—all adding up to what would usually be a promising environment for an incumbent. His Democratic opponent was Senator George McGovern of South Dakota. The choice of McGovern as nominee was somewhat surprising, as he didn't have many strong allies among national Democrats, but nonetheless he'd managed to navigate the new nomination system that stressed doing well in early contest states like New Hampshire and Iowa. McGovern's left-wing political stances, including calls for dramatic reductions in

American troop numbers, were easily caricatured by the Nixon campaign, making the senator appear to be an out-of-touch socialist.

Instead of rallying around their nominee, as many key Republican leaders did in 2016, several key Democratic constituencies abandoned McGovern in 1972. The Teamsters Union, a long-standing Democratic ally, swung its support to Nixon, and the head of the AFL-CIO called McGovern "an apologist for the Communist world."[17] Former Democratic governor John Connally of Texas organized a "Democrats for Nixon" campaign, enlisting many prominent Democratic officeholders to publicly back the Republican president. (Connally later became a Republican himself and ran for the party's presidential nomination in 1980.)

All these prominent members of the Democratic coalition abandoning their party's nominee sent a strong message to Democratic voters. While 95 percent of Republicans voted for Nixon that year, only 67 percent of Democrats voted for McGovern. Nixon ended up winning in a landslide, with a popular vote of 61 percent to McGovern's 38 percent. Nixon won 520 of 538 electoral votes, with McGovern claiming only Massachusetts and the District of Columbia. In this case, the party's activity made a big difference in the outcome; by failing to back its nominee, it all but ensured his defeat.

2003: The Party Finds a Way In

The California recall election of 2003 was an unusual election in many ways, but it turns out to be surprisingly instructive in how parties function and what purposes they serve. In October of 2003, Californians voted to recall their twice-elected Democratic governor, Gray Davis. One of the unusual features of California's recall laws is that the replacement vote is on the same ballot. So voters in that election saw a ballot with two questions:

1. Should the governor be recalled?
2. If he is recalled, who should replace him?

The second question was followed by a list of 135 replacement candidates spread across four pages. This list included a number of prominent politicians, several B-, C-, and D-list celebrities, and dozens of unknowns. Somehow, though, the resulting election produced a remarkably normal-looking outcome: three candidates—a moderate Republican, a conservative Republican, and a mainstream Democrat—split 94 percent of the vote. The moderate Republican, actor Arnold Schwarzenegger, nearly won an outright majority, claiming 49 percent of the vote. How did so much of the partisan vote coalesce around just a few key candidates?

A large part of the answer is that the parties structured the election that way. They were operating at a disadvantage—there was no primary to weed out candidates and signal to partisan voters the one true nominee of the party. But the parties could do similar work behind the scenes.

Republicans faced the possibility of a split vote, as former gubernatorial candidate Bill Simon, former Major League Baseball commissioner Peter Ueberroth, and state senator Tom McClintock joined Schwarzenegger on the ballot. All four had statewide name recognition and considerable access to money. But the risk of all four running full-throated campaigns was that the Republican vote would be split, handing the election to the Democrats. Republicans within the state party addressed this issue by coalescing around Schwarzenegger. Conservative interest group leaders, Republican consultants, and state party officials publicly endorsed Schwarzenegger, and several directly appealed to the other candidates to drop out of the race. Major donors, even very conservative ones, contributed to Schwarzenegger, signaling to the other candidates that they couldn't get the support they needed. In the end, Ueberroth and Simon dropped out and endorsed Schwarzenegger. Many of these same party leaders pressured McClintock to drop out as well. McClintock resisted, but ended up only pulling 13 percent of the vote.

On the Democratic side, the party first attempted to discourage anyone from joining the replacement ballot, figuring that the best way to defeat the recall was to give voters no decent Democratic options. Party leaders, prominent Democratic politicians, liberal interest group leaders, and others discouraged potential Democratic candidates from jumping into the race. But Lieutenant Governor Cruz Bustamante, who had a series of long-standing grudges with Governor Davis, entered the race. Ultimately, party resources converged on Bustamante as though he were the nominee, providing him the money and backing he needed to mount a competitive race. It wasn't enough to secure a win, but he did receive 31 percent of the vote in that crowded field of candidates.[18]

2006: Recruitment to Take Advantage of Favorable Winds

Two thousand and six looked to be a favorable midterm environment for Democrats. The unpopularity of the Iraq War was dragging down President George W. Bush's approval ratings, and Republican members of Congress were plagued with a string of ethical violations, including Representative Mark Foley's (R-FL) text solicitations to underage congressional pages. But promising **fundamentals** (the state of the economy and any other background conditions beyond the control of the candidates, but which voters will care about) don't guarantee a big victory, which was what the Democrats needed in order to take over the House and the Senate.

This was where U.S. Representative Rahm Emanuel came in. Emanuel, the brash former Clinton White House staffer who would later serve as Barack Obama's chief of staff and then as Chicago's mayor, was appointed by House

Minority Leader Nancy Pelosi in 2005 to head the Democratic Congressional Campaign Committee. Emanuel then turned to DNC chair Howard Dean and discussed ways to implement Dean's "50-state plan" in an effort to make the party more competitive in areas where Democrats don't generally win. Emanuel took on the task of recruiting strong candidates to run for Congress in those areas, even in more-conservative districts. One such candidate was former NFL quarterback Heath Shuler, an anti-abortion evangelical Christian, who agreed to run as a Democrat in North Carolina. According to campaign accounts, Shuler was hesitant to run because he worried about being away from his family in Congress all the time. Emanuel responded by calling Shuler repeatedly from his own kids' soccer games and school plays to demonstrate that it was possible to simultaneously work in politics and be a good parent.[19]

Emanuel set a goal of recruiting strong Democratic candidates for 50 House seats and raising enough funds for all of them to be competitive. He maintained close contact with the candidates throughout the election season and advised them extensively on tactics and messaging, seeking to tailor the candidates and their messages to local interests and concerns. In the end, Democrats picked up 30 House seats—15 more than they needed to take over the chamber—installing Nancy Pelosi as the first female House Speaker. Similar efforts by Senator Chuck Schumer (D-NY) in the Senate led to Democrats taking that chamber as well. Democrats held both chambers of Congress for the first time since 1994.

This was a substantial victory for the Democratic Party. While candidate recruitment and aggressive fund-raising were obviously important, they would not have led to such a substantial victory without the fundamental conditions of the political world that left Republicans, and President Bush specifically, so unpopular. But it also requires party activity to take advantage of these kind of conditions.

2016: Signaling a Favorite in California

Beginning in 2012, California began using a new approach to electing partisan candidates to office, known as the top-two primary (see Chapter 9). The primary elections held in June are actually a contest between every candidate across every party interested in a particular office, and voters may choose among them regardless of their own party registration. The top two vote-getters from that contest go on to the November general election, even if they are of the same political party.

The parties have seen this system as a potential threat to their control over election outcomes. If too many of their own candidates enter the race, that could split their vote and hand the election to the other party. This happened in California's 31st Congressional District in 2012, a moderate- to left-leaning district east of Los Angeles that had been represented by Democrat Xavier Becerra. Four Democrats and only two Republicans ran in the primary. Since the Democrats failed to coordinate and encourage one candidate or discourage others, the Democratic vote was split among the four candidates, and the two Republicans moved on to the fall runoff election. Both parties have been more cautious since then and usually issue very clear endorsements for a favorite candidate prior to the primary. This party endorsement has been shown to be associated with a 5- to 10-point boost for the anointed candidate—not an enormous bump, but certainly a big help in a close contest.[20]

There have nonetheless continued to be several interesting same-party run-offs at the congressional and state legislative levels, usually in very liberal or very conservative districts. But November of 2016 saw a statewide runoff between two California Democrats for an open U.S. Senate seat: California Attorney General Kamala Harris and U.S. Representative Loretta Sanchez. Sanchez was generally considered more conservative than Harris, and the Democratic Party did everything it could to publicly signal its preference for Harris, both in the primary and in the runoff election. Harris garnered the endorsements of the state Democratic Party, President Barack Obama and Vice President Joe Biden, the *Los Angeles Times* and the *San Francisco Chronicle*, Senators Diane Feinstein and Barbara Boxer, Governor Jerry Brown, a massive number of Democratic state and local officeholders, and a host of Democratic clubs and left-leaning interest groups. Sanchez received a number of officeholder and newspaper endorsements but nothing close to what Harris had.

In the end, the Democratic-leaning state seemed to get the party's message. Harris trounced Sanchez 62 to 38 percent. Any hopes that Sanchez would win over the support of more-moderate Republican voters seemed dashed as many Republicans declined to cast a vote in the race. Only 12.2 million Californians voted in the Senate race, compared to the 14.1 million who voted in the presidential race—a rolloff of 13 percent.

2016: Making an Extraordinary Election Look Ordinary

We've referred to the 2016 general election quite a bit in this book, and political observers will undoubtedly be analyzing it for many years to come. It was certainly an unusual election, featuring two of the least popular major party nominees in modern political history, with one of them seemingly going out of his way to act unlike previous candidates for office, to offend key constituencies, and to dismiss all previously held rules and norms. What's more, that candidate—Donald Trump—won office despite losing the popular vote.

Despite the seeming uniqueness of the 2016 campaign, one of the more striking features of this election was how normal the results were. Months prior to the election, political science forecasts, looking only at the typical behavior of voters and the strength of the economy, suggested it would be a close election with a narrow Republican victory.[21] The actual results adhered very closely to these forecast models. Ninety percent of Republicans and 89 percent of Democrats voted for their party's nominee, just as they have in other modern elections. Those unaffiliated with a party largely voted as they have in previous elections—in periods of modest economic growth with the incumbent party seeking a third term in office, many turned against that party.

The election ended up with such typical results largely because of the activities of the parties. While a number of Republican officeholders expressed concerns about Donald Trump's behavior and comments, the bulk of them stood behind him, and almost none of Trump's most open detractors within the Republican Party urged a vote for his opponent. Conservative activists and interest groups largely rallied for Trump, and Senate Majority Leader Mitch McConnell's decision to leave a Supreme Court seat open throughout 2016 helped remind party voters of the importance the election would have on the makeup of the Court. Had more Republican leaders publicly opposed Trump and advocated for his defeat, we might well have seen more party voters following that cue. Instead, their support for Trump helped keep party voters in line.

2017: Pointing to the "Real" Democrat

The city of San Antonio, Texas, holds nonpartisan municipal elections. Yet the 2017 election, in which the incumbent mayor, Ivy Taylor, sought a second term, took on a decidedly partisan flavor, especially after traditionally partisan groups and individuals weighed in. Although a registered Democrat, Taylor had managed to anger a number of Democratic constituencies during her two-year term as mayor, especially through some stances perceived as unsupportive of the city's LGBT community. She had additionally made some statements that detractors saw as suggesting that atheism leads to poverty.[22]

A large pool of candidates challenged Taylor's reelection campaign in 2017, including the county's Democratic Party chair. However, the runoff election came down to Taylor and city councilman Ron Nirenberg. Despite Taylor's past association with Democrats, and Nirenberg's self-professed independence, Taylor was quickly portrayed as the conservative Republican, while Nirenberg came to be perceived as the liberal Democrat. Taylor received endorsements from some of the more conservative groups in the city, including the city's police officer's association, while Nirenberg was backed by former mayor and Obama cabinet official Julián Castro, as well as a former leader of the AFL-CIO and the Sierra Club of Texas. Taylor's campaign began derisively referring to Nirenberg as "Liberal Ron" following those endorsements.

Nirenberg ended up defeating Taylor by 10 points in the majority-Democratic city. Although the race remained nonpartisan, the activities of the broader party coalitions helped voters see the underlying partisan nature of the race and ended up structuring the results of the election. A similar pattern occurred in 2019 when Nirenberg won a narrow reelection over city councilman Greg Brockhouse. Nirenberg continued to campaign as a Democrat, defending his two years in office during a prosperous time for the city, while Brockhouse emphasized more conservative, Republican-style messaging, such as tax cuts and support for law enforcement. Nirenberg was again backed by labor unions and the state Democratic party, while police associations backed Brockhouse. Again, the race was officially nonpartisan, but it was easy to see this as a race between Democrats and Republicans.

THE PARTIES' PERSISTENT PRESENCE IN ELECTIONS

As we've highlighted in this chapter and others, the role of parties in campaigns, and the role of the campaigns themselves, is difficult to measure precisely and is often overstated. There's a great deal of regularity in voting behavior that describes a large percentage of voting outcomes. For example, voters usually reward the president's party during good times and punish it during bad times. Despite this regularity, we tend to look back on elections and assume that whatever the winning candidate did was brilliant and we admire their ability to connect with voters, while we assume that the loser lost because of some poor campaign choices or because they were inauthentic or ineffective. Those narratives often fail to hold up under much scrutiny.

That said, it is clear that party activities play vital roles in affecting the outcomes of elections. In this chapter, we saw examples of the party issuing powerful endorsements to help their candidates (the 2016 presidential election and California senate election, the 2003 California recall) or very notably refusing to endorse one of their candidates (the 1972 presidential election). We saw the party aggressively recruiting candidates (the 2006 congressional midterms) and helping voters understand which candidates were the true Democrats and Republicans (the San Antonio mayoral race). We looked at their role in organizing money and voter turnout drives for their candidates.

And if elections largely end up following the fundamental conditions of the political environment, including the economy, the state of war or peace, and more, that's in part due to actions taken by the parties. If voters are upset with one party because they blame it for poor economic growth, that is in part because the other party has been reminding voters of that poor economic growth and blaming the first party for it.[23] If a party flips control of the Congress or of many state legislatures, that's in part because that party was able to recruit a strong group of candidates to challenge the incumbents and give those candidates the funds they needed to be effective. And if a party underperforms in an election, that may be a result of the party's leaders not enthusiastically supporting their nominees.

As you watch the next round of general elections, it is worth looking to see just what a party may be doing behind the scenes to affect the outcome. As always, we encourage you to see the party not simply as those formal party groups with the word "Democrat" or "Republican" in their title. The interest groups, major donors, activists, consultants, and others who are loyal to a party are integral to the party's activities, help create the partisan environment we see today, and can shape the outcomes of general elections.

Discussion Questions

1. Special congressional elections are obviously unusual, but what can they tell us about the national political parties?

2. Based on what you've read in this chapter, how would you describe the role of money in campaigns? Is money everything? Is it overrated?

3. Think about the different types of campaign expense tools described in this chapter. Which of these seems the most useful for a political party trying to influence the outcome of an election? Why?

4. Drawing on what you read in the Toolkit section, try to imagine what national politics would be like if parties could be eliminated from Congress. How might this affect elections? Would it change who votes? Who wins?

5. In 2020, several prominent Republicans, including former Republican National Committee chair Michael Steele and former Ohio governor John Kasich, publicly endorsed Democrat Joe Biden's presidential bid. Is this an example of a party active in a general election? Why or why not?

12

Parties and Voters

The COVID-19 virus that emerged in late 2019 and showed up in the United States in early 2020 posed a threat to all Americans, but the level of its threat was not perceived equally by the population. In April 2020, when the virus was killing more than a thousand Americans a day and most states were operating under shelter-in-place or stay-at-home orders, one of the starkest divisions in people's perceptions of the illness, and of the economic consequences of stay-at-home orders, was across party lines.

As a Pew Research Center study demonstrated, Democrats were far more likely to take the virus seriously than Republicans were.[1] Seventy-eight percent of Democrats, but only 52 percent of Republicans, agreed that the outbreak was a threat to the U.S. population as a whole; and by a margin of 41 to 30 percent, Democrats were more likely than Republicans to view the virus as a personal threat. Republicans were 14 more points likely to say Americans were overreacting to the threat, while Democrats were 17 points more likely to say that Americans weren't taking the threat seriously enough.

These differences in opinion were not unexpected. Some of the positions described above were indirectly related to people's partisan leanings. For one, the virus hit first—and most forcefully—in more-densely populated states with more international airports and port cities. Such concentrated urban areas were

In spring 2020, as COVID-19 hit the United States, partisanship affected how seriously Americans took the virus. In Michigan, as well as several other states, conservative groups protested the stay-at-home orders.

more likely to implement strict social-distancing restrictions. For reasons unrelated to the virus, Democratic voters are more likely to live in those areas, so they were more likely to be immediately affected by the disease and by efforts to combat it.

Perhaps most importantly, the parties' leaders also communicated vastly different messages about the dangers of the virus. As we saw in Chapter 4, across the nation, Democratic governors reacted to the crisis differently than did Republican governors. Leadership at the presidential level differed as well. In late January 2020, when the virus was detected within the United States, President Trump said, "We have it very well under control" and "It will all work out well"; while leading Democratic presidential candidate Joe Biden said that the country was in the middle of "a crisis with the coronavirus" that would "get worse before it gets better."[2] As the 2020 presidential campaigns went on, Trump continued conducting his large political rallies, with only a brief pause in the spring. After the president himself contracted COVID-19 and recovered in early October, he continued to downplay the seriousness of the disease. Trump backed out of the second debate in October when the debate commission decided it would be held remotely to minimize the spread of the disease.

Meanwhile, as early as March, Biden and his Democratic rival Bernie Sanders were canceling rallies and even moved a scheduled television debate to a CNN studio with no audience to avoid viral transmission. Trump and other conservatives mocked Biden for wearing a face mask, as recommended by health experts. The Biden campaign opened no field offices from which to conduct door-to-door get-out-the-vote operations, reversing the previous trend for Democratic candidates to have more field offices than Republicans.

Unsurprisingly, at this point the public had vastly different impressions of President Trump's management of the pandemic, with 83 percent of Republicans, and 18 percent of Democrats, describing it as excellent or good. In mid-April, citizen groups in several cities organized protests against state governments' stay-at-home orders, arguing that the virus was not enough of a threat to warrant such infringement on personal liberties and damage to the economy. Although the protests were covered by the national media, polls taken at the time showed that the majority of Americans agreed with state lockdown policies and opposed these citizen protests—but partisan differences emerged again, with the protests opposed by 47 percent of Republicans and by 75 percent of Democrats.[3]

At least part of the difference in these early partisan responses may lie in how party leaders appealed to their different constituencies, with Democratic leaders responding more sharply to hotspots that first emerged in Democratic areas. But the pandemic eventually shifted. By the summer, cases were growing in the other states, and the country was not following other developed democracies in getting the virus under control. The only places that seemed to be recovering were Democratic states that were hit hard early (New York, New Jersey, among others). By then, the partisan division in attitudes toward the virus had been established. The administration's handling of the virus became a regular line of attack from the Biden campaign, and Trump ended the campaign complaining that the media were exaggerating its impact, despite the fact that, by Election Day, infection rates and deaths were on the rise.

Partisan impressions of the pandemic are just one example of what is often referred to as the **party in the electorate**. The party in the electorate refers to the beliefs and behavior of the voters themselves, which can play an important role in determining what parties can and can't do. Up until now, we've focused on a lot of the major decision makers in parties—politicians, activists, party officials, donors, and others. And we've made a point of keeping voters to the side, as they're not really the ones that organize parties. But in this chapter, we're bringing the voters back in, as they do have a role to play.

Voters often have sharply partisan opinions, as they did during the pandemic, and these may shape and constrain how their elected officials behave. But the behavior of those officials also strongly affects what those voters believe. It's a tricky question as to whether we should consider voters as part of the party, a discussion that we'll get into later in this chapter. But voters are obviously important to the party, to many of its key tasks like nominating candidates, and to its central goal of controlling government.

This chapter will also investigate the role voters play in polarization, whether voters are causing it or being affected by it, and whether voters are more or less polarized than other aspects of the party system. We'll look at the concept of party identification—what causes voters to consider themselves part of a party or not. And we'll look at the growing numbers of independent voters and try to glean just how influential they are in the party system and modern American politics.

DO PARTIES REALLY HAVE MEMBERS?

Are you a member of a political party? That question isn't as easy to answer as it might sound. To be sure, American political parties want people to think of themselves as members. Every convention speech, advertisement, and e-mail solicitation from a party tries to evoke a sense of shared purpose and camaraderie. And some people even call themselves "card-carrying" Republicans or Democrats. (To our knowledge, there aren't really any cards to carry.) But how do you become a member of a party? One way is to register with a party when registering to vote. But that isn't a real guarantee of any loyalty; in a number of states, voters may switch their party registration to participate in one party's primary and then switch right back when it's over. If you're only a Republican for a few days, or even a few hours, chances are you're not a very loyal one.

You could also give money to a party; that surely conveys some sort of commitment to it. In some democracies, citizens must donate to a party in order to have the privilege of voting in a primary or otherwise participating in the party's decisions. But in the United States, very few people actually do this. According to surveys, about 10 percent of Americans donate to political candidates, and only about 6 percent donate to local, state, or national political party committees.[4] One might also consider themselves a member of a party simply by promising to support that party's nominee, whomever that may be, in the November election. Most voters are very loyal to the party they favor. In fact, quite a few Americans who refuse to consider themselves members of a party still vote loyally for the party they are closest to. But this is not strictly the same thing as being a "member" of the party.

Political scientist E. E. Schattschneider famously critiqued the idea of party membership in his 1942 book *Party Government*. As he noted, "membership" in an American political party is unlike membership in any other club or organization. You may call yourself a member of a party, and that party has no ability to challenge your claim. It can't kick you out of the party even if you refuse to donate to it or support its candidates. Such a membership surely has little value if it carries no dues, no obligations, and if the organization has no say over whether you can become or remain a member.[5]

Nonetheless, over the decades these "members" of American parties have increasingly asserted a right to control the party. The history of the parties is one of movement toward increasing **intra-party democracy**, the idea that the parties themselves should be ruled by the people, just as democratic governments are. The days of congressional caucus rule of the parties eventually yielded to bosses and conventions, which eventually yielded to primary elections. With each shift, rank-and-file voters have assumed a greater role in making the most important decision a party makes—deciding whom to nominate for office.

Perhaps the ultimate expression of the shift toward rank-and-file members having a greater role in party decision-making can be seen in primary elections. As we saw in Chapter 5, primaries are rare worldwide; parties in most democracies select their nominees through far less democratic means, and voters simply choose between the choices presented by the parties. But as we noted in Chapter 9, primaries have been a standard means for parties to select nominees in the United States since the turn of the twentieth century.

Rules for participation in primaries vary considerably across states. Some state parties allow nonparty members to participate in the contests. New Hampshire, for example, has a semi-closed primary system that allows unaffiliated voters to select a party primary to participate in on the day of the contest. Some states have closed systems, mandating that only established party registrants may participate. Still others open up the primaries completely: California, Louisiana, and Washington State have top-two primaries, in which voters may pick their favorite candidate among all candidates from all parties; the top two vote-getters go on to a runoff contest, even if they're of the same party.

These different primary rules make the concept of party membership challenging. Advocates of open primaries maintain that many of the important decisions about who will represent us are made at the primary stage. After all, many districts lean heavily toward one party or the other; the general election is relatively meaningless there, but who wins the primary is clearly very important. Thus a broad swath of voters should be allowed to participate in the primary. However, as the U.S. Supreme Court declared, "[A] single election in which the party nominee is selected by nonparty members could be enough to destroy the party."[6] Do people who have never registered to vote with a party have a right to participate in its selection of nominees? Does their right to participate outweigh the rights of long-standing party registrants to pick their own nominees? More generally, do the party's rank and file actually have a claim to governance of a party?

HOW DO VOTERS DECIDE?

Political scientists, psychologists, journalists, and campaign consultants have spent decades trying to figure out just what it is that leads a voter to make up their mind in an election. To watch the behavior of campaigns and the reporting of political journalists, one might get the impression that voters are paying close attention to what politicians say and do every day. Much has been written about the colors of Al Gore's suits, the fit of George W. Bush's pants, the Obamas' vacation destinations, Hillary Clinton's efforts to "humanize" herself on the campaign trail, and Joe Biden's age. And maybe in an electorate of 100 million people or more, such matters affect a significant number of votes. But how many? Are we so easily swayed by such superficial matters?

Rational Ignorance

One of the most reliable findings in the vast literature on voting behavior is that voters just don't know a whole lot about the political system (see Figure 12.1). Only about a third of Americans can name their member of the House of Representatives. Roughly 20 percent can name their state legislator. Less than half of Americans know which party controls their state legislature. Even the

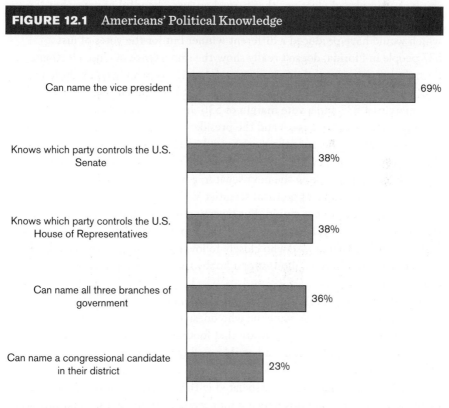

FIGURE 12.1 Americans' Political Knowledge

Can name the vice president — 69%

Knows which party controls the U.S. Senate — 38%

Knows which party controls the U.S. House of Representatives — 38%

Can name all three branches of government — 36%

Can name a congressional candidate in their district — 23%

Source: American National Election Studies, Annenberg Policy Center, Pew Research Center, http://cdn .annenbergpublicpolicycenter.org/wp-content/uploads/Civics-survey-press-release-09-17-2014-for-PR -Newswire.pdf.

name of the vice president is a mystery to 3 out of 10 Americans.[7] Such intricate matters as which level of government is most in charge of which policy area or how an executive order might be overturned surely escape most Americans' grasp.

This may sound like a damning assessment of the American people, but it shouldn't be taken as one. For one thing, Americans are hardly less educated about politics and government than other citizens around the globe. Citizens of other nations appear to be just as prone to ignorance and error about their political systems.[8] For another, why should voters actually know all that much? Yes, a political system that rests on the idea of "consent of the governed" presumes that voters have the knowledge and ability to hold governing officials accountable, but just how important is it for them to be closely informed about politics and government?

In Chapter 9, we discussed Anthony Downs's formula suggesting that voting is costly, in terms of time and effort spent learning about the candidates and going to a polling place. Voters have a pretty good sense that their vote is unlikely to actually determine the outcome of an election. Sure, we can all probably think of examples of elections that turned on just a handful of votes, but the overwhelming majority of them do not. Even the 2000 presidential election, which would have produced a different winner but for the votes of just 537 people in Florida, doesn't really show the importance of close elections. Even if you were one of the 5.7 percent of Americans who lived in Florida in 2000, your deciding to vote would have at most been the difference between a vote margin of 537 and a vote margin of 536. In both cases, Bush would have won the state's electoral votes and the presidency.

People may vote because they've been asked to or because they believe it's their civic responsibility to do so, but they still know that they're not the one person in charge of picking the next senator, governor, or president. This is why voters are, in the words of political scientist V. O. Key, *rationally ignorant*. For the most part, they're not stupid. But investing their brainpower in their job, their family, and even their dinner just makes more sense and yields a much higher payoff. Indeed, those who closely follow politics might well be regarded as irrational—it's more an interest or a hobby than a requirement of citizenship.[9]

It might be helpful to think of the typical American's relationship with politics as roughly the same as someone who doesn't care about professional football. Such a person is of course aware that football exists, probably has some idea when it's football season, and could possibly name two or three current players, but beyond that has little idea of which teams are doing well or poorly or why. The hype and coverage associated with the playoffs or the Super Bowl might actually penetrate this person's indifference, as might a scandal such as a coverup over concussions or deflated game balls. They might even be able to pick a favorite team if pressed. But for the most part, the football season just goes on almost completely outside the awareness of our hypothetical person. So it is with politics for most people.

We should digress here to note, emphatically, that we *do* think that it is important to vote, and especially that it is important for you to vote. Please vote. There is evidence suggesting that having the paradox of voting explained to you makes you less likely to vote, and in that, we are doing you a disservice. People vote not because the election might be one of those very rare ones settled by one vote, but because as citizens in a democracy they're supposed to. A democracy in which most people vote is far better and healthier than one in which very few do. But it's also worth understanding why and how people vote, and recognizing that those decisions may be driven by seemingly unimportant considerations, because the considerations many assume to be important turn out not to matter as much as we might think.

Partisans

What is it that draws people's attention to the political process? In presidential elections, more than 100 million people vote—the vast majority of whom are poorly informed about political matters. How do they make up their minds?

Partisanship is a very strong predictor of vote choice. A series of studies conducted in the mid-twentieth century and published in a book called

Partisans are often extremely loyal to the party they identify with. Here, a delegate wears a decorative hat to show her support for Donald Trump.

The American Voter found that the vast majority of voters simply vote with the party they've identified with since their youth. Campaigns, the authors found, don't actually do that much persuasion. Instead, they largely remind people of the things they like about the party they already identify with and provide a rationale for voting that way.[10] Voters, as such, are largely partisans, whether they identify that way or not. We'll explain more below about how people become partisans. But we should note that simply voting your party without much thought isn't inherently wrong. A party is a very useful **cue**, or a guide to making a complex decision. Knowing whether a candidate is a Democrat or a Republican tells you a great deal about their views on taxes, abortion, gun control, business regulation, rights for same-sex couples, and many other issues. If you're looking for a shortcut to understand how candidates will behave in office, you could do a lot worse than just looking at their party label.

This means that prior to any given national election, about 80 percent of the electorate has already made up their minds. In fact, it's made up even for those who say that it isn't. Voters who claim that they want to learn about the candidates first, or even who claim that they will not vote for their party in the general election if their own preferred candidate does not win the nomination, usually end up voting for their party's candidate anyway.

This explains why "landslide" presidential elections usually have splits of around 60 to 40. Ronald Reagan demolished Walter Mondale in 1984 with 59 percent of the vote, and Lyndon Johnson's epic defeat of Barry Goldwater in 1964 only got him around 61 percent of the vote. President Herbert Hoover managed to pull almost 40 percent of the vote in his 1932 reelection bid despite the economy having shrunk by 25 percent that year. History suggests about 80 percent of the electorate would vote for their party's presidential candidate no matter what.

Political scientists call this long-standing, stable attachment to a political party a voter's **party identification**, and "identity" is a good way to think about it. Just as a person thinks of themselves as a man or a woman or a Korean or an Italian or Black or White or Hindu or Jewish or a Californian or a Virginian or a Bruin or a Trojan or, almost always, some combination of many things like these, most American voters also say they think of themselves as a "Republican" or a "Democrat."

By nearly every measure, even those who don't follow politics very closely identify with a political party. For the most part, we get our party affiliation from our parents—roughly three-quarters of Americans have the same party identification as their mother and father—and we adopt it pretty early, years before we are old enough to vote.[11] There is a myth that we are political blank slates until we are 18 years old, and then we dispassionately survey the political system to find a party affiliation that suits our views. This is not an accurate depiction of the way we form our party identities.

In fact, we gain much of our party identification before we know much about politics (although we may update that identification as new information arises over the course of our lives). To a large extent, instead of our beliefs leading us to join a particular party, our party affiliation leads us to interpret issues in different ways. We see the world through partisan glasses. To give an example, consider a survey conducted at the end of Ronald Reagan's presidency. A majority of Democrats in the survey said that inflation had gotten worse during Reagan's time in office. In fact, annual inflation dropped from 10.3 percent during Reagan's first year in office to 4.8 percent when he left. Consider also that a majority of Republicans in a 1996 survey claimed that the deficit had grown larger during Bill Clinton's first term in office when it had, in fact, dropped from $255 billion to $107 billion during that time.[12] The people in these surveys aren't trying to be manipulative or deceptive; they simply don't know the right answer and are using their beliefs about parties and presidents to make what seems like an informed view. In general, Democrats thought Reagan a bad president, so they just assumed that any economic indicator during his time in office must have been bad. Republicans did the same for Clinton.

What should we make of this? Are partisans just tuning out reality, substituting talking points for actual evidence? It's more complicated than that. Research by political scientists Philip Converse, John Zaller, and others shows that loyal partisans actually tend to be much better informed about government and politics than moderates and independents.[13] Partisans are much more likely to know the answers to basic questions about the political system, such as which party controls the Senate, who the vice president is, what the three branches of government are, and so forth. They are also more likely to look at the world through partisan blinders. Partisans have more knowledge and background than others do but are also least likely to use that experience to process new information.

There are several reasons why the most knowledgeable voters tend to be loyal partisans. For one thing, caring about politics means you've simply been exposed to more information about it, and that information could lead you to make decisions about a range of issues. Also, as Zaller's research has shown, highly informed people tend to actively filter the information they receive. They'll tend to believe a message that aligns with their worldview, and they'll tend to dismiss or even forget one that doesn't. This is because they remember the things that shaped their worldview in the first place. It takes a lot of new information to override it.

Less informed people might be more accepting of new political information—such as that a war is going poorly, the economy is slowing down, a pandemic response is failing—but they're also far less likely to even hear it in the first place. Political scientists have actually studied voters' brains and found that more-partisan people tend to develop specialized centers of their brains for processing political information. It's easier for them to answer political questions and it takes less time, but they end up putting less thought into it than others do.[14]

So, somewhat paradoxically, those who are most aware and knowledgeable about political issues tend to be the ones who use their brains the least in coming up with answers. They quickly learn to process the world through partisan filters. The ones who are most open to listening to different ideas are actually the ones least likely to hear them in the first place.

We believe it is possible to be a regular, even avid, consumer of political news, to be a strong supporter of one political party, *and* to critically evaluate new information and not simply interpret everything in a way that helps the party we like and hurts the party we dislike. But we recognize that this is a challenge in today's polarized media environment. Selecting news from a range of different sources, and not just ones we are inclined to agree with, can be a healthy way of understanding the political world and keep us from falling into the informational traps that often face partisans.

Independents

"Independent" is one of the more popular terms in American politics. People like to consider themselves independent—free of external influence, capable of making up their own minds, not beholden to one party or another. When asked about their party affiliation, roughly 40 percent of Americans claim to be **independents**, not associated with either party, and that figure has been growing in recent decades (see Figure 12.2).

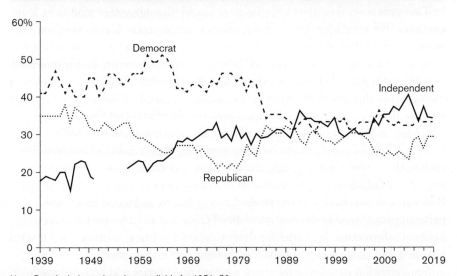

FIGURE 12.2 Party Identification over Time

Note: Data for Independents is unavailable for 1951–56.
Source: Pew Research Center, "Trends in Party Identification," www.people-press.org/interactives/party-id -trend/.

While there may be more self-identified independents today, the claim that voters are increasingly independent is misleading. Many people who claim to be independents actually end up voting in a very partisan fashion. They may even be more loyal to one party than self-identified partisans are.[15] They have made a definite choice between the major parties; they just don't like to think of themselves as the sort of people that do so. Thus the growth in the number of independents over time can give the impression that there's less party loyalty among the voters than there used to be. This isn't the case.[16]

The American National Election Studies have addressed this problem over the years by asking self-identified independents follow-up questions. When a respondent says they're independent, they're asked whether they lean toward one of the parties or not. (Those who say no are considered "true" independents; those who say yes are independent leaners.) People who identify with a party are asked whether they feel weakly or strongly toward that party. Figure 12.3 shows how these four categories of Americans break down over time. Interestingly, the proportion of "true" independents among the population hasn't changed much, hovering between 10 and 15 percent since the 1950s. There is an increasing proportion of independents who lean toward one of the parties, however, and most likely they're the sort of people who used to consider themselves "weak" partisans.

This doesn't mean that people who call themselves independent are the same as partisans. Simply by refusing to identify with a party, they're indicating a difference. In some cases, voters really are carefully judging the candidates without reference to the parties. Some may have strong preferences that are inconsistent with both parties, and so they evaluate each candidate without the help of party cues. In other cases, they are simply disengaged from politics, and so cannot choose a side any more than non-sports fans can choose a favorite team.

A large part of what makes people identify as independent is a negative view of political parties and partisan politics. Political scientists Samara Klar and Yanna Krupnikov argue that many voters are reluctant to identify with a party because parties are seen negatively.[17] They show that when respondents are reminded of the hostility and disagreement between the parties, they are less likely to say they are partisan and instead report being independent. Many Americans actually believe it is socially undesirable to report being partisan, even if they are. This is why many independents end up acting like partisans; they really are partisan, but they don't want to admit it. That, of course, has consequences. If being a partisan is seen as undesirable, some people won't participate in a partisan democracy.

One of the more interesting features of the electorate is that just as the number of people declaring themselves free of the parties is on the rise, the electorate is actually becoming more partisan. People are actually less likely to

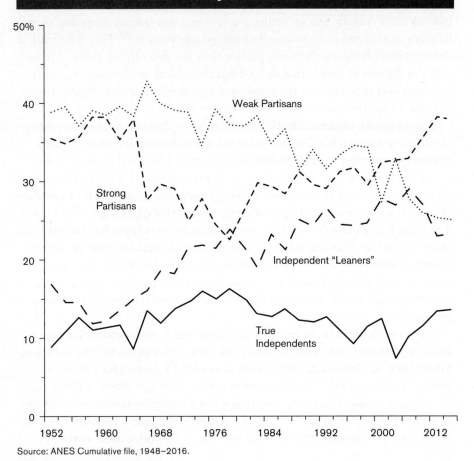

FIGURE 12.3 Partisans and Independents over Time

Source: ANES Cumulative file, 1948–2016.

split their tickets than they used—that is, people are more likely to vote for the same party for president as they do for Congress, governor, and other offices.[18] In the 1970s and 1980s, between 25 and 30 percent of survey respondents in the American National Election Study reported voting for a different party for president and for their member of Congress. In the 2000s and 2010s, that number fell to between 10 and 20 percent. This suggests that people's congressional votes are increasingly aligning with their presidential votes.

Despite their lower average engagement with politics, independent voters play a critical role in holding elected officials accountable. Because they're not tied to a political party, their votes are less certain, and thus they functionally determine the winner. How do they make their voting decisions? Despite their

importance, these same people aren't usually carefully weighing the party platforms and characteristics for the candidates. As we noted above, that's because
independents are among the least informed voters.[19] For the most part, they just
don't follow the political news very much, and they couldn't tell you a lot about
each of the candidate's priorities or much about their biographies.

Even when voters do not vote loyally for one of the two parties, however, they
are still evaluating their choices in partisan terms. That is, they recognize that
the president, his or her supporters, and other candidates and elected officials
aligned with him or her are part of the governing party, and to the extent that
voters follow what is going on in the country, they are likely to give the governing party and its candidates credit or blame for it.

One thing we do know is that voters—even relatively uninformed ones—
respond to the state of the economy. In survey after survey, voters generally
list the economy and jobs as the thing that they care about most.[20]
Figure 12.4 plots economic performance and presidential election results
since World War II. Economic performance here is measured by the percent
growth in per capita real disposable income from the third quarter of the year
preceding the election to the third quarter of the election year. The election
variable is a bit less straightforward. We have looked at the vote share won by
the party currently in control of the White House, based on the idea that voters
will give credit or blame to the party in power. So, for example, the data point
for 2016 is based on Hillary Clinton's performance relative to the state of the
economy, since Democrats were the party in control of the White House at that
point.

The overall shape of the data here suggests the economy is very important in
determining people's votes. Voters hold the president's party responsible for the
performance of the economy, and unlike their knowledge of politics, voters have
a pretty good idea of how the economy is doing. When the economy is humming
along, as it was in 1964 and 1984, voters reward the president with reelection.
When the economy is actually contracting, as it was in 1980 and 2008, voters
throw that party out and try a new one.

For candidates who are not incumbents, the relationship between the economy and voter choice is weaker, but still present. In 2008, when John McCain
distanced himself from incumbent George W. Bush and claimed to be a maver-
ick Republican and advocate for reform, he was still the Republican candidate,
and he still did poorly in the context of a poor economy. The year 2020 was a
notable outlier. Real disposable income grew at a healthy clip in 2020, in large
part thanks to stimulus payments by the federal government at the beginning of
the COVID-19 pandemic. Those payments were sent to the American people
mainly to offset dramatic income losses and business closures as the pandemic
transformed American life. So the economy rode something of a roller coaster
during 2020, with a sharp initial recession followed by rapid growth, and many

> **FIGURE 12.4** The Incumbent Party, the Economy, and the Vote, 1956–2020

One way voters evaluate the choices in a presidential election is by asking how well the incumbent, or the incumbent's party, has taken care of the economy. When the economy is doing better, measured here by growth in the income that consumers have to spend on themselves, they are more likely to vote for the incumbent party's candidate for president, here measured by that candidate's share of the vote for the two major parties. (Votes for minor parties are excluded.)

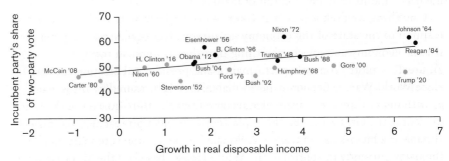

Source: Bureau of Economic Analysis, September 2020, www.bea.gov; Dave Leip's Atlas of U.S. Election Results, www.uselectionatlas.org.

people paradoxically suddenly both out of work and having money to spend. For this and other reasons, the relationship between income growth and the vote was not particularly strong in 2020.

The relationship between the state of the economy and election outcomes is an important corrective to a lot of campaign lore. Consultants and journalists might suggest that, for example, Reagan won reelection in 1984 because he was funny, strong, attractive, and gave great speeches, and his opponent Walter Mondale was unappealing, weak, and promised to raise taxes. These descriptions may well be accurate, but there's little evidence that they molded people's votes. Reagan did about as well as we'd expect given the performance of the economy. And maybe some of Barack Obama's charisma and youth relative to his opponent, John McCain, did help put him in the White House, but again, the 2008 result is very close to the line. Hillary Clinton, a scandal-free John Edwards, and practically any other mainstream Democrat would likely have done just about as well in 2008, given the state of the economy at the end of Bush's final term.

But what about the data points that don't fit the line in Figure 12.4? They also have stories to tell. Note, for example, that the Democratic nominees in 1952 (Adlai Stevenson) and 1968 (Hubert Humphrey) didn't do as well as we might expect, given economic growth. Why those years? It's probably no coincidence that the incumbent party's candidate underperformed during the wars in Korea and Vietnam—bloody, lengthy conflicts with relatively little support at home. Voters appear to blame the party in power when a lot of U.S. soldiers are dying.

Ideological extremism seems to matter as well. Relatively moderate incumbents like Lyndon Johnson (1964) and Richard Nixon (1972) substantially outperformed the economy when they had the good fortune of running against candidates perceived as out of step with the American people. Barry Goldwater (Johnson's rival) had talked openly about using nuclear weapons in China and Southeast Asia, and George McGovern (Nixon's rival) was widely believed to have socialist leanings. It's difficult to know just how large the extremism penalty in elections is—Johnson and Nixon would likely have defeated much more moderate opponents anyway—although evidence from congressional elections suggests that ideologically extreme or overtly partisan behavior is bad for reelection efforts.[21] Donald Trump's policy positions were somewhat difficult to pin down in 2016, but his extreme campaign rhetoric, which included overtly prejudiced comments about women, immigrants, and Muslims, likely caused him to underperform somewhat in that election.

So economic growth, war, and, possibly, ideological extremism appear to have some impact on the way undecided voters ultimately make up their minds in a presidential election. That is, they credit or blame not only the president for these aspects of the political environment, but also other candidates of the president's party up and down the ticket. But we see little evidence that voters are heavily swayed by other factors, such as personality, likability, charisma, or a desire to have a beer with the candidate. (Richard Nixon, not known for his charisma or overly warm personality, nonetheless outperformed the economy all three times he ran.)

We should note here that in Figure 12.4 Al Gore appears to have notably underperformed against George W. Bush in 2000. Despite a strong economy and conditions of relative peace, Gore could not secure a third consecutive term for the Democrats although he did prevail narrowly in the popular vote. This is something of a puzzle for political scientists, but it could well be an example where the campaign truly made a difference. Bush substantially outspent Gore in swing states, and character attacks against Gore appear to have been effective. What's more, Gore's integrity may well have been smeared by his service with and defense of Bill Clinton, who had been impeached less than two years before the election. Besides, it is difficult for a party to hold on to the presidency for three consecutive terms—since World War II, both parties have done it just once, the Democrats in 1948, and the Republicans in 1988. So our read here is that overall, campaign activities and qualities don't broadly change election outcomes, but we can't rule out that they can be pivotal once in a while.[22]

The fact that candidate qualities, campaign spending, or the quality of a campaign doesn't massively influence how people vote is certainly not consistent with how elections are covered by the news media, but it's actually a very encouraging sign. It suggests that, even though most of the independent voters going into an election season don't actually follow politics very closely, they do base their decisions on rather large and important factors. The fact that they hold the party in power responsible for the strength of the economy and the death of troops means that presidents have incentives to promote economic growth and keep lengthy military conflicts to a minimum. That voters seem to like moderation and reject extremism means that presidents who want their party to stay in power would be wise to work with the other side once in a while to secure broad legislative achievements, and to not give their own party everything it wants.

There are also reasons to be discouraged. For one thing, the economy appears to be voters' biggest concern, and they appear to hold the president and his party accountable for it, despite the fact that the president has only marginal influence over the economy's performance. No president wants a recession on their watch, but they occur with some regularity anyway, meaning that presidents are often held responsible for things they can't really control. Voters also tend to overweight the importance of the economy in the last year or even last several months, rather than evaluate the incumbent for their entire term. It is more likely that voters are simply rewarding incumbents when they are happy and booting them out when they are unhappy. Several scholars have found that presidents appear to be given credit or blame for things completely outside their control, from shark attacks to the performance of their favorite football team.[23]

A further problem is that voting decisions don't just affect the presidency. People casting votes for members of Congress, governors, and state legislators follow the same cues. If they're generally happy with the way things are going, they'll reward the party in power with their vote. If they're unhappy—even if the president and his party had nothing to do with their misfortune—the party in power may well get turned out of office.[24]

DO CAMPAIGNS MATTER?

As suggested in the previous section, campaigns may not exert an enormous influence over people's votes. This is consistent with what political scientists call the **minimal effects** school.[25] The idea is that campaigns generally don't cause us to change our minds about our votes; at best, they remind us to do what we were probably going to do anyway. That is, the campaign reminds Democrats to vote Democratic and reminds Republicans to vote Republican.

As political scientists John Sides and Lynn Vavreck note, however, campaign effects on voters may be obscured by the fact that both the Republican and the Democratic campaigns are exerting pressure on voters simultaneously, and they're usually well matched against each other. The authors liken campaigns to a tug of war—as long as both sides are pulling evenly, it doesn't look like the rope is moving very much, but there's actually a great deal of energy being exerted to keep the rope in that position. If one side stops trying, the rope suddenly moves a great distance. In fact, if you look at places and times where just one campaign is active, you can find quite a bit of voter responsiveness, but it's surprisingly short-lived. In some areas of the country, for example, Barack Obama's 2012 reelection campaign ran many ads while Mitt Romney ran none. This actually moved polls in Obama's direction by a few points, but the effect was gone within a few days of the ads going off the air.[26]

One thing we know from a great deal of research on voting behavior is that voters rely on cues when making decisions. After all, as we have noted, voters generally don't internalize all the information that's available about candidates. It probably isn't worth their effort. Instead, they look for shortcuts that can give them a fairly good sense of what candidates would do once in office. By far the most reliable cue is the candidate's party. For the most part, voters can make a decision as though they're informed about a great many matters simply by relying on the party label.

POLITICAL SCIENCE TOOLKIT
Who Is in the Parties?

We have claimed that parties can be thought of as coalitions. In Chapter 2, we noted that labor unions, racial and ethnic groups, and secular activists tend to be in the Democratic Party, while business interests and religious leaders tend to be in the Republican Party. At the level of activists, these coalitions shift around somewhat from year to year, but they are remarkably durable over time.

What do these coalitions look like? There's no one definitive way to examine them, and they look different whether you're examining them at the level of voters or of political elites. But public opinion can be a useful guide. It often lags what party leaders and coalitions are doing, but it also tends to be fairly stable over time, giving us an ability to see which coalitions identify with which parties.

The figure on the next page shows how voters' party allegiances have changed, or remained the same, over the past half century. Each demographic subgroup (e.g., White women, union households, frequent church attendees) is shown at two time periods: the presidential elections from 1968 to 1976, and the presidential elections from 2008 to 2016.

As we can see, race is an important component of party identification and has become more important over time. White Americans lean Republican overall, particularly White men, and have moved strongly in the Republican direction since the 1970s. Black voters, meanwhile, have identified strongly with the Democratic Party for decades, and Black women have become even more Democratic in recent years. Today, more than 85 percent of African Americans identify as Democrats. (Interestingly, roughly a third of African Americans consider themselves conservative ideologically but still identify with the Democratic Party.)[27] Latinos additionally lean Democratic, although not to such a strong degree. The results all show a persistent *gender gap* since at least the 1960s, with women leaning 5 to 10 points more Democratic than men.

Members of union households have traditionally been more Democratic than nonunion households, even when controlling for race, income, and other factors. In the figure, we see that union households have consistently been about 10 points more Democratic than nonunion households over time, although White union members now lean somewhat Republican. (Also, notably, union membership overall is down substantially over the past few decades.) Region continues to be relevant, with White southerners moving dramatically in the Republican direction since the 1970s and African American southerners moving toward the Democrats. White southerners are, indeed, one of the most consistently Republican groups in this analysis today, although they were the bedrock of Democratic Party strength for decades after the Civil War.

In addition, we see an increasing polarization across several categories. Younger voters have been more Democratic than older ones for decades. Income divisions remain, with wealthier Americans continuing to vote more often Republican than poorer Americans, though the divisions have decreased slightly. We've seen substantial polarization by religiosity: those who say they attend church at least once a week have become about 10 points more Republican—about 30 points more among White frequent churchgoers. There were no such differences in the 1970s. This polarization, incidentally, has occurred across many different religions and denominations; the more observant tend to be more Republican.

Partisanship by Groups over Time

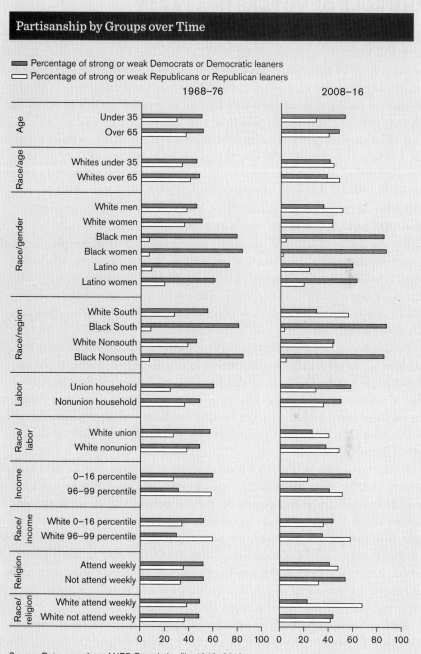

▬ Percentage of strong or weak Democrats or Democratic leaners
▭ Percentage of strong or weak Republicans or Republican leaners

Source: Data come from ANES Cumulative file, 1948–2016.

THE ROLE OF VOTERS IN A PARTY

We've seen that voters can be very loyal to their party, even if they don't necessarily think of themselves as partisans. We've also seen that voters don't actually follow politics all that closely. As discussed, voters aren't completely ignorant of important political events—they know if the economy is doing well or poorly, or whether or not we're at war, and they have an idea which party is in power and who to credit or blame for the way things are going.

And, as we've mentioned before, evidence suggests that voters don't much like ideological extremism. Moving things too far in one direction or another can irk them. Voters act in some ways like a thermostat.[28] If public policy moves too far in a liberal direction, the public responds by voting more Republicans into office. If things get too conservative, they'll vote more Democrats into office. On average, voters tend to act as a force for moderation.

But the reality of "rational ignorance" among voters is worth keeping in mind. It suggests that voters don't monitor politics too closely. They have what some party scholars call a "blind spot." In other words, they'll notice unusually bad things—a major scandal, an economic catastrophe, and in particular a very liberal or very conservative politician—but for anything less egregious, they may not notice at all.

Parties depend on that blind spot. Parties, after all, consist of an array of political actors who want the government to do things and move in a certain direction, and they're seeking candidates who will deliver on those goals. But they also know that the public may punish the candidate if they catch them acting on these party goals. So parties look for candidates who are just at the edge of the blind spot. They want a nominee who will fulfill many party goals without angering voters.

President George W. Bush is a good example of the type of candidate parties tend to look for. Running in 2000, he gave every indication that he was a serious conservative and would deliver the sorts of policies that Republican party leaders wanted, from rollbacks on environmental regulations to tax cuts and aggressive foreign policy stances. But he also came off as enough of a reasonable moderate, with a record of bipartisanship as Texas' governor, to not frighten voters too much. The fact that he won the presidency by the slenderest of margins and enacted a wide range of conservative policies once in office suggests the party successfully threaded the needle in nominating him.

Donald Trump is probably an example of a party choosing someone outside the voters' blind spot. While most of his policy stances (other than immigration) weren't seen as particularly extreme, voters noticed his bombastic campaigning style and insulting language; they offended people and drew more detractors than supporters. He likely underperformed what a more conventional Republican nominee would have managed in 2016,[29] and he was less popular throughout his

President George W. Bush's "compassionate conservativism" made him an ideal choice for the Republican Party in the 2000 election. While he touted conservative values and had a track record to support them, he also showed the ability to be moderate and bipartisan.

first term than other incumbents have been with similar economic conditions, even before the effects of the COVID-19 pandemic began to be felt.[30]

This concept of the blind spot suggests that voters impose some sort of constraint on what parties can do. Parties can't just nominate anyone they want—there are risks to nominating someone outside the blind spot, possibly costing the party an election. Again, voters, for the most part, don't pay very close attention to politics, and parties have some leeway in picking nominees. But voters occasionally notice outlandish or extreme behavior and punish parties for it, and the parties have to keep this in mind.

But just as the mass of voters can impose constraints on parties, the more partisan and active voters can *place* demands on parties. We saw the potential power of voter demand in late 2008 when Republican and Democratic officeholders largely worked together on a financial sector bailout to prevent a complete collapse of the economy. A more active and conservative group of Republican voters strongly objected to this and formed what would be known as the Tea Party. By demanding more-conservative behavior from Republican officeholders and threatening those who wouldn't provide it with primary challenges, these voters helped chart a path for the Republican Party that would move it further to the right in the following years. Similarly, progressive activists and officeholders within the Democratic coalition helped moved that party leftward after 2016.

Polarization and the Electorate

Americans can sense that the parties are becoming more polarized with time. The differences between Democratic and Republican officeholders have been growing, and the parties are becoming more disciplined. There just aren't as many moderate politicians as there used to be.

How much of a role have voters played in this **polarization**? If politicians are more polarized, have the voters followed them, or have they led them? This is a difficult question. Our measures of voters' partisanship are far from perfect, and there are several trends in voter behavior that make it hard to sort out. In particular, it can be difficult to tell just what form of polarization voters are experiencing. Journalists and political scientists who talk about polarization often disagree about what polarization is exactly. We think there are at least four different phenomena that might count as polarization (see also Figure 12.5):

1. Voters might be moving further apart in their views on the issues, or on an ideological dimension. We call that **ideological distance**. This could happen if the moderates become extreme or if the extremes become even more extreme. What is important is that, if we think in terms of the spatial model we introduced in Chapter 3, Democrats and Republicans are moving farther and farther away from each other in that space.[31]

2. Voters might be becoming more ideologically consistent in their views. That is, people who take, say, the liberal position on one issue are more likely to take the liberal position on another issue. For example, a voter who supports restrictions on gun access may be more likely to support access to abortion services than she was a few years earlier. Political scientists refer to this as **constraint** or issue consistency.[32]

3. Voters might be **sorting** themselves ideologically, so that Democrats are more likely to be liberal and Republicans conservative. In the past, there were liberals who were Republicans and conservatives who were Democrats, but today, liberals and conservatives have sorted themselves into separate parties, which makes the parties more distinctive.[33]

4. Voters might just dislike the other side more. We call that **negative polarization**. Their policy positions might not have changed at all, but their attitudes toward those who disagree have.[34]

The word "polarization" could refer to any of these phenomena. We think that when many people use the word, they may be thinking of the first example— distance. But the idea of polarization in physics, in which the molecules of a substance are all aligned with one another, is much closer to examples 2 or 3. To make matters worse, it can be hard to measure people's attitudes in a way that can distinguish each of these different kinds of polarization.

FIGURE 12.5 Kinds of Polarization

Ideological distance: Voters (or politicians) have become further apart in an ideological space, as in the spatial model we've introduced in earlier chapters.
Constraint: Voters (or politicians) have become more ideologically consistent in their views, so that their position on one issue is aligned with their position on other issues.
Sorting: Voters' (or politicians') ideological or issue positions are more aligned with their party. Liberals are more likely to be Democrats and conservatives are more likely to be Republicans.
Negative polarization: Voters (or politicians) more intensely dislike those who disagree with them, even if they haven't changed their policy positions at all.

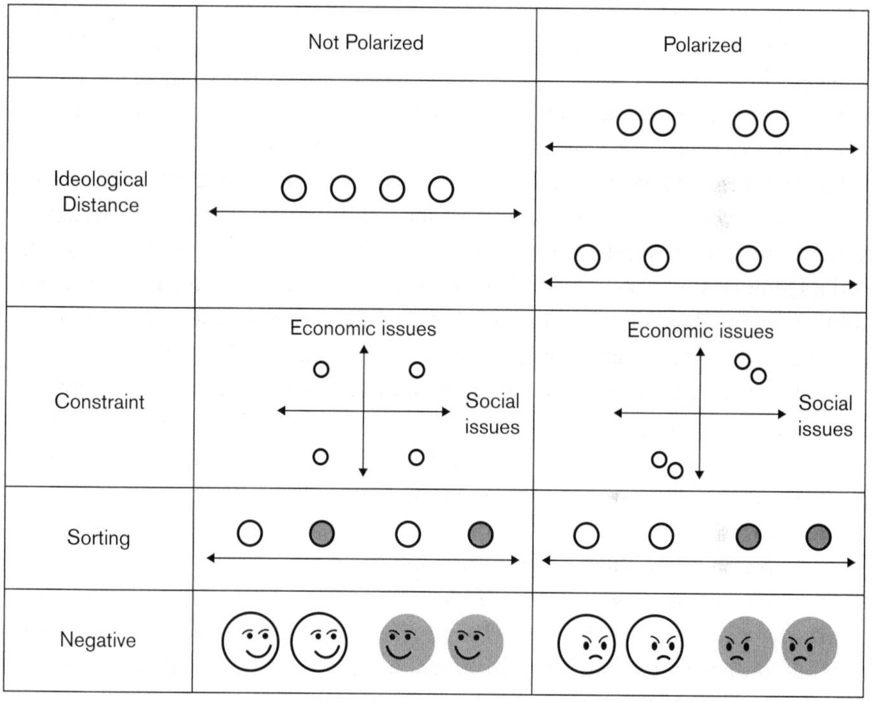

So which of these kinds of polarization has actually happened? Among voters, there is little evidence of increased *distance*. It is true that some people take more extreme positions on some issues than anyone used to take. Voters in the 1950s were unlikely to favor gay marriage or privatized Social Security, and some voters now do. But it is just as likely that voters have become less extreme on individual issues. Few voters are as extremely opposed to civil rights as many conservatives were in the 1950s, and there are fewer liberals who favor the extreme interventions in the economy that were on the table in the 1950s.[35]

In its annual reports, Pew finds an increasing ideological consistency across issues, or constraint.[36] If we measure ideology as the percent of liberal or conservative positions that people take, this can look like increased distance, but the many remaining moderates are not in the middle. They are simply less consistent across issues. Indeed, there is some evidence that these moderates are more extreme on their issues, just not consistently liberal or conservative.[37]

The greatest evidence we have on polarization is for sorting.[38] In the 1950s, politicians, voters, and activists who considered themselves liberals or conservatives could be found in both parties. Today, this is rare at all levels. Most committed liberals have shifted to the Democratic Party, and most committed conservatives are now Republicans. And many who didn't change sides have changed their political views. People who identified with the Democratic Party and were not deeply committed to their conservatism became more liberal, and vice versa. Newcomers to the parties match ideology to party.

There is also evidence of increased negative polarization. A 2019 survey found that 45 percent of Democrats would be unhappy if their child married a Republican, and 35 percent of Republicans would be unhappy if their child married a Democrat.[39] These figures have grown considerably over time. When political scientists ask survey respondents to list things they like or dislike about the parties, the main change over the past several years has been more and more respondents listing more and more things they dislike about the other party.

PARTIES AND VOTER TURNOUT

As mentioned earlier, there's a cost to voting, from taking the time to learn about candidates to actually going to a polling place and filling out a ballot. To determine whether it's worth their time to do this, voters consider the material benefits to their voting (such as how much more money they'll make if one candidate wins as opposed to the other) multiplied by the chance that their own vote will make the difference, which is nearly zero. They also consider their own feelings about voting, like whether they believe it's an important thing for them to do as citizens in a democracy.

Given this logic, it is perhaps surprising that anyone votes at all. Around 60 percent of eligible voters have shown up to vote in recent presidential elections. This number is substantially lower in midterm congressional elections, and it is far lower in municipal elections, when as little as 10 percent might show up. Part of the reason voters show up at all is parties, which are fantastic organizations for motivating voter turnout. They maintain impressive lists of voters and party registrants and deploy armies of volunteers every election cycle to make sure their supporters show up. Indeed, this is one of the best reasons for a candidate to join a political party: it means that a large percentage of the electorate will be energized to show up and pull the lever for you.[40] Not being part of a party means you have to do all that mobilization yourself.

Yet voter turnout is significantly lower in the United States than it is in most major democracies (Table 12.1).[41] The reason for that discrepancy is fairly simple: the United States is one of the only major democracies that requires voter registration. Except for those in a very few states, American voters must "opt-in" to registering to vote, often as much as a month in advance of the election. As Figure 12.6 shows, voter turnout dropped substantially in the early 1900s just as states adopted voter registration laws as part of a series of Progressive Era reforms. Turnout has fluctuated a good deal since then but has never come close to the levels it experienced in the late 1800s. There were certainly valid reasons for imposing these rules—party machines were reaching high turnout numbers by compelling or paying people to vote, sometimes multiple times in the same election—but a century later, the legacy of those reforms is voter participation that is low by global standards.

The parties, interestingly, have different attitudes toward voter turnout. For decades, Republicans have tended to turn out in higher numbers than Democrats, in part due to their demographic profiles. Republicans tend to be older, more educated, and wealthier than Democrats, and such people are simply more likely to vote. Unsurprisingly, perhaps, recent efforts to tighten voting rules, such as by requiring photo identification, tend to be favored by Republicans,[42] and evidence suggests that such laws have a disproportionate impact on Democratic voters. Poorer people in urban areas are simply less likely to have a driver's license (they can't afford cars and often rely on public transportation), and thus face more of a barrier to voting.

The differences of turnout and the effects of voter restrictions across party lines raise an important question: What if everyone voted? What if we abolished voter registration and adopted mandatory turnout laws like those used in Australia and other nations, which charge citizens a fine for failing to vote, and boosted turnout to nearly 100 percent? Given that Democrats are currently less likely to vote than Republicans, would such a change give a big advantage to Democrats?

Surprisingly, the answer is not really.[43] One study of Senate elections found that universal turnout would help Democrats marginally but not actually change the outcome of many contests.[44] A simulation of presidential elections found that universal turnout could have flipped some very close elections, such as 1980 and 2000, but for the most part would have produced the same results.[45] Voters and nonvoters do differ in their beliefs, but the latter is only slightly more Democratic than the former.

nation, and when they get a chance to put those ideas into practice, it's the voters (like you) who ultimately determine whether those ideas succeed or fail and whether that party should be allowed more time in power. The public has the final say in deciding which party was right and which was wrong. It's a blunt tool, but an incredibly powerful one.

Discussion Questions

1. Do you consider yourself a member of a political party? If so, what makes you a member? If not, what do you feel you'd need to do to become one?

2. Many civic education programs focus on the idea that Americans need to know a great deal about their government to be good citizens. Yet we know from surveys that Americans do not follow politics or government very closely. Is this a problem? Is education failing, or are people behaving rationally?

3. This chapter talks about partisanship and the stability of many people's voting behavior over time. What did the 2020 election tell us about the stability of partisanship?

4. As we saw in this chapter, many people who call themselves "independent" actually vote pretty consistently for just one party. What are the consequences of voters increasingly calling themselves independent, even if they prefer one party?

5. Consider the four different types of polarization discussed in this chapter. Which do you feel best explains what's happened in American politics in recent decades? What are the consequences of that?

Endnotes

Chapter 1: You Can't Understand Politics without Understanding Parties

1. E. Schattschneider, *Party Government: American Government in Action* (1942. New York: Routledge, 2017), 1.
2. Schattschneider, *Party Government*, 52.
3. American Political Science Association, "Toward a More Responsible Two-Party System," Part 2, Suppl., *American Political Science Review* 44, no. 3 (September 1950), i–ix, 1–99.
4. Lilliana Mason, *Uncivil Agreement: How Politics Became Our Identity* (Chicago: University of Chicago Press, 2018).
5. Steven Levitsky and Daniel Ziblatt, *How Democracies Die* (New York: Crown, 2018).
6. David Karol, *Red, Green, and Blue: The Partisan Divide on Environmental Issues* (Cambridge: Cambridge University Press, 2019).
7. John Aldrich, *Why Parties? The Origin and Transformation of Political Parties in America* (Chicago: University of Chicago Press, 1995). Aldrich's book built on an unpublished essay by Thomas Schwartz, also called "Why Parties?" (Thomas Schwartz, "Why Parties?" Research memorandum, 1989.)
8. And as others have shown—for example: Thomas Schwartz, "Why Parties?" Research memorandum, 1989. Kathleen Bawn, "Constructing 'Us': Ideology, Coalition Politics, and False Consciousness," *America Journal of Political Science* 43, no. 2 (1999): 303–34. Hans Noel, *Political Ideologies and Political Parties in America* (New York: Cambridge University Press, 2013).

Chapter 2: American Political Parties: A Brief History

1. Dinesh D'Souza, "The Switch That Never Happened: How the South Really Went GOP," American Greatness, July 29, 2018, https://amgreatness.com/2018/07/29/the-switch -that-never-happened-how-the-south-really-went-gop/.
2. Kevin Kruse, Twitter post, July 31, 2018, 2:27 P.M., https://twitter.com/KevinMKruse /status/1024360878760779776.
3. Viktor Winetrout, Twitter post, May 29, 2018, 11:19 P.M., https://twitter.com/Cpin42 /status/1001664483687915520.
4. James Sterling Young, *The Washington Community, 1800–1828* (New York: Columbia University Press, 1966).

5. Originally the top five; this was also changed in the Twelfth Amendment.
6. Jeffery Jenkins and Brian Sala, "The Spatial Theory of Voting and the Presidential Election of 1824," *American Journal of Political Science* 42, no. 4 (1994): 1157–79.
7. Cas Mudde and Cristobal Rovira Kaltwasser, *Populism: A Very Short Introduction* (New York: Oxford University Press, 2017).
8. Eric Schickler, *Racial Realignment: The Transformation of American Liberalism, 1932–1965* (Princeton, NJ: Princeton University Press, 2016).
9. Keneshia N. Grant, *The Great Migration and the Democratic Party: Black Voters and the Realignment of American Politics in the 20th Century* (Philadelphia: Temple University Press, 2020).
10. Frances Lee, *Insecure Majorities: Congress and the Perpetual Campaign* (Chicago: University of Chicago Press, 2016).
11. See also Chapter 6, on the Powell Amendments.
12. Brian D. Feinstein and Eric Schickler, "Platforms and Partners: The Civil Rights Realignment Reconsidered," *Studies in American Political Development* 22, no. 1 (2008): 1–31; Eric Schickler, *Racial Realignment: The Transformation of American Liberalism, 1932–1965* (Princeton, NJ: Princeton University Press, 2016).
13. John Sides, Michael Tesler, and Lynn Vavreck, *Identity Crisis: The 2016 Presidential Campaign and the Battle for the Meaning of America* (Princeton, NJ: Princeton University Press, 2018).

Chapter 3: Parties in Congress

1. David Karol, "It's Really Democratic Care, Not Obamacare," *The Monkey Cage* (newsletter), *Washington Post*, September 27, 2013, www.washingtonpost.com/news/monkey-cage/wp/2013/09/27/its-really-democratic-care-not-obamacare/.
2. Jennifer N. Victor, Nils Ringe, and Christopher J. Carman, *Bridging the Information Gap: Legislative Member Organizations as Social Networks in the United States and the European Union* (Ann Arbor: University of Michigan Press, 2013).
3. M. Veera Pandiyan, "How the term 'Whip' came to be used in Parliament," The Star, May 14, 2006, www.thestar.com.my/news/nation/2006/05/14/how-the-term-whip-came-to-be-used-in-parliament/Harvard Fox Hounds, "Fox Hunting Terms," accessed June 22, 2020.
4. Gary W. Cox and Mathew D. McCubbins, *Legislative Leviathan: Party Government in the House* (Berkeley: University of California Press: 1993).
5. Barbara Sinclair, *Unorthodox Lawmaking: New Legislative Processes in the U.S. Congress* (Washington, DC: CQ Press, 2012).
6. Eric Schickler, *Racial Realignment: The Transformation of American Liberalism, 1932–1965* (Princeton, NJ: Princeton University Press, 2016); Hans Noel, *Political Ideologies and Political Parties in America* (New York: Cambridge University Press, 2014).
7. This example follows William Riker's analysis in *The Art of Political Manipulation* (New Haven, CT: Yale University Press, 1986), 114–28. Riker deduces preferences from votes. But as he notes, strategic voting and sincere voting will lead to different choices for people with the same preferences. So we cannot be sure. Table 3.1 simplifies his analysis somewhat.
8. Cited in Riker, *The Art of Political Manipulation*, 126.
9. For that reason, amendments like these are sometimes described as "killer amendments," in that they kill the bill. But killing the bill wasn't Powell's intention. Getting attention to civil rights issues was.
10. Cox and McCubbins, *Legislative Leviathan* (Cambridge: Cambridge University Press, 1993), 90. See also Steven N. S. Cheung, "The Contractual Nature of the Firm," *Journal of Law and Economics* 26, no. 1 (April 1983): 1–21.

11. Thomas Hobbes, *Leviathan*, 1651.
12. Cox and McCubbins, *Legislative Leviathan*.
13. John H. Aldrich and David W. Rohde, *The Logic of Conditional Party Government: Revisiting the Electoral Connection* (East Lansing, MI: Political Institutions and Public Choice, 2000).
14. John Patty, "Equilibrium Party Government," *American Journal of Political Science* 52, no. 3 (July 2008): 636–55.
15. Frances Lee, *Beyond Ideology* (Chicago: University of Chicago Press, 2009).
16. Gregory Koger and Matthew J. Lebo, *Strategic Party Government: Why Winning Trumps Ideology* (Chicago: University of Chicago Press, 2017).
17. Koger and Lebo, *Strategic Party Government*, 169.
18. Koger and Lebo, *Strategic Party Government*, 11.
19. This assumption is not necessary for most of the conclusions we will discuss, but it does make it easier to illustrate them. Very sophisticated uses of the spatial model make other assumptions, but we will keep things simple here. For a longer and more technical discussion see Anthony Downs, *An Economic Theory of Democracy* (New York: HarperCollins, 1957); James Enelow and Melvin Hinich, "A General Spatial Model of Candidate Competition," in *The Spatial Theory of Voting*, eds. James Enelow and Melvin Hinich (Cambridge: Cambridge University Press, 1984); James Enelow and Melvin Hinich, "The Theory of Predictive Mappings," in *Advances in the Spatial Theory of Voting*, eds. James Enelow and Melvin Hinich (Cambridge: Cambridge University Press, 1989), 167–78.
20. Jeff Zeleny, "In Health Vote, Democrats Weigh Success vs. Survival," *New York Times*, March 10, 2010, www.nytimes.com/2010/03/19/health/policy/19memo.html (accessed 3/10/2020).
21. Sean Theriault, *Party Polarization in Congress* (New York: Cambridge University Press, 2008); Frances Lee, *Beyond Ideology* (Chicago: University of Chicago Press, 2009).
22. Gary Cox and Mathew D. McCubbins, *Setting the Agenda: Responsible Party Government in the U.S. House of Representatives* (New York: Cambridge University Press, 2005).
23. Gregory Koger, "Cloture Reform and Party Government in the Senate, 1918–1925," *Journal of Politics* 68, no. 3 (August 2006): 708–19.
24. Sean M. Theriault, *The Gingrich Senators: The Roots of Partisan Warfare in Congress* (New York: Oxford University Press, 2013); Sean M. Theriault, "Party Warriors: The Ugly Side of Party Polarization in Congress," in *American Gridlock: The Sources, Character, and Impact of Political Polarization*, eds. James A. Thurber and Antoine Yoshinaka (New York: Cambridge University Press, 2015), 152–70.
25. Gregory Koger, *Filibustering: A Political History of Obstruction in the House and Senate* (Chicago: University of Chicago Press, 2010).
26. Matthew Green, *Underdog Politics* (New Haven, CT: Yale University Press, 2015): 127–28.
27. Seth Masket, *No Middle Ground: How Informal Party Organizations Control Nominations and Polarize Legislatures* (Ann Arbor: University of Michigan Press, 2009).

Chapter 4: Parties and the Executive

1. NBC News, "Trump Defends Handling of Coronavirus Response," March 30, 2020, 10:19 P.M. www.nbcwashington.com/news/coronavirus/trump-defends-handling-of-coronavirus-threat/2258840/.
2. Donald Trump, Daily Coronavirus Pandemic Briefing, March 17, 2020, https://factba.se/transcript/donald-trump-press-conference-coronavirus-briefing-march-17-2020; Hope Yen, Calvin Woodward, and Tom Krisher, "AP Fact Check: Trump Says He Always Knew Virus Was Pandemic," Associated Press, March 23, 2020, https://apnews.com/dbddbcf6cb4b17420e4a08820b73d4be.

3. David Jackson, "Trump Says Impeachment 'Probably' Distracted Him from Fighting Coronavirus," *USA Today*, March 31, 2020, www.usatoday.com/story/news/politics/2020 /03/31/coronavirus-trump-says-impeachment-distracted-him-coronavirus/5100694002 /; Felicia Sonmez, "McConnell Claims Impeachment 'Diverted the Attention' of Trump Administration from Coronavirus Response," *Washington Post*, March 31, 2020, www .washingtonpost.com/politics/mcconnell-claims-impeachment-diverted-the-attention -of-trump-administration-from-coronavirus-response/2020/03/31/6cd84128-736f-11ea -a9bd-9f8b593300d0_story.html.

4. Violet Ikonomova, "'Failing Michigan Governor': Trump Takes Shot at Whitmer on Twitter," Deadline Detroit, www.deadlinedetroit.com/articles/24691/failing_michigan _governor_trump_takes_shot_at_whitmer_on_twitter; Kevin Breuninger, "Trump Attacks Cuomo Again on Coronavirus Response: 'Andrew, Keep Politics Out of It,'" CNBC, March 16, 2020, www.cnbc.com/2020/03/16/trump-and-cuomo-fight-over -coronavirus-response.html; Brett Samuels, "Trump Touts Cooperation with States on Coronavirus after Criticizing Democratic Governors," *The Hill*, March 17, 2020, https:// thehill.com/homenews/administration/487976-trump-touts-cooperation-with-states-on -coronavirus-after-criticizing.

5. Michael Crowley, Katie Thomas, and Maggie Haberman, "Ignoring Expert Opinion, Trump Again Promotes Use of Hydroxychloroquine," *New York Times*, April 5, 2020, www.nytimes.com/2020/04/05/us/politics/trump-hydroxychloroquine-coronavirus .html; Richard Luscombe, "Fauci: No Evidence Anti-Malaria Drug Pushed by Trump Works against Virus," *The Guardian*, April 6, 2020, www.theguardian.com/world/2020 /apr/05/coronavirus-fauci-trump-anti-malaria-drug.

6. Marty Johnson, "Trump Blames Obama for Coronavirus Testing Issues, Says 'Changes Have Been Made,'" *The Hill*, March 13, 2020, https://thehill.com/homenews/administration /487404-trump-blames-obama-for-coronavirus-testing-issues-says-changes-have.

7. Seth Masket, "Democratic and GOP Governors Enacted Stay-at-Home Orders on the Same Timeline. But All Holdouts Are Republicans," FiveThirtyEight, April 9, 2020, https://fivethirtyeight.com/features/democratic-and-gop-governors-enacted-stay-at-home -orders-on-the-same-timeline-but-all-holdouts-are-republicans/.

8. John Gerring, *Party Ideologies in America, 1828–1996* (Cambridge: Cambridge University Press, 2001).

9. Ronald Reagan, "A Time for Choosing," October 27, 1964, www.americanrhetoric.com /speeches/ronaldreaganatimeforchoosing.htm.

10. Kristen Lee, "Rick Santorum Tells Audience That 'Smart People' Will Never Be on His Side," *New York Daily News*, September 17, 2012.

11. https://factba.se/transcript/donald-trump-speech-scranton-pa-november-7-2016.

12. Keith T. Poole and Howard Rosenthal, "A Spatial Model for Legislative Roll Call Analysis," *American Journal of Political Science* 29, no. 2 (1985): 357–84.

13. William Welch, "AARP 'Dead Set against' Bush's Social Security Plan," *USA Today*, January 24, 2005, A4.

14. Julia R. Azari, *Delivering the People's Message: The Changing Politics of the Presidential Mandate* (Ithaca, NY: Cornell University Press, 2014).

15. Samuel Kernell, *Going Public: New Strategies of Presidential Leadership* (Washington, DC: CQ Press, 2006).

16. Brandice Canes-Wrone, *Who Leads Whom? Presidents, Policy, and the Public* (Chicago: University of Chicago Press, 2010).

17. George C. Edwards, *On Deaf Ears: The Limits of the Bully Pulpit* (New Haven, CT: Yale University Press, 2006).

18. Office of the Governor, "Read Gov. Walker's State of the State Address as Prepared for Delivery," *Wisconsin State Journal*, February 1, 2011, http://host.madison.com/wsj

/news/local/govt-and-politics/read-gov-walker-s-state-of-the-state-address-as/article
_6a42ad28-2e5e-11e0-9f9e-001cc4c03286.html.

19. Jonathan Bernstein, "Stepping Back a Bit (Jobs Speech 2)," *A Plain Blog about Politics*, http://plainblogaboutpolitics.blogspot.com/2011/09/stepping-back-bit-jobs-speech-2_09 .html.

20. Jim VandeHei and Jonathan Weisman, "Republicans Split with Bush on Ports," *Washington Post*, February 23, 2006, www.washingtonpost.com/wp-dyn/content/article/2006/02/22 /AR2006022201609.html.

21. Richard S. Conley, "The Legislative Presidency in Political Time: Party Control and Presidential-Congressional Relations," in *Rivals for Power*, 3rd ed., edited by James Thurber (Lanham, MD: Rowman & Littlefield, 2005), 151–82.

22. Margaret Robertson Ferguson, "Chief Executive Success in the Legislative Arena," *State Politics & Policy Quarterly* 3, no. 2 (2003): 158–82.

23. Doris Kearns Goodwin, *Team of Rivals: The Political Genius of Abraham Lincoln* (New York: Simon and Schuster, 2005).

24. Richard M. Skinner, "George W. Bush and the Partisan Presidency," *Political Science Quarterly* 123, no. 4 (2008): 605–22.

25. Daniel J. Galvin, *Presidential Party Building: Dwight D. Eisenhower to George W. Bush* (Princeton, NJ: Princeton University Press, 2010).

26. Katherine Krimmel, "The Efficiencies and Pathologies of Special Interest Partisan-ship," *Studies in American Political Development* 31, no. 2 (2017): 149–69, https://doi.org /10.1017/S0898588X17000104.

27. Daniel Schlozman, *When Movements Anchor Parties: Electoral Alignments in American History* (Princeton, NJ: Princeton University Press, 2015).

28. Sidney M. Milkis, Daniel J. Tichenor, and Laura Blessing, "Rallying Force: The Modern Presidency, Social Movements, and the Transformation of the American Party Politics" (presented at the Annual Meeting of the American Political Science Association in Chicago, IL, September 1, 2013).

29. Martin Luther King Jr., *The Autobiography of Martin Luther King, Jr.* (New York: Warner Books, 1998).

30. Steven Rogers, "Accountability in a Federal System" (PhD diss., Vanderbilt University, 2014).

31. Peter Nicholas, "Gov. Criticizes Legislators as 'Girlie Men,'" *Los Angeles Times*, July 18, 2004, www.latimes.com/archives/la-xpm-2004-jul-18-me-arnold18-story.html.

32. Brendan Nyhan, Eric McGhee, John Sides, Seth Masket, and Steven Greene, "One Vote Out of Step? The Effects of Salient Roll Call Votes in the 2010 Election," *American Politics Research* 40, no. 5 (2012): 844–79.

33. Frances E. Lee, *Insecure Majorities: Congress and the Perpetual Campaign* (Chicago: University of Chicago Press, 2016).

Chapter 5: U.S. Parties in Comparative Perspective

1. Giovanni Sartori, *Parties and Party Systems* (Cambridge: Cambridge University Press, 1976).

2. Maurice Duverger, *Political Parties: Their Organization and Activity in the Modern State*, trans. Barbara North and Robert North (London: Methuen & Co., 1955), 217.

3. The Electoral College is not strictly single member, but it operates similarly. Each state has more than one elector, but those electors are still awarded as a block to whichever candidate comes in first place. (Even Nebraska and Maine, which do not award all of their electors to the statewide winner, still use plurality at the congressional district level, so coming in first is still necessary to win any electors.)

4. David Freedlander, "AOC Has Already Changed DC. It Hasn't Changed Her Much," *New York Magazine*, January 6, 2020, https://nymag.com/intelligencer/2020/01/aoc-first-year -in-washington.html (accessed 4/1/2020).

5. For a thorough discussion of counting rules, see Matthew Shugart and Rein Taagepera, *Votes from Seats: Logical Models of Electoral Systems* (Cambridge: Cambridge University Press, 2017).

6. Duverger, *Political Parties*.

7. For example, Patrick Dunleavy argues that Duverger's law is wrong enough that political scientists should abandon it, and that those of us who keep it around are ignoring the evidence against it. We agree that most cases of first past the post are not strictly two-party systems, but the evidence is strong that the system does tend to produce *fewer* parties. See Patrick Dunleavy, "Duverger's Law Is a Dead Parrot," *European Politics and Policy* (blog), London School of Economics and Political Science, June 20, 2012, http://blogs.lse .ac.uk/europpblog/2012/06/20/duvergers-law-is-dead/.

8. William Roberts Clark and Matt Golder, "Rehabilitating Duverger's Theory: Testing the Mechanical and Strategic Modifying Effects of Electoral Laws," *Comparative Political Studies* 39, no. 6 (August 2006): 679–708, https://doi.org/10.1177/0010414005278420.

9. John Whitesides, "Trump Blasts 'Rigged' Rules on Picking Republican Delegates," Reuters, April 11, 2016, www.reuters.com/article/us-usa-election/trump-blasts-rigged -rules-on-picking-republican-delegates-idUSKCN0X81HE.

10. John Wagner, "Not Continuing to Run Would Be 'Outrageously Undemocratic,' Bernie Sanders Says," *Washington Post*, March 17, 2016; Yamiche Alcindor, "Bernie Sanders Says Superdelegates Should Follow Voters' Will in Landslide States," *New York Times*, May 1, 2016.

11. Jonathan Chait, "Sanders Claims 2016 Primary Was Rigged, Won't Commit to Supporting Winner," *New York Magazine*, June 26, 2019, http://nymag.com/intelligencer/2019/06 /bernie-sanders-2016-rigged-wont-pledge-support-winner.html.

12. Trip Gabriel, "Bernie Sanders Backers March against Hillary Clinton in Philadelphia," *New York Times*, July 24, 2016.

13. William Cross and Jean-Benoit Pilet, eds., *The Politics of Party Leadership: A Cross-National Perspective* (Oxford: Oxford University Press, 2015).

14. Gloria Galloway, "300,000 Eligible to Vote in Federal Liberal Leadership Race: Party," *Globe and Mail*, March 6, 2013, www.theglobeandmail.com/news/politics/300000 -eligible-to-vote-in-federal-liberal-leadership-race-party/article9336372/ (accessed 3/3/2020); Leslie MacKinnon, "Liberals' 'Supporter' Experiment Put to the Test," CBC News, April 13, 2013, www.cbc.ca/news/politics/liberals-supporter-experiment-put-to -the-test-1.1366977 (accessed 3/3/2020).

15. Steven L. Taylor, Matthew S. Shugart, Arend Lijphart, and Bernard Grofman, *A Different Democracy* (New Haven, CT: Yale University Press, 2013).

16. Bernie Sanders, "Full Text: Bernie Sanders' DNC speech," *Politico*, July 25, 2016, www.politico.com/story/2016/07/full-bernie-sanders-dnc-speech-226187 (accessed 3/3/2020); Andrew Prokop, "Bernie Sanders's DNC Speech Methodically Dismantled the 'Bernie or Bust' Argument," *Vox*, July 25, 2016, www.vox.com/2016/7/25/12282962 /bernie-sanders-dnc-speech-analysis (accessed 3/3/2020).

17. ANSA, "Mattarella Calls for Unity on Terror at Nazi Massacre Site," ANSA, January 31, 2015, www.ansa.it/english/news/2015/01/31/mattarella-calls-for-unity-on-terror-at -nazi-massacre-site_4fa9baf2-f1f1-4e31-8798-6a9a8618d722.html (accessed 3/3/2020); Associated Press, "German President Visits Site of Rome's WWII-Era Massacre," Fox News, May 3, 2017, www.foxnews.com/world/german-president-visits-site-of-romes -wwii-era-massacre (accessed 3/3/2020).

18. Arend Lijphart, *Patterns of Democracy: Government Forms and Performance in Thirty-Six Countries* (New Haven: Yale University Press, 2012).

19. *Almost* all. Americans in the District of Columbia have a vote for president, but they do not elect full members of the House or Senate. Americans in U.S. overseas territories do not vote for president and do not send full members to the House or Senate.
20. Josh Chafetz, "The Real 'Resistance' to Trump? The GOP Congress," *Politico Magazine*, June 6, 2017, www.politico.com/magazine/story/2017/06/06/the-real-resistance-to -trump-the-gop-congress-215230 (accessed 3/3/2020).
21. Kathleen Bawn and Frances Rosenbluth, "Short versus Long Coalitions: Electoral Accountability and the Size of the Public Sector," *American Journal of Political Science* 50, no. 2 (April 2006): 251–65, https://doi.org/10.1111/j.1540-5907.2006.00182.x.

Chapter 6: Party Machines

1. Mike Royko, *Boss: Richard J. Daley of Chicago* (New York: New American Library, 1971).
2. It's worth noting that the comparison is best when we look at the romanticized version of the Mafia that we see in movies like *The Godfather*, rather than at the Mafia of American history.
3. James P. Walsh, "Abe Ruef Was No Boss: Machine Politics, Reform, and San Francisco," *California Historical Quarterly* 51, no. 2 (Spring 1972): 3–16.
4. Arthur H. Samish, *The Secret Boss of California: The Life and High Times of Art Samish* (New York: Crown, 1971).
5. Seth E. Masket, *No Middle Ground: How Informal Party Organizations Control Nominations and Polarize Legislatures* (Ann Arbor: University of Michigan Press, 2009).
6. William A. Bullough, *The Blind Boss & His City: Christopher Augustine Buckley and Nineteenth-Century San Francisco* (Berkeley: University of California Press, 1979).
7. Terry Golway, *Machine Made: Tammany Hall and the Creation of Modern American Politics* (New York: W. W. Norton, 2014).
8. Golway, *Machine Made: Tammany Hall*, 170.
9. Golway, 106.
10. Golway, 107.
11. Golway.
12. Golway, 203.
13. Walton Bean, *Boss Ruef's San Francisco: The Story of the Union Labor Party, Big Business, and the Graft Prosecution* (Berkeley: University of California Press, 1974).
14. Frank R. Kent, *The Great Game of Politics: An Effort to Present the Elementary Human Facts about Politics, Politicians, and Political Machines, Candidates and Their Ways* (Garden City, NY: Doubleday, Page, 1924).
15. Mike Royko, *Boss: Richard J. Daley of Chicago* (New York: New American Library, 1971).
16. Joseph P. Lyford, *Candidate* (New York: Henry Holt, 1959).
17. Samish, *The Secret Boss of California*.
18. William L. Riordan, *Plunkitt of Tammany Hall: A Series of Very Plain Talks on Very Practical Politics* (New York: Signet Classics, 1995).
19. Golway, *Machine Made: Tammany Hall*.
20. Jessica Trounstine, *Political Monopolies in American Cities: The Rise and Fall of Bosses and Reformers* (Chicago: University of Chicago Press, 2008).
21. David R. Mayhew, *Placing Parties in American Politics* (Princeton, NJ: Princeton University Press, 1986).
22. James Q. Wilson, *The Amateur Democrat: Club Politics in Three Cities* (Chicago: University of Chicago Press, 1966).
23. Seth E. Masket, *No Middle Ground: How Informal Party Organizations Control Nominations and Polarize Legislatures* (Ann Arbor: University of Michigan Press, 2009).

Chapter 7: Formal Party Organizations

1. Michael Bennet (@MichaelBennet), Twitter post, August 23, 2019, 12:07 P.M., https://twitter.com/MichaelBennet/status/1164977491901059072.

2. Marianne Williamson (@marwilliamson), Twitter post, August 31, 2019, 8:24 P.M., https://twitter.com/marwilliamson/status/1168001717331537921.

3. Bill Scher (@billscher), Twitter post, December 2, 2019, 4:35 A.M., https://twitter.com/billscher/status/1201483033175457792?s=20.

4. Tal Axelrod, "Booker Leads Other 2020 Dems in Petition Urging DNC to Change Debate Qualifications," *The Hill*, December 14, 2019, https://thehill.com/homenews/campaign/474592-booker-asks-other-2020-dems-to-sign-petition-urging-dnc-to-change-debate.

5. Ralph Volney Harlow, *The History of Legislative Methods in the Period before 1825* (New Haven, CT: Yale University Press, 1917), 51.

6. Harlow, *History of Legislative Methods*, 56.

7. Andrew Goldman, *The National Party Chairmen and Committees: Factionalism at the Top* (New York: Routledge, 2019), 26.

8. Daniel Walker Howe, *What Hath God Wrought: The Transformation of America, 1815–1848* (Oxford: Oxford University Press, 2007).

9. Daniel P. Klinghard, "Grover Cleveland, William McKinley, and the Emergence of the President as Party Leader," *Presidential Studies Quarterly* 35, no. 4 (2005): 736–60.

10. Robert H. Wiebe, *The Search for Order, 1877–1920* (New York: Hill and Wang, 1967), 28.

11. Klingard, "Grover Cleveland," 750.

12. Herbert Croly, *Marcus Alonzo Hanna: His Life and Work* (New York: Macmillan, 1912), 218.

13. John Morton Blum, *Liberty, Justice, Order: Essays on Past Politics* (New York: W. W. Norton, 1993), 93.

14. Klinghard, "Grover Cleveland," 739–40.

15. Allen Fraser Lovejoy, *La Follette and the Establishment of the Direct Primary in Wisconsin, 1890–1904* (New Haven, CT: Yale University Press, 1941), 36.

16. Cornelius C. Cotter, James L. Gibson, John F. Bibby, and Robert J. Huckshorn, *Party Organizations in American Politics* (Pittsburgh: University of Pittsburgh Press, 1989); Paul S. Herrnson, "Do Parties Make a Difference? The Role of Party Organizations in Congressional Elections," *Journal of Politics* 48, no. 3 (1986): 589–615; Xandra Kayden and Edie Mahe, *The Party Goes On: The Persistence of the Two-Party System in the United States* (New York: Basic Books, 1985); Paul R. Abramson, John H. Aldrich, Philip Paolino, and David W. Rohde, "Challenges to the American Two-Party System: Evidence from the 1968, 1980, 1992, and 1996 Presidential Elections," *Political Research Quarterly* 53, no. 3 (2000): 495–522; Todd Donovan, Daniel A. Smith, and Christopher Z. Mooney, *State and Local Politics: Institutions and Reform* (Stamford, CT: Cengage Learning, 2009).

17. Melody Crowder-Meyer, "The Party's Still Going: Local Party Strength and Activity in 2008," in *The State of the Parties*, 6th ed., edited by John Green and Daniel Coffey (Lanham, MD: Rowman & Littlefield, 2010).

18. Douglas D. Roscoe and Shannon Jenkins, *Local Party Organizations in the Twenty-First Century* (Albany: State University of New York Press, 2016).

19. Marian Currinder, *Money in the House: Campaign Funds and Congressional Party Politics* (Boulder, CO: Westview Press, 2009), 34–39.

20. Burgess Everett and Kevin Robillard, "DSCC Endorses McGinty in Pennsylvania Primary," *Politico*, March 23, 2016, www.politico.com/story/2016/03/dscc-endorses-katie-mcginty-221148.

21. Lee Fang, "Secretly Taped Audio Reveals Democratic Leadership Pressuring Progressive to Leave Race," *The Intercept*, April 26, 2018, https://theintercept.com/2018/04/26/steny-hoyer-audio-levi-tillemann/.

22. Josh Kraushaar, "NRSC Endorses Crist," *Politico*, May 12, 2009, www.politico.com/blogs/scorecard/0509/NRSC_to_endorse_Crist.html.

23. Ray La Raja and Brian Schaffner, *Campaign Finance and Political Polarization: When Purists Prevail* (Ann Arbor: University of Michigan Press, 2015).

24. Adam Schrager and Robert Witwer, *The Blueprint: How Democrats Won the West (and Why Republicans Should Care)* (Golden, CO: Fulcrum, 2010).

25. David E. Broockman, Nicholas Carnes, Melody Crowder-Meyer, Christopher Skovron, "2013 National Survey of Party Leaders," 2013.

26. Jon Ward, "The Koch Brothers and the Republican Party Go to War—with Each Other," *Yahoo News*, June 11, 2015, www.yahoo.com/news/the-koch-brothers-and-the-republican-party-go-to-121193159491.html.

27. Rasmus Kleis Nielsen, *Ground Wars: Personalized Communication in Political Campaigns* (Princeton, NJ: Princeton University Press, 2012).

28. Molly Ball, "Obama's Edge: The Ground Game That Could Put Him over the Top," *The Atlantic*, October 24, 2012, www.theatlantic.com/politics/archive/2012/10/obamas-edge-the-ground-game-that-could-put-him-over-the-top/264031/.

29. Michael Zoorob and Theda Skocpol, "The Overlooked Organizational Basis of Trump's 2016 Victory," in Skocpol and Caroline Tervo, eds., *Upending American Politics* (New York: Oxford University Press, 2020), 79–100.

30. Joshua P. Darr, "In 2020, the Ground Game Is All Trump," *Mischiefs of Faction*, October 9, 2020, www.mischiefsoffaction.com/post/2020-ground-game.

31. Philip A. Klinkner, *The Losing Parties: Out-Party National Committees 1956–1993* (New Haven, CT: Yale University Press, 1994), 3.

32. William Crotty, *Party Reform* (New York: Longman, 1983).

33. Republican National Committee, *Growth and Opportunity Project*. 2012. 4

34. RNC, *Growth*, 5

35. Julia Azari and Seth Masket, "Intraparty Democracy and the 2016 Election," in *Conventional Wisdom, Parties, and Broken Barriers in the 2016 Election*, eds. Jennifer C. Lucas, Christopher J. Galdieri, and Tauna S. Cisco (Lanham, MD: Lexington Books, 2018), 137–62.

36. Klinkner, *The Losing Parties*.

37. Daniel J. Galvin, *Presidential Party Building: Dwight D. Eisenhower to George W. Bush* (Princeton, NJ: Princeton University Press, 2010).

38. Daniel J. Galvin, "Obama Built a Policy Legacy. But He Didn't Do Enough to Build the Democratic Party," The Monkey Cage (blog), *Washington Post*, November 16, 2016, www.washingtonpost.com/news/monkey-cage/wp/2016/11/16/obama-built-a-policy-legacy-but-didnt-do-enough-to-build-the-democratic-party.

39. Daniel Galvin, "The Transformation of Political Institutions: Investments in Institutional Resources and Gradual Change in the National Party Committees," *Studies in American Political Development* 26, no. 1 (April 2012):50–70.

40. Boris Heersink, "Beyond Service: National Party Organizations and Party Brands in American Politics" (PhD diss., University of Virginia, 2016).

41. Suzanne O'Dea, *Madam Chairman: Mary Louise Smith and the Republican Revival after Watergate* (Columbia: University of Missouri Press, 2012).

Chapter 8: Party Activists

1. Ira Glass, "This Party Sucks," *This American Life*, episode 417 (transcript), aired October 29, 2010, www.thisamericanlife.org/radio-archives/episode/417/transcript.

2. Jessica Glenza, Vanessa Thorpe, and Hannah Summers, "'I Saw Myself in Dr. Ford's Words': Protesters Tell of Jeff Flake Elevator Confrontation," *The Guardian*, September 29, 2018, www.theguardian.com/us-news/2018/sep/29/abuse-survivors-say-flake-lift-protest-in-solidarity-with-ford (accessed 4/3/2020).

3. Anthony Downs, *An Economic Theory of Democracy* (New York: Harper and Row, 1957); William Riker and Peter Ordeshook, "A Theory of the Calculus of Voting," *American Political Science Review* 62, no. 1 (1968): 25–42.

4. S. Verba, K. L. Schlozman, and H. E. Brady. (1995). *Voice and Equality: Civic Voluntarism in American Politics*. Cambridge, MA: Harvard University Press; Alan I. Abramowitz, John McGlennon, and Ronald B. Rappaport. 2015. "Incentives for Activism." In Alan I. Abramowitz, John McGlennon, and Ronald B. Rappaport, eds., *The Life of the Parties: Activists in Presidential Politics*. University Press of Kentucky.

5. Joanne M. Miller and Kyle L. Sanders. 2016. "It's Not All about Resources: Explaining (or Not) the Instability of Individual-Level Political Participation." American Politics Review (44(6): 94381 doi: 10.1177/1532673X15599480; Joanne M. Miller. 2013. "The Motivational Underpinnings of Political Participation." In New Directions in American Politics, ed., Raymond J. La Raja. New York: Routledge.

6. John Zaller, *The Nature and Origins of Mass Opinion* (Cambridge: Cambridge University Press, 1992).

7. John D. May, "Opinion Structure of Political Parties: The Special Law of Curvilinear Disparity," *Political Studies* 21, no. 2 (1973): 135–51.

8. Walter J. Stone and Alan I. Abramowitz, "Winning May Not Be Everything, but It's More Than We Thought: Presidential Party Activists in 1980," *American Political Science Review* 77, no. 4 (1983): 945–56; Seth Masket, *Learning from Loss: The Democrats 2016–2020* (Cambridge: Cambridge University Press, 2020).

9. Robert M. Bond et al., "A 61-Million-Person Experiment in Social Influence and Political Mobilization," *Nature* 489 (2012): 295–98.

10. Frank Kent, *The Great Game of Politics* (New York: Arno Press, 1923).

11. Michael Heaney and Fabio Rojas, "The Partisan Dynamics of Contention: Demobilization of the Antiwar Movement in the United States, 2007–2009," *Mobilization: An International Journal* 16, no. 1 (2011): 45–64.

12. E. E. Schattschneider, *Party Government* (New York: Farrar and Rinehart, 1942), 64.

13. Gregory Koger, Seth Masket, and Hans Noel, "Partisan Webs: Information Exchange and Party Networks," *British Journal of Political Science* 39, no. 3 (2009): 633–53.

14. Seth Masket, *No Middle Ground: How Informal Party Organizations Control Nominations and Polarize Legislatures* (Ann Arbor: University of Michigan Press, 2009).

15. Nicholas Confessore, "Welcome to the Machine," *Washington Monthly*, July/August 2003, https://washingtonmonthly.com/magazine/julyaugust-2003/welcome-to-the-machine/.

16. Kathleen Bawn, Marty Cohen, David Karol, Seth Masket, Hans Noel, and John Zaller, "A Theory of Political Parties: Groups, Policy Demands and Nominations in American Politics," *Perspectives on Politics* 10, no. 3 (2012): 571–97.

17. Richard Skinner, Seth Masket, and David Dulio, "527 Committees and the Political Party Network," *American Politics Research* 40, no. 1 (2012): 60–84.

18. David Mayhew, *Congress: The Electoral Connection* (New Haven, CT: Yale University Press, 1974), 5.

19. Mayhew, *Congress*, 37.

20. David Broockman, "Mobilizing Candidates," *Journal of Experimental Political Science* 1, no. 2 (2014): 104–19.

21. James Q. Wilson, *The Amateur Democrat: Club Politics in Three Cities* (Chicago: University of Chicago Press, 1962), 188.

22. Jo Freeman, "The Political Culture of the Democratic and Republican Parties," *Political Science Quarterly* 101, no. 3 (1986): 327–56.

23. Ryan W. Miller and John Bacon, "Thousands of Pro-gun Protesters, Many Heavily Armed, Rally Peacefully in Richmond," *USA Today*, January 20, 2020.

24. Seth Masket, *No Middle Ground: How Informal Party Organizations Control Nominations and Polarize Legislatures* (Ann Arbor: University of Michigan Press, 2009).

25. Laurel Bliss and Brian Schaffner, "Not All Democratic Primary Voters Are as 'Woke' as Your Twitter Feed," *Mischiefs of Faction* (blog), December 3, 2019, www .mischiefsoffaction.com/post/not-all-democratic-primary-voters-are-as-woke-as-your -twitter-feed/.

26. Max Weber, "Politics as a Vocation," in *From Max Weber: Essays in Sociology.*, ed. H. H. Gerth and C. Wright Mills (New York: Oxford University Press, 1946), 77–128.

27. Jonathan Bernstein, "Hard Boards," *A Plain Blog about Politics*, December 9, 2009, plainblogaboutpolitics.blogspot.com/2009/12/hard-boards.html.

28. Erica Chenoweth, "How Can We Know When Popular Movements Are Winning? Look to These Four Trends," *Political Nonviolence at a Glance*, November 15, 2016, http://politicalviolenceataglance.org/2016/11/15/how-can-we-know-when-popular -movements-are-winning-look-to-these-four-trends/.

29. Jo Freeman, "The Political Culture of the Democratic and Republican Parties," *Political Science Quarterly* 101, no. 3 (1986): 327–56.

30. As with many colorful quotes that seem to capture a politician's character, this one may be apocryphal. But it is widely attributed to Roosevelt; see, for example, Richard Kirsch, *Fighting for Our Health: The Epic Battle to Make Health Care a Right in the United States* (Albany, New York: Rockefeller Institute Press. 2012), 261.

Chapter 9: Nominations

1. Lewis L. Gould, *Four Hats in the Ring* (Lawrence: University Press of Kansas, 2008), 73–74; Richard Harding Davis, "The Two Conventions in Chicago," *Scribner's Magazine* 50, no. 3 (September 1912): 259–73.

2. "Stephanopoulos Defends Debate Performance: 'We Asked Tough but Appropriate Questions,'" *Politico*, April 17, 2008, www.politico.com/blogs/michaelcalderone/0408 /Stephanopoulos_defends_debate_performance_We_asked_tough_but_appropriate _questions.html (accessed 5/20/2020).

3. Abraham Lincoln, "Letter to Samuel Galloway, March 24, 1860" in *The Complete Works of Abraham Lincoln*, vol. 6, John G. Nicolay and John Hay, eds. (New York: Francis D. Tandy, 1894/1860). Permission: Northern Illinois University. Persistent link to this document, http://lincoln.lib.niu.edu/file.php?file=nh660f.html.

4. Marty Cohen, David Karol, Hans Noel, and John Zaller, *The Party Decides: Presidential Nominations Before and After Reform* (Chicago: University of Chicago Press, 2008).

5. Theodore H. White, "Kefauver Rides Again," *Colliers*, May 11, 1956, 28.

6. Randall R. Calvert, *Models of Imperfect Information in Politics* (London: Harwood Press, 1986); Kathleen Bawn, Martin Cohen, David Karol, Seth Masket, Hans Noel, and John Zaller "A Theory of Parties: Groups, Policy Demanders and Nominations in American Politics," *Perspectives on Politics* 10, no. 3 (2012): 571–97.

7. Taylor E. Dark, *The Unions and the Democrats: An Enduring Alliance* (Ithaca, NY: Cornell University Press, 1999), 191.

8. Seth Masket, *Learning from Loss*, (New York: Cambridge University Press, 2020).

9. Seth Masket, *No Middle Ground: How Informal Party Organizations Control Nominations and Polarize Legislatures* (Ann Arbor: University of Michigan Press, 2009).

10. Nelson Polsby, *The Consequences of Party Reform* (Oxford: Oxford University Press, 1983), 66.

11. E. E. Schattschneider, *Party Government* (New York: Farrar and Rinehart, 1942), 64.

12. Mike Royko, *Boss* (London: Penguin, 1971), 81.

13. Royko, *Boss*, 82.

14. Note that this "caucus" is different from the caucuses that some states use to nominate delegates to their party conventions. We will discuss those institutions in Chapter 10

when we discuss the modern mixed system for nominating U.S. presidential candidates. For now, note that the word "caucus" simply refers to a meeting of the members of a political party (Republicans in Congress sometimes refer to these meetings as a "conference"). Its precise origins are unknown, but any group of people of the same party meeting to discuss anything might be called a caucus. The party in the legislature is called a caucus, as we saw in Chapter 3.

15. See Alan Ware, *The American Direct Primary: Party Institutionalization and Transformation in the North* (Cambridge: Cambridge University Press, 2002).

16. Todd Donovan, "The Limbaugh Effect: A Rush to Judging Cross-Party Raiding in the 2008 Democratic Nomination Contests," *The Forum* 6, no. 2 (2008), https://doi-org.du .idm.oclc.org/10.2202/1540-8884.1232.

17. Thad Kousser, Seth Masket, Eric McGhee, and Scott Lucas, "Kingmakers or Cheerleaders? Party Power and the Causal Effects of Endorsements," *Political Research Quarterly* 68, no. 3 (2015), https://doi.org/10.1177/1065912915595882.

18. Eric McGhee, Seth Masket, Nolan McCarty, Boris Shor, and Steve Rogers, "A Primary Cause of Partisanship? Nomination Systems and Legislator Ideology," *American Journal of Political Science* 58, no. 2 (2014): 337–51.

19. Jeff Stein, "Closed Primaries Are Hurting Bernie Sanders. But They're Not Why He's Losing," *Vox*, April 28, 2016, www.vox.com/2016/4/28/11528764/closed-primaries -bernie-sanders.

20. Casey Dominguez, "Does the Party Matter? Endorsements in Congressional Primaries," *Political Research Quarterly* 64, no. 3 (2011): 534–44.

Chapter 10: Presidential Nominations

1. Mark Sanford, Joe Walsh, and Bill Weld, "We Are Trump's Republican Challengers. Canceling GOP Primaries Is a Critical Mistake," *Washington Post*, September 13, 2019, www .washingtonpost.com/opinions/we-are-trumps-republican-challengers-canceling-gop -primaries-is-a-critical-mistake/2019/09/13/7a951c84-d665-11e9-86ac-0f250cc91758 _story.html.

2. Dan Merica, "DNC Doubles Threshold for Third, Fourth Democratic Debates," CNN, May 29, 2019, www.cnn.com/2019/05/29/politics/dnc-threshold-democratic-debates /index.html.

3. Ezra Klein, "Why Iowa Gets to Go First, and Other Facts about Tonight's Caucus," *Washington Post*, January 3, 2012, www.washingtonpost.com/blogs/ezra-klein/post/why -iowa-gets-to-go-first-and-other-facts-about-tonights-caucus/2011/08/25/gIQAJtygYP _blog.html (accessed 6/2/2020).

4. The Green Papers: 2020 Presidential Primaries, Caucuses, and Conventions, Iowa Republican: Presidential Nominating Process, www.thegreenpapers.com/P20/IA-R; The Green Papers: 2020 Presidential Primaries, Caucuses, and Conventions, Iowa Democrat: Presidential Nominating Process, www.thegreenpapers.com/P20/IA-D; Richard E. Berg-Andersson, The Green Papers, thegreenpapers.com (accessed July 8, 2020).

5. Lydia Saad, "McCain and Gore Emerge as Front-Runners in New Hampshire Primary," Gallup News Service, January 25, 2000, https://news.gallup.com/poll/3310/mccain -gore-emerge-frontrunners-new-hampshire-primary.aspx; CNN, "Exit Polls: McCain's New Hampshire Support Ran Deeper Than Just Independents," CNN.com, February 2, 2000, www.cnn.com/2000/ALLPOLITICS/stories/02/02/exitpolls.cnn/index .html.

6. The Green Papers, www.thegreenpapers.com/P16/NH-R.

7. Steve Benen, "Sanders Says Southern States 'Distort Reality,'" *The Rachel Maddow Show*, April 14, 2016, www.msnbc.com/rachel-maddow-show/sanders-says-southern-primaries

-distort-reality; Steve Benen, "The Relevance of the South in the Democratic Presidential Race," *The Rachel Maddow Show*, April 11, 2016, www.msnbc.com/rachel-maddow-show/the-relevance-the-south-the-democratic-presidential-race; Rebecca Traister, "Why Clinton Voters Say They Won't Support Obama," Salon.com, June 23, 2008, www.salon.com/2008/06/23/pumas/.

8. Ismail K. White and Chryl N. Laird, *Steadfast Democrats* (Princeton, NJ: Princeton University Press, 2020).

9. Daniel Klinghard, *The Nationalization of the American Party System, 1880–1896* (New York: Cambridge University Press, 2010), 200–201.

10. Marty Cohen, David Karol, Hans Noel, and John Zaller, *The Party Decides: Presidential Nominations Before and After Reform* (Chicago: University of Chicago Press, 2008).

11. Nelson W. Polsby, *Consequences of Party Reform* (Oxford: Oxford University Press, 1983), pp. 23–24.

12. Austin Ranney, *Curing the Mischiefs of Faction: Party Reform in America* (Berkeley: University of California Press, 1975).

13. The concept of momentum applied to primaries is different from momentum in the physical sciences, where objects in motion tend to maintain their speed and direction. When journalists talk about momentum in the context of presidential primaries, they're saying that winning a little bit early means winning *even more* later.

14. David Redlawsk, Caroline Tolbert, and Todd Donovan, *Why Iowa? How Caucuses and Sequential Elections Improve the Presidential Nominating Process* (Chicago: University of Chicago Press, 2010).

15. Larry Bartels, *Presidential Primaries and the Dynamics of Public Choice* (Princeton, NJ: Princeton University Press, 1988); Nelson W. Polsby, *Consequences of Party Reform* (Oxford: Oxford University Press, 1983).

16. William G. Mayer, "Forecasting Presidential Nominations," in *In Pursuit of the White House: How We Choose Our Presidential Nominees*, ed. William G. Mayer (London: Chatham House, 1996).

17. Marty Cohen, David Karol, Hans Noel, and John Zaller, *The Party Decides: Presidential Nominations Before and After Reform* (Chicago: University of Chicago Press, 2008).

18. "Dean Statement on Florida and Michigan," Democratic Party, press release, March 5, 2008, http://web.archive.org/web/20080308173709/http://democrats.org/a/2008/03/dean_statement_45.php.

19. Caitlin E. Jewitt. *The Primary Rules: Parties, Voters, and Presidential Nominations* (Ann Arbor: University of Michigan Press, 2019).

20. Marty Cohen, David Karol, Hans Noel, and John Zaller, "Party versus Faction in the Reformed Presidential Nominating System," *PS: Political Science and Politics* 43, no. 4 (2016): 701–8.

21. Byron E. Shafer, *Quiet Revolution: The Struggle for the Democratic Party and the Shaping of Post-reform Politics* (New York: Russell Sage Foundation, 1983).

Chapter 11: The Party in General Elections

1. Larry J. Sabato, *The Rise of Political Consultants* (New York: Basic Books, 1981).

2. David Halberstam, *The Fifties* (New York: Ballantine Books, 1994).

3. Alexander Heard, *The Costs of Democracy* (Chapel Hill: University of North Carolina Press, 1960).

4. American Association of Political Consultants, "About Us," https://theaapc.org/about-us/.

5. Joseph William Doherty, "The Candidate-Consultant Network in California Legislative Campaigns: A Social Network Analysis of Informal Party Organization" (PhD diss., University of California, Los Angeles, 2006).

6. These words are widely attributed to Hanna, although they may be apocryphal. Quoted in Costas Panagopoulos and Aaron C. Weinschenk, *A Citizen's Guide to U.S. Elections: Empowering Democracy in America* (New York: Routledge, 2016), 31, and David Schultz, ed., *Money in American Politics: An Encyclopedia* (Santa Barbara: ABC-CLIO, 2018), xiii, among others.

7. "Colbert Super PAC: Not Coordinating with Stephen Colbert," *The Daily Show with Jon Stewart*, filmed January 17, 2012, www.cc.com/video-clips/3pwzi5/the-daily-show-with -jon-stewart-colbert-super-pac---not-coordinating-with-stephen-colbert.

8. Christina Cauterucci, "There's No Need to Slut-Shame Melania in Political Ads. Trump Is Horrible Enough!" *Slate*, March 22, 2016, www.slate.com/blogs/xx_factor/2016/03/22 /anti_trump_ads_try_to_win_over_mormons_by_slut_shaming_melania.html.

9. Richard Skinner, Seth Masket, and David Dulio, "527 Committees and the Political Party Network," *American Politics Research* 40, no. 1 (2011): 60–84.

10. Philip Rucker, "Profile of Stephanie Schriock, Campaign Adviser to Sen. Al Franken," *Washington Post*, July 13, 2009, www.washingtonpost.com/wp-dyn/content/article/2009 /07/12/AR2009071202209.html.

11. GOPAC, www.gopac.org/history/.

12. Seth Masket, "You Can't Buy Your Way around the Party," Mischiefs of Faction, February 19, 2015, https://mischiefsoffaction.blogspot.com/2015/02/you-cant-buy-your-way -around-party.html.

13. Seth Masket, John Sides, and Lynn Vavreck, "The Ground Game in the 2012 Presidential Election," *Political Communication* 33, no. 2 (2016): 169–87; Seth Masket, "Did Obama's Ground Game Matter? The Influence of Local Field Offices during the 2008 Presidential Election," *Public Opinion Quarterly* 73, no. 5 (2009): 1023–39, https://doi.org/10.1093 /poq/nfp077; Joshua P. Darr and Matthew S. Levendusky, "Relying on the Ground Game: The Placement and Effect of Campaign Field Offices," *American Politics Research* 42, no. 3 (2014): 529–48.

14. Van Jones, *Rebuild the Dream* (New York: Nation Books, 2013).

15. Brian Schaffner, Matthew Streb, and Gerald Wright, "Teams without Uniforms: The Nonpartisan Ballot in State and Local Elections," *Political Research Quarterly* 54, no. 1 (2001): 7–30.

16. Sarah F. Anzia, *Timing and Turnout: How Off-Cycle Elections Favor Organized Groups* (Chicago: University of Chicago Press, 2013).

17. Dylan Matthews, "Was George McGovern Doomed to Lose in 1972?" *Washington Post*, October 22, 2012, www.washingtonpost.com/news/wonk/wp/2012/10/22/was-george -mcgovern-doomed-to-lose-in-1972/?utm_term=.ceaf6152f996.

18. Seth Masket, *The Inevitable Party: Why Attempts to Kill the Party System Fail and How They Weaken Democracy* (New York: Oxford University Press, 2016).

19. Naftali Bendavid, "The House That Rahm Built," *Chicago Tribune*, Special Report, November 12, 2016, www.chicagotribune.com/news/ct-xpm-2006-11-12-0611170492 -story.html.

20. Thad Kousser, Scott Lewis, Seth Masket, and Eric McGhee, "Kingmakers or Cheerleaders? Party Power and the Causal Effects of Endorsements," *Political Research Quarterly* 68, no. 3 (2015): 443–56.

21. James Campbell, "How Accurate Were the Political Science Forecasts of the 2016 Presidential Election?" *Sabato's Crystal Ball*, UVA Center for Politics, November 17, 2016, http://centerforpolitics.org/crystalball/articles/how-accurate-were-the-political-science -forecasts-of-the-2016-presidential-election/.

22. Tré Goins-Phillips, "Did the San Antonio Mayor Really Say That Atheism Leads to Poverty?" *The Blaze*, April 25, 2017, www.theblaze.com/news/2017/04/25/did-the-san -antonio-mayor-really-say-that-atheism-leads-to-poverty.

23. Lynn Vavreck, *The Message Matters: The Economy and Presidential Campaigns* (Princeton, NJ: Princeton University Press, 2009).

Chapter 12: Parties and Voters

1. Ted Van Green and Alec Tyson, "5 Facts about Partisan Reactions to COVID-19 in the U.S.," Pew Research Center, April 2, 2020, www.pewresearch.org/fact-tank/2020/04/02/5-facts-about-partisan-reactions-to-covid-19-in-the-u-s/.
2. Greg Sargent, "Trump vs. Biden on Coronavirus: The Timeline Is Utterly Damning," *Washington Post*, April 6, 2020, www.washingtonpost.com/opinions/2020/04/06/trump-versus-biden-coronavirus-timeline-is-utterly-damning/.
3. Yahoo! News, Coronavirus poll of 1,597 U.S. Adults, conducted April 17–19, 2020, published April 19, 2020, https://docs.cdn.yougov.com/rjneitr3jm/20200419_yahoo_coronavirus_crosstabs.pdf.
4. American National Election Studies, 2016 Time Series.
5. By contrast, European party membership does come with dues, rights, and responsibilities. It is also something that not all European citizens are interested in having.
6. *California Democratic Party v. Jones*, 530 U.S. 567 (2000).
7. Steven Rogers, "Accountability in a Federal System" (PhD diss., Princeton University, 2013); Liz Farmer, "Who's Your Governor? 1 in 3 Americans Don't Know," December 21, 2018, *Governing*, www.governing.com/topics/politics/gov-americans-knowledge-state-government.html.
8. Ilya Somin, "Political Ignorance around the World," *Volokh Conspiracy* (blog), *Washington Post*, November 3, 2014, www.washingtonpost.com/news/volokh-conspiracy/wp/2014/11/03/political-ignorance-around-the-world/.
9. Eitan Hersh, *Politics Is for Power: How to Move beyond Political Hobbyism, Take Action, and Make Real Change* (New York: Scribner, 2020).
10. Angus Campbell, Philip E. Converse, Warren E. Miller, and Donald E. Stokes, *The American Voter* (Chicago: University of Chicago Press, 1960).
11. Duane F. Alwin and Jon A. Krosnick, "Aging, Cohorts, and the Stability of Sociopolitical Orientations over the Life Span," *American Journal of Sociology* 97, no. 1 (1991): 169–95; Christopher Ojeda and Peter K. Hatemi, "Accounting for the Child in the Transmission of Party Identification," *American Sociological Review* 80, no. 6 (2015): 1150–74.
12. Christopher H. Achen and Larry M. Bartels, *Democracy for Realists: Why Elections Do Not Produce Responsive Government* (Princeton, NJ: Princeton University Press, 2017).
13. Philip E. Converse, "The Nature of Belief Systems in Mass Publics," *Critical Review* 18, no. 1–3 (1964): 1–74, https://doi.org/10.1080/08913810608443650; John Zaller, *The Nature and Origins of Mass Opinion* (Cambridge: Cambridge University Press, 1993).
14. Matthew D. Lieberman, Darren Schreiber, and Kevin N. Ochsner, "Is Political Cognition Like Riding a Bicycle? How Cognitive Neuroscience Can Inform Research on Political Thinking," *Political Psychology* 24, no. 4 (2003): 681–704.
15. Bruce E. Keith, David B. Magleby, Candice J. Nelson, Elizabeth A. Orr, Mark C. Westlye, and Raymond E. Wolfinger, *The Myth of the Independent Voter* (Berkeley: University of California Press, 1992).
16. Keith et al., *The Myth*.
17. Samara Klar and Yanna Krupnikov, *Independent Politics: How American Disdain for Parties Leads to Political Inaction* (New York: Cambridge University Press, 2016).
18. Daniel Donner, "As Partisan Polarization Has Increased, Split-Ticket Voting Has Declined Precipitously," *Daily Kos*, March 19, 2015, www.dailykos.com/story/2015/3/19/1370206/-As-partisan-polarization-has-increased-split-ticket-voting-has-declined-precipitously.
19. Philip E. Converse, "The Nature of Belief Systems in Mass Publics," *Critical Review* 18, no. 1–3 (1964): 1–74, https://doi.org/10.1080/08913810608443650; John Zaller, *The Nature and Origins of Mass Opinion* (Cambridge: Cambridge University Press, 1993).
20. "Most Important Problem," In Depth: Topics A–Z, Gallup polls, https://news.gallup.com/poll/1675/most-important-problem.aspx.

21. Jamie Carson, Gregory Koger, Matthew Lebo, and Everett Young, "The Electoral Costs of Party Loyalty in Congress," *American Journal of Political Science* 54, no. 3 (2010): 598–616; Brandice Canes-Wrone, David W. Brady, and John F. Cogan, "Out of Step, Out of Office: Electoral Accountability and House Members' Voting," *American Political Science Review* 96, no. 1 (2002): 127–40.

22. D. Sunshine Hillygus and Simon Jackman, "Voter Decision Making in Election 2000: Campaign Effects, Partisan Activation, and the Clinton Legacy," *American Journal of Political Science* 47, no. 4 (2003): 683–96; Richard Johnston, Michael G. Hagen, and Kathleen Hall Jamieson, *The Dynamics of Election: The 2000 Presidential Election and the Foundations of Party Politics* (Cambridge University Press, 2004).

23. Christopher H. Achen and Larry M. Bartels, *Democracy for Realists: Why Elections Do Not Produce Responsive Government* (Princeton, NJ: Princeton University Press, 2016); Andrew J. Healy, Neil Malhotra, and Cecilia Hyunjung Mo, "Irrelevant events affect voters' evaluations of government performance," Proceedings of the National Academy of Sciences, July 20, 2010, 107 (29) 12804–12809; https://doi.org/10.1073/pnas.1007420107.

24. Steven Rogers, "Accountability in a Federal System" (PhD diss., Princeton University, 2013).

25. Douglas A. Hibbs, *The American Political Economy* (Cambridge, MA: Harvard University Press, 1989); Steven Rosenstone, *Forecasting Presidential Elections* (New Haven, CT: Yale University Press, 1983); Michael S. Lewis-Beck and Tom W. Rice, "Forecasting Presidential Elections: A Comparison of Naive Models," *Political Behavior* 6, no. 1 (1984): 9–21.

26. John Sides and Lynn Vavreck, *The Gamble: Choice and Chance in the 2012 Presidential Election* (Princeton, NJ: Princeton University Press, 2013).

27. Ismail K. White and Chryl N. Laird, *Steadfast Democrats: How Social Forces Shape Black Political Behavior* (Princeton, NJ: Princeton University Press, 2020); Tasha S. Philpot, *Conservative but Not Republican: The Paradox of Party Identification and Ideology among African Americans* (New York: Cambridge University Press, 2017).

28. Christopher Wlezien, "The Public as Thermostat: Dynamics of Preferences for Spending" *American Journal of Political Science* 39, no. 4 (1995): 981–1000.

29. James Campbell, "Introduction," *PS: Political Science & Politics* 49, no. 4 (2016): 649–54.

30. John Sides, Michael Tesler, and Lynn Vavreck, *Identity Crisis: The 2016 Presidential Campaign and the Battle for the Meaning of America* (Princeton, NJ: Princeton University Press, 2019).

31. DiMaggio et al. distinguish between these two kinds of polarization—fewer people in the middle, and the extremes becoming more extreme—but we treat them as the same, especially since they are hard to tell apart in the data. See Paul DiMaggio, John Evans, and Bethany Bryson, "Have Americans' Social Attitudes Become More Polarized?" *American Journal of Sociology* 102, no. 3 (1996): 690–755. See also Hans Noel, *Political Ideologies and Political Parties in America* (Cambridge: Cambridge University Press, 2013).

32. Michael Barber and Jeremy C. Pope, "Who Is Ideological? Measuring Ideological Consistency in the American Public," *Forum* 16, no. 2 (2018): 97–122.

33. Matt Levendusky, *The Partisan Sort: How Liberals Became Democrats and Conservatives Became Republicans* (New York: Cambridge University Press, 2009).

34. Alan I. Abramowitz and Steven Webster, "The Rise of Negative Partisanship and the Nationalization of U.S. Elections in the 21st Century," *Electoral Studies* 41 (March 2016): 12–22.

35. Hans Noel, *Political Ideologies and Political Parties in America* (Cambridge: Cambridge University Press, 2014).

36. Pew Research Center, U.S. Politics & Policy, "A Wider Ideological Gap between More and Less Educated Adults: Political Polarization Update," April 26, 2016, www.people-press.org/2016/04/26/a-wider-ideological-gap-between-more-and-less-educated-adults/.

37. Douglas J. Ahler and David E. Broockman, "The Delegate Paradox: Why Polarized Politicians Can Represent Citizens Best," *Journal of Politics* 80, no. 4, (2018): 1117–33.

38. Lilliana Mason, *Uncivil Agreement: How Politics Became Our Identity* (Chicago: University of Chicago Press, 2018).

39. Maxine Najle and Robert P. Jones, "American Democracy in Crisis: The Fate of Pluralism in a Divided Nation," PRRI (Public Religion Research Institute), February 19, 2019, www.prri.org/research/american-democracy-in-crisis-the-fate-of-pluralism-in-a-divided -nation/.

40. John Aldrich, *Why Parties?* (Chicago: University of Chicago Press, 1995).

41. Drew DeSilver, "U.S. Trails Most Developed Countries in Voter Turnout," Pew Research Center, May 21, 2018, www.pewresearch.org/fact-tank/2018/05/21/u-s-voter-turnout -trails-most-developed-countries/.

42. Emily Guskin and Scott Clement, "Poll: Nearly Half of Americans Say Voter Fraud Occurs Often," *The Fix* (blog), *Washington Post,* September 15, 2016, www.washington post.com/news/the-fix/wp/2016/09/15/poll-nearly-half-of-americans-say-voter-fraud -occurs-often/.

43. James DeNardo, "Turnout and the Vote: The Joke's on the Democrats," *American Political Science Review* 74, no. 2 (1980): 406–20.

44. Jack Citrin, Eric Schickler, and John Sides, "What If Everyone Voted? Simulating the Impact of Increased Turnout in Senate Elections," *American Journal of Political Science* 47, no. 1 (2003): 75–90.

45. Thomas Brunell and John DiNardo, "A Propensity Score Reweighting Approach to Estimating the Partisan Effects of Full Turnout in American Presidential Elections," *Political Analysis* 12, no. 1 (2004): 28–45.

46. Nancy Rosenblum, *On the Side of the Angels: An Appreciation of Parties and Partisanship* (Princeton, NJ: Princeton University Press, 2008), 354–55.

Appendix

President George Washington's Farewell Address (1796)

While, then, every part of our country thus feels an immediate and particular interest in union, all the parts combined can not fail to find in the united mass of means and efforts greater strength, greater resource, proportionably greater security from external danger, a less frequent interruption of their peace by foreign nations, and what is of inestimable value, they must derive from union an exemption from those broils and wars between themselves which so frequently afflict neighboring countries not tied together by the same governments, which their own rivalships alone would be sufficient to produce, but which opposite foreign alliances, attachments, and intrigues would stimulate and imbitter. Hence, likewise, they will avoid the necessity of those overgrown military establishments which, under any form of government, are inauspicious to liberty, and which are to be regarded as particularly hostile to republican liberty. In this sense it is that your union ought to be considered as a main prop of your liberty, and that the love of the one ought to endear to you the preservation of the other. * * *

In contemplating the causes which may disturb our union it occurs as matter of serious concern that any ground should have been furnished for characterizing parties by *geographical* discriminations—*Northern* and *Southern, Atlantic* and *Western*—whence designing men may endeavor to excite a belief that there is a real difference of local interests and views. One of the expedients of party to acquire influence within particular districts is to misrepresent the opinions and aims of other districts. You can not shield yourselves too much against the jealousies and heart-burnings which spring from these misrepresentations; they tend to render alien to each other those who ought to be bound together by fraternal affection. * * *

To the efficacy and permanency of your union a government for the whole is indispensable. * * * This Government, the offspring of our own choice, uninfluenced and unawed, adopted upon full investigation and mature deliberation, completely free in its principles, in the distribution of its powers, uniting security with energy, and containing within itself a provision for its own amendment, has a just claim to your confidence and your support. Respect for its authority, compliance with its laws, acquiescence in its measures, are duties enjoined by the fundamental maxims of true liberty. The basis of our political systems is the right of the people to make and to alter their constitutions of government. But the constitution which at any time exists till changed by an explicit and authentic act of the whole people is sacredly obligatory upon all. The very idea of the power and the right of the people to establish government presupposes the duty of every individual to obey the established government.

I have already intimated to you the danger of parties in the State, with particular reference to the founding of them on geographical discriminations. Let me now take a more comprehensive view, and warn you in the most solemn manner against the baneful effects of the spirit of party generally.

This spirit, unfortunately, is inseparable from our nature, having its root in the strongest passions of the human mind. It exists under different shapes in all governments, more or less stifled, controlled, or repressed; but in those of the popular form it is seen in its greatest rankness and is truly their worst enemy. * * *

It serves always to distract the public councils and enfeeble the public administration. It agitates the community with ill-founded jealousies and false alarms; kindles the animosity of one part against another; foments occasionally riot and insurrection. It opens the door to foreign influence and corruption, which find a facilitated access to the government itself through the channels of party passion. Thus the policy and the will of one country are subjected to the policy and will of another.

There is an opinion that parties in free countries are useful checks upon the administration of the government, and serve to keep alive the spirit of liberty. This within certain limits is probably true; and in governments of a monarchical cast patriotism may look with indulgence, if not with favor, upon the spirit of party. But in those of the popular character, in governments purely elective, it is a spirit not to be encouraged. From their natural tendency it is certain there will always be enough of that spirit for every salutary purpose; and there being constant danger of excess, the effort ought to be by force of public opinion to mitigate and assuage it. A fire not to be quenched, it demands a uniform vigilance to prevent its bursting into a flame, lest, instead of warming, it should consume.* * *

Observe good faith and justice toward all nations. Cultivate peace and harmony with all. Religion and morality enjoin this conduct. And can it be that good policy does not equally enjoin it? It will be worthy of a free, enlightened, and at no distant period a great nation to give to mankind the magnanimous and too novel example of a people always guided by an exalted justice and benevolence. Who can doubt that in the course of time and things the fruits of such a plan would richly repay any temporary advantages which might be lost by a steady adherence to it? Can it be that Providence has not connected the permanent felicity of a nation with its virtue? The experiment, at least, is recommended by every sentiment which ennobles human nature. Alas! is it rendered impossible by its vices?

In the execution of such a plan nothing is more essential than that permanent, inveterate antipathies against particular nations and passionate attachments for others should be excluded, and that in place of them just and amicable feelings toward all should be cultivated. The nation which indulges toward another an habitual hatred or an habitual fondness is in some degree a slave. It is a slave to its animosity or to its affection, either of which is sufficient to lead it astray from its duty and its interest. Antipathy in one nation against another disposes each more readily to offer insult and injury, to lay hold of slight causes of umbrage, and to be haughty and intractable when accidental or trifling occasions of dispute occur. * * *

So, likewise, a passionate attachment of one nation for another produces a variety of evils. Sympathy for the favorite nation, facilitating the illusion of an imaginary common interest in cases where no real common interest exists, and infusing into one the enmities of the other, betrays the former into a participation in the quarrels and wars of the latter without adequate inducement or justification. It leads also to concessions to the favorite nation of privileges denied to others, which is apt doubly to injure the nation making the concessions by unnecessarily parting with what ought to have been retained, and by exciting jealousy, ill will, and a disposition to retaliate in the parties from whom equal privileges are withheld; and it gives to ambitious, corrupted, or deluded citizens (who devote themselves to the favorite nation) facility to betray or sacrifice the interests of their own country without odium, sometimes even with popularity, gilding with the appearances of a virtuous sense of obligation, a commendable deference for public opinion, or a laudable zeal for public good the base or foolish compliances of ambition, corruption, or infatuation. * * *

Against the insidious wiles of foreign influence (I conjure you to believe me, fellow-citizens) the jealousy of a free people ought to be *constantly* awake, since history and experience prove that foreign influence is one of the most baneful foes of republican government. But that jealousy, to be useful, must be impartial, else it becomes the instrument of the very influence to be avoided, instead of a defense against it. Excessive partiality for one foreign nation and excessive dislike of another cause those whom they actuate to see danger only on one side, and serve to veil and even second the arts of influence on the other. Real patriots who may resist the intrigues of the favorite are liable to become suspected and odious, while its tools and dupes usurp the applause and confidence of the people to surrender their interests.

The great rule of conduct for us in regard to foreign nations is, in extending our commercial relations to have with them as little *political* connection as possible. So far as we have already formed engagements let them be fulfilled with perfect good faith. Here let us stop.

Europe has a set of primary interests which to us have none or a very remote relation. Hence she must be engaged in frequent controversies, the causes of which are essentially foreign to our concerns. Hence, therefore, it must be unwise in us to implicate ourselves by artificial ties in the ordinary vicissitudes of her politics or the ordinary combinations and collisions of her friendships or enmities.

Our detached and distant situation invites and enables us to pursue a different course. If we remain one people, under an efficient government, the period is not far off when we may defy material injury from external annoyance; when we may take such an attitude as will cause the neutrality we may at any time resolve upon to be scrupulously respected; when belligerent nations, under the impossibility of making acquisitions upon us, will not lightly hazard the giving us provocation; when we may choose peace or war, as our interest, guided by justice, shall counsel.

Why forego the advantages of so peculiar a situation? Why quit our own to stand upon foreign ground? Why, by interweaving our destiny with that of any part of Europe, entangle our peace and prosperity in the toils of European ambition, rivalship, interest, humor, or caprice?

It is our true policy to steer clear of permanent alliances with any portion of the foreign world, so far, I mean, as we are now at liberty to do it; for let me not be understood as capable of patronizing infidelity to existing engagements. I hold the maxim no less applicable to public than to private affairs that honesty is always the best policy. I repeat, therefore, let those engagements be observed in their genuine sense. But in my opinion it is unnecessary and would be unwise to extend them.

Taking care always to keep ourselves by suitable establishments on a respectable defensive posture, we may safely trust to temporary alliances for extraordinary emergencies.

Harmony, liberal intercourse with all nations are recommended by policy. humanity, and interest. But even our commercial policy should hold an equal and impartial hand, neither seeking nor granting exclusive favors or preferences; consulting the natural course of things; diffusing and diversifying by gentle means the streams of commerce, but forcing nothing; establishing with powers so disposed, in order to give trade a stable course, to define the rights of our merchants, and to enable the Government to support them, conventional rules of intercourse, the best that present circumstances and mutual opinion will permit, but temporary and liable to be from time to time abandoned or varied as experience and circumstances shall dictate; constantly keeping in view that it is folly in one nation to look for disinterested favors from another; that it must pay with a portion of its independence for whatever it may accept under that character; that by such acceptance it may place itself in the condition of having given equivalents for nominal favors, and yet of being reproached with ingratitude for not giving more. There can be no greater error than to expect or calculate upon real favors from nation to nation. It is an illusion which experience must cure, which a just pride ought to discard.

The Federalist Papers

NO. 10: MADISON

Among the numerous advantages promised by a well constructed Union, none deserves to be more accurately developed than its tendency to break and control the violence of faction. The friend of popular governments never finds himself so much alarmed for their character and fate, as when he contemplates their propensity to this dangerous vice. He will not fail therefore to set a due value on any plan which, without violating the principles to which he is attached, provides a proper cure for it. The instability, injustice, and confusion introduced into the public councils have, in truth, been the mortal diseases under which popular governments have everywhere perished, as they continue to be the favorite and fruitful topics from which the adversaries to liberty derive their most specious declamations. The valuable improvements made by the American constitutions on the popular models, both ancient and modern, cannot certainly be too much admired; but it would be an unwarrantable partiality to contend that they have as effectually obviated the danger on this side, as was wished and expected. Complaints are everywhere heard from our most considerate and virtuous citizens, equally the friends of public and private faith and of public and personal liberty, that our governments are too unstable, that the public good is disregarded in the conflicts of rival parties, and that measures are too often decided, not according to the rules of justice and the rights of the minor party, but by the superior force of an interested and overbearing majority. However anxiously we may wish that these complaints had no foundation, the evidence of known facts will not permit us to deny that they are in some degree true. It will be found, indeed, on a candid review of our situation, that some of the distresses under which we labor have been erroneously charged on the operation of our governments; but it will be found, at the same time, that other causes will not alone account for many of our heaviest misfortunes; and, particularly, for that prevailing and increasing distrust of public engagements and alarm for private rights which are echoed from one end of the continent to the other. These must be chiefly, if not wholly, effects of the unsteadiness and injustice with which a factious spirit has tainted our public administration.

By a faction I understand a number of citizens, whether amounting to a majority or minority of the whole, who are united and actuated by some common impulse of passion, or of interest, adverse to the rights of other citizens, or to the permanent and aggregate interests of the community.

There are two methods of curing the mischiefs of faction: the one, by removing its causes; the other, by controlling its effects.

There are again two methods of removing the causes of faction: the one, by destroying the liberty which is essential to its existence; the other, by giving to every citizen the same opinions, the same passions, and the same interests.

It could never be more truly said than of the first remedy, that it is worse than the disease. Liberty is to faction what air is to fire, an aliment without which it instantly expires. But it could not be a less folly to abolish liberty, which is essential to political life, because it nourishes faction, than it would be to wish the annihilation of air, which is essential to animal life, because it imparts to fire its destructive agency.

The second expedient is as impracticable, as the first would be unwise. As long as the reason of man continues fallible, and he is at liberty to exercise it, different opinions will be formed. As long as the connection subsists between his reason and his self-love, his opinions and his passions will have a reciprocal influence on each other; and the former will be objects to which the latter will attach themselves. The diversity in the faculties of men, from which the rights of property originate, is not less an insuperable obstacle to a uniformity of interests. The protection of these faculties is the first object of Government. From the protection of different and unequal faculties of acquiring property, the possession of different degrees and kinds of property immediately results; and from the influence of these on the sentiments and views of the respective proprietors, ensues a division of the society into different interests and parties.

The latent causes of faction are thus sown in the nature of man; and we see them everywhere brought into different degrees of activity, according to the different circumstances of civil society. A zeal for different opinions concerning religion, concerning Government, and many other points, as well of speculation as of practice; an attachment to different leaders ambitiously contending for pre-eminence and power; or to persons of other descriptions whose fortunes have been interesting to the human passions, have in turn divided mankind into parties, inflamed them with mutual animosity, and rendered them much more disposed to vex and oppress each other, than to co-operate for their common good. So strong is this propensity of mankind to fall into mutual animosities, that where no substantial occasion presents itself, the most frivolous and fanciful distinctions have been sufficient to kindle their unfriendly passions, and excite their most violent conflicts. But the most common and durable source of factions has been the various and unequal distribution of property. Those who hold and those who are without property have ever formed distinct interests in society. Those who are creditors, and those who are debtors, fall under a like discrimination. A landed interest, a manufacturing interest, a mercantile interest, a moneyed interest, with many lesser interests, grow up of necessity in civilized nations, and divide them into different classes, actuated by different sentiments and views. The regulation of these various and interfering interests forms the principal task of modern Legislation, and involves the spirit of party and faction in the necessary and ordinary operations of Government.

No man is allowed to be judge in his own cause, because his interest would certainly bias his judgment and, not improbably, corrupt his integrity. With equal, nay with greater reason, a body of men are unfit to be both judges and parties at the same time; yet what are many of the most important acts of legislation but so many judicial determinations, not indeed concerning the rights of single persons, but concerning the rights of large bodies of citizens; and what are the different classes of legislators but advocates and parties to the causes which they determine? Is a law proposed concerning private debts? It is a question to which the creditors are parties on one side and the debtors on the other. Justice ought to hold the balance between them. Yet the parties are, and must be, themselves the judges; and the most numerous party, or in other words, the most powerful faction must be expected to prevail. Shall domestic manufacturers be encouraged, and in what degree, by restrictions on foreign manufacturers? are questions which would be differently decided by the landed and the manufacturing classes, and probably by neither with a sole regard to justice and the public good. The apportionment of taxes on the various descriptions of property is an act which seems to require the most exact impartiality; yet there is, perhaps, no legislative act in which greater opportunity and temptation are given to a predominant party to trample on the rules of justice. Every shilling with which they overburden the inferior number is a shilling saved to their own pockets.

It is in vain to say that enlightened statesmen will be able to adjust these clashing interests and render them all subservient to the public good. Enlightened statesmen will not always be at the helm. Nor, in many cases, can such an adjustment be made at all without taking into view indirect and remote considerations, which will rarely prevail over the immediate interest which one party may find in disregarding the rights of another or the good of the whole.

The inference to which we are brought is that the *causes* of faction cannot be removed and that relief is only to be sought in the means of controlling its *effects*.

If a faction consists of less than a majority, relief is supplied by the republican principle, which enables the majority to defeat its sinister views by regular vote. It may clog the administration, it may convulse the society; but it will be unable to execute and mask its violence under the forms of the Constitution. When a majority is included in a faction, the form of popular government, on the other hand, enables it to sacrifice to its ruling passion or interest both the public good and the rights of other citizens. To secure the public good and private rights against the danger of such a faction, and at the same time to preserve the spirit and the form of popular government, is then the great object to which our enquiries are directed. Let me add that it is the great desideratum by which alone this form of government can be rescued from the opprobrium under which it has so long labored and be recommended to the esteem and adoption of mankind.

By what means is this object attainable? Evidently by one of two only. Either the existence of the same passion or interest in a majority at the same time must be prevented, or the majority, having such co-existent passion or interest, must be rendered, by their number and local situation, unable to concert and carry into effect schemes of oppression. If the impulse and the opportunity be suffered to coincide, we well know that neither moral nor religious motives can be relied on as an adequate control. They are not found to be such on the injustice and violence of individuals, and lose their efficacy in proportion to the number combined together, that is, in proportion as their efficacy becomes needful.

From this view of the subject it may be concluded that a pure Democracy, by which I mean a Society consisting of a small number of citizens, who assemble and administer the Government in person, can admit of no cure for the mischiefs of faction. A common passion or interest will, in almost every case, be felt by a majority of the whole; a communication and concert results from the form of Government itself; and there is nothing to check the inducements to sacrifice the weaker party or an obnoxious individual. Hence it is that such Democracies have ever been spectacles of turbulence and contention; have ever been found incompatible with personal security or the rights of property; and have in general been as short in their lives as they have been violent in their deaths. Theoretic politicians, who have patronized this species of Government, have erroneously supposed that by reducing mankind to a perfect equality in their political rights, they would at the same time be perfectly equalized and assimilated in their possessions, their opinions, and their passions.

A Republic, by which I mean a Government in which the scheme of representation takes place, opens a different prospect and promises the cure for which we are seeking. Let us examine the points in which it varies from pure Democracy, and we shall comprehend both the nature of the cure and the efficacy which it must derive from the Union.

The two great points of difference between a Democracy and a Republic are: first, the delegation of the Government, in the latter, to a small number of citizens elected by the rest; secondly, the greater number of citizens and greater sphere of country over which the latter may be extended.

The effect of the first difference is, on the one hand, to refine and enlarge the public views by passing them through the medium of a chosen body of citizens, whose wisdom may best discern the true interest of their country and whose patriotism and love of justice will be least likely to sacrifice it to temporary or partial considerations. Under such a regulation it may well happen that the public voice, pronounced by the representatives of the people, will be more consonant to the public good than if pronounced by the people themselves, convened for the purpose. On the other hand, the effect may be inverted. Men of factious tempers, of local prejudices, or of sinister designs, may, by intrigue, by corruption, or by other means, first obtain the suffrages, and then betray the interests of the people. The question resulting is, whether small or extensive Republics are most favorable to the election of proper guardians of the public weal; and it is clearly decided in favor of the latter by two obvious considerations.

In the first place it is to be remarked that however small the Republic may be, the Representatives must be raised to a certain number in order to guard against the cabals of a few; and that however large it may be they must be limited to a certain number in order to guard against the confusion of a multitude. Hence, the number of Representatives in the two cases not being in proportion to that of the Constituents, and being proportionally greatest in the small Republic, it follows that if the proportion of fit characters be not less in the large than in the small Republic, the former will present a greater option, and consequently a greater probability of a fit choice.

In the next place, as each Representative will be chosen by a greater number of citizens in the large than in the small Republic, it will be more difficult for unworthy candidates to practise with success the vicious arts by which elections are too often carried; and the suffrages of the people being more free, will be more likely to centre on men who possess the most attractive merit and the most diffusive and established characters.

It must be confessed that in this, as in most other cases, there is a mean, on both sides of which inconveniencies will be found to lie. By enlarging too much the number of electors, you render the representative too little acquainted with all their local circumstances and lesser interests; as by reducing it too much, you render him unduly attached to these, and too little fit to comprehend and pursue great and national objects. The Federal Constitution forms a happy combination in this respect; the great and aggregate interests being referred to the national, the local and particular to the State legislatures.

The other point of difference is the greater number of citizens and extent of territory which may be brought within the compass of Republican than of Democratic Government; and it is this circumstance principally which renders factious combinations less to be dreaded in the former than in the latter. The smaller the society, the fewer probably will be the distinct parties and interests composing it; the fewer the distinct parties and interests, the more frequently will a majority be found of the same party; and the smaller the number of individuals composing a majority, and the smaller the compass within which they are placed, the more easily will they concert and execute their plans of oppression. Extend the sphere and you take in a greater variety of parties and interests; you make it less probable that a majority of the whole will have a common motive to invade the rights of other citizens; or if such a common motive exists, it will be more difficult for all who feel it to discover their own strength and to act in unison with each other. Besides other impediments, it may be remarked, that where there is a consciousness of unjust or dishonorable purposes, communication is always checked by distrust in proportion to the number whose concurrence is necessary.

Hence, it clearly appears that the same advantage which a Republic has over a Democracy in controlling the effects of faction is enjoyed by a large over a small republic—is enjoyed by the Union over the States composing it. Does this advantage consist in the substitution of representatives whose enlightened views and virtuous sentiments render them superior to local prejudices and to schemes of injustice? It will not be denied that the representation of the Union will be most likely to possess these requisite endowments. Does it consist in the greater security afforded by a greater variety of parties, against the event of any one party being able to outnumber and oppress the rest? In an equal degree does the increased variety of parties comprised within the Union increase this security? Does it, in fine, consist in the greater obstacles opposed to the concert and accomplishment of the secret wishes of an unjust and interested majority? Here again the extent of the Union gives it the most palpable advantage.

The influence of factious leaders may kindle a flame within their particular States but will be unable to spread a general conflagration through the other States: a religious sect may degenerate into a political faction in a part of the Confederacy; but the variety of sects dispersed over the entire face of it must secure the national Councils against any danger from that source: a rage for paper money, for an abolition of debts, for an equal division of property, or for any other improper or wicked project, will be less apt to pervade the whole body of the Union than a particular member of it; in the same proportion as such a malady is more likely to taint a particular county or district than an entire State.

In the extent and proper structure of the Union, therefore, we behold a republican remedy for the diseases most incident to Republican Government. And according to the degree of pleasure and pride we feel in being republicans ought to be our zeal in cherishing the spirit and supporting the character of federalist.

PUBLIUS

November 22, 1787

NO. 51: MADISON

To what expedient, then, shall we finally resort, for maintaining in practice the necessary partition of power among the several departments as laid down in the constitution? The only answer that can be given is that as all these exterior provisions are found to be inadequate the defect must be supplied, by so contriving the interior structure of the government as that its several constituent parts may, by their mutual relations, be the means of keeping each other in their proper places. Without presuming to undertake a full development of this important idea I will hazard a few general observations which may perhaps place it in a clearer light, and enable us to form a more correct judgment of the principles and structure of the government planned by the convention.

In order to lay a due foundation for that separate and distinct exercise of the different powers of government, which to a certain extent is admitted on all hands to be essential to the preservation of liberty, it is evident that each department should have a will of its own; and consequently should be so constituted that the members of each should have as little agency as possible in the appointment of the members of the others. Were this principle rigorously adhered to, it would require that all the appointments for the supreme executive, legislative, and judiciary magistracies should be drawn from the same fountain of authority, the people, through channels having no communication whatever with one another. Perhaps such a plan of constructing the several departments would be less difficult in practice than it may in contemplation appear. Some difficulties, however, and some additional expense would attend the execution of it. Some deviations, therefore, from the principle must be admitted. In the constitution of the judiciary department in particular, it might be inexpedient to insist rigorously on the principle: first, because peculiar qualifications being essential in the members, the primary consideration ought to be to select that mode of choice which best secures these qualifications; second, because the permanent tenure by which the appointments are held in that department must soon destroy all sense of dependence on the authority conferring them.

It is equally evident that the members of each department should be as little dependent as possible on those of the others for the emoluments annexed to their offices. Were the executive magistrate, or the judges, not independent of the legislature in this particular, their independence in every other would be merely nominal.

But the great security against a gradual concentration of the several powers in the same department consists in giving to those who administer each department the necessary constitutional means and personal motives to resist encroachments of the others. The provision for defence must in this, as in all other cases, be made commensurate to the danger of attack. Ambition must be made to counteract ambition. The interest of the man must be connected with the constitutional rights of the place. It may be a reflection on human nature that such devices should be necessary to control the abuses of government. But what is government itself but the greatest of all reflections on human nature? If men were angels, no government would be necessary. If angels were to govern men, neither external nor internal controls on government would be necessary. In framing a government which is to be administered by men over men, the great difficulty lies in this: You must first enable the government to control the governed; and in the next place oblige it to control itself. A dependence on the people is, no doubt, the primary control on the government; but experience has taught mankind the necessity of auxiliary precautions.

This policy of supplying, by opposite and rival interests, the defect of better motives, might be traced through the whole system of human affairs, private as well as public. We see it particularly displayed in all the subordinate distributions of power, where the constant aim is to divide and arrange the several offices in such a manner as that each may be a check on the other; that the private interest of every individual may be a sentinel over the public rights. These inventions of prudence cannot be less requisite in the distribution of the supreme powers of the State.

But it is not possible to give to each department an equal power of self-defense. In republican government, the legislative authority necessarily predominates. The remedy for this inconveniency is to divide the legislature into different branches; and to render them, by different modes of election and different principles of action, as little connected with each other as the nature of their common functions and their common dependence on the society will admit. It may even be necessary to guard against dangerous encroachments by still further precautions. As the weight of the legislative authority requires that it should be thus divided, the weakness of the executive may require, on the other hand, that it should be fortified. An absolute negative on the legislature appears, at first view, to be the natural defense with which the executive magistrate should be armed. But perhaps it would be neither altogether safe nor alone sufficient. On ordinary occasions it might not be exerted with the requisite firmness, and on extraordinary occasions it might be perfidiously abused. May not this defect of an absolute negative be supplied by some qualified connection between this weaker branch of the stronger department, by which the latter may be led to support the constitutional rights of the former, without being too much detached from the rights of its own department?

If the principles on which these observations are founded be just, as I persuade myself they are, and they be applied as a criterion to the several State constitutions, and to the federal Constitution, it will be found that if the latter does not perfectly correspond with them, the former are infinitely less able to bear such a test.

There are, moreover, two considerations particularly applicable to the federal system of America, which place that system in a very interesting point of view.

First. In a single republic, all the power surrendered by the people is submitted to the administration of a single government; and usurpations are guarded against by a division of the government into distinct and separate departments. In the compound republic of America, the power surrendered by the people is first divided between two distinct governments, and then the portion allotted to each subdivided among distinct and separate departments. Hence a double security arises to the rights of the people. The different governments will control each other, at the same time that each will be controlled by itself.

Second. It is of great importance in a republic not only to guard the society against the oppression of its rulers, but to guard one part of the society against the injustice of the other part. Different interests necessarily exist in different classes of citizens. If a majority be united by a common interest, the rights of the minority will be insecure. There are but two methods of providing against this evil: The one by creating a will in the community independent of the majority— that is, of the society itself; the other, by comprehending in the society so many separate descriptions of citizens as will render an unjust combination of a majority of the whole very improbable, if not impracticable. The first method prevails in all governments possessing an hereditary or self-appointed authority. This, at best, is but a precarious security; because a power independent of the society may as well espouse the unjust views of the major as the rightful interests of the minor party, and may possibly be turned against both parties. The second method will be exemplified in the federal republic of the United States. Whilst all authority in it will be derived from and dependent on the society, the society itself will be broken into so many parts, interests and classes of citizens, that the rights of individuals, or of the minority, will be in little danger from interested combinations of the majority. In a free government the security for civil rights must be the same as that for religious rights. It consists in the one case in the multiplicity of interests, and in the other in the multiplicity of sects. The degree of security in both cases will depend on the number of interests and sects; and this may be presumed to depend on the extent of country and number of people comprehended under the same government. This view of the subject must particularly recommend a proper federal system to all the sincere and considerate friends of republican government: Since it shows that in exact proportion as the territory of the Union may be formed into more circumscribed Confederacies, or States, oppressive combinations of a majority will be facilitated; the best security, under the republican form, for the rights of every class of citizens, will be diminished; and consequently the stability and independence of some member of the government, the only other security, must be proportionally increased. Justice is the end of government. It is the end of civil society. It ever has been and ever will be pursued until it be obtained, or until liberty be lost in the pursuit. In a society under the forms of which the stronger faction can readily unite and oppress the weaker, anarchy may as truly be said to reign as in a state of nature, where the weaker individual is not secured against the violence of the stronger: And as, in the latter state, even the stronger individuals are prompted, by the uncertainty of their condition, to submit to a government which may protect the weak as well as themselves: So, in the former state, will the more powerful factions or parties be gradually induced, by a like motive, to wish for a government which will protect all parties, the weaker as well as the more powerful. It can be little doubted that if the State of Rhode Island was separated from the Confederacy and left to itself, the insecurity of rights under the popular form of government within such narrow limits would be displayed by such reiterated oppressions of factious majorities that some power altogether independent of the people would soon be called for by the voice of the very factions whose misrule had proved the necessity of it. In the extended republic of the United States, and among the great variety of interests, parties, and sects which it embraces, a coalition of a majority of the whole society could seldom take place on any other principles than those of justice and the general good; and there being thus less danger to a minor from the will of the major party, there must be less pretext, also, to provide for the security of the former, by introducing into the government a will not dependent on the latter, or, in other words, a will independent of the society itself. It is no less certain than it is important, notwithstanding the contrary opinions which have been entertained, that the larger the society, provided it lie within a practicable sphere, the more duly capable it will be of self-government. And happily for the *republican cause*, the practicable sphere may be carried to a very great extent by a judicious modification and mixture of the *federal principle*.

PUBLIUS

February 6, 1788

Party Control of Congress, 1789–2023

Unified Control of Government | Divided Government

Congress	Years	Senate			House			President
		Pro-Administration	Anti-Administration	Other	Pro-Administration	Anti-Administration	Other	
1	1789–91	18	8	—	37	28	—	George Washington
2	1791–93	16	13	—	39	30	—	Washington
3	1793–95	16	14	—	51	54	—	Washington
		Federalists	Jeffersonian Republicans	Other	Federalists	Jeffersonian Republicans	Other	
4	1795–97	21	11	—	47	59	—	Washington
5	1797–99	22	10	—	57	49	—	John Adams
6	1799–1801	22	10	—	60	46	—	Adams
7	1801–03	15	17	—	38	68	—	Thomas Jefferson
8	1803–05	9	25	—	39	103	—	Jefferson
9	1805–07	7	27	—	28	114	—	Jefferson
10	1807–09	6	28	—	26	116	—	Jefferson
11	1809–11	7	27	—	50	92	—	James Madison
12	1811–13	6	30	—	36	107	—	Madison
13	1813–15	8	28	—	68	114	—	Madison
14	1815–17	12	26	—	64	119	—	Madison
15	1817–19	12	30	—	39	146	—	James Monroe
16	1819–21	9	37	—	26	160	—	Monroe
17	1821–23	4	44	—	32	155	—	Monroe
		Adams-Clay Republicans	Jackson Republicans	Other	Adams-Clay Republicans	Jackson Republicans	Other	
18	1823–25	17	31	—	72	64	77	Monroe
19	1825–27	22	26	—	109	104	—	John Quincy Adams
20	1827–29	21	27	—	100	113	—	Quincy Adams
		Anti-Jacksons	Jacksons	Other	Anti-Jacksons	Jacksons	Other	
21	1829–31	23	25	—	72	136	5	Andrew Jackson
22	1831–33	22	24	2	66	126	21	Jackson

(continued)

Party Control of Congress, 1789–2023 *(continued)*

Congress	Years	Senate			House			President
23	1833–35	26	20	2	63	143	34	Jackson
24	1835–37	24	26	2	75	143	24	Jackson
		Democrats	**Whigs**	**Other**	**Democrats**	**Whigs**	**Other**	
25	1837–39	35	17	—	128	100	12	Martin Van Buren
26	1839–41	30	22	—	125	109	8	Van Buren
27	1841–43	22	29	—	98	142	2	William Henry Harrison/John Tyler
28	1843–45	23	29	—	147	72	4	Tyler
29	1845–47	34	22	—	142	79	6	James K. Polk
30	1847–49	38	21	1	110	116	4	Polk
31	1849–51	35	25	2	113	108	11	Zachary Taylor/ Millard Fillmore
32	1851–53	36	23	3	127	85	21	Fillmore
33	1853–55	38	22	2	157	71	6	Franklin Pierce
		Democrats	**Oppositions**	**Other**	**Democrats**	**Oppositions**	**Other**	
34	1855–57	39	21	2	83	100	51	Pierce
		Democrats	**Republicans**	**Other**	**Democrats**	**Republicans**	**Other**	
35	1857–59	41	20	5	132	90	15	James Buchanan
36	1859–61	38	26	2	83	116	39	Buchanan
37	1861–63	15	31	3	44	108	31	Abraham Lincoln
38	1863–65	10	33	9	72	85	27	Lincoln
39	1865–67	11	39	4	38	136	16	Lincoln/Andrew Johnson
40	1867–69	9	57	—	47	173	4	Johnson
41	1869–71	12	62	—	67	171	5	Ulysses S. Grant
42	1871–73	17	56	1	104	136	3	Grant
43	1873–75	19	47	7	88	199	5	Grant
44	1875–77	28	46	1	182	103	8	Grant
45	1877–79	35	40	1	155	136	2	Rutherford B. Hayes

Congress	Years	Senate			House			President
		Democrats	Republicans	Other	Democrats	Republicans	Other	
46	1879–81	42	33	1	141	132	21	Hayes
47	1881–83	37	37	2	128	151	14	James A. Garfield/ Chester A. Arthur
48	1883–85	36	38	2	196	117	12	Arthur
49	1885–87	34	42	—	182	141	2	Grover Cleveland
50	1887–89	37	39	—	167	152	6	Cleveland
51	1889–91	37	51	—	152	179	1	Benjamin Harrison
52	1891–93	39	47	—	238	86	8	Harrison
53	1893–95	44	40	4	218	124	14	Cleveland
54	1895–97	40	44	6	93	254	10	Cleveland
55	1897–99	34	44	12	124	206	27	William McKinley
56	1899–1901	26	53	10	161	187	9	McKinley
57	1901–03	31	55	4	151	197	9	McKinley/Theodore Roosevelt
58	1903–05	33	57	—	178	208	—	T. Roosevelt
59	1905–07	33	57	—	136	250	—	T. Roosevelt
60	1907–09	31	61	—	164	222	—	T. Roosevelt
61	1909–11	32	61	—	172	219	—	William Howard Taft
62	1911–13	41	51	—	228	161	1	Taft
63	1913–15	51	44	1	291	127	17	Woodrow Wilson
64	1915–17	56	40	—	230	196	9	Wilson
65	1917–19	53	42	—	216	210	6	Wilson
66	1919–21	47	49	—	190	240	3	Wilson
67	1921–23	37	59	—	131	301	1	Warren G. Harding
68	1923–25	43	51	2	205	225	5	Calvin Coolidge
69	1925–27	39	56	1	183	247	4	Coolidge
70	1927–29	46	49	1	195	237	3	Coolidge
71	1929–31	39	56	1	167	267	1	Herbert Hoover

(continued)

Party Control of Congress, 1789–2023 *(continued)*

Congress	Years	Senate			House			President
		Democrats	Republicans	Other	Democrats	Republicans	Other	
72	1931–33	47	48	1	220	214	1	Hoover
73	1933–35	60	35	1	313	117	5	Franklin D. Roosevelt
74	1935–37	69	25	2	319	103	10	F.D. Roosevelt
75	1937–39	76	16	4	331	89	13	F.D. Roosevelt
76	1939–41	69	23	4	261	164	4	F.D. Roosevelt
77	1941–43	66	28	2	268	162	5	F.D. Roosevelt
78	1943–45	58	37	1	218	208	4	F.D. Roosevelt
79	1945–47	56	38	1	242	190	2	Harry S. Truman
80	1947–49	45	51	—	188	245	1	Truman
81	1949–51	54	42	—	263	171	1	Truman
82	1951–53	49	47	—	234	199	1	Truman
83	1953–55	47	48	1	211	221	1	Dwight D. Eisenhower
84	1955–57	48	47	1	232	203	—	Eisenhower
85	1957–59	49	47	—	233	200	—	Eisenhower
86	1959–61	65	35	—	284	153	—	Eisenhower
87	1961–63	65	35	—	263	174	—	John F. Kennedy
88	1963–65	67	35	—	258	177	—	Kennedy/ Lyndon B. Johnson
89	1965–67	68	32	—	295	140	—	Johnson
90	1967–69	64	36	—	247	187	—	Johnson
91	1969–71	57	43	—	243	192	—	Richard M. Nixon
92	1971–73	54	44	2	254	180	—	Nixon
93	1973–75	56	42	2	239	192	1	Nixon/Gerald R. Ford
94	1975–77	60	37	2	291	144	—	Ford
95	1977–79	61	38	1	292	143	—	Jimmy Carter
96	1979–81	58	41	1	276	157	—	Carter
97	1981–83	46	53	1	243	192	—	Ronald Reagan

Congress	Years	Senate			House			President
		Democrats	Republicans	Other	Democrats	Republicans	Other	
98	1983–85	45	55	—	267	168	—	Reagan
99	1985–87	47	53	—	252	183	—	Reagan
100	1987–89	55	45	—	258	177	—	Reagan
101	1989–91	55	45	—	260	175	—	George H.W. Bush
102	1991–93	57	43	—	268	166	1	Bush
103	1993–95	56	44	—	258	176	1	Bill Clinton
104	1995–97	47	53	—	204	230	1	Clinton
105	1997–99	45	55	—	207	227	1	Clinton
106	1999–2001	45	55	—	211	223	1	Clinton
*107	2001–03	50	49	1	210	222	3	George W. Bush
108	2003–05	48	51	1	205	229	1	Bush
109	2005–07	44	55	1	202	232	1	Bush
110	2007–09	49	49	2	233	202	—	Bush
111	2009–11	58	40	2	257	178	—	Barack Obama
112	2011–13	51	47	2	193	242	—	Obama
113	2013–15	53	45	2	200	233	—	Obama
114	2015–17	44	54	2	188	247	—	Obama
115	2017–19	47	51	2	193	236	—	Donald Trump
116	2019–21	45	53	2	235	199	1	Trump
117	2021–23	48	50	2	222	212	—	Joseph R. Biden

he Republicans controlled the Senate in the 107th Congress, and thus had unified majority control of government until May 24, 2001, hen Senator Jim Jeffords (VT) left the Republican Party to become an Independent and caucus with the Democrats. The Jeffords switch ave the Democrats organizational control of the Senate for the remainder of the Congress.

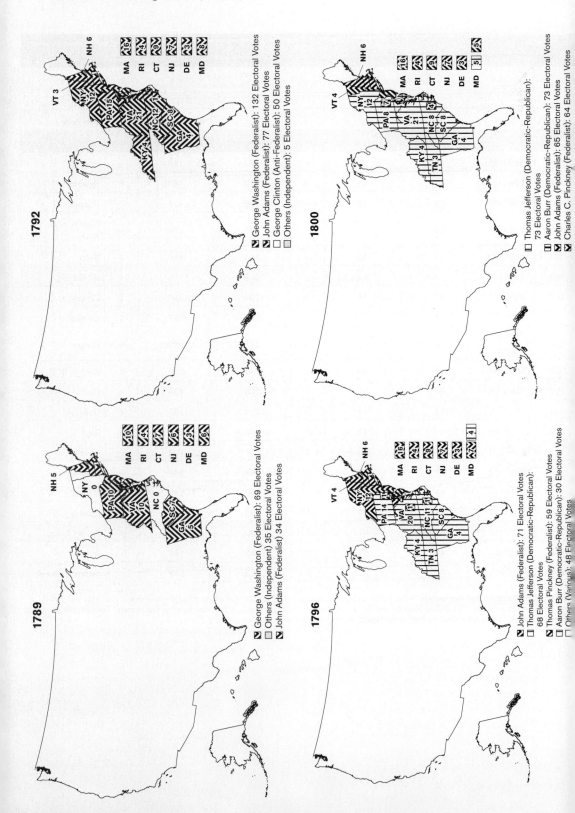

1789

NH 5
NY 0
PA 10
VA 10
NC 0
SC 7
GA 5

MA 10
RI 4
CT 7
NJ 6
DE 3
MD 6

- George Washington (Federalist): 69 Electoral Votes
- Others (Independent) 35 Electoral Votes
- John Adams (Federalist) 34 Electoral Votes

1792

VT 3
NH 6
NY 12
PA 15
VA 21
KY 4
NC 12
SC 8
GA 4

MA 16
RI 4
CT 9
NJ 7
DE 3
MD 8

- George Washington (Federalist): 132 Electoral Votes
- John Adams (Federalist): 77 Electoral Votes
- George Clinton (Anti-Federalist): 50 Electoral Votes
- Others (Independent): 5 Electoral Votes

1796

VT 4
NH 6
NY 12
PA 14
VA 20
KY 4
TN 3
NC 11
SC 8
GA 4

MA 16
RI 4
CT 9
NJ 7
DE 3
MD 7   4

- John Adams (Federalist): 71 Electoral Votes
- Thomas Jefferson (Democratic-Republican): 68 Electoral Votes
- Thomas Pinckney (Federalist): 59 Electoral Votes
- Aaron Burr (Democratic-Republican): 30 Electoral Votes
- Others (Various): 48 Electoral Votes

1800

VT 4
NH 6
NY 12
PA 8   7
VA 21
KY 4
TN 3
NC 8   4
SC 8
GA 4

MA 16
RI 4
CT 9
NJ 7
DE 3
MD 5   5

- Thomas Jefferson (Democratic-Republican): 73 Electoral Votes
- Aaron Burr (Democratic-Republican): 73 Electoral Votes
- John Adams (Federalist): 65 Electoral Votes
- Charles C. Pinckney (Federalist): 64 Electoral Votes

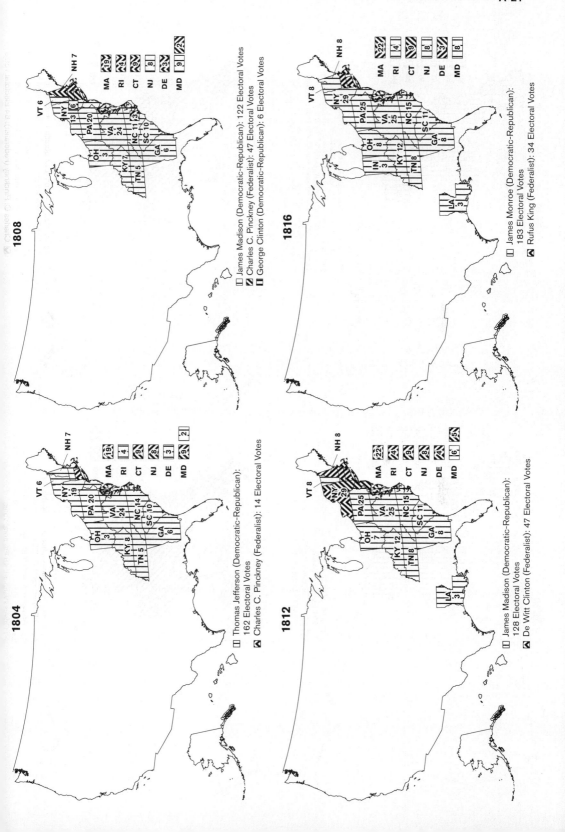

1804

- ☐ Thomas Jefferson (Democratic–Republican): 162 Electoral Votes
- ◪ Charles C. Pinckney (Federalist): 14 Electoral Votes

1808

- ☐ James Madison (Democratic–Republican): 122 Electoral Votes
- ◪ Charles C. Pinckney (Federalist): 47 Electoral Votes
- ▨ George Clinton (Democratic–Republican): 6 Electoral Votes

1812

- ☐ James Madison (Democratic–Republican): 128 Electoral Votes
- ◪ De Witt Clinton (Federalist): 47 Electoral Votes

1816

- ☐ James Monroe (Democratic–Republican): 183 Electoral Votes
- ◪ Rufus King (Federalist): 34 Electoral Votes

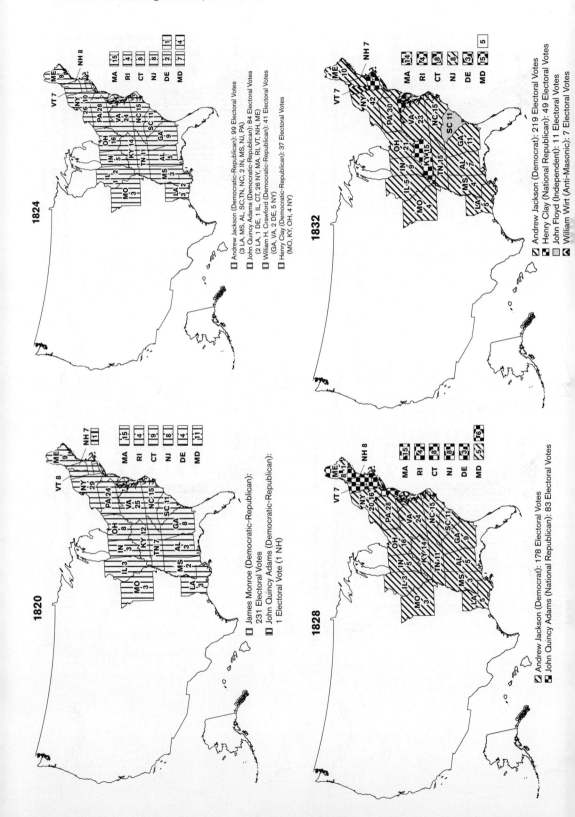

1824

MA 15
RI 4
CT 8
NJ 8
DE 2 1
MD 7 4

☐ Andrew Jackson (Democratic-Republican): 99 Electoral Votes
(3 LA, MS, AL, SC,TN, NC, 2 IN, MS, NJ, PA)
▨ John Quincy Adams (Democratic-Republican): 84 Electoral Votes
(2 LA, 1 DE, 1 IL, CT, 26 NY, MA, RI, VT, NH, ME)
▥ William H. Crawford (Democratic-Republican): 41 Electoral Votes
(GA, VA, 2 DE, 5 NY)
▦ Henry Clay (Democratic-Republican): 37 Electoral Votes
(MO, KY, OH, 4 NY)

1820

MA 15
RI 4
CT 9
NJ 8
DE 4
MD 11

☐ James Monroe (Democratic-Republican):
231 Electoral Votes
▣ John Quincy Adams (Democratic-Republican):
1 Electoral Vote (1 NH)

1832

MA 14
RI 4
CT 8
NJ 8
DE 3
MD 5
5

☐ Andrew Jackson (Democrat): 219 Electoral Votes
◰ Henry Clay (National Republican): 49 Electoral Votes
▨ John Floyd (Independent): 11 Electoral Votes
◆ William Wirt (Anti-Masonic): 7 Electoral Votes

1828

MA 15
RI 4
CT 8
NJ 8
DE 3
MD 5 6

◇ Andrew Jackson (Democrat): 178 Electoral Votes
▨ John Quincy Adams (National Republican): 83 Electoral Votes

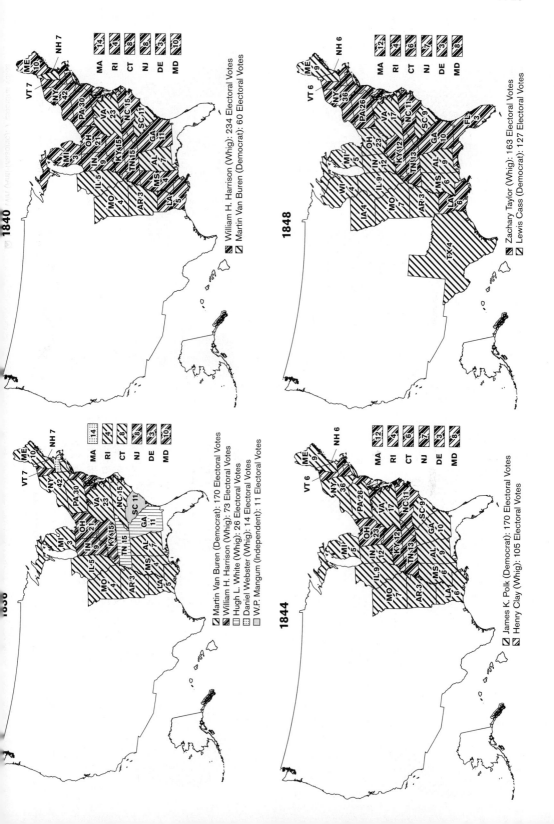

1840

ME 10, NH 7, VT 7, NY 42, PA 30, VA 23, NC 15, SC 11, GA 11, OH 21, IN 9, IL 5, MI 3, KY 15, TN 15, AL 7, MS 4, LA 5, MO 4, AR 3

MA 14, RI 4, CT 8, NJ 8, DE 3, MD 10

☑ William H. Harrison (Whig): 234 Electoral Votes
☑ Martin Van Buren (Democrat): 60 Electoral Votes

1836

ME 10, NH 7, VT 7, NY 42, PA 30, VA 23, NC 15, SC 11, GA 11, OH 21, IN 9, IL 5, MI 3, KY 15, TN 15, AL 7, MS 4, LA 5, MO 4, AR 3

MA 14, RI 4, CT 8, NJ 8, DE 3, MD 10

☑ Martin Van Buren (Democrat): 170 Electoral Votes
☑ William H. Harrison (Whig): 73 Electoral Votes
▦ Hugh L. White (Whig): 26 Electoral Votes
▨ Daniel Webster (Whig): 14 Electoral Votes
☒ W.P. Mangum (Independent): 11 Electoral Votes

1848

ME 9, NH 6, VT 6, NY 36, PA 26, VA 17, NC 11, SC 9, GA 10, FL 3, OH 23, IN 12, IL 9, MI 5, WI 4, IA 4, KY 12, TN 13, AL 9, MS 6, LA 6, MO 7, AR 3, TX 4

MA 12, RI 4, CT 6, NJ 7, DE 3, MD 8

☑ Zachary Taylor (Whig): 163 Electoral Votes
☑ Lewis Cass (Democrat): 127 Electoral Votes

1844

ME 9, NH 6, VT 6, NY 36, PA 26, VA 17, NC 11, SC 9, GA 10, OH 23, IN 12, IL 9, MI 5, KY 12, TN 13, AL 9, MS 6, LA 6, MO 7, AR 3

MA 12, RI 4, CT 6, NJ 7, DE 3, MD 8

☑ James K. Polk (Democrat): 170 Electoral Votes
☑ Henry Clay (Whig): 105 Electoral Votes

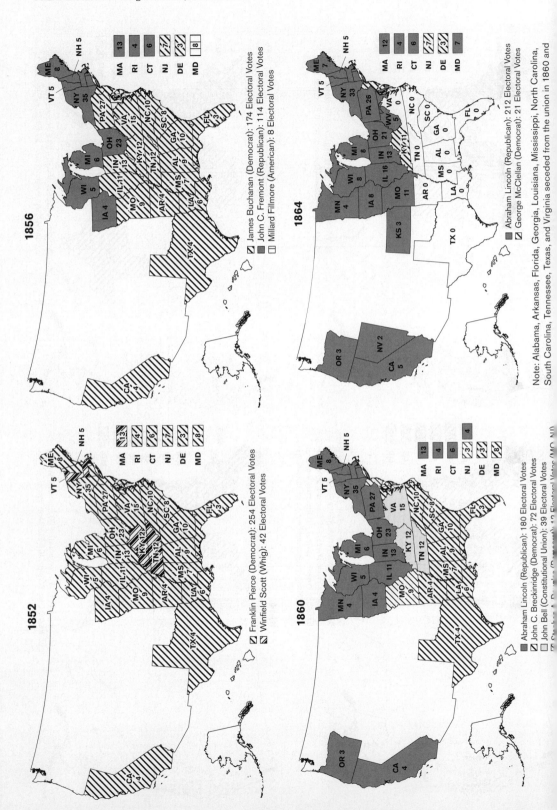

1856

- ☑ James Buchanan (Democrat): 174 Electoral Votes
- ■ John C. Fremont (Republican): 114 Electoral Votes
- ☐ Millard Fillmore (American): 8 Electoral Votes

MA	13
RI	4
CT	6
NJ	7
DE	3
MD	8

1852

- ☑ Franklin Pierce (Democrat): 254 Electoral Votes
- ▨ Winfield Scott (Whig): 42 Electoral Votes

MA	13
RI	4
CT	6
NJ	7
DE	3
MD	8

1864

- ■ Abraham Lincoln (Republican): 212 Electoral Votes
- ☑ George McClellan (Democrat): 21 Electoral Votes

MA	12
RI	4
CT	6
NJ	7
DE	3
MD	7

Note: Alabama, Arkansas, Florida, Georgia, Louisiana, Mississippi, North Carolina, South Carolina, Tennessee, Texas, and Virginia seceded from the union in 1860 and

1860

- ■ Abraham Lincoln (Republican): 180 Electoral Votes
- ☑ John C. Breckinridge (Democrat): 72 Electoral Votes
- ☐ John Bell (Constitutional Union): 39 Electoral Votes
- ▨ Stephen A. Douglas (Democrat): 12 Electoral Votes (MO, NJ)

MA	13
RI	4
CT	6
NJ	3
DE	3
MD	6
	4

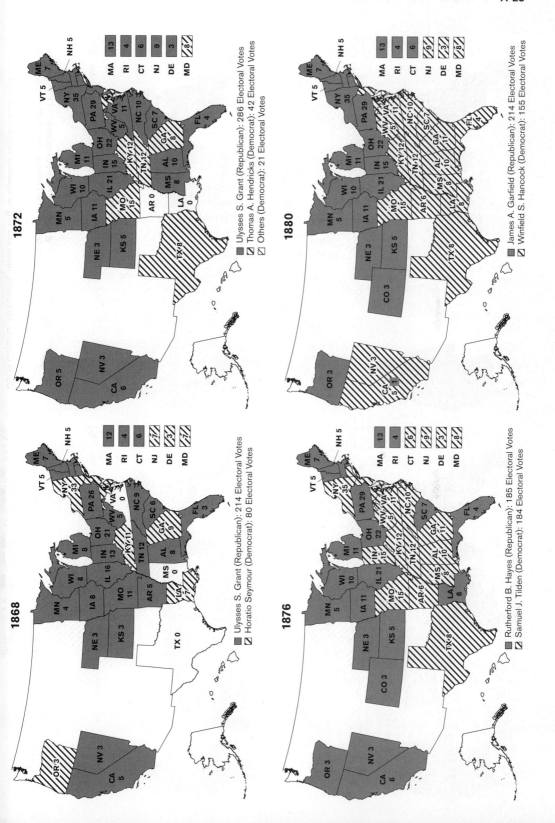

1872

Ulysses S. Grant (Republican): 286 Electoral Votes

Thomas A. Hendricks (Democrat): 42 Electoral Votes

Others (Democrat): 21 Electoral Votes

MA 13 RI 4 CT 6 NJ 9 DE 3 MD 8

1880

James A. Garfield (Republican): 214 Electoral Votes

Winfield S. Hancock (Democrat): 155 Electoral Votes

MA 13 RI 4 CT 6 NJ 9 DE 3 MD 8

1868

Ulysses S. Grant (Republican): 214 Electoral Votes

Horatio Seymour (Democrat): 80 Electoral Votes

MA 12 RI 4 CT 6 NJ 7 DE 3 MD 7

1876

Rutherford B. Hayes (Republican): 185 Electoral Votes

Samuel J. Tilden (Democrat): 184 Electoral Votes

MA 13 RI 4 CT 6 NJ 9 DE 3 MD 8

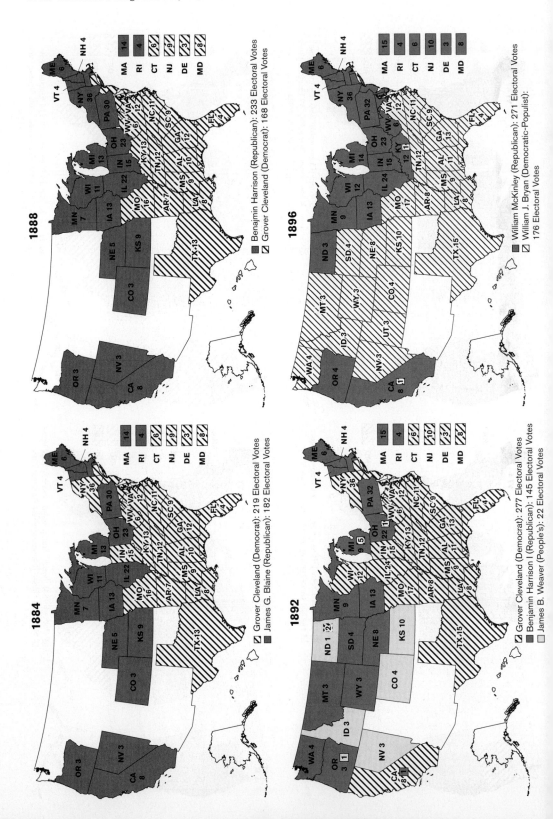

1888

MA 14
RI 4
CT 6
NJ 9
DE 3
MD 8

☐ Benjamin Harrison (Republican): 233 Electoral Votes
☐ Grover Cleveland (Democrat): 168 Electoral Votes

1896

MA 15
RI 4
CT 6
NJ 10
DE 3
MD 8

☐ William McKinley (Republican): 271 Electoral Votes
☐ William J. Bryan (Democratic-Populist): 176 Electoral Votes

1884

MA 14
RI 4
CT 6
NJ 9
DE 3
MD 8

☐ Grover Cleveland (Democrat): 219 Electoral Votes
☐ James G. Blaine (Republican): 182 Electoral Votes

1892

MA 15
RI 4
CT 6
NJ 10
DE 3
MD 8

☐ Grover Cleveland (Democrat): 277 Electoral Votes
☐ Benjamin Harrison I (Republican): 145 Electoral Votes
☐ James B. Weaver (People's): 22 Electoral Votes

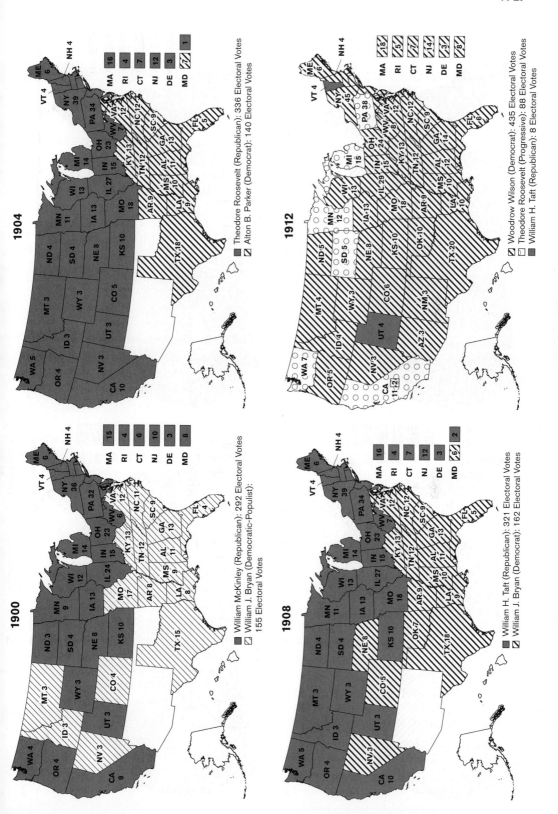

1904

Theodore Roosevelt (Republican): 336 Electoral Votes

Alton B. Parker (Democrat): 140 Electoral Votes

1900

William McKinley (Republican): 292 Electoral Votes

William J. Bryan (Democratic-Populist): 155 Electoral Votes

1912

Woodrow Wilson (Democrat): 435 Electoral Votes

Theodore Roosevelt (Progressive): 88 Electoral Votes

William H. Taft (Republican): 8 Electoral Votes

1908

William H. Taft (Republican): 321 Electoral Votes

William J. Bryan (Democrat): 162 Electoral Votes

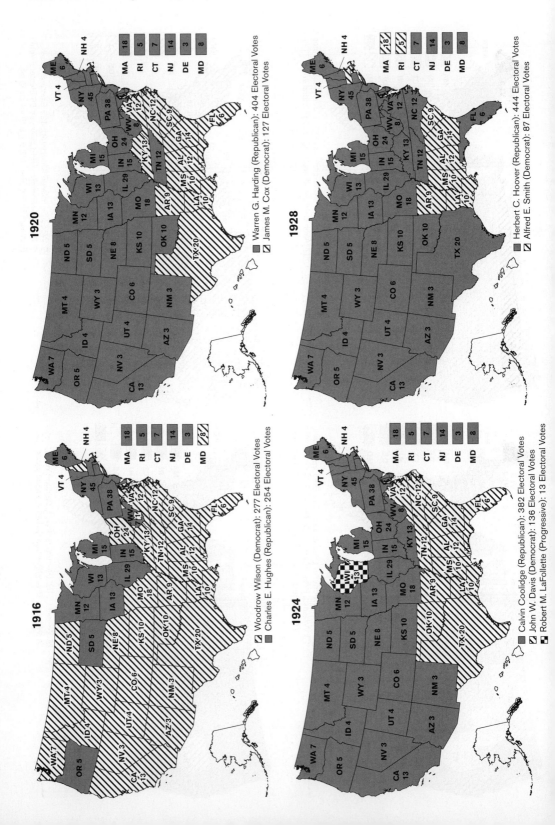

1920

MA 18 · RI 5 · CT 7 · NJ 14 · DE 3 · MD 8

☐ Warren G. Harding (Republican): 404 Electoral Votes
⬛ James M. Cox (Democrat): 127 Electoral Votes

1928

MA 18 · RI 5 · CT 7 · NJ 14 · DE 3 · MD 8

⬛ Herbert C. Hoover (Republican): 444 Electoral Votes
☐ Alfred E. Smith (Democrat): 87 Electoral Votes

1916

MA 18 · RI 5 · CT 7 · NJ 14 · DE 3 · MD 8

☐ Woodrow Wilson (Democrat): 277 Electoral Votes
⬛ Charles E. Hughes (Republican): 254 Electoral Votes

1924

MA 18 · RI 5 · CT 7 · NJ 14 · DE 3 · MD 8

⬛ Calvin Coolidge (Republican): 382 Electoral Votes
☐ John W. Davis (Democrat): 136 Electoral Votes
▨ Robert M. LaFollette (Progressive): 13 Electoral Votes

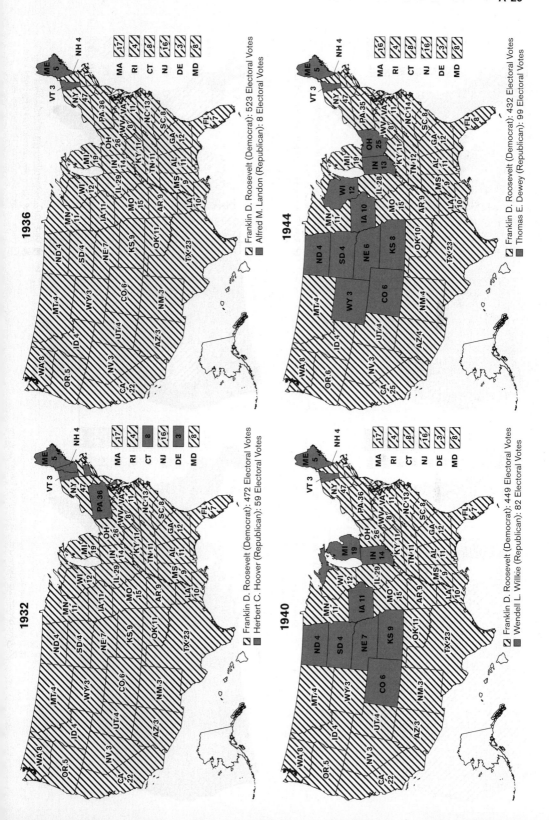

1936

Franklin D. Roosevelt (Democrat): 523 Electoral Votes

Alfred M. Landon (Republican): 8 Electoral Votes

MA 17 · RI 4 · CT 8 · NJ 16 · DE 3 · MD 8

1944

Franklin D. Roosevelt (Democrat): 432 Electoral Votes

Thomas E. Dewey (Republican): 99 Electoral Votes

MA 16 · RI 4 · CT 8 · NJ 16 · DE 3 · MD 8

1932

Franklin D. Roosevelt (Democrat): 472 Electoral Votes

Herbert C. Hoover (Republican): 59 Electoral Votes

MA 17 · RI 4 · CT 8 · NJ 16 · DE 3 · MD 8

1940

Franklin D. Roosevelt (Democrat): 449 Electoral Votes

Wendell L. Willkie (Republican): 82 Electoral Votes

MA 17 · RI 4 · CT 8 · NJ 16 · DE 3 · MD 8

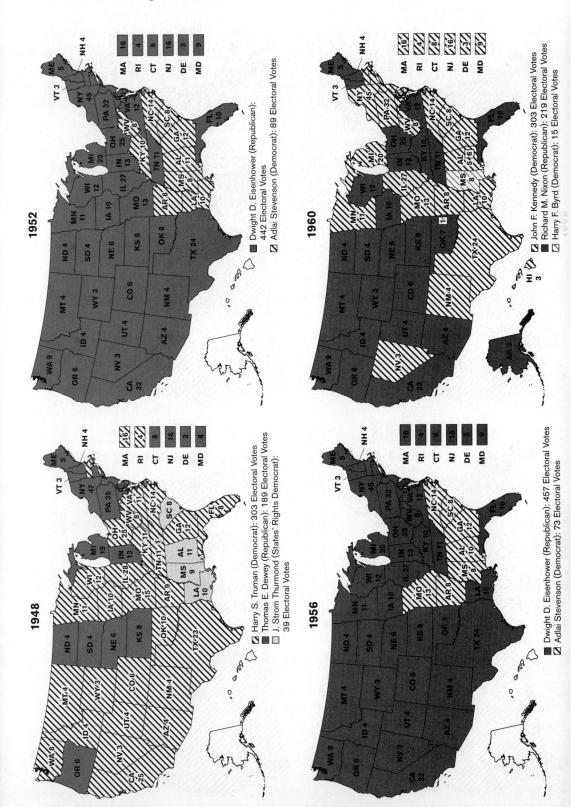

1952

Dwight D. Eisenhower (Republican): 442 Electoral Votes

Adlai Stevenson (Democrat): 89 Electoral Votes

1948

Harry S. Truman (Democrat): 303 Electoral Votes

Thomas E. Dewey (Republican): 189 Electoral Votes

J. Strom Thurmond (States' Rights Democrat): 39 Electoral Votes

1960

John F. Kennedy (Democrat): 303 Electoral Votes

Richard M. Nixon (Republican): 219 Electoral Votes

Harry F. Byrd (Democrat): 15 Electoral Votes

1956

Dwight D. Eisenhower (Republican): 457 Electoral Votes

Adlai Stevenson (Democrat): 73 Electoral Votes

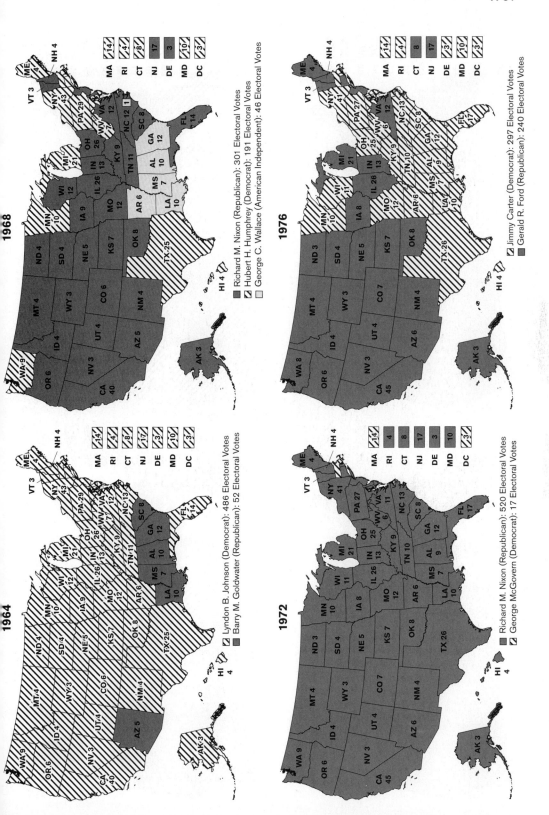

1964

MA 14
RI 4
CT 8
NJ 17
DE 3
MD 10
DC 3

☑ Lyndon B. Johnson (Democrat): 486 Electoral Votes
■ Barry M. Goldwater (Republican): 52 Electoral Votes

1968

MA 14
RI 4
CT 8
NJ 17
DE 3
MD 10
DC 3

■ Richard M. Nixon (Republican): 301 Electoral Votes
☑ Hubert H. Humphrey (Democrat): 191 Electoral Votes
☐ George C. Wallace (American Independent): 46 Electoral Votes

1972

MA 14
RI 4
CT 8
NJ 17
DE 3
MD 10
DC 3

■ Richard M. Nixon (Republican): 520 Electoral Votes
☑ George McGovern (Democrat): 17 Electoral Votes

1976

MA 14
RI 4
CT 8
NJ 17
DE 3
MD 10
DC 3

☑ Jimmy Carter (Democrat): 297 Electoral Votes
■ Gerald R. Ford (Republican): 240 Electoral Votes

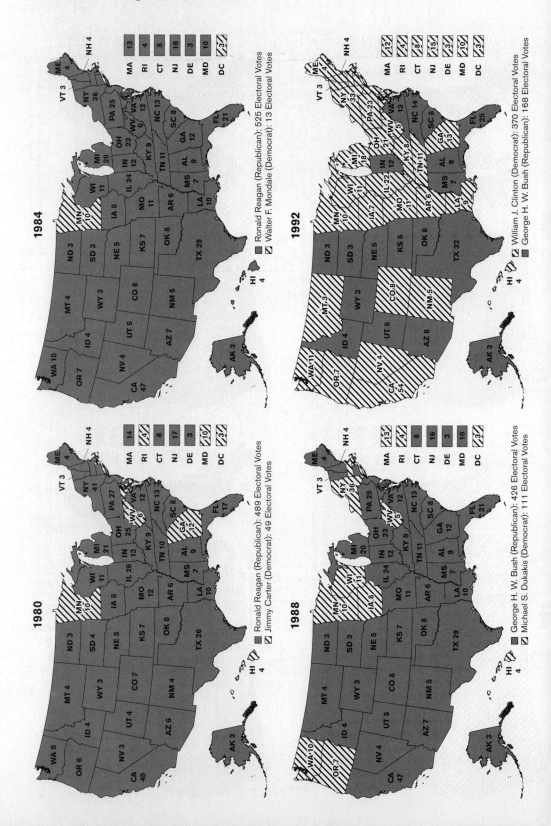

1984

MA	13	
RI	4	
CT	8	
NJ	16	
DE	3	
MD	10	
DC	3	

☐ Ronald Reagan (Republican): 525 Electoral Votes
▨ Walter F. Mondale (Democrat): 13 Electoral Votes

1980

MA	14	
RI	4	
CT	8	
NJ	17	
DE	3	
MD	10	
DC	3	

☐ Ronald Reagan (Republican): 489 Electoral Votes
▨ Jimmy Carter (Democrat): 49 Electoral Votes

1992

MA	12	
RI	4	
CT	8	
NJ	15	
DE	3	
MD	10	
DC	3	

▨ William J. Clinton (Democrat): 370 Electoral Votes
☐ George H. W. Bush (Republican): 168 Electoral Votes

1988

MA	13	
RI	4	
CT	8	
NJ	16	
DE	3	
MD	10	
DC	3	

☐ George H. W. Bush (Republican): 426 Electoral Votes
▨ Michael S. Dukakis (Democrat): 111 Electoral Votes

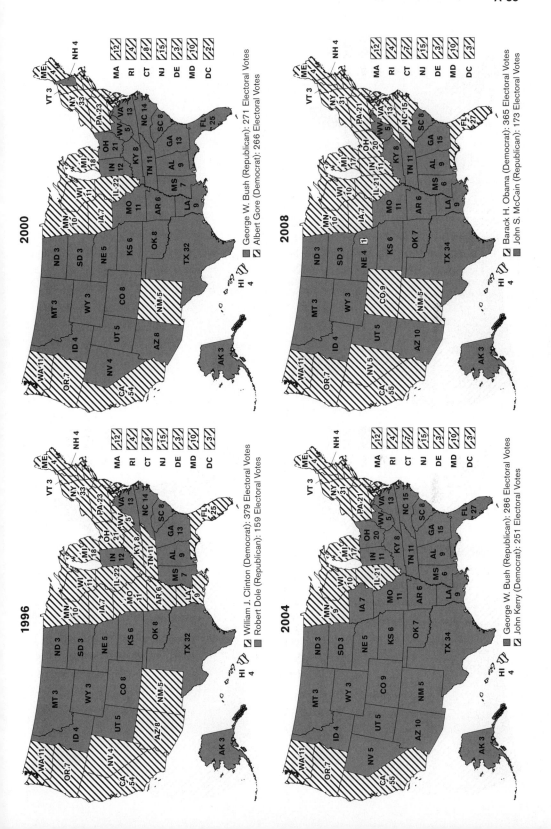

2000

MA 12 RI 4 CT 8 NJ 15 DE 3 MD 10 DC 2

☐ George W. Bush (Republican): 271 Electoral Votes
▨ Albert Gore (Democrat): 266 Electoral Votes

1996

MA 12 RI 4 CT 8 NJ 15 DE 3 MD 10 DC 3

▨ William J. Clinton (Democrat): 379 Electoral Votes
☐ Robert Dole (Republican): 159 Electoral Votes

2008

MA 12 RI 4 CT 7 NJ 15 DE 3 MD 10 DC 3

▨ Barack H. Obama (Democrat): 365 Electoral Votes
☐ John S. McCain (Republican): 173 Electoral Votes

2004

MA 12 RI 4 CT 7 NJ 15 DE 3 MD 10 DC 3

☐ George W. Bush (Republican): 286 Electoral Votes
▨ John Kerry (Democrat): 251 Electoral Votes

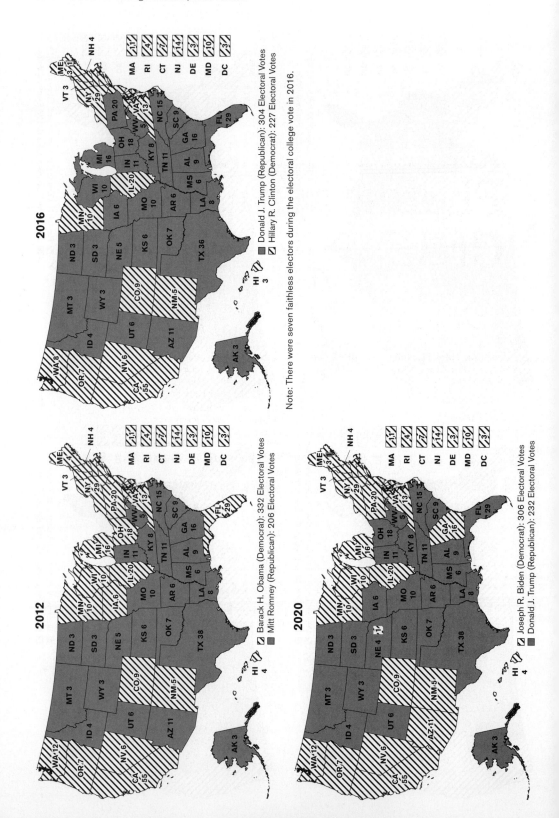

2016

Donald J. Trump (Republican): 304 Electoral Votes

Hillary R. Clinton (Democrat): 227 Electoral Votes

Note: There were seven faithless electors during the electoral college vote in 2016.

2012

Barack H. Obama (Democrat): 332 Electoral Votes

Mitt Romney (Republican): 206 Electoral Votes

2020

Joseph R. Biden (Democrat): 306 Electoral Votes

Donald J. Trump (Republican): 232 Electoral Votes

Photograph and Text Credits

Glossary/Index

Terms and page numbers in **bold** refer to main discussions of glossary terms.
Page numbers in *italics* refer to material in figures or tables.